DESIGN AND LAYOUT OF FOODSERVICE FACILITIES

DESIGN AND LAYOUT OF FOODSERVICE FACILITIES

JOHN C. BIRCHFIELD

ENDORSED BY THE FOODSERVICE CONSULTANTS SOCIETY INTERNATIONAL

VAN NOSTRAND REINHOLD
NEW YORK

Printed in the United States of America

Designed by Karolina Harris

Van Nostrand Reinhold
115 Fifth Avenue
New York, New York 10003

Van Nostrand Reinhold (International) Limited
11 New Fetter Lane
London EC4P 4EE, England

Van Nostrand Reinhold
480 La Trobe Street
Melbourne, Victoria 3000, Australia

Macmillan of Canada
Division of Canada Publishing Corporation
164 Commander Boulevard
Agincourt, Ontario M1S 3C7, Canada

16 15 14 13 12 11 10 9 8 7 6 5 4 3 2 1

Library of Congress Cataloging-in-Publication Data

Birchfield, John C.
  Design and layout of foodservice facilities/John C.
    Birchfield. p. cm.
  Bibliography: p.
  ISBN 0–442–21042–6
  1. Food service management. 2. Food service—Equipment
and supplies. I. Title. II. Title: Design and layout of food
service facilities.
TX911.3.M27B57 1988   87–31655
647'.95'068—dc19   CIP

Josalee Birchfield, Vice President of Birchfield Foodsystems, Inc., proofreader of this book and my best friend, has often pointed out that the company could not run profitably nor could this book have been completed successfully without the support team behind John Birchfield. This book is dedicated to the wonderful staff, past and present, at Birchfield Foodsystems, Inc.

CONTENTS

PREFACE

Foodservice is unique as a large industry because it combines both the service and the manufacturing sectors of industry. Whereas most goods are manufactured at one place, sold at a second place, and consumed in a third place, the modern hotel, restaurant, and institutional food operation accomplishes all three of these functions in one place. As an added challenge, foodservice people must handle a perishable product served to an ever-changing number of people. To manufacture, sell, and serve a perishable product to be consumed on the premises to a changing number of people requires highly specialized equipment and dedicated, hard-working people.

The hospitality industry has demonstrated a steady pattern of growth over the past forty years. The number of restaurants, fast-food chains, and hotels continues to increase, together with the number of meals eaten out of the home by each person in the United States. The public shows little apparent resistance to paying for the convenience of eating a meal away from home, even during periods when the economy is on a downswing. Although several years in the 1970s and 1980s saw no net growth, the foodservice industry as a whole shows a rising trend in food sales in hotels, restaurants, and institutions over the long term.

This growth requires owners and managers of all types of foodservice facilities to construct new food outlets and to renovate their existing operations on an ongoing basis. Even during the difficult recession of 1982, construction and renovation projects in many food companies continued at a brisk pace. Large corporations such as Marriott, Hyatt, Sheraton, McDonalds, Burger King, and others continued to add food facilities and to renovate old ones during such periods. Even at the best of times, owners and managers are faced with the need to control increased energy, labor, and operating costs while continuing to maintain high standards of quality for their guests. The steady growth of the foodservice industry combined with a need to control costs through more efficient facilities has created a continuing demand for well-designed food operations.

In this volume, the task of designing foodservice facilities is presented step by step, beginning with the initial concept and planning of the project. Principles of design, the design process itself, financing, construction, equipment, and final inspections are all considered. A chapter on interior design gives an overview of the subject and stresses the importance of engaging a professional interior design person to guide the owner toward a quality finished product.

This book was written to provide a reference for managers and owners who need to understand the process of designing or renovating a foodservice facility, and for students in hotel, restaurant, and institutional management, and in dietetics studies. It is hoped that experienced design consultants may also find this book useful as a tool in developing working relationships with the clients they serve.

The title *Design and Layout of Foodservice Facilities* was chosen because the book covers the broad range of topics that should be considered when developing a foodservice facility. In the field of architecture, the terms *design* and *layout* have distinct meanings. *Design* refers to the overall relationship of space within and outside a building, while the *layout* of a particular space within a building is smaller in scope and more specific to the expected function of the space.

ACKNOWLEDGMENTS

The author would like to acknowledge the work of those whose skills and expertise have contributed to the creation of this book. Members of the Foodservice Consultants Society International (FCSI), food equipment manufacturers, members of the Birchfield Foodsystems staff, students at Michigan State University, and many others have had a role in the collection of data, the development of drawings, and the sharing of photographs. The information on lighting design in chapter 6 was provided largely by Richard E. Hopkins, Associate member of FCSI, Chevy Chase, Maryland, who wrote an article in *The Consultant* on the subject.

At the FCSI board meeting in May of 1985, the association approved the endorsement of this book, which was reviewed by highly qualified professionals in the association. These persons read the manuscript and offered valuable suggestions and additions to the text. The author would like to acknowledge, in particular, the following FCSI members: Arthur Avery (Purdue University), William Eaton (Cini-Little), C. Russell Nickel (FCSI), and Ted Waskey (University of Houston).

ABOUT THE AUTHOR

John C. Birchfield is the founder and a principal of Birchfield Foodsystems, Inc., a foodservice consulting and design firm with offices in Annapolis, Maryland, and Okemos, Michigan. His background includes educational and operational aspects of the foodservice industry. Mr. Birchfield has been an Associate Professor of Hotel, Restaurant, and Institutional Management at Michigan State University, Vice President of Westminster Choir College in New Jersey, and has had operational experience in hotels, clubs, restaurants, and colleges. In 1973, Mr. Birchfield won the International Foodservice Manufacturer's Association Silver Plate Award as Foodservice Operator of the year. He is a past-president of the National Association of College and University Food Services and was awarded the Distinguished Service Award by that association in 1973. A graduate of Cornell University's School of Hotel and Restaurant Management, Mr. Birchfield also holds a master's degree from Rutgers University in the field of Institutional Management and Nutrition.

Mr. Birchfield is the author of many articles and two books on foodservice and management, including *The Contemporary Quantity Recipe File*, published by Cahners Books (now Van Nostrand Reinhold), and "A New Plan for College Food Services," published in the Cornell Hotel and Restaurant Quarterly. The work he is perhaps best known for is the comprehensive *Foodservice Operations Manual*, published by Van Nostrand Reinhold. He served on the advisory board of Cahners Publishing Company for three years and has been guest columnist for *Food Management Magazine*.

Mr. Birchfield has designed numerous foodservice operations and has served as an operations consultant to numerous institutions, hotels, and clubs in the continental United States and Europe.

Design and Layout of Foodservice Facilities was reviewed during its development by four members of the Foodservice Consultants Society International.

CHAPTER 1

PRELIMINARY PLANNING

THIS CHAPTER WILL:

▶ Assist the reader in determining the scope of a project, which will in turn determine the complexity of the planning process

▶ Explain the process of concept development for hotels, chains, restaurants, and institutions

▶ Guide the person who is contemplating a design or equipment replacement project through the decision-making process regarding menu, market, management, money, and method of execution

▶ Introduce the elements of a feasibility study and outline the different kinds of feasibility research that are necessary before designing a foodservice facility

▶ Introduce to the reader the professional persons who can best assist the owner or manager with the renovation or construction of a food facility

THE SCOPE OF A PROJECT

The size and complexity of the project will greatly influence the design approach taken by the owner or manager. If the project involves only the layout of a new hot food production area for an existing restaurant, the approach used and the planning process will be fairly simple. If the project entails the construction of a new restaurant or the complete renovation of an existing facility, the planning process becomes more difficult. And if the project includes the construction of a new facility that is to serve as the prototype for a chain or franchise, the planning process is even more complex.

Scope can be divided into three levels of complexity, each of which requires different individuals' involvement and different amounts of planning time. Determining the scope of the project is an important first step before the planning begins.

LEVEL I

Scope At this level, the project involves no more than the selection of a major piece of equipment or the replacement of a small area of a food facility.

Persons Likely to Be Involved

- *The owner or manager:* Assuming that this person is reasonably familiar with foodservice equipment and has a good grasp of the workings of the food facility, he or she will be responsible for choosing the necessary equipment and making other installation and layout decisions.
- *Kitchen equipment dealer or manufacturer's representative:* The dealer usually has a small stock of equipment on display in the store and will certainly have a wide range of catalogs to assist with equipment selection. The manufacturer's representative, who may represent only a small number of equipment companies, has detailed technical knowledge about each piece of equipment that he or she handles.
- *Food facilities design consultant:* If the project involves the rearrangement of equipment or the selection of several pieces of equipment, a food facilities design consultant may be needed. The help of a design consultant is especially important if the foodservice operator lacks a working knowledge of available kitchen equipment.

Planning Time Three or four days of research and shopping for the needed pieces of equipment plus a week to determine engineering and utility needs should be sufficient planning time for the project. Obtaining bids on equipment and installing it will add more time, depending on the complexity of the project. Delivery time for equipment ordered from a catalog (usually four to eight weeks) is another factor that must be considered.

LEVEL II

Scope The project is the construction of a new food facility or a major renovation of an existing facility. The scope and complexity of a new facility is nearly always underestimated by those who go through the planning process for the first time. At Level II, the planning process for a major renovation may be even more complex than a new facility, because of the difficulty of dealing with existing walls, structural members, utilities, and space, and the demolition of parts of the existing structure. Moreover, decisions must be made about which pieces of existing equipment should or could be used in the newly renovated facility.

Persons Likely to Be Involved

- owner or manager
- foodservice facilities design consultant
- architects/engineers
- interior designer
- others (see the discussion under "Design and Planning Professionals" later in this chapter)

Planning Time A Level II project could take from two months to two years to plan, depending on the size of the project and the availability of funds.

LEVEL III

Scope The development of a chain or franchise prototype, in addition to the considerations relating to Level II projects, involves a corporate strategy, a well-researched marketing plan, complex financial planning, and a strong management team. The food facility design at Level III must fit the needs of the menu, market, strategy, and financial package that is being developed by the corporation.

Persons Likely to Be Involved

- investors and/or owners of the corporation
- foodservice facility design consultant
- architects/engineers
- corporate officers and specialists
- interior designer
- marketing consultants
- financial planners
- bankers
- others (see the section on "Design and Planning Professionals" later in this chapter)

CONCEPT DEVELOPMENT

It is not unusual for a person to consider a new restaurant or, in fact, to open a new restaurant without knowing what type of food facility will have the best chance of succeeding. The potential entrepreneur may have some investment money, a location or a theme in mind, and a great amount of enthusiasm for the food business, but has not really thought through the total concept of the operation. Concept development, applied to the foodservice industry, means the planning of a menu, a decor, and a method of serving food in harmony with an identified market to achieve a profitable operation. For the corporation, concept development should also include a strategy for growth and financial return on investment.

Hotel Food and Beverage Concept Development

The development of a foodservice concept for hotels has evolved in recent years, from the traditional view that considered the food and beverage department as a necessary evil to the modern idea that the food and beverage department is an important profit center. Some large hotels have food and beverage sales of over $35 million per year, an amount that exceeds room sales and creates in management a high expectation of profit from these two departments.

The Hilton Hotel in Atlanta, Georgia, has developed a concept for its first-class rooftop restaurant that goes beyond the idea of a foodservice facility as a profit center. The restaurant, called Nikolai's Roof, was conceived as a luxury dining room and was marketed to the city of Atlanta as well as to hotel guests. The decor was exquisite, the food was served with flair and showmanship, and the entire theme captured the imagination of the residents of the city. The concept was developed with such success that the guests of the hotel had great difficulty getting reservations to dine. A hotel restaurant so overcrowded that it could not serve the guests of the hotel would have been unthinkable in earlier days of hotel keeping in the United States.

Nikolai's Roof is an excellent example of the execution of a hotel dining concept that complements the hotel itself as well as drawing a significant number of guests from the community.

Hotel managers have known for many years that the hotel restaurants must have certain desirable features if they are to be successful. These features include:

- availability of parking
- unique theme or decor (differing from the decor of the hotel itself)
- strong promotion to the community
- a menu and a method of service that are distinctive

The developers of hotel properties and in some cases, hotel chains, have used outside foodservice facilities and interior design consultants to create unique specialty restaurants that can be successfully marketed to both hotel guests and the community.

Restaurant Chain and Fast-Food Concept Development

When Dave Thomas, who is now chairman of the board of Wendy's, traveled around the country with Colonel Sanders in the mid 1950s trying to promote a chicken franchise, he learned many of the do's and don'ts of food franchise marketing. Thomas certainly picked up good ideas about concept development for chain restaurants and franchises, as the success of Kentucky Fried Chicken and then Wendy's demonstrates. The basic concepts he developed, which led to the formation of Wendy's, were the following:

- Produce a "cadillac" hamburger with a large number of available condiments.
- Limit the menu to the smallest number of items possible, as most restaurants can prepare only a few food items extremely well.

- Create an image different from major competitors. In the case of Wendy's, distinctive features included
  - an old-fashioned nostalgic theme
  - carpet on the floor
  - service personnel to clear the tables
  - marketing directed at adults
  - a larger hamburger than the competitions', at a lower price per ounce.

The concept development of Wendy's was more comprehensive than that for a single restaurant. The franchise strategy was carefully thought out to create a balance between company-owned stores and franchised stores. In 1970, only two stores were open, both company owned and operated. By 1975, 83 company-owned stores and 169 franchised stores were in operation. A ratio of 30 to 40 percent company-owned stores to 60 to 70 percent franchised stores permitted a balance of control and greater financial return from company-owned properties. The strategy entailed rapid expansion by the franchise and heavy promotion of the Wendy's name through national advertising. In 1988, Wendy's had a total of 3,816 operations, 1,229 being company owned and 2,587 franchised.

The Wendy's concept of development included:

- limited menu
- strong market penetration
- attractive facilities and decor
- corporate control to maximize profits
- corporate control of quality
- planned expansion

Restaurant chain concept development often follows the same pattern as the Wendy's example, although usually the growth is much less dramatic. Gilbert/Robinson, Inc., and Continental Restaurant Systems, Inc., are two examples of successful restaurant chains that have developed multitheme restaurant concepts. These two companies each use several different themes, and each restaurant is promoted with its theme rather than by using the corporate name. For instance, Continental Restaurant Systems has a group of restaurants named J. Ross Browne's Whaling Station, with heavy emphasis on seafood. The company also has a group of restaurants called Mountain Jack's, which offer prime

rib and steaks. The development of these restaurant concepts through excellent marketing, well-planned menus, and good design comes about through the efforts of a very sophisticated management team.

Institutional Concept Development

Institutional foodservice is usually conceived as a service to an organization, and most often has a "not for profit" philosophy. Most institutional food operations are expected to break even, and all are expected to budget and operate within well-defined ranges of costs, so that they do not become a financial burden on the organization they serve. In some cases, the institutional food operation is expected to make a profit and to pay for all of its direct and indirect operational costs.

The development of an operational concept for the institution is often ignored, and this is usually a serious mistake. The institution must accurately interpret its market and must "sell" its products, even when the food is indirectly paid for by the customer. For instance, in hospital foodservice, an unattractive meal presentation will cause dissatisfaction and complaining on the part of the patient and possibly adverse health effects as well, for if he does not eat a meal, the patient will lack nourishment. In a college or university dining hall, a comprehensive concept of service and decor can greatly influence financial success. Attractive cafeteria service or "scramble" design, for example, can increase the popularity of a college foodservice operation. A dining facility operated by a corporation for its employees should also have a well-planned concept and decor. The ability of corporate foodservice operations to attract employees may influence the degree of subsidy that a company is willing to contribute to the operation.

Individual Restaurant Concept Development

The client who most frequently comes to the food facilities design consultant for help with concept development is the individual restaurant owner. The restaurant owner typically organizes a corporation comprised of a small number of local business people and then begins to develop a concept that will eventually become a freestanding restaurant. The success or failure of the venture often depends on how well the concept was planned and how well the plan was followed.

The Five M's of Concept Development

The successful foodservice operation combines the following elements of concept development:

- menu
- market
- money
- management
- method of execution

MENU

The importance of the menu to the design of the food facility cannot be overemphasized. The subject of menu writing is too broad to be addressed adequately in a book on food facilities design. The owner or manager is encouraged to seek additional sources of information as a part of the process of developing a menu for a new or renovated food operation.

The menu has a tremendous influence on the design and success of a food operation. From a design and layout consideration, these are just some of the factors determined by the menu:

- amount of floor space needed
- type and size of seating
- method of designing service areas
- dishwashing area size and dishmachine capacity
- type of cooking equipment
- capacity of each piece of cooking equipment
- size of refrigeration and storage areas
- number of employees
- selling price of food
- amount of investment

MARKET

The importance of conducting market studies before proceeding with the construction of a food facility cannot be too heavily stressed. The basic marketing questions that must be answered are:

- To whom is the food operation being marketed?
- Is the market large enough to generate sales and produce a profit?
- How will the market be identified?
- What method will be used to communicate to this market?
- Will the potential customer want or need the food product?
- Will a quality assurance plan be developed that will encourage the customer to return because of superior service and/or product quality?
- Will internal marketing successfully sell the customer additional services or products after he or she arrives at the food facility?

A classic mistake made by both large corporations and individual restaurant operators is to conduct the market analysis and then fail to act on the basis of the information obtained. There are several cases in which extensive marketing feasibility studies were conducted by outside marketing firms, but the owners and managers made their decisions on "gut" feelings rather than from the hard data derived from the study.

Even owners (or potential owners) of food operations who have no marketing background can conduct their own market research, with a small amount of guidance and a large amount of energy and common sense. Do-it-yourself marketing and the limitations of this approach are discussed later in this chapter.

MONEY

The proper capitalization of a food facility must include funds for:

- planning costs
- building construction or renovation
- equipment (fixed)
- china, glassware, utensils
- furniture and fixtures
- decor
- operating costs

These funds must be identified and committed before serious planning can begin. Yet, in concept development, the commitments may not be made in the early planning stage because the costs are not yet known. Therefore, the planning for capital funds is a two-step process:

1. The financial needs are estimated and sources of financial support are contacted to determine the possibility of obtaining investment funds.
2. After concept development has taken place, preliminary designs and construction estimates have been made, and market research is completed, financial commitments are made by lenders and investors.

MANAGEMENT

The quality of the management of the foodservice operation will be the most important element in achieving success. Following are typical questions to be addressed by the owners:

- Who will operate the food facility?
- What kind of food experience and educational background must this person have?
- Who will assist this person in covering the long hours that are usually required to operate a foodservice facility?
- What kind of pay will this person receive?
- Will this person be rewarded in some way for excellent sales and profit results?
- How will the owners set operational policies and communicate these to the management staff?

The answer to these questions will determine the organizational structure and the kind of management team that will be used to operate the food facility.

The successful restaurant often is owned and operated by one individual whose personality becomes a part of the guests' dining experience. On the other hand, the management of a food and beverage department of a hotel may be under the control of more than one person and usually is part of a more complex organizational team. In this case, the poli-

cies and procedures of the food facility should be described in an operations manual to assure consistent implementation of management policy.

From the point of view of the investor or the institutional administrator, the management of a food facility must follow traditional management principles of good communication, strong controls, and sound personnel relations regardless of the number of people operating the facility. The operational philosophy and specific management guidelines to be used in foodservice operations must be carefully considered by the investors in a foodservice facility. Failure to develop management guidelines will very likely lead to the financial failure of the operation.

METHOD OF EXECUTION

The last step in concept development involves operational matters. Although the opening date might seem to be in the distant future to the person planning a food facility, decisions about operating methods must be made during the concept development phase on matters such as production methods, control systems, and personnel.

Production methods: Will convenience foods or traditional "from scratch" cookery be used? This decision will have a great influence on the size of refrigerated and dry storage areas and on the size of the kitchen. Production methods will also determine the number of employees in the kitchen and the skill level of these employees.

Control systems: Food and beverage controls involve many different parts of the facility, and planning for these controls before the project is under construction is strongly recommended. The following areas of control should be carefully considered:

- cash control
- sales analysis
- guest check control
- food production forecasting
- storeroom and refrigeration control
- back door security
- labor control
- purchasing and receiving control
- quality control
- portion control

Personnel: The development of financial feasibility studies cannot begin until the amount of labor required is known. The employee schedules, operation hours, staffing patterns, staff benefits, skill levels, and level of supervision of employees must all be determined before serious development of the food facility begins. As part of its concept development, the fast-food industry based its low labor costs on the use of hourly unskilled labor, scheduled to work short periods of time. When the food operation is busy, part-time employees are scheduled to work. The traditional eight-hour day is seldom used in the fast-food industry, except for supervisors and managers. The use of part-time employees in fast-food restaurants has also significantly reduced the cost of benefits. The use of part-time employees was an important part of the concept development in the fast-food industry.

FEASIBILITY

Many terms are commonly used in the hospitality industry to describe the process of determining whether or not a food facility is likely to return a profit to its owners. The following is a partial list of these terms:

> market or marketability study
> market-segmentation analysis
> market and operations analysis
> appraisal report
> economic study
> timeshare feasibility study
> feasibility study, report, or analysis
> financial feasibility study
> ROI (return on investment) analysis
> sales/performance study

Although each term has a slightly different meaning or involves a slightly different approach, they all share the goal of determining the potential of a facility to generate sales and a profit. In the case of the financial feasibility or ROI (return on investment) analysis, the emphasis is on financial matters such as capital needs, operating funds, cash flow, and return on investment. However, even financial feasibility reports have, as their primary focus, the determination of whether or not a facility under good management can give investors or owners a return on their investment. For purposes of explaining the feasibility studies and of guiding the owner, manager, or student into a common-sense approach to these studies, they are classified here into two general categories: those dealing with market feasibility and those that attempt to determine financial feasibility.

The Market Feasibility Study

Market feasibility studies can best be developed by following the step-by-step process presented—in simplified and shortened form—in the following list. (This do-it-yourself version, however, would not be appropriate for the investor considering a large investment in a hotel or restaurant property with complex financial implications. In such a case, a leading accounting firm or marketing consultant should be engaged to conduct a study.)

STEPS FOR CONDUCTING A MARKET FEASIBILITY STUDY

1. Demographic data
   a. Determine the population for the trading area by age, sex, income level, household size, occupation.
   b. Determine the population within a short (walking distance), medium (2- to 10-minute drive), or long (15- to 30-minute drive) distance.
2. Traffic patterns
   a. Determine highway accessibility, traffic counts, visibility from nearby roads.
   b. Determine future highway or street routings.

3. Area employment and industry growth
   a. Locate large employers in the area.
   b. Estimate future growth for new industries.
4. Other economic factors
   a. Check on access to present or future recreational facilities.
   b. Determine land costs and taxes.
   c. Ask about growth patterns in the geographic area.
   d. Determine the parking availability.
5. Potential customers
   a. Make a list of your competition.
   b. Determine the similarities between your menu, prices, and decor and the competitors'.
   c. Try to find out whether other competing operations are likely to be built in the future.
   d. Count the number of seats in nearby food operations.
   e. Collect menus from competitors' operations, and study the variety and prices.
6. Sales projection
   a. Develop a questionnaire (a sample is provided in this chapter).
   b. Use a formula, described later in this chapter, for projecting sales.

DEMOGRAPHIC DATA, TRAFFIC COUNTS, AND INDUSTRIAL GROWTH

Food facility customers usually are near the area where such operations conduct most of their business: most people will not walk or drive long distances to eat a meal. The trading area for the food operation must be carefully analyzed. Several methods can be used for analyzing the immediate trading area, including:

· door-to-door canvassing
· direct-mail questionnaires
· telephone canvassing
· sidewalk canvassing
· personal surveys of business people in the area
· questionnaires filled out by the employees of nearby noncompeting businesses

Some fast-food chains have developed very exact specifications for locating a good site for the foodservice facilities. For instance, one of the guidelines for placement of a Kentucky Fried Chicken outlet is that it be located on the "going-home side of the street," for obvious sales reasons. Other chains have minimum community size, minimum traffic count, and minimum average income standards that must be met before consideration will be given to building or franchising on a particular site.

Traffic counts and demographic data can usually be obtained free of charge from the local chamber of commerce, highway department, mayor's office, tourist agency, or other municipal offices. Local government officials are usually very helpful in pointing out zoning requirements, tax rates, and other information about the immediate geographic area. Planned new industry construction projects and existing employment statistics are also usually available from the chamber of commerce or the other agencies mentioned.

POTENTIAL CUSTOMERS AND SALES

The weakness in many feasibility studies can be found within the sales projection section. This part of the feasibility report is often the first place that a banker will look to determine the accuracy of the financial forecast. The forecaster who projects sales at a very high level but does not recognize that sales can significantly drop during economically difficult periods or during slow times of the year will overstate the sales potential. Bankers always appreciate conservative sales projections that reflect the restaurateur's planning for sales fluctuations during difficult periods.

The dining habits and patterns of the people who reside or work near a food facility will have a significant impact on the volume of sales for any commercial foodservice operation. There is usually a minimum and maximum average guest check range for each community or geographic area. The best way to determine this range is to develop a questionnaire and distribute it to those who reside or work in the area. A questionnaire is helpful in determining such things as:

· eating-out patterns

- favorite eating places for lunch or business dining
- age, income, and size of family of potential diners
- average price paid for lunch and dinner

The questionnaire beginning on page 10 was developed by Birchfield Foodsystems, Inc., to determine the eating patterns of a small community in Michigan. The questionnaire was distributed in two ways. A direct mailing was made to the community at large, by enclosing the questionnaire in the monthly utility bill. (The utility company permitted this because community interest in the project was strong.) And individual interviews were conducted by the consultants in the shopping areas and along the sidewalks, with the same questionnaire being completed by the interviewer. The purpose of the questionnaire was to determine the feasibility of opening a restaurant located near the center of town. The time required to mail the questionnaire and conduct the sidewalk interviews was approximately one week, with three persons assisting two consultants. Students from a nearby college were used to conduct the interviews. Much was learned by careful examination of the answers to the questions. The data was then converted to a sales projection.

To determine the sales projection for a feasibility study, first, multiply the number of anticipated seats by the seat turnover to determine the customer count for each meal. Take into consideration that all seats will not be 100 percent occupied, and therefore some will not turn over at all. For example, a college dining hall seating 200 persons turns over 2.2 times during a one-hour meal period for breakfast, lunch, and dinner.

200 seats × 2.2 turnovers = 440 customers
440 customers × 3 meals = 1320 customers/day

Recognize that all seats will not be occupied and will not turn over and reduce the number of customers by 20 percent.

440 customers/meal − 88 = 352 customers/meal

Second, determine the average check by using the actual average check if the operation is existing, or the prices from the new menu, if one is anticipated. If a new operation is being planned, check the questionnaire results and the average check for similar operations or restaurants in the area. Multiply the average check by the projected number of customers for each meal. For example, in the college dining hall discussed above,

Average breakfast check:	$2.75 × 352 =	$ 968.00
Average lunch check:	$4.00 × 352 =	$1,408.00
Average dinner check:	$5.00 × 352 =	$1,760.00
Average snacks check:	$0.55 × 352 =	$ 193.60

Total estimated sales per day $4,845.50
Average check per day
(excluding snacks) $ 3.92

Third, determine the number of days that the facility will operate, and project the slow and busy days of the week, estimating the number of persons who will eat at each meal:

	SUN.	MON.	TUES.	WED.	THURS.	FRI.	SAT.	TOTAL
Breakfast	Closed	200	225	250	250	220	100	1,245
Lunch	Closed	300	350	375	375	300	200	1,900
Dinner	Closed	320	350	350	300	200	150	1,670
					Total customers per week			4,815

The corrected estimated sales per week is then:

Breakfast:
    1245 customers × $2.75 = $ 3,423.75
Lunch:
    1900 customers × $4.00 =   7,600.00
Dinner:
    1670 customers × $5.00 =   8,350.00
            Total sales/week $19,373.75
Corrected average/day: $ 3,228.95
Corrected average check
    (excluding snacks): $ 4.02

Multiply the weekly sales by the number of

▼

RESTAURANT QUESTIONNAIRE

This questionnaire was approved by the town council for distribution to local citizens to determine the feasibility of constructing a restaurant in the center of town. Please assist us by answering the following questions.

1. How often per week do you eat out?

   <u> 0 </u>   <u> 1 </u>   <u> 2 </u>   <u> 3 </u>   <u> 4 </u>   <u> 5 </u>   <u> 6+ </u>

   Breakfast
   Lunch
   Dinner

2. What type of restaurant do you eat out in most often?

3. List the restaurants you most frequently patronize (from most to least often visited).

   a.
   b.
   c.
   d.
   e.
   f.

4. When you eat out, are you usually with:

   Family
   Business associates
   Friends

5. How many people do you usually eat with?

   <u> 0 </u>   <u> 1 </u>   <u> 2 </u>   <u> 3 </u>   <u> 4 </u>   <u> 5 </u>   <u> 6 </u>   <u> 7+ </u>

   Family
   Business associates
   Friends

6. When you eat out, how much do you usually spend per person?

   Lunch:
   Dinner:

7. How many minutes does it usually take to get to the food establishment?

   <u> 0 </u>   <u> 1-2 </u>   <u> 3-5 </u>   <u> 5-10 </u>   <u> 10-15 </u>   <u> 15-20 </u>   <u> 20-30 </u>   <u> 30+ </u>

   Lunch
   Dinner

RESTAURANT QUESTIONNAIRE *(continued)*

8. Who are you? (Circle your selection).

    Age
    18-25
    26-34
    35-40
    41-64
    65+

    Income
    0-$10,000
    11,000-$15,900
    16,000-$25,900
    26,000-$35,000
    36,000-$50,000
    $50,000+

9. What kind of food facility would you like in the center of town?

10. What price range per person do you think would be acceptable for this food facility for lunch?

    $3.00-$3.99
    $4.00-$4.99
    $5.00-$5.99
    $6.00-$6.99
    $7.00+

11. What price range per person do you think would be acceptable for this food facility for dinner?

    $4.00- $4.99
    $5.00- $5.99
    $6.00- $6.99
    $7.00- $7.99
    $8.00- $8.99
    $9.00- $9.99
    $10.00-$12.99
    $13.00-$15.99
    $16.00+

▼

RESTAURANT QUESTIONNAIRE *(continued)*

12. Would you like to see the facility offer beer, wine, or liquor?

    Beer, wine, and liquor
    Beer and wine
    Beer
    Liquor
    None

13. What type of foods do you think would be popular for this restaurant if the food facility

    a. were designed as a snack bar?

    b. were designed as a light lunch and dinner restaurant, appealing to both the local citizens and the tourist trade?

    c. were designed as a "special occasion" restaurant for dinner, with a full luncheon menu?

Comments:

Thank you.

operating weeks, recognizing that some weeks will have greater sales than others. For example, the college dining hall would have the following sales potential during a regular nine-month (thirty-week) college year:

$$30 \times \$19,373.75 = \$581,121.50$$

and during the ten weeks of summer school, which has a 50 percent sales potential:

$$10 \times \$9686.00 = \$96,860.00$$

The college is closed for twelve weeks. Therefore, the projected annual sales is $677,981.50.

For a hotel, the sales pattern would be influenced by the house count (number of persons who occupy the guest rooms). The calculation, therefore, should be based on the projected occupancy. Excellent data on occupancy for hotels is available from two of the leading hospitality industry accounting firms: Pannell, Kerr, Forster & Company or Laventhol and Horwath. These two firms publish the results of hotel operations from all parts of the country and different segments of the hotel field (resorts, transient hotels, and motels). *Trends*, put out by Pannell, Kerr, Forster, and *U.S. Lodging Industry*, published by Laventhol and Horwath, contain excellent historical information, including data for the food and beverage departments of the hotel.

By utilizing these annual publications, one should be able to make accurate sales projections that will be creditable to the lending institution or investor.

Projections for hospitals and nursing homes are based on patient room occupancy data, but in the health care field a feasibility study usually does not include any data on sales. Foodservice in hospitals and other health care institutions is a service and support arm of the facility, with the primary management and financial considerations focused on the quality of the service and cost containment of the operation.

This overview of marketing feasibility studies should give the manager, owner, investor, or student a basic understanding of the process, as well as the confidence to conduct such a study if the project is not too large in scope. Excellent sources of more detailed information on the subject are available.

The Financial Feasibility Study

The lending institution, investor, owner, and manager will all want to know the financial projections for the planned new or renovated food facility. Each of these persons will, of course, have a different set of reasons for seeking the projections and each will want data from the projections presented in a different manner. For instance, the banker will be looking in part for the ratio of invested capital to borrowed capital. The banker may also want to know the amount of operating cash and the cash flow from sales that will be involved in the operation. The manager needs to know what his or her budget is and what the expectation of the owners is concerning profit and loss. The manager and the banker probably will not be using the same financial reports and projections, but they certainly will be getting their information from the same original source, which will probably be the financial feasibility study. Usually in the financial feasibility study two basic documents—the projected balance sheet and the pro forma profit and loss statement—are prepared, along with other supporting reports and schedules. A good outline of the kind of information that must be projected can be made by examining the line items on each of these documents.

PROJECTED BALANCE SHEET

A simple comparative balance sheet, like that shown on page 14, will illustrate the kind of data that must be determined. This balance sheet is a simplification of the projected comparative balance sheet that should be developed under the guidance of the firm's accountant. Note that the balance sheet shows a projected comparison between the assets, liabilities, and capital for a twelve-month period. The balance sheet illustrates the following projections that must be made by the person or firm preparing the financial feasibility study:

ON THE ASSET SIDE OF THE BALANCE SHEET

- The amount of cash needed as operating funds
- The amount of cash tied up in food inventory
- The investment in land and building
- The cash needed for down payment on land and building
- The cost of furniture, fixtures, equipment, and utensils
- The cost of parking lots, driveways, lighting, and other improvements to the property

ON THE LIABILITIES AND CAPITAL SIDE OF THE BALANCE SHEET

- Necessary short-term funds that must be borrowed
- The amount of payables
- The amount of long-term mortgages on building and land
- The amount of funds that will represent the owner's net worth (capital)
- Decisions regarding
  - The type of business organization (proprietorship, partnership, corporation, and so forth)
  - Control of ownership (closely held, limited number of investors, the sale of common stock, and so forth)

PRO FORMA PROFIT-AND-LOSS STATEMENT

The pro forma profit-and-loss (P&L) statement should be prepared by the owner, manager, or other persons who will be involved in the management of the food facility. This statement is a docu-

JOE'S GRILL
PROJECTED COMPARATIVE BALANCE SHEET
FOR THE YEAR ENDED DECEMBER 31, 19—

ASSETS	JANUARY, 19—	DECEMBER 19—
Current assets		
Cash	$ 12,000	$ 14,000
Food inventory	6,000	7,000
Total	**$ 18,000**	**$ 21,000**
Fixed assets		
Building	$ 220,000	$ 220,000
Furniture and fixtures	60,000	65,000
Land improvements	10,000	10,000
Total	**$308,000**	**$316,000**
Liabilities and capital		
Current liabilities		
Note to bank	$ 40,000	$ 35,000
Accounts payable	8,000	13,000
Long-term liabilities		
Mortgage, building	$ 180,000	$ 175,000
Capitalization	$ 80,000	$ 93,000
Total liabilities and capital	**$308,000**	**$316,000**

ment that projects the income and expense for a particular period of time. For the financial feasibility study, a three-year projection would be considered sufficient. The format for the P&L should follow the Uniform System of Accounts developed for hotels and restaurants for income and expense categories that fit the needs of the food operation. An example of a pro forma P&L is on page 15.

SUPPORTING SCHEDULES TO THE P&L STATEMENT

The computation of the information from each line item should be explained in a series of short schedules or charts. A few examples of these schedules follow.

Sales: The projection and calculation of sales have been illustrated earlier in this chapter.

Cost of sales: After the menu is designed, the price for each food item should be established. The owner or manager of a food facility often determines menu prices by deciding on a "reasonable markup" or by "checking the competition." These pricing methods are unacceptable and can only lead to financial loss or limited profits. To determine the selling price of food requires knowledge of the cost of the entire meal that is presented to the customer. The use of a menu costing form is the easiest way to arrive at the cost. The form provides the following information:

· a list of all food ingredients
· the portion size of each ingredient
· the cost of each ingredient
· the total cost

An example of costing a menu item follows.

JOE'S GRILL
PRO FORMA STATEMENT OF PROFIT AND LOSS

	1987	1988	1989
Food sales	$ 400,000	$ 500,000	$ 600,000
Cost of food sales (40%)	160,000	200,000	240,000
Beverage sales	200,000	300,000	400,000
Cost of beverage sales (30%)	60,000	90,000	120,000
Gross profit on sales	**$380,000**	**$510,000**	**$640,000**
Controllable expenses			
Salaries	$ 60,000	$ 70,000	$ 80,000
Wages	120,000	140,000	160,000
Benefits	3,600	5,200	6,000
Supplies	2,000	3,000	4,000
Insurance	3,000	3,500	4,000
Entertainment	4,000	4,500	5,000
Utilities	30,000	32,000	34,000
Maintenance	10,000	15,000	20,000
Replacement, china and glass	3,000	7,000	8,000
General	2,000	3,000	4,000
Total	**$237,600**	**$283,200**	**$325,000**
Fixed expenses			
Real estate taxes	$ 15,000	$ 15,000	$ 15,000
Lease on land	12,000	12,000	12,000
Total	**$ 27,000**	**$ 27,000**	**$ 27,000**
Total controllable and fixed expenses	**$264,600**	**$310,200**	**$352,000**
Net profit (loss) before taxes	**$115,400**	**$199,800**	**$288,000**

MENU ITEM: HAM AND CHEESE SANDWICH

INGREDIENTS	PORTION SIZE	COST	TOTAL
Ham	2 oz.	$2.00/lb.	$ .25
Swiss cheese	2 oz.	2.40/lb.	.30
Rye bread	2 slices	.80/loaf, 20 slices/loaf	.08
Mustard	¼ oz.	3.60/gal.	.01
Mayonnaise	½ oz.	4.80/gal.	.02
Lettuce	1/20 head	.80/head	.04
Pickle chip	2 slices	4.00/gal.	.02
		Total	**$ .72**

If the menu price includes the meat, vegetable, dessert, and beverage, then the above example would necessarily include a complete list of all foods that are a part of this meal. A small amount ($.05) might be added to cover the cost of seasonings and other condiments. After the cost of an individually priced item (à la carte menu) or the cost of an entire meal (table d'hôte menu or institutional cycle menu) is determined, a reasonable markup must be added to cover labor and other overhead, taxes, and profit.

Two pricing methods for arriving at the selling price (including overhead, taxes, and profit) are summarized below.

Menu Pricing as a Percentage of Sales

This is the traditional pricing method in which the cost of food is multiplied by a factor that the manager feels will cover the cost of food, labor, other expenses, and taxes and that will yield a profit. For example, a factor of 2, 2.5, 3, or 3.5 might be used. If a factor of 3, for instance, is used, the selling price for the ham and cheese sandwich would be:

$$3 \times .72 = \$2.16$$

Rounded up, the selling price would be $2.20. This would yield a food cost as a percentage of sales of 32.7 percent, calculated by dividing the selling price into the food cost:

$$\frac{.720}{2.20} = 32.7\%$$

Menu Pricing by Adding a Dollar Gross Profit

Adding a standard dollar amount to the cost of a food item on the menu is another method often used for menu pricing. To illustrate, the manager might decide to mark up all dinners on the menu $5.00 above the calculated food cost. This technique would create the following prices:

MENU ITEM	COST	SELLING PRICE
Roast beef	$3.00	$8.00
Chicken	1.75	6.75
Lobster	4.50	9.50

In this example, the $5.00 is considered the "gross profit" or is referred to as the "contribution margin." This method of arriving at the selling price tends to create a better range of selling prices on the menu than the percentage method.

Many management people search for a "standard" for gross profit on sales, a percentage of food cost, or a percentage of labor cost. While no standard exists in the food industry that would cover all segments, it is possible to establish standards within luxury table service restaurants, fast-food chains, or institutions that serve a similar menu to similar customers. To establish a standard requires the collection of data from friends and competitors who operate a similar type of food facility.

Regardless of the menu pricing method used, the calculation for the cost of sales line item would be:

Cost of the menu item ÷ Selling price
= Cost of food sold

For example, for the roast beef in the table above,

$$\frac{\$3.00}{\$8.00} = 37.5\%$$

This calculation would be done for every item on the menu, and the average percentage food cost calculated for all food items. The projected food cost would then be multiplied by the projected sales: projected sales (from the P&L statement) × calculated average food cost = cost of sales.

Salaries and wages: The method of projecting the total labor costs for the pro forma P&L is to write the employee schedule, after deciding, of course, on the number of persons needed in each job category. Salary and wage levels should be estimated, and the annual cost of labor computed. A small amount, perhaps 10 to 12 percent should be added for overtime. The labor schedule might appear as follows:

POSITION	NUMBER OF PERSONS	HOURS/WEEK	WEEKLY COST
Manager	1	40–50	$ 400.00
Assistant manager	1	40–50	250.00
Chef	1	40	275.00
Cook	2	80	400.00
Cook's helper	1	40	160.00
Dishwasher	3	120	480.00
Waitress	4	160	400.00
Total weekly cost			$2,365.00

Weekly labor $2,365 × 52 weeks	$122,980
Overtime at 10%	12,298
Benefits at 25%	30,745
Total Labor and Benefits	$166,023

The examples illustrated are very simple to construct and take a common-sense approach to providing the backup data that is often required for a financial feasibility study. Other major costs, such as utilities and taxes, should be obtained from local utility and government agencies, to be sure of accurate projections. The estimates of other expense categories should be made by using comparative data from the National Restaurant Association; Laventhol and Horwath; Pannell, Kerr, Forster; or any of the following professional associations:

L. Edwin Brown, Executive Director
American Culinary Federation
10 San Bartolla Road
P.O. Box 3466
St. Augustine, FL 32084
(904) 824-4336

Julian Haynes, Executive Director
American Dietetic Association
430 North Michigan Avenue
Chicago, IL 60611
(312) 280-5000

Ann G. Smith, Executive Director
American School Food Service Association
4101 East Iliff Avenue
Denver, CO 80222
(303) 757-8555

Robert L. Richards, Executive Vice President
American Hotel and Motel Association
888 Seventh Avenue
New York, NY 10019
(212) 265-4506

Kathleen Pontius, Director
American Society for Hospital Foodservice
   Administrators
840 North Lake Shore Drive
Chicago, IL 60611
(312) 280-6417

Horace G. Duncan, Executive Director
Club Managers Association of America
7615 Winterberry Place
Washington, DC 20034
(301) 229-3600

Jean Denwood, Executive Director
Dietary Managers Association
4410 West Roosevelt Road
Hillside, IL 60162
(312) 449-2770

Barbara Chalik, Executive Vice-President
International Foodservice Executives Association
111 East Wacker Drive
Chicago, IL 60601
(312) 644-6610

Clark E. DeHaven, Executive Director
National Association of College and University Food
   Services
7 Olds Hall
Michigan State University
East Lansing, MI 48824
(517) 353-8711

Charles A. Winans, Executive Director
National Association of Concessionaires
35 East Wacker Drive
Chicago, IL 60601
(312) 236-3858

The Go/No Go Decision

After completing the market and financial feasibility studies and presenting these to bankers and potential investors, the owners can make a good judgment as to the potential success of the food facility project. Further contacts with zoning boards, liquor license agencies, and other municipal groups will bring the project to a point of decision. The accumulation of the data contained in the feasibility studies together with encouragement or discouragement from lenders, investors, and municipal agencies will lead the owner to the first go/no go decision. In other words, if the project looks financially sound, the market is identified, a need for the foodservice exists, and the capital is obtainable, the decision to go ahead can be made.

If one or more of the elements of the go/no go decision are uncertain, there are three alternative courses to explore. The first is to correct the problem area that has been identified. Is the facility too large? Are the labor costs too high? Is the menu wrong for the market? Is the competition too strong in the immediate trading area?

The second option is to abandon the project and look for another place to invest the funds. The third alternative is to delay the decision until the final go/no go decision. This alternative is financially risky, because to progress from this point will cost money for foodservice facilities design consultants, architects, lawyers, accountants, and other professionals.

The final section of this chapter describes some of the outside assistance that will be needed to assure a successful foodservice project. The biggest mistake that could be made at this point in the process is to try to do the planning without the help of professionals.

DESIGN AND PLANNING PROFESSIONALS

Preliminary planning on most projects must be carried out with the help of those who are trained as professional planners. The alternatives to the engagement of professional planners for the renovation or construction of a foodservice facility are:

- To buy a franchise package that has been planned by a large corporation. A high percentage of successful food operations have been opened through franchising because of the excellent guidance available before construction and the excellent management methods that are imposed by the franchising company.
- To purchase or lease an existing facility and "do it yourself." This alternative is often chosen and is one of the reasons for the high bankruptcy rate for restaurants.
- To construct a food facility with the help of a building contractor, a small amount of money, and a great amount of enthusiasm. This alternative is also often chosen and frequently results in failure.
- To plan a foodservice facility with the help of an architect, but without the use of a foodservice facilities design consultant. This alternative is frequently selected in an effort to save money. The architect may design the food facility in his or her own firm or ask a friendly equipment dealer to submit a layout. This alternative can cost the client many thousands of dollars in poor layout, improper equipment selection, or inefficiency in operations.

Cost Justification for Professional Planners

How much will it cost to retain an architect or foodservice facilities design consultant, and how can the cost of these services be justified? These are questions frequently asked by those who are contemplating a major foodservice project. These same questions are also asked by the restaurateur or foodservice director who is thinking of refurbishing a department in the kitchen or rearranging a service area. To answer these questions, the prospective owner or manager should consider the cost of a single piece of kitchen equipment. A double-deck convection oven might cost approximately $5,500, or a walk-in refrigerator/freezer may cost $15,000 to $25,000, depending on size and finish. A hood over the range section of a medium-sized kitchen may cost $30,000 to $45,000, depending on size, construction, and features specified. If the cost of the hood is calculated by the foot, the cost would be:

$$\$30,000 \neq 20\text{-foot hood} = \$1,500 \text{ per linear foot}$$

A compact arrangement for the equipment under the hood could save 4 or 5 linear feet of hood construction. The correct size and shape of the walk-in refrigerator/freezer could reduce the needed refrigeration and floor space by 20 percent. The selection of the correct amount of oven capacity and the most efficient use of floor space occupied by a compact oven could reduce the size of the kitchen. In this example, the savings to the client might be:

Hood: 4 linear ft. × $1500	= $ 6,000
Walk-in: 20% × $20,000	= 4,000
Oven: one compact convention oven rather than two	= 5,500
Savings in floor space: 70 sq. ft. × $100/foot (construction cost)	= 7,000
Total savings	$22,500

The fee for the foodservice facilities consultant is usually computed on an hourly basis and often ranges between 6 and 10 percent of the cost of the equipment. On a foodservice project with equipment costs of $200,000, the fee would be between $12,000 and $20,000. As illustrated in the example, it takes very few errors in a kitchen design to waste this amount of money. The financial loss that comes about through poor design in labor, maintenance, and other operational costs cannot be easily estimated. The loss of funds through a failure to develop proper specifications, resulting in the purchase of equipment at a high price, is also difficult to estimate.

The value received from a professional food facilities design consultant can be summarized as follows:

- Savings in operational costs as a result of layout and design efficiencies
- Savings in equipment costs as a result of proper selection
- Savings in construction costs as a result of the efficient use of space
- Savings in purchase price as a result of properly written specifications and bid documents
- And, finally, although not measured in dollars, the owner's satisfaction in knowing that the planning and design group provided the best teamwork possible for developing an outstanding foodservice facility.

Professional Planners

The scope of the project, as described earlier in this chapter (Level I, II, or III), requires different professional people to assist in the planning. The specialists who are usually associated with the development of a food facility are:

	SCOPE OF PROJECT		
SPECIALISTS	LEVEL I	LEVEL II	LEVEL III
Foodservice facilities design consultants	X	X	X
Architects		X	X
Engineers	X	X	X
Interior designers		X	X
Bankers		X	X
Lawyers		X	X
Accountants		X	X
Equipment dealers	X	X	X
Manufacturers representatives	X		
Realtors		X	X
General contractors		X	X
Subcontractors	X	X	X

Some of the professional people who play an important part in the planning process are discussed below. (Other specialists are consulted on specific planning aspects but do not play a central role.) The foodservice facility design consultant's role is described in some detail in chapter 2.

ARCHITECTS

The professional architect is usually a graduate of a school of architecture, a member of the American Institute of Architects (AIA), and is licensed to practice in the state where he or she works. The architect should be selected carefully because of the complexity of the process of designing, bidding, and constructing a commercial building. Architects are often specialists in one segment of the construction industry, such as home, or industrial or commercial structures. Experience in working with large commercial buildings and membership in a firm larger than a one-man office are minimum qualifications for working on a food facility. It is advisable to examine buildings that the architect has designed and talk with that building's owner to gain insight into the quality and detail that can be expected from the architect.

The architect is the person primarily responsible for the design, preparation of specifications, engineering, bidding, construction, and final inspection and acceptance of a new building or renovated facility. He or she will usually engage other professional people such as engineers to handle electrical work, plumbing, heating, and air conditioning, and structural and other special skills needed for the project. The architect is usually paid:

- A percentage of the construction costs (or total project costs)
- A fixed fee
- Or some combination of the above

Percentage fees usually range from 4 to 8½ percent of costs, depending on the complexity and the number of repeated elements (in a multifloor project, for example, many design elements are used over and over). Fees for engineers are usually included in the architectural fee, but special consultants are often paid an additional fee by the client, through the architect.

INTERIOR DESIGNERS

Interior design may or may not be handled by the architect. For a renovated facility, the owner should engage an interior designer, and the selection should be based on the quality of the work that the designer has done.

For a new facility, the interior design should be discussed first with the architect to determine whether or not this service is included in the architectural fees. If the fees are not included, the owner must then decide whether or not to use an outside interior designer or the architect. Often, the architect will select all interior building finishes, and an interior designer will select the furniture, draperies, and wall hangings.

One excellent method of finding a good interior designer is to find a restaurant, hotel interior, or institutional food operation that the owner feels is especially attractive, and then find out who designed it. Another method is to have several interior designers submit preliminary design sketches and furniture photographs and then select the one whose work appeals to the owners. The designer should be told that the presentation to the owner must be done without obligation, and that he or she will be competing with other design firms. The fee arrangements should be presented in writing at the time of the presentation.

The interior designer will select floor finishes, wall colors and finishes, fixtures, furniture, graphics for walls, and lighting. Samples and choices of color schemes are submitted by the designer until the client is satisfied with the layout and atmosphere or "feel" of each room. The designer then writes the specifications, prepares bid documents, and oversees the installation. Some design firms provide the furnishings as well as design services. This dual role may introduce a conflict of interest or result in higher prices for furniture, carpeting, draperies, and fixtures.

For more information on the use of interior designers, see chapter 7, "Foodservice Interior Design."

LAWYERS, BANKERS, AND ACCOUNTANTS

These professional people have already been mentioned in this chapter in connection with feasibility studies. The services that lawyers and accountants provide usually involve the beginning and end of the project. Their participation in the planning process is brief, but essential to success. The owner should seek a good lawyer and accountant and then use the advice and counsel that they offer. Banking relationships, of course, include both planning and operating activity and are extremely important to the project. Conrad Hilton often said that his success in innkeeping revolved mostly around banking relationships and his ability to use other people's money to purchase and operate hotels.

SUMMARY

A food facilities design project, regardless of its scope and complexity, must start with a preliminary plan. If the owner or manager follows the planning method suggested in this chapter, a successful food facility is not necessarily guaranteed, but the chances of its success are greatly enhanced. The preliminary planning process should include:

- *Careful consideration of the scope and complexity of the project:* This will enable the selection of an appropriate planning team. If the project is simply a replacement of equipment, the team will be small or perhaps consist of only the food facilities design consultant and the manager. If the scope involves major renovation or construction, a larger group of professional people would be drawn into the project.
- *Concept development:* For hotels, restaurants, and institutions this is now recognized as an important planning stage. It includes consideration of menu, market, money, management, and the method of execution of the plan.
- *Feasibility studies:* Marketing and financial feasibility studies are often requested by bankers, investors, and others before financial commitments can be made. For large projects these may be conducted by professional accounting firms; in other instances the owners or managers may want to undertake them themselves. A go/no go decision to proceed with the project should be made only after the marketing and feasibility studies have been completed.
- *Design and planning professionals:* The services of these necessary members of the team should be viewed by the owner as a good financial investment.

CHAPTER 2

FOODSERVICE DESIGN

THIS CHAPTER WILL:

▶ Explain the role of the professional *foodservice facilities design consultant*

▶ Outline the step-by-step design sequence for developing a food facility

▶ Describe the design sequence, so that the client (owner or manager) or student will understand each of the steps in the sequence

▶ Illustrate the work that is typically done by a food facilities design consultant, as outlined in a proposal to a client

▶ Describe the method of compiling a cost estimate for a food facility project

THE FOOD FACILITIES DESIGN CONSULTANT

With the tremendous expansion in the use of consultants throughout the economy in recent years, the demand for a high quality of services has become pressing. In response to this need, professional associations have been formed to establish performance criteria and create a code of ethics that members are expected to follow. One such organization, the Foodservice Consultants Society International (FCSI), has established itself as a recognized group of professionals in the field of foodservice design and consulting. Membership requirements are stringent, and the members are expected to have extensive experience in designing and coordinating small and large foodservice projects. The complexities of foodservice design have forced the consultants in this field to broaden the scope of services offered. William Caruso, past president of FCSI, described some of those services in an article published in *The Consultant*, in the fall issue of 1983.

Numerous technological advances have occurred in the field of foodservice planning. Gone are the days of limited equipment lines, traditional system approaches and space availabilities that once made planning an easily defined task.

Energy, labor and space costs have played havoc in almost every industry, but these particular problems have had an exaggerated effect on the foodservice business, an industry that has historically placed in the top three for numbers of annual business failures.

As costs have increased, so has Owner involvement in demanding that a new array of specific professional planning services be provided as a prerequisite for the design and construction services that for years had been the "mainstay" of most foodservice consultants. The "traditional" roasted turkey with mashed potatoes was suddenly being replaced with freeze-dried, soya injected, reconstituted, blast frozen products and technologies beyond the experience of most foodservice operators. It became fashionable almost overnight to try "Nouvelle Cuisine," smoked eel and alfalfa sprouts in restaurants. Not only was the foodservice consultant faced with unending line-ups of "I can do it better" equipment to meet these new challenges, but also suddenly in Consultant offices everywhere, business words were being used such as: Return on Investment, Target and Segmented Market Demand, Pert Chart Scheduling, Long Range Planning, and on and on.

The understanding of increased client demands and how best to serve them has recently been discussed openly at professional society meetings (the Foodservice Consultants Society International—FCSI). A number of members actively set about to form working Advisory service divisions within their already functioning design firms.

Now, after a decade of refinement and alteration to meet ever-changing market needs, many foodservice consultants provide full-scope services ranging from front-end Master Planning and Systems Development packages, through Design and into the actual monitoring and reporting of client operating and financial efficiencies and effectiveness.

New services are developed and offered as client needs arise and increase. Research by FCSI and its professional member firms on new ways to provide top quality products and services to clients continues. It is now safe to say that through the years a basic portfolio of "most demanded" management services has evolved.

In an article in the November 1981 issue of *Restaurant Hospitality*, entitled, "In Defense of Consulting" Ron Kooser, past president of FCSI, explained the importance of foodservice consultants.

The role of the foodservice consultant is a good example of the changing business structure in the foodservice industry. A restaurateur can no longer take the hit-or-miss approach in determining where, and indeed, if, he should build a facility. He needs to employ a more sophisticated method-market study, feasibility study, analysis, and implementation programs.

I believe that today's foodservice consultant best represents the source that can help the restaurateur become more sophisticated. A perfect example is the new type of members that are joining the Foodservice Consultants Society International (FCSI). More and more members are food and business oriented: computer experts; food technologists, chefs, dietitians who are consulting, marketing pros, and motivational and productivity experts. They're consulting on many different aspects of the foodservice industry. When the two original consultants societies began over 25 years ago (they merged in 1979), members were primarily foodservice planners and kitchen designers. Today, the membership of the consulting society is representative of what is happening in the foodservice industry. The background of the people involved is expanding.

The architect may select his or her own foodservice consultant or the client may need assistance for early planning before naming the architect. The food facilities design consultant should become involved with the project at the beginning—ideally, even before the architect is named. The reason for the early selection of a design consultant is to seek assistance with concept development and the feasibility studies.

The most demanded types of service the consultant provides are discussed in the following pages.

Master Planning

Approaching the development of foodservice facilities haphazardly, without making a careful study of the long-range goals, can lead to inefficiency of operation and waste of capital funds. A master plan should be written for the foodservice that includes alternative locations and different types of services. A master plan usually examines long-range growth, evaluates the market to be served, and incorporates space and architectural considerations.

System(s) Recommendations

Systems are defined as a series of interacting parts (subsystems) that must be considered to achieve the most satisfactory and efficient result. An example in foodservice is the "warewashing system," which involves delivering dishes to the warewashing area, scraping soiled dishes, transporting dishes back to service areas, washing pots and pans, and sanitizing large carts. The system may utilize conveyors, dishmachines, pot and pan machines, cart wash rooms, dish carts, and many other pieces of expensive equipment. Because of the large amount of both capital and operating funds involved, a careful study should be made to determine the best systems to use. Tray delivery systems for hospitals, fast-food systems, and warehouse/food delivery systems are examples of complex foodservice systems that usually require the services of a foodservice facilities consultant.

Financial Evaluations

Feasibility studies, discussed in chapter 1, may be a part of the consultant's work on a foodservice project. Consultants are also often requested to conduct an evaluation of existing food operations. An evaluation of the financial condition of the foodservice is usually the most important part of "management advisory" or "operations analysis" work conducted by the consultant.

Space/Equipment Budgeting

Space planning and budgeting is described briefly in this chapter under programming. Equipment budgeting may involve the assessment of existing equipment, determining the cost of repairs, and estimating the cost of new equipment.

Feasibility Studies

Feasibility studies should be done from market, economic, and financial standpoints. These help to insure that the "dreams" of an owner or operator can be realized in a tough, competitive business world.

Design Programming

A prerequisite to design development of foodservice facilities, design programming is a narrative presentation of the way a particular projected foodservice facility is intended to operate. The consultant's specific objective is to highlight space and room usage and to define the flow of people and material through the proposed facility. The following topics are usually covered in this type of program document:

- objective of the foodservice operation
- types and numbers of persons to be served
- hours of facility operation
- basic staffing requirements
- type(s) of menus to be served
- system selected for serving
- handling and storage systems for food and supplies
- area requirements for production and service
- preliminary food and beverage service equipment gross budget estimate

Operations Consulting

The consultant's services are solicited when the owner/operator is having problems. The most common analyses include:

- Space utilization analysis to increase seats,

turnover, or production/storage capacity
- Layout and equipment efficiency
- Studies of the control and security system to reduce costs and losses

- Marketing/menu assistance to increase profits and customer counts
- Operations concept assistance to assure optimum use of facilities

THE DESIGN SEQUENCE

A planning model or design sequence used by both architects and food facilities design consultants breaks down the process into the following sequential functions:

1. Proposal and client contact
2. Feasibility*
3. Programming
4. Schematic design and cost estimates
5. Design development engineering and specifications
6. Bidding and awarding the contract
7. Construction and coordination

8. Inspection/acceptance
9. Implementation and training*

*Note: These functions are usually performed by a foodservice facilities design consultant rather than an architect.

(A graphic presentation of a similar model, showing both the steps in the process and the roles of the consultant and other team members in a typical foodservice project, is provided in figure 2-1.)

The following pages outline the food facilities design consultant's role in the traditional design sequence listed above.

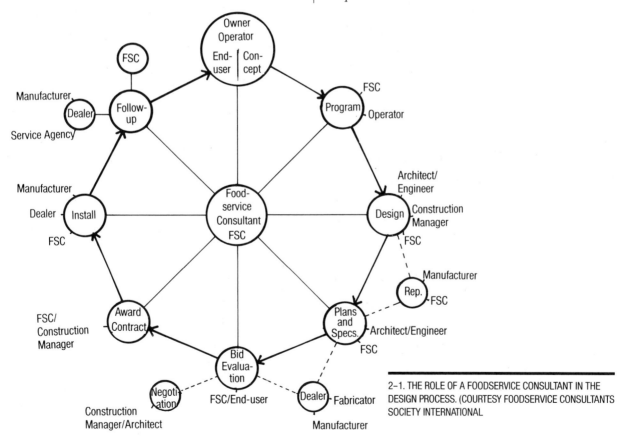

2–1. THE ROLE OF A FOODSERVICE CONSULTANT IN THE DESIGN PROCESS. (COURTESY FOODSERVICE CONSULTANTS SOCIETY INTERNATIONAL

Step 1: Proposal and Client Contact

The client will wish to explore with a consultant what services are provided and the cost of those services. The food facilities design consultant usually meets with the client to discuss the project and to determine the scope and gather enough information to prepare the proposal. Often there is no charge for this first contact. However, if out-of-town travel is required and the evaluation of the project will take more than one day, a fee might be charged for the initial meeting with the client. The proposal is written for three primary purposes:

1. To establish (sell) the credentials of the design consultant
2. To describe the work to be accomplished
3. To set the fee

The Foodservice Consultants Society International (FCSI) has adapted a standard client contract, which is included in the appendix. This document establishes the working relationship between the client and the consultant. The specific work to be done by the consultant must be carefully described so that a clear understanding exists. A typical list of the items included under "work to be accomplished" from the files of Birchfield Foodsystems is shown on page 27. In this example, the client is given a clear idea of the technical work that will be done by the food facilities design consultant. It is helpful to the client and the architect to have the tasks to be accomplished listed in detail, so that their functions will not overlap.

Step 2: Feasibility

The discussion of space analysis in chapter 3 contains a "Client Survey Form" that should be used at this point to summarize the important data from the client concerning the project. This data, useful during the entire planning process, is especially helpful in developing the feasibility study, writing the program, and in the schematic design phase.

Step 3: Programming

A building program describes in words the function of each space in a building, how that space will be most frequently used, and the number of square feet needed to serve these needs. A program for a foodservice facility is the same as a building program except that a greater amount of detail is furnished for the former. An example of a program description of a space in a building appears on page 28.

A "bubble diagram," such as the relatively simple example shown in figure 2-2, is a commonly used method of establishing space relationships during the early planning stages. It is particularly helpful in identifying design problems.

In this diagram the position of the ballroom—between the kitchen and the dining room and the private dining room—clearly must be changed. The kitchen should conveniently serve the main dining room, and the space relationship to the ballroom should be viewed as a secondary consideration.

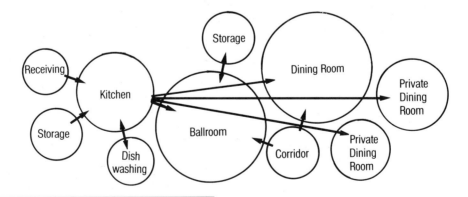

2-2. BUBBLE DIAGRAM SHOWING SPACE RELATIONSHIPS IN A FOODSERVICE FACILITY.

▼ WORK TO BE ACCOMPLISHED*

A. Meet with the architect, client, and other personnel to review preliminary plans for the new facility.

B. Meet with the architect and mechanical engineers to review schematic drawings to ascertain the adequacy of space, and to determine the characteristics of the available utility services.

C. Present preliminary drawings for the foodservices areas in ⅛ inch = 1 foot scale as often as necessary until the architect, client, and other members of the project team are satisfied with the design.

D. Develop a ¼ inch = 1 foot scale drawing of the kitchen, serving areas, and support foodservice areas indicating the placement of the equipment.

E. Furnish to the architect, engineers, and client specification sheets of standard catalog equipment recommended for purchase. Develop utility requirements for each piece of equipment.

F. Develop elevation drawings for major fabricated equipment.

G. Prepare a ¼ inch = 1 foot scale drawing indicating plumbing and electrical spot connections for each piece of equipment and the utilities for each piece of equipment.

H. Review shop drawings and mechanical drawings prepared by the successful Kitchen Equipment Contractor and other contractors, and work with the client in seeking agency approvals for the design.

I. Inspect the installation of the kitchen and foodservice equipment, and prepare a list of all items that do not meet the specifications.

J. Submit equipment guarantees and manuals to the client, and demonstrate to the employees the proper operation of each piece of equipment. Meet with manager and supervisors to explain the design.

*From a proposal prepared by Birchfield Foodsystems for furnishing design services

After the space relationships are established and the program is summarized, the total square footage requirements, the net square feet of space needed, are presented to the client. This measurement is converted to gross square feet, the total of net square feet plus the space that will be taken up by:

· wall thickness (exterior and interior)
· pipe chases
· mechanical rooms
· stairwells and fire escapes
· corridors
· entrances
· wasted space

The total square feet must fit the financial means of the owner or investor and the needs of the foodservice program described in the concept development phase of the project. Since the amount of space needed almost always exceeds the resources available, the food facilities design consultant must work with the owner and architect to reduce it. This is usually a difficult process, because those involved may feel very strongly about the size of a given space. The following questions are examples of the type that might be asked at this point:

· Can we reduce the number of seats in the dining room?

· Do we really need three walk-in refrigerators?
· Can we reduce the size of the dishroom?
· Are we required to have a cart and garbage can washdown room?
· Should we reduce the size of the lounge or eliminate it totally?

The one word that describes this space and cost-cutting exercise is "compromise." After the program is approved in writing by the client, then and only then should the design process begin.

Step 4: Schematic Design (Preliminary Drawings) and Cost Estimates

The primary purpose of the schematic design is to show the shape of the building, the entrances and flow patterns, and the location of the dining rooms, kitchen, and other major components. Drawings at this stage will show elevations of the outside of the building, site plans for the building lot and the location of roads, sidewalks, and parking lots. The owner may ask the architect and/or the design consultant to rework the schematic designs several times before they are accepted. Schematic designs are often used to gain preliminary approval from zoning officials, or for public relations purposes in selling stock to potential investors. For institutions, schematic designs would be used to seek approval from boards of trustees or other governing boards.

Schematic designs are usually presented in small scale ($1/16$ inch or $1/32$ inch = 1 foot), so that the entire facility and the surrounding property will fit onto one piece of paper. Templates, which are usually colored pieces of paper cut to the correct size and approximate shape for each planned room in the facility, are excellent planning tools for arriving at the proper arrangement for the rooms before the schematics are drawn. Templates are often used for designing the kitchen or service area of a food facility (at a scale of $1/8$ inch = 1 foot) because of the ease of rearranging the component parts of the food operation; the templates can simply be shifted until the best arrangement possible is found.

Acceptance of the schematic design should be in writing by the owner and architect on the actual floor plan of the building or food facility. The implications of acceptance are:

1. The foodservice facilities design consultant is assured that the basic layout is acceptable, so that further development of the project can be undertaken without fear of major changes by the client.
2. The architect can proceed with cost estimates for the entire facility with some assurance that major changes that would affect the cost will not be made.
3. After acceptance, if the client makes major changes because of high cost estimates or for other reasons, the foodservice consultant and/or the architect may request additional compensation. This provision should be included in the original contract between the consultant and the client.
4. The internal walls of the facility are laid out in the general shape that they will take in the final drawings, but changes to these walls can still be made without incurring additional costs.

COST ESTIMATES FOR A FOOD FACILITIES PROJECT

The owner or investor must have some idea of the cost of a project before financing can be obtained and before a final decision is made to build. The cost estimate will usually be made twice.

First estimate: The first estimate of the cost of the project will often be a joint effort by the architect, engineers, and the food facilities design consultant. The architect will gather information from the building program (Step 3) as to the quality of finish of each space and will then use standard price per-square-foot data that is available from outside commercial publications. The engineers will also look at the size of the space, the type of HVAC (heating, ventilation, and air conditioning) system needed, and the amount and kind of equipment needed in the foodservice areas. Of course, the consultant does not know at this time what equipment will be needed, but an educated guess must be made.

The design consultant must give the engineers an estimate of the electrical loads, steam requirements, and special ventilation needs so that the cost of all utilities for the foodservice area can be calculated. The final cost estimate, compiled by the architect includes:

· Building cost estimates
· Land cost
· Electrical, plumbing, and other mechanical costs
· Land development costs
· Foodservice equipment costs
· Interior design and furnishing costs
· Cost of a construction loan
· Professional fees and other costs that will occur during planning and construction

Second estimate: After the completion of the preliminary drawings (Step 4) and when the go/no go decision is about to be made, a second cost estimate is often done. This estimate will be more accurate than the first, because the architect, engineers, and design consultant will have a much better idea of the scope of the project and of the details of construction. At this stage, a preliminary foodservice drawing would have been developed in ⅛ inch = 1 foot scale, identifying the equipment, but showing very little detail.

A typical cost estimate for foodservice equipment includes:

· cost of the equipment
· model number of the equipment, unless fabricated
· price estimate for each piece of equipment not connected, but delivered to the job site, uncrated and set in place

The estimate is usually considered to represent a "budget price," that is, an amount between the list price and the dealer's cost of the equipment. Skill in developing accurate price estimates usually comes from years of experience by the food facilities design consultant. Sources of information are:

· List prices from the manufacturer's catalog, and an estimate of the discount that the dealer

may receive. These discounts typically range between 30 and 50 percent.
- Price bids from recent projects.
- A written estimate from the manufacturer. This is usually obtained for complex equipment such as hoods, conveyor systems, or dishwashing systems.

The dealer is of course expected to make a profit on each piece of equipment and to cover the costs of overhead, handling, freight, setting in place, and cleaning. Some contracts require that the dealer (kitchen equipment contractor) also connect the equipment to the utility source. The client should expect to pay a markup on the equipment of approximately 15 to 25 percent, depending on the size of the project and the amount of equipment being purchased.

THE GO/NO GO DECISION

Before the final decision to proceed with a project, there must be a compilation of all cost estimates for the project with the expert help of members of the planning team. Engineers must consider the amount of plumbing, electrical loads, HVAC, and mechanical systems needed. Structural engineers must determine the quantity of steel, prestressed concrete, or roof trusses that will be needed. The food facilities design consultant must do a preliminary layout and estimate the cost of all of the equipment. The architect must obtain price estimates on all of the construction costs, including material and labor.

As soon as these costs are compiled, the final preliminary drawings and a brief set of specifications, along with a summary of the cost of the facility, are presented to the client. The decision to proceed, to cut back on the scope, or to abandon the project can then be made.

Step 5: Design Development/ Engineering and Specifications

The design consultant, architect, and engineers begin the detailed work in the planning process in step five. Working drawings, the detailed plans that will guide those who actually build the facility, are developed during the design development phase. The selection of equipment, the accumulation of food equipment brochures, and the development of utility schedules all occur in this step of the planning. All of this information is forwarded to the engineers.

The food facilities design consultant will be in frequent contact with the client or manager of the food operation during design development, to share ideas concerning equipment selection, the detail of a particular work area, or the method of service to the guest. Many decisions are made during these exchanges, and the consultant is well advised to follow up each of these meetings with a good set of minutes. The consultant must be sure that communication with the client is very clear at this point. It is extremely embarrassing if the client is surprised by the appearance of an expensive piece of fabricated equipment. Stainless steel is difficult and expensive to alter after it leaves the fabrication shop. Ranges, ovens, and other large pieces of equipment are very difficult to return to the dealer or manufacturer.

Equipment specification is one of the most important parts of the design development process. Establishing the quantity, quality, accessories, and utility requirements for each piece of equipment, the specifications become a part of the contract documents (see Step 6) and are the primary legal evidence in any dispute that may arise between the client and the contractor. Types of specifications covered in these documents are shown in figure 2-3. Chapter 3 contains more detailed information concerning equipment specifications.

GENERAL CONDITIONS AND SPECIFICATIONS

The purpose of setting up "General Conditions and Specifications," a phrase used by both the architect and the food facilities design consultant, is to:

1. Establish the relationship between the owner, architect, foodservice consultant, and contractor. In this instance, the contractor may be the kitchen equipment contractor.
2. Set out the conditions for bidding, such as the

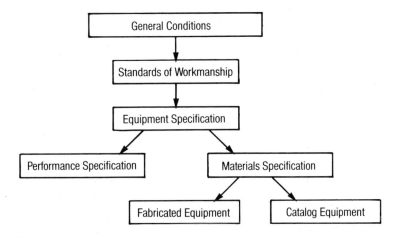

2-3. TYPES OF SPECIFICATIONS.

date the bids will be opened, the name that should be on the outside of the bid envelope, and the form that the bid should be written on.

3. Describe the scope of the project and the person to contact for answers to questions regarding the bid or specification.

4. Describe the delivery data and the penalty for late delivery.

5. Describe the requirements for:
   · Supervision of the work
   · Cleanup during and after installation
   · Storage of equipment before installation
   · Assigning of responsibility for damage to the building during delivery or installation
   · Guarantee of equipment
   · Insurance

6. Describe the payment schedule for all materials, equipment, and labor.

7. Establish the requirements to adhere to local codes, laws, and equal employment expectations.

8. Describe the "or equal" provision, which encourages the dealer to bid equipment of equal quality, if there is a price advantage.

STANDARDS OF WORKMANSHIP

The purpose of the "Standards of Workmanship" section of the specification is to describe, in considerable detail, the expectations as to how the fabricated equipment and catalog equipment will be built and installed. Most food facilities design consultants have a set of Standards of Workmanship specifications that they use over and over, modifying them to comply with local codes. Obviously, the catalog equipment will be the standard construction and quality established by the manufacturer. However, there are often many different options in the equipment catalog to choose from, and workmanship description simplifies establishing the quality and other characteristics desired. This section of the specification may be as long as twenty or thirty pages. The following excerpt will illustrate the nature of a Standards of Workmanship specification.

a. *Steam Pressure.*
   All steam operated pressure vessels such as kettles, steamers, urns, etc., shall be constructed to ASME and local code requirements and shall bear labels and certificates of compliance therewith.

b. *Steam Thermostats.*
   Steam thermostats or temperature regulators are to be furnished by the foodservice contractor on all items of steam-heated equipment if required for proper operation of the piece of equipment.

.c. *Steam Coils.*
   1. All steam coils shall be installed in sufficient quantity to provide ample heat at the steam pressure hereinbefore specified. They shall be tested for 100 pounds psi working pressure.
   2. In fixtures having coils under more than

one shelf, all coils shall be connected together with inlet and outlet extended down through base of fixture to point indicated on drawings and left ready for installation of stop valves and final connection.

3. Unless otherwise specified, coils are to be ⅞-inch-O.D. hard copper tubing with brazed fittings. Where immersed in water, coils are to be mounted on strap type brackets or feet with a clearance of not less than 1 inch below coils for cleaning purposes. These feet are to be soldered watertight to the bottom of the pan in which coils are mounted. Couplings shall be welded or brazed in the bottom or sides of fixtures for steam inlet and outlet, and shall extend through fixture ready for final connections.

d. *Sinks.*

1. Sinks shall be of size, shape, and dimensions as indicated and as hereinafter specified. Unless otherwise specified, they shall be constructed throughout of no. 14-gauge stainless steel, having front, bottoms, and rear—including splashback—constructed of one (1) sheet of metal. The front shall extend up 2¾ inches higher than the drainboard line and be finished with a 1¾-inch wide channel rim, running full length, with ends of sink constructed for welding to drainboards where such are specified.

2. Where drainboards are required, they shall be electrically welded to the sink body so that fixture appears to be an integral unit.

3. Where the sink is free-standing without drainboards, the channel rims shall continue around both ends with the corners of the channel edge rounded to conform with the radius of the inside vertical corner of the sink. Corners shall be electrically welded.

4. The rear of splashback shall extend to a height as detailed above the drainboard's working surface with the top edge formed to 45 degrees providing a 2¼-inch wide pipe chase.

5. The ends of the sinks shall be electrically welded to the body of the sink with all vertical and horizontal corners formed on a ¾-inch radius with welds ground and polished smooth.

6. Each compartment of sink shall be fitted with a 2-inch quick-opening lever handle drain set into a die-depression in center of each compartment, without use of rivets. Waste shall be cast bronze, and fastening flange on inside of sink shall be stainless steel casting fitted with a perforated no. 14-gauge stainless steel strainer plate. At rear of drain body, under sink, shall be a threaded connection for overflow outlet below drain valve ground seat.

7. At top center rear of each compartment below the drainboard line a polished cast nickel bronze overflow shall be provided, with 1¼-inch-O.D. brass tubing connection to outlet at back of drain.

8. In the case of two (2) and three (3) compartment sinks, the front, bottom, and rear, including splashback, shall be formed from one (1) sheet of material and then have the ends and intermediate double wall partitions welded in to form the number of compartments required by the specifications. Partitions shall have 1-inch air space between double walls to prevent temperature transfer between compartments. Where sinks are specified to set into counter tops, the sinks shall have a raw edge around entire top. The counter top or table shall be electrically welded to top with continuous weld, ground smooth and polished.

EQUIPMENT SPECIFICATION

The equipment specification can be written in several different ways, but the most important thing to be considered is whether or not the exact requirements for the equipment are clearly written. The equipment should be described in such a manner that the bidder is encouraged to bid the best possible equipment at the lowest possible price. In this instance, the "best" equipment is the piece that exactly matches the specification. The dealer, who is anxious to submit the lowest price possible, will often substitute an inferior product that may not meet the quality described in the specification. The burden of proof of quality rests on the dealer (kitchen equipment contractor), and the responsibility for acceptance of the quality recommended rests on the consultant and client. To avoid unpleasantness in the negotiations, most equipment dealers will bid the model number and brand name that is mentioned in the specification. Pages 34-35 show fabricated and catalog equipment specifications.

SPECIFICATION CHECKLIST

In the examples given, notice the format for writing the equipment specification. This format can be summarized in an easy-to-follow checklist that helps to eliminate errors and omissions. The following are elements of the checklist:

- *Item number:* The number used on the drawing, in the specifications, and on the equipment schedule.
- *Name:* The generic name of the equipment (work table, grill, oven, walk-in freezer, etc.).
- *Number:* The quantity to be furnished (listed, for example, as "two (2)" to help eliminate errors in typing).
- *Model and manufacturer:* The model number, name and location of manufacturer. This indicates the first choice of the client and/or consultant.
- *Measurement (size):* Width, length, and height.
- *Description:* Specification of the quality and standards of fabrication along with a description of the standard parts normally furnished with the equipment.
- *Utility requirements:* Listing of the electrical, plumbing, steam, and ventilation requirements for the equipment.
- *Accessories:* The optional finishes, features, and parts that have a substantial impact on the price.
- *Approvals:* Underwriter Laboratories (UL), National Sanitation Foundation (NSF), American Society of Mechanical Engineers (ASME), and American Gas Association (AGA), and other recognized associations that have established standards of construction and safety.

Other notes: Special installation notes or instructions that will assist the bidder and/or contractor in understanding the desires of the client or consultant; special local codes or regulations for this particular piece of equipment.

PERFORMANCE SPECIFICATIONS

A performance specification describes an amount of work that must be done by or the capacity of equipment and establishes a standard of performance. Performance specifications are more common in the building industry than in the foodservice industry. Performance specification wording, however, does frequently appear in equipment catalog materials. For instance, "Fryer must be capable of preparing 100 pounds of french fries per hour" is clearly a performance specification. The problem with this type of specification is that it is very difficult to measure or judge. When the fryer is installed, how can the consultant or owner measure the actual results? Frying 100 pounds of french fries in one hour might be possible, but to what degree of doneness? Are the french fries frozen or fresh? A specification that includes the materials to be furnished seems to be more definitive and easier to judge. The words "material specifications" are not commonly used, but are included in this section to clarify the two types of equipment specifications.

CONTRACT DOCUMENTS

The design development/engineering step in the design sequence is usually concluded by the preparation of the contract documents. The contract documents usually include:

- Final drawings, including site drawings, floor plans, mechanical drawings, elevations, schedules, and other graphic data needed to construct or renovate the facility
- Specifications, broken into sections according to general construction, landscaping, electrical, HVAC, plumbing, structural, demolition, foodservices (kitchen equipment), and other parts of the project

▼

EXAMPLE OF A FABRICATED EQUIPMENT SPECIFICATION

Item D-3 Dish Scraping Table

Provide one (1) dish scraping table, "L" shape as shown on plan, measuring 8 feet four inches long × 3 feet 0 inches wide × 10 feet 0 inches long × 2 feet 6 inches wide × 34 inches high. Construct top of no. 14-gauge stainless steel with all edges formed to a raised 3-inch high edge. Table shall be mounted on eight (8) 1⅝-inch diameter stainless steel tubular legs with adjustable stainless steel feet and cross bracing, as shown on plan.

Where shown on plan, provide a cutout for a disposer, and fit the opening with an 18-inch stainless steel cone cover. As a part of this item, provide a model FD-125 waste disposer as manufactured by Hobart. Electrical characteristics shall be 208/3 phase, 1¼ HP, 3.3 AMP. Provide an 18-inch cone, vinyl silver saver splash guard ring, and vacuum breaker (Group B). Fabricate scraping troughs from table to flow into cone. Weld and polish the troughs to the cone. Provide electrical control group number 2, and mount on a stainless plate under dish table.

Provide two troughs, as shown on plan, with coved corners, measuring 8 inches wide × 4 feet and 2 feet long, with depth that varies from 4 inches on one end to 6½ inches on the disposer end. The troughs shall be fitted with a ½-inch chrome plated faucet under table with a fitting at the end of each trough for washing garbage into disposer. A 6-×-8-inch depression, 2 inches deep, shall be made at the lower end of each trough to prevent silverware from washing into disposer.

Provide a cutout in table sized as shown on plan. The cutout shall have a ½-inch raised edge on all four sides, and shall have a stainless steel chute 1 inch deep. As a part of this item, provide a mobile undercounter soak sink 25 inches × 27 inches × 18 inches high, Model 3474 without chute, as manufactured by Seco. The kitchen equipment contractor can fabricate the soak sink of no. 14-gauge stainless steel, and meet the Seco specifications, if desired.

Provide overhead shelf for 20-×-20-inch dish racks, measuring 8 feet 0 inches long × 21 inches deep, located as shown on plan. Construct shelf of no. 16-gauge stainless steel, turn shelf up on bottom edge 2 inches and top of shelf down 1½ inches, and connect a drain from shelf to dish table of stainless steel tubing. The end of the shelf should have a ½-inch edge to prevent glass racks from falling off the end. The front edge of the shelf should be 56 inches AFF and the back end 62 inches AFF; and the shelf shall be supported with six (6) stainless tubular legs, welded to dish table in a rigid manner.

Sound deaden underside of table with ¼-inch layer of mastic and spray paint with an aluminum paint.

Construct table to NSF standards.

The kitchen equipment contractor shall deliver table to job site in no more than two pieces, one if possible. Field welding and polishing shall be done so that the weld is not visible. Final electrical and plumbing connections shall be by others.

EXAMPLE OF A CATALOG EQUIPMENT SPECIFICATION

Item K-12 Grill

Provide one (1) grill, measuring 48 inches long × 33⅛ inches deep × 37½ inches high (height of cooking surface above floor), Model 48 BLFD, Miraclean Gas Griddle as manufactured by Keating of Chicago, Bellwood, Illinois.

Grill shall have exterior of welded and reinforced stainless steel at front, sides, and rear. Griddle shall be supplied with cooking surface of ¾-inch thick, hardened 40/50 carbon steel polished mirror bright and coated with trivalent chromium. Cooking surface to measure 30 inches deep × 45 inches long.

Temperature to be controlled by two thermostats as standard.

Grill to have full width, 2-inch grease trough along the front, 3-inch grease trough along the left, and a 4- × ½-inch drain located in the front section of the left trough draining into a 2-gallon grease drawer.

Integral splash guards to be provided at sides and rear.

As a part of this item, provide a standard stand. Grill shall be without legs suitable for mounting on modular stand, and shall be sealed to this stand so that grease will not accumulate between stand and bottom of grill.

Grill stand shall be constructed of stainless steel with bullet type feet. The grill mounted on the stand shall measure 37½ inches from the floor to the cooking surface and be 48 inches in width.

All controls shall be mounted on the front panel of unit.

Utility requirements: 160,000 Btu each unit.

Provide UL and NSF approval and AGA certification.

· Special instructions to bidders, including the required legal documents, such as building permits and other licenses

As the name implies, "contract documents" become a part of the contract between the owner and general contractor or kitchen equipment contractor. If the food facilities part of the project is separated from the general contract, then the contract documents would be written separately for the kitchen equipment contractor and the general contractor.

Step 6: Bidding and Awarding the Contract

The bidding process and award of the contract take a few days even for a simple project such as the replacement of an oven or range. For purchasing a section of a kitchen, the process may take three weeks, with a requirement that dealers return their bids in two weeks. For a large project (Level III) the bidding may take four to six weeks, and the award of contract two weeks, for a total time of two months. The reason that the time period increases as the scope of the project increases is that each bidder must obtain prices from each company that will furnish labor and/or materials on the project.

Contract documents must be carefully examined to be sure that no item is overlooked. When discovered after the contract is signed, the omission of a single item by the contractor can result in an unexpected cost of thousands of dollars.

After awarding the contract and obtaining the necessary permits, construction or renovation can begin.

Step 7: Construction

During the construction phase, the food facilities design consultant will:

· Review shop drawings for fabrication of equipment
· Answer questions from the contractor or architect
· Attend job site meetings, if requested
· Inspect fabricated equipment while it is in the fabrication shop
· Approve drawings prepared by the contractor

Step 8: Inspection/Acceptance

The food facility will be inspected at least twice during the final phase of construction. The first inspection will probably occur after all the equipment has been set in place and most of the pieces are connected. The inspection usually involves the food facilities design consultant, the dealer (kitchen equipment contractor), and a representative of the architectural firm. Any problems seen during the inspection are noted and compiled into what is termed a "punch list." The items on the list must be corrected by the dealer before a second inspection is made. The second inspection (or third, if necessary) should be made after all equipment has been connected, tested, and is ready for food preparation. The second punch list should be much shorter than the first. A letter to the owner and architect prepared by the design consultant, recommending acceptance of the food facility, is often the final step in the design sequence.

Step 9: Implementation and Training

Demonstration of the equipment and training sessions to explain the layout and design to the employees are helpful last steps. When an employee remarks, "I wonder who designed this mess?" (a frequently heard remark), one can assume that the people who use the kitchen probably do not understand the concepts that were put into the design by the consultant. Training employees in the proper use of the equipment is often handled by either the consultant, manufacturer's representative, or the kitchen equipment dealer.

SUMMARY

The planning team for the development of a foodservice facility project can work together most effectively if each member of the team understands the role of the others. This chapter clarifies the functions of the various team members and provides the owner, manager, or client with a description of the work normally accomplished by the foodservice design consultant. The chronology of events that typically occur when a project is being planned and constructed is described in some detail under the heading "The Design Sequence." Architects and food facilities design consultants work together during many stages in this sequence. Two of the steps, however, the feasibility study and the implementation and training, are frequently the sole responsibility of the design consultant.

Contract documents establish the legal relationship between the client and the contractor and are frequently used to interpret the quality of work that must be accomplished by the contractor. Specifications that are a part of the contract documents must be carefully written so that the quantity and quality of each piece of equipment is clearly understood. A standard format for writing the specifications provides clarity and assists all persons who must read and interpret the contract documents.

The manager or other foodservice professionals can obtain maximum benefit from the food facilities design consultant if the role of the consultant is clearly understood.

CHAPTER 3

THE PRINCIPLES OF DESIGN

THIS CHAPTER WILL:

▶ Describe the basic principles of design for all food facilities

▶ Focus on human engineering in design

▶ Develop the method for analyzing the space in each major part of a food operation, to assure a balance of space in the final design

▶ List the general description of each functional area of the food facility, its relationship to other areas, the amount of space needed, and special design features

BASIC DESIGN PRINCIPLES

Although there are significant differences in the physical layout, menu, and method of service of various food facilities, there are underlying design principles that are followed by a food facilities designer in any type of situation. These principles lead to efficiency and a pleasant environment for the worker and customer, but do not result in one particular layout. Prototype restaurants of the three leading hamburger chains are quite different in layout, each for its own reason, but all follow a set of design principles.

A common misconception about design is that there is only one "right" way to lay out the equip-ment and arrange the space. There are, in fact, many designs that would be acceptable and work-able for the same facility. A competent designer will approach a facilities design project knowing that in each project a different set of variables will prevail. Each food facility is treated as unique, with its own design problems to be solved.

The reader should understand the difference between "design" and "layout." Design encompasses the entire facility, with all the considerations that were discussed in chapter 1 on concept development. Layout involves a consideration of each small unit or work space in a food facility. In the field of architecture or food facilities design we speak of "designing" a building or a foodservice operation and of "laying out" a range section or bakery.

Compromise

In every design project, conflicting needs will give rise to a series of compromise conditions that the designer must be able to work with. Certainly the number of compromises should be kept to a minimum, but it is certain that they will always exist. For example, in the design of a dining area, it might be highly desirable to include a private dining room that could be closed off for special groups. Should this room be near the customer entrance for easy public access or near the kitchen for convenience to the hot food production area? The answer might be "both"! However, if placing the private dining room near both the entrance and the kitchen interferes with other major components of the design, the best alternative may be to move it to another part of the dining area. Conflicting needs always arise in the design process, and only the skilled and experienced person will be able to balance priorities so that the resulting compromises are logical and defensible. Since the owner's priorities may not be the same as the designer's, frank discussion and give-and-take by all parties are often needed to create a satisfactory working relationship.

The designer will be basing his or her work on a set of principles that should be clearly described to the client before the project begins. If the client insists on making choices that depart from principles of good design, the designer has three choices.

1. Resign and bill the client for the work completed as of the day of the disagreement.
2. Formally protest the change and give in to the client's demand. The change should be put in writing for all to see, but not in such a way that the client would be embarrassed.
3. Resubmit the design, hoping that an agreement can be reached that will satisfy the client and that will preserve the principles of good design.

Resubmission is quite common, and it is not unusual to resubmit at least four to eight times for the design of a major project. Resubmission should be viewed as a healthy approach to the idea that a good design represents the best thinking of many people.

Each design professional has a set of guidelines that he or she has found helpful in approaching the design of a food facility. Thus, while certain principles are universally accepted, there is no standard set of design rules for all professionals working in the foodservice field. The following principles, which are based on the author's own experience as a food facilities design professional, are intended to provide a general framework for approaching the design process. The design should:

- have flexibility and modularity
- have simplicity
- create efficient flow of materials and personnel
- facilitate ease of sanitation
- create ease of supervision
- use space efficiently

The Principle of Flexibility and Modularity

The use of heavy-gauge stainless steel in the construction of kitchen equipment is almost universally accepted by the foodservice industry. Stainless steel does not rust, is easy to clean, is not porous, and does not easily wear out. Stainless steel has the major fault of being very inflexible, however. A stainless steel table in the kitchen cannot be modified easily to accommodate a change in the design. If, for instance, a work area 14 feet in length is required, the principle of flexibility would lead the designer to specify two tables, one 6 feet long and one 8 feet long. These two lengths would permit rearrangement of the kitchen, without the necessity of cutting the table to accommodate a new design. The principle of flexibility requires components that can be rearranged to meet changing conditions, such as new management, different methods of service, a new menu, or a new preparation method. Designing for change is the primary means of achieving flexibility.

In the dining area, flexibility can be achieved

by dividing movable walls. In the service area, the space can be divided to accommodate both table service and buffet service.

An inflexible construction method that was popular in the past was the construction of concrete pads as a base for kitchen equipment. These bases were used in the place of legs for refrigerators, ovens, or other heavy pieces of equipment to eliminate the difficulty in cleaning under the equipment. The problem with these bases is that as the equipment was replaced or the kitchen was rearranged, the bases were then the wrong shape or were in the wrong spot. A concrete base is difficult to eliminate and almost impossible to move. Concrete bases are now infrequently seen in commercial kitchens.

Modularity in design provides standardized sizes and functions of space and equipment. For example, in the construction industry doors are "modular" because they are sized according to an industry standard. Reach-in refrigerators in the foodservice industry usually are modular in size and function. In a free-flow or "scramble" cafeteria, the service components should be modular, so that the service lines can be easily shifted, as menu and customer tastes change. Modular range sections, which are commonly used, permit the designer to select from many types of equipment and to arrange these in a smooth and continuous lineup. "Quick disconnect" utility lines that allow inexpensive changes and easy disconnection of the equipment are an excellent example of flexibility and modularity. The modular pieces can be designed for "off-the-floor" installation, with the entire range section mounted on legs for ease in cleaning. In future years, if a piece of equipment needs to be replaced, the modular unit can be removed without disturbing other pieces of equipment.

The Principle of Simplicity

In the designing of a food facility, striving for simplicity offers a great many advantages. Foodservices facilities seem to invite clutter, and clutter leads to poor sanitation, confusion, and inefficiency in the work areas, as well as an environment that customers may find uncomfortable and overcrowded.

The principle of simplicity can be incorporated into the design of foodservice components and systems in various ways. Some examples are:

- Clean uncluttered lines for range sections
- Simple wall-hung tables in areas where a heavy grease or soil condition exists
- The use of modular or drop-in cooking equipment that eliminates corners, edges, and unnecessary undershelves or overshelves
- The elimination of wheels on equipment that will seldom be moved
- The elimination of utility connections that penetrate the floor (rather than the wall behind the equipment), creating dirt pockets and clutter
- The selection of a piece of equipment without unnecessary accessories
- Convenient waiter/waitress stations near the serving area in the dining room
- The arrangement of tables in the dining room to create natural and comfortable aisle space for waiters and guests

Examples of the violation of the principle of simplicity exist in many restaurant kitchens. For instance, the large stainless steel equipment stands for fryers and grills sold by equipment manufacturers are very expensive and difficult to clean. A better solution is a simple, flat stainless steel table with drop-in fryers and grills. This would save thousands of dollars in the original installation and make the cleaning process much simpler for the employees.

The Principle of Flow of Materials and Personnel

The movement of food through a foodservice facility should follow a logical sequence beginning with receiving and ending with waste disposal. Since both receiving and waste disposal usually occur at the back dock of a food operation, the food moves through the food facility in a circle, as illustrated in figure 3-1.

If the food does not move in the order shown, then backtracking by the personnel will occur, resulting in lower productivity and wasted labor.

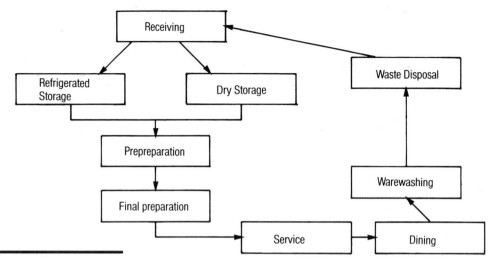

3-1. THE FLOW OF MATERIALS AND PERSONNEL.

The following are examples of some flow considerations in design:

- The movement of employees from one section of the kitchen to another
- The flow of dishes through the dishwashing system, back to the service area.
- In a restaurant, the flow of customers from the entrance to the cocktail lounge and/or to the main dining room
- In a cafeteria, the flow of customers from the entrance through the service cafeteria to the dish drop-off point
- The flow of raw food ingredients through the main traffic aisles of the kitchen to the preparation area

It is helpful for the designer to diagram the flow patterns on the preliminary floor plan, showing the movement of customers, food, dishes, trash, and garbage. Color coding the flow-lines makes the patterns easier to distinguish and assists the designer in arriving at a design solution that accommodates the proper flow of materials and personnel.

The Principle of Ease of Sanitation

In virtually every type of facility, more employee labor hours are spent cleaning the food operation than are spent preparing the food. A food facility designed with sanitation in mind can be cleaned more quickly and easily and thus require fewer labor hours for this aspect of operation. Some examples of sanitation design considerations are described below:

- *Building finishes* that are durable and easy to clean. Structural glazed tile on the walls is the most desirable building finish because of ease of cleaning and damage resistance. Ceramic tile is easy to clean and can be purchased in colorful patterns that make the kitchen a pleasant place to work. Epoxy paint on cement block is the least expensive wall finish, but will turn brown around areas that are exposed to high heat. The painted surface is also easily chipped by rolling equipment. The use of bright colors in the kitchen will improve the general appearance of the space and encourage cleanliness. Quarry tile is the standard floor finish for the industry because it does not wear, is grease resistant, and is less slippery than other floors when wet.
- *Wall-hung equipment.* The use of equipment that is attached to the wall, eliminating the use of legs, makes an excellent sanitation design (fig. 3-2). A space is created under the equipment, allowing for ease of cleaning.
- *Equipment racks* with a minimum number of legs.

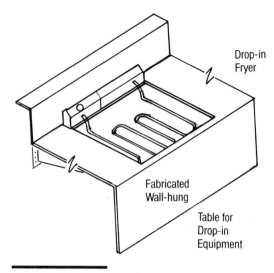

Drop-in
Fryer

Fabricated
Wall-hung

Table for
Drop-in
Equipment

3-2. WALL-HUNG FRYER.

- *Garbage disposals* in work areas to facilitate waste disposal.
- *Shelf storage design.* Portable storage shelving systems and open shelving under tables can be cleaned easily.

The subject of sanitation of food preparation equipment will be covered in some detail in chapter 5.

The Principle of Ease of Supervision

Many hotels and foodservice institutions built during the 1920s and 1930s had vegetable preparation areas that were remote from the main kitchen or separated by partitions and were therefore difficult to supervise. The open type of design, which is now preferred, allows the supervisor to oversee the production areas more efficiently. The elimination of walls and partitions also permits workers to move and communicate with each other more easily and tends to reduce the number of people needed.

The separation of production areas by floor level not only violates the ease-of-supervision principle by increasing the amount of supervision needed, but it also creates cumbersome flow patterns between the floors. The designer should avoid separating the production areas by floor whenever possible.

It is often desirable to put a half-wall under hoods and between work departments. A 4-foot half-wall provides separation and defines workspace, but does not block the view of the supervisor, who needs to maintain contact with production workers. A half wall is also very useful as:

- a place to attach wall-hung equipment
- a sanitary site for utility connections
- a containment device for spilled water (around stock kettles)

The Principle of Space Efficiency

As costs of building construction and maintenance rise, designers are constantly striving to incorporate space-saving ideas into their work. In this case, necessity can be turned to advantage—space saving is translated into space efficiency in the design of a small, well-equipped food facilities work area.

The principle of space efficiency can, of course, be carried to the extreme. Small, efficient kitchens are a pleasure to use, but kitchens that are too small can be most unpleasant for cooks and other kitchen workers. How can the designer know the difference between "small and efficient" and "too small"? Providing the following components will help ensure that each section of the kitchen has the necessary equipment and storage space to enable employees to work efficiently:

- a work surface (table)
- a sink
- a cutting surface
- storage for utensils
- storage for pans
- storage for raw ingredients
- storage for the finished product
- proper aisle space for movement

If each work area includes the above features, and the work area is arranged efficiently and is adequate for their utilization, the food facility will be space efficient. (Space efficiency and the proper layout of work areas will be developed more fully later in this chapter.)

HUMAN ENGINEERING

A work environment that is designed with the comfort and safety of the workers in mind will have a tremendous effect on worker productivity. If workers have a pleasant place to work, with the proper equipment and tools at hand, they will be likely to enjoy the job and function more efficiently. The primary factors that influence the quality of the workplace are:

- proper levels of temperature and humidity
- sufficient work space
- properly designed equipment
- availability of materials handling tools
- control of noise levels
- proper lighting levels
- proper equipment height

Temperature and Humidity

The relationship between temperature, humidity, and air movement is a technical subject that is the responsibility of the engineer on the design project. However, the food facilities design consultant needs to be aware of this aspect of environmental design, which affects the comfort of the building occupants. The range of temperature and humidity in which most of the people who use the building will be comfortable is referred to as the "comfort zone." In the winter, if the temperature is too high and the humidity too low, an unpleasant dryness results. In winter, outside air usually contains very little moisture. When this air is drawn into a building and heated to 70°F (21.1°C), the humidity drops to a very low level. In the summer, the reverse condition often exists. Moist air from the outside is drawn in and cooled, resulting in high humidity. Air conditioning reduces the amount of moisture in the hot humid air and provides a comfortable combination of low temperature and low humidity in the summer.

In foodservice facilities, very few kitchens or dishwashing rooms are air conditioned. Air movement is therefore essential for comfort. If the temperature is slightly high but air movement is rapid, skin evaporation will usually keep the body cool enough for comfort. Dishwashing rooms and range sections of a food facility are usually the most difficult areas to keep comfortable. In the dishroom, the high humidity produced by the moisture and steam from the automatic dishwashing equipment creates two problems: the workers are uncomfortable, and the dishes do not air dry.

The designer must work closely with the engineers to be sure that air movement is sufficient and that ventilation ducts are provided for both the feed (entrance) and discharge ends of the dishmachine. Typical vent requirements recommended by commercial dishwasher manufacturers are 200 CFM (cubic feet per minute) at the entrance to the machine and 400 CFM at the discharge of the machine (Hobart Manufacturing Company, Model C-44 Dishwasher). It is suggested that these levels of air movement be increased slightly above the recommended levels, since dishwashing rooms themselves often do not have enough "room exhaust." The additional exhaust will keep the room more comfortable.

The range section of a kitchen is often uncomfortable for the cooks because of the heat generated by broilers, hot top ranges, and other pieces of equipment that produce (and waste) large amounts of energy. The high heat condition is usually the result of inadequate exhaust ventilation by the hood equipment. (This problem is discussed in detail in chapter 6.)

Sufficient Workspace

There are many different workspaces that must be considered in an overall design of a food facility. The amount of space needed by a dishwasher is far different from that needed by a waitress at a beverage station. In the dishwasher's situation, the worker needs to move back and forth, stooping, gathering carts and racks, and performing other tasks that require a considerable amount of space. The waitress may need only enough room to pass by a beverage station and pick up a coffee pot or glass of milk, en route to the dining room.

The information provided below on workspace can be used as a general guideline. It is no substitute, however, for a common-sense evaluation of the unique requirements of any given foodservice facility. The amount of space that an individual worker needs is influenced by:

- the number of people working in the space
- the amount and type of equipment
- the clearance required for equipment doors
- the type of food being processed
- the amount of space needed for storage

AISLE SPACE

The aisle space needed for different types of work areas is listed below:

DESCRIPTION OF THE SPACE	AISLE WIDTH NEEDED
Single aisle with limited equipment	2 feet 6 inches to 3 feet 0 inches
Double aisle with limited equipment	3 feet 6 inches to 4 feet 6 inches
Single aisle with protruding equipment	3 feet 6 inches to 4 feet 6 inches
Double aisle with protruding equipment	4 feet 6 inches to 5 feet 6 inches
Aisle with little traffic	3 feet 0 inches to 4 feet 0 inches
Aisle with major traffic	4 feet 0 inches to 6 feet 0 inches

An example of a double aisle with protruding equipment is shown in figure 3-3.

As noted in the preceding list, the width of major traffic aisles should range between 4 and 6 feet. A major traffic aisle is used for the movement of people and material from storage to production areas, or from production areas to the point of service. A piece of equipment with a protruding door should never be located in a major traffic aisle that is only 4 feet wide. An aisle 6 feet wide can accommodate a refrigerator door or other protruding equipment.

It is important that aisles be the proper size, because they have a significant influence on the

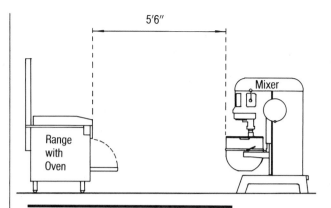

3-3. A DOUBLE AISLE WITH PROTRUDING EQUIPMENT.

total size of the food facility and on operating efficiency. If the aisle is too narrow, employees will have a difficult time working in the space. If the aisle is too wide, the employees will be required to take many extra steps during the day, and fatigue and low productivity will result.

WORK SURFACES

In its Standard Number 1 (revised June 1984), the National Sanitation Foundation (NSF) lists three types of surfaces used for foodservice equipment: food contact surfaces, splash contact surfaces, and nonfood contact surfaces. NSF describes the materials that may be used as follows:

Food contact surfaces: Surface materials in the food zone shall be smooth, corrosion resistant, nontoxic, stable, and nonabsorbent under use condition. They shall not impart an odor, color, taste, or contribute to the adulteration of food.

Splash contact surfaces: shall be smooth, easily changeable, and corrosion resistant or rendered corrosion resistant with a material which is noncracking and nonchipping.

Nonfood contact surfaces: shall be smooth, corrosion resistant or rendered corrosion resistant.

Work surfaces should be arranged within easy reach of the worker. Table tops are often 30 inches wide in production areas, because the average worker can reach out only 30 inches from a standing position. The height of the working surface should permit the worker to chop or to do other hand work without stooping over. The height of a work surface must be adjusted for the height of the worker and the type of material that is placed on the work surface. A thick cutting board, for instance, will raise the surface height by as much as 1¾ to 3 inches.

The standard used by most designers for the height of a work surface is 34 to 37 inches (fig. 3-4). If a work area will be used for heavy bulky objects, a lower height should be selected. Some height variations can be created for the worker by the use of mats on the floor, cutting boards on the table, or adjustable table feet.

The amount of space needed from one side of a work surface to the other will depend on the size of the materials used and the layout of the work area. For example, if standard 18- by 26-inch sheet pans are used as trays for holding individual tossed salads, space would be needed for:

- empty bowls
- bulk tossed salad
- empty sheet pans
- sheet pans filled with salads

In this example, 6 linear feet of space is provided, even though the worker cannot reach that far from one position (fig. 3-5).

The most important guideline for good workplace layout is to think through the steps in a process and provide a space for the food and equipment needed to carry out these steps. For instance, a sandwich makeup table in a cold food production area needs

- storage for plates
- refrigerated storage for food
- storage for bread

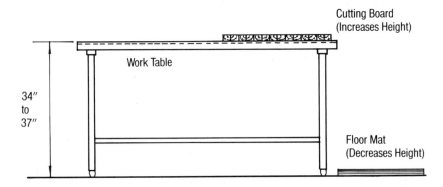

3-4. STANDARD HEIGHT FOR WORK SURFACE.

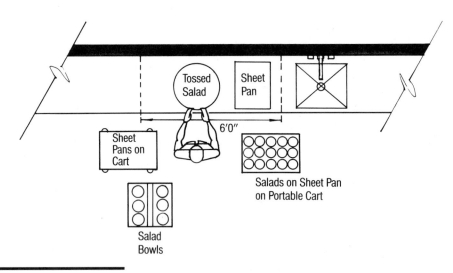

3-5. SPACE NEEDS FOR PREPARING TOSSED SALADS.

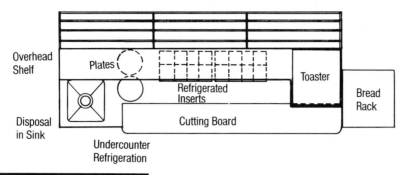

3-6. PIZZA TABLE DESIGNED INTO A SANDWICH WORK STATION.

- utensil drawer or rack
- cutting surface
- toaster
- refrigerated compartments for condiments
- sink with hot and cold water
- garbage disposal or can
- pick up area for waiters/waitresses

A pizza makeup table satisfies most of these requirements—it has many refrigerated compartments, a wide cutting surface, and space for many of the other pieces of equipment needed (fig. 3-6).

Properly Designed Equipment

The design of equipment from the human engineering point of view is also a consideration of the professional food facilities design consultant.

This section will discuss fabricated equipment specified by the designer and how it affects the people working in foodservice facilities. (The use of manufactured equipment is covered in detail in chapter 4.)

The National Sanitation Foundation has established standards for constructing foodservice equipment that are primarily concerned with safety and sanitation. The reader can consult NSF publications, which are available at a small cost from NSF in Ann Arbor, Michigan.

The checklist beginning on page 46 can be used as a guide to human engineering in equipment design. Although it is not intended as a comprehensive check for all design features that should be in a food facility, the list does contain items that are often overlooked in designing a foodservice facility. The use of the checklist will help assure a food operation that is engineered for comfort, safety, and sanitation.

Materials Handling Tools

The lifting of heavy objects by foodservice workers will lead to accidents and personal injury. Materials handling tools and equipment that can greatly reduce or eliminate worker injury include:

- forklift trucks
- hand forklift trucks (mules)
- carts
- hand trucks
- portable receiving ramps
- skate wheel conveyors

The materials handling tool that will be most frequently used for assembling ingredients in the kitchen will be a simple cart. The cart is often abused by the worker, through heavy use and the dropping of full cases of food onto the top shelf. The designer should specify the heaviest cart (600-1,000-pound capacity) possible to prevent damage and abuse.

Forklift trucks are normally reserved for large foodservice warehouses, but the hand-operated forklift is frequently used in the storeroom and kitchen of medium-sized and large foodservice operations. Hand-operated forklifts raise pallets of food a few inches off the floor, permitting easy transport to a freezer or storeroom. Hand trucks are simple L-shaped two-wheeled devices that permit the worker to balance a stack of case goods on two wheels and to move it in or out of storage.

Receiving ramps and skate wheel conveyors

Floors
( ) Adequate number of floor drains to keep floors dry
( ) Carborundum chips in quarry tile in slippery or wet areas
( ) Slip-resistant wax on vinyl floors
( ) Ramps and handrails in receiving area and storage space for carts and hand trucks
( ) Floor mats for comfort of workers who must stand in one place for long periods of time
( ) Kitchen floor level with walk-in refrigerator floor
( ) Heavy slope of floor around steam-jacketed kettles to encourage quick drain off of hot liquids to floor drains
( ) Coved corners of floors, where they meet the wall for ease of cleaning

Materials handling
( ) Hand trucks and carts for moving all foods
( ) Strong, easy-to-clean shelving
( ) Portable shelving
( ) Ladders for reaching stored goods on high shelves
( ) Carts for the movement of processed foods from production area to refrigeration and then to service area

Utensil handling
( ) Knife racks
( ) Easy-to-clean utensil drawers with removable inserts
( ) Utensil drawers at every work station and table
( ) Overhead utensil racks

Food production equipment
( ) Compliance with NSF standards
( ) Portable equipment, if needed in more than one department
( ) Portable bins for flour, sugar, and salt
( ) Wall hung or mounted on legs for ease of cleaning
( ) Free of burrs, sharp edges, or difficult-to-reach areas
( ) Safety equipment and guards on equipment such as shields for mixing machine
( ) Disposals in all production areas (if permitted by local codes)
( ) Open rail type undershelving that will permit crumbs and small particles of food to fall to the floor
( ) Marine edge on all tables with sinks (to prevent water from spilling on floor)
( ) Adequate space for parking equipment from other departments (bread racks, raw ingredients from stores, etc.)

Warewashing equipment
( ) Pot storage racks beside pot-washing station and in or near each work area
( ) Storage containers for soiled linen
( ) Box, glass, and metal can container in each major work area

( ) Utensil sorting table
( ) Paper and bone container at dishwashing station
( ) Prerinse, power or hand
( ) Cleaning supply storage
( ) Hose reel
( ) Cart wash down area

Service and Dining

( ) Condiments and support service equipment available near the point of service
( ) Convenient dish dropoff
( ) Easy-to-clean chairs with absence of cracks that accumulate crumbs
( ) Minimum number of steps from food pickup to point of service
( ) Well-designed waiter/waitress station to reduce the number of trips to the kitchen
( ) Dishes, glasses, and cups on under-counter portable carts to eliminate double handling of dishes
( ) Linen storage convenient to dining area

permit the movement of materials from one level to the next, without lifting. Receiving docks are the wrong height for some of the different types of delivery trucks that bring goods to the receiving area. A portable receiving ramp, constructed of lightweight aluminum, is very helpful in solving the height variation problem. Motorized "load leveler" devices are often designed into the ramp to solve this same problem. Motor driven belts, dumb waiters, and elevators are also used to transport materials from one level to the next.

Adequate Lighting

The standard measure of light is the footcandle, which is equivalent to the amount of light from a standard candle that strikes a 1-foot-square surface from a distance of 1 foot. The farther away a light is placed from the surface to be lighted, the lower the number of footcandles. For this reason, lighting needs to be spaced at frequent intervals in a food production area. The following chart should be used as a guide in selecting the proper light levels for food facilities.

SPACE	FOOTCANDLES
Kitchen work area	30–40
Classroom	40–50
Cashier	50–60
Storeroom	10–15
Landing platform	20–25
Building entrance	10–20
Bathroom	10–30
Hotel: general areas	10–20
Accounting and bookkeeping	100–150
Foodservice dining room	
Fast-food	40–50
Moderate price	10–20
High price	5–15

In service areas that will be seen by the public, one very effective means of lighting is to provide a high intensity of light on the food and low intensity for the main part of the room. High-intensity lighting for food display is illustrated in figure 3-7.

Control of Noise Levels

High noise levels are very unpleasant for the worker in a foodservice facility. It has been demonstrated in industrial settings that excessive noise causes

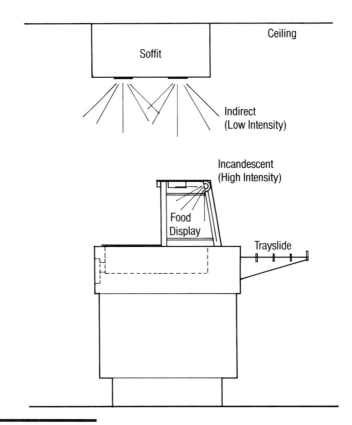

3-7. LIGHTING OVER A CAFETERIA SERVICE COUNTER.

fatigue, accidents, and low productivity in a direct relationship to the volume of the noise. Some techniques that will help to reduce noise in a foodservice facility are:

- Sound-deadening materials sprayed onto the underside of all tables and counters.
- The separation of areas (other than production) in the food facility department, especially warewashing. The construction of walls between the kitchen and warewashing will restrict noise transmission.
- Designing conveyors to create a sound barrier between dish drop-off points and warewashing. An illustration of a sound barrier that might be used in a self-bussing application for a restaurant or cafeteria is illustrated in figure 3-8.
- Acoustic ceilings that are grease or moisture resistant.
- Carpeting in dining rooms in the seating areas.
- Carpeting on the walls in dining areas. This is an excellent wall finish because it not only absorbs sound, but will take the punishment of chairs and tables that often scar wooden, papered, or painted wall finishes.
- Double doors between the dining room and the kitchen.
- Background music in both the public areas and the back of the establishment (kitchen, warewashing, service areas).
- Remote refrigeration compressors.

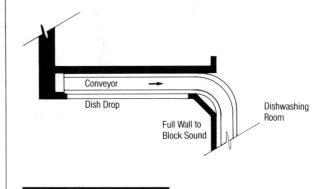

3-8. CONTROLLING DISHROOM NOISE.

SPACE ANALYSIS

How large should a food facility be? Should the kitchen be half the size of the dining room? How much space will be needed for warewashing and storage? These and related questions must be answered during the early phase of the design project, since the answers will determine the size and thus the total cost of the facility. By knowing space requirements in advance, the owner or architect can make realistic preliminary estimates of construction costs.

It is the design consultant's job to determine the space requirements for each section of the foodservice facility before the actual design can begin. This early but difficult estimate of space is achieved by gathering basic data about the nature of the planned food operation. The chart on pages 50-51, used by Birchfield Foodsystems, shows the type of data that should be collected to determine space needs. Once this information has been obtained, the space requirements of each functional part of a foodservice facility are analyzed. The areas that need to be considered are the following:

Receiving
Storage
  dry storage
  paper and cleaning supplies storage
  refrigerated storage
  utensil and cleaning equipment storage
Office
Preparation areas
  prepreparation
  hot food preparation
  cold food preparation
  final preparation
Bakery
Employee locker room toilet
Service areas
Dining rooms
Warewashing

For purposes of easy reference, the description of each of these functional foodservice areas is divided into four sections entitled:

- General Description of the Space
- Relationship to Other Areas
- Amount of Space Needed
- Special Design Features

Receiving

GENERAL DESCRIPTION OF THE SPACE

The receiving area is located with easy access to driveways and street entrances to the property. Usually the architect will decide where major ingress/egress for people, delivery trucks, and service vehicles will be located. The food facilities design consultant must work with the architect to be sure that sufficient space is allocated for the movement of large tractor-trailer trucks and other vehicles that need access to the receiving area. Consideration must be given to proper screening of the receiving dock and especially to trash and garbage storage containers. It is desirable to screen the receiving area so that persons looking out of the building windows or walking along the street will not have a full view of the receiving dock and garbage containers.

RELATIONSHIP TO OTHER AREAS

The primary relationship of receiving is to the storage areas, which are often scattered and may in fact be located at different building levels. Regardless of the location of storage, easy access must be available for the movement of heavy materials from the receiving dock. The receiving dock must also be accessible to the kitchen for the following reasons:

- Many food products will go directly from receiving to the production areas in the kitchen.
- Refrigerated storage areas are often located adjacent to the kitchen and will be stocked directly from the receiving dock.
- Since in small- to medium-sized foodservice facilities, supervisory personnel such as the chef, manager, or assistant managers will personally be responsible for receiving the food,

CLIENT SURVEY FORM, BIRCHFIELD FOODSYSTEMS, INC.

1. Name of project _____
    Address _____
    _____
    Client's name _____
    Client's phone _____

2. Architect's name _____
    Address _____
    _____
    Phone _____

3. Engineer's name _____
    Phone _____

4. Number of persons to be served

	Total Number	Seats	Seat Turnover	Serving Hours
Breakfast				
Lunch				
Dinner				
Other				

5. Seating Capacity

	Seats	Recommended Sq. Ft.
Number of seats, main dining room		
Number of seats, snack bar		

Number of private dining rooms: _____

Number of seats in each PDR:

Seats	Sq. Ft.
_____	_____
_____	_____
_____	_____

Number of seats in ballroom _____ sq. ft.: _____

6. Method of cookery (scratch, convenience, mixture)

▼

7. Frequency of food deliveries (number per week)

   Grocery   Produce
   Meats   Dairy

8. Bakery products: Purchased? Made on the premises: (Describe extent of baking.)

9. Form of service (circle)

   Table   Counter
   Table with salad bar   Tray service
   Cafeteria   Banquet
   Scramble   Other
   Mini mall

10. Existing equipment capacities (if any)

    Oven   Steamer
    Kettle   Range
    Grill   Broiler
    Fryer   Dishwasher

11. The menu (describe or attach a copy)

    Breakfast

    Lunch

    Dinner

    Other

12. Utilities in new facility

    Electric
    1 & 3 phase
    Natural gas
    Hot water temperature
    Steam
    Who will design vent system?

easy access from the kitchen to the dock is highly desirable.

Other important relationships for the receiving area include access to trash containers, washdown rooms, and cleaning equipment.

AMOUNT OF SPACE NEEDED

Space needs in the receiving area vary with the volume of food to be received, frequency of delivery, and the distance between the receiving area and the storage spaces. If the receiving clerk must transport food products great distances before placing them in storage, the accumulation of food products on the back dock may require the allocation of additional space. Often, too much space is provided for the receiving dock, resulting in the accumulation of miscellaneous equipment and debris that add clutter to the food operation. The following chart provides general guidelines for allocating the proper amount of space for the receiving dock.

TYPE OF FOOD OPERATION	SPACE NEEDED[a] Sq. Ft.	(Sq. M.)	NUMBER OF TRUCKS
Fast-food	40–60	(3.72–5.58)	1
Small restaurant (under 75 seats)	60–80	(5.58–7.44)	1
Medium restaurant (75–150 seats) OR Small institution (300–1,000 meals per day)	80–100	(7.44–9.30)	1
Large restaurant (150–400 seats) OR Medium institution (1,000–2,000 meals per day)	120–150	(11.16–13.95)	2
Large institution (over 2,000 meals per day)	150–175	(13.95–16.28)	2
Large hotel, restaurant, or institution with complex menu, catering facilities, snack bars	175–200	(16.28–18.60)	3

[a]Does not include space for trash removal truck or trash container. Space for this equipment (approximately 40-60 sq. ft.—3.72-5.58 sq. m.) should be added to the receiving dock.

SPECIAL DESIGN FEATURES

The receiving dock can be designed as an elevated platform for tractor-trailer trucks, at street level, or at any level in between these two heights. The decision on receiving dock height will probably be determined by the architect on the basis of site development and the placement of the building on the property. The depth of the dock (distance from front to back) should permit a person to walk back and forth, with space for goods stored temporarily on wooden pallets. Usually 8 or 10 feet is sufficient. The length of the dock should accommodate the number of delivery trucks that are likely to be unloading at one time. For most foodservice operations, a receiving clerk can check in only one or two trucks at a time, and a single or at the most a double truck width is usually sufficient. A third truck width for a trash/garbage vehicle is also desirable. A range of 10 to 15 feet per truck should be used as a standard, depending on the angle for backing to the dock (fig. 3-9).

The following design features must be considered in the planning process for the receiving area:

- control
- protection from the weather
- scales
- materials handling equipment

Control: The control of food and supplies moving in and out of the receiving area will be of concern to the foodservice management staff. Visibility of the receiving area from an office window is highly desirable if the food facility is large enough to justify a receiving office. For a small food facility that does not have a receiving office, visual control from the kitchen or manager's office should be a design consideration. It is often necessary to construct a stairway at the back dock for the use of employees coming and going from the workplace. This presents a serious control problem because it permits easy access to food and supplies by employees as they enter or exit the building. If possible, a separately controlled entrance for employees should be incorporated into the building design. If this is not possible, the next best solution is to design a separate door and connected corridor from the receiving area to the interior of the building.

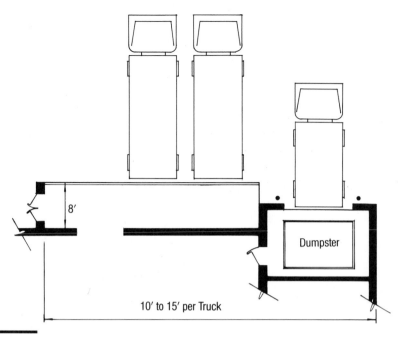

3-9. LAYOUT OF RECEIVING DOCK.

Protection from the weather: Receiving personnel must be protected from rain, cold, and excessive heat as they perform their duties on the back dock. Typical architectural solutions include a simple roof overhang, placement of the receiving dock in a recess under the exterior wall of the building, or the enclosure of the entire receiving area with a heavy-duty folding door. Unless weather conditions are extremely severe, the enclosure of the entire receiving area is excessively expensive. The door from the receiving area should be 5 feet wide when two doors are used and a minimum of 4 feet wide for a single door entrance. Double entry doors should be used for proper screening to prevent flies and other insects from entering the food production area. Air curtains, which are simple centrifugal fans located over the door entrances, are somewhat effective in discouraging the entry of flies.

Scales: The importance of scales adjacent to the receiving dock is often overlooked by many foodservice managers. Meats and most products are often prepackaged and weighed, with the weights clearly marked on the meat containers. It is often assumed—falsely—that these weights are always accurate. All foodservice facilities should have a scale for use by the receiving clerk to verify the weights of foods that are purchased by the pound or kilogram. The location of the scale should be in the break-out area inside the building, so that the scale is protected from the weather. (The types of scales that are most useful in foodservice facilities are described in chapter 5.)

Materials handling equipment: Several types of materials handling equipment are commonly used in foodservice receiving areas for efficient transport and to avoid stress and injury to employees. Hand trucks (two-wheeled vehicles for moving small stacks of case goods), platform hand trucks (four-wheeled flat vehicles) that are strong enough to hold the weight of fifteen or twenty cases of food goods, and wooden or steel pallets are all a part of the equipment needs for the receiving clerk. Large numbers of wooden pallets (skids) often accumulate in the receiving area because they are commonly used in the food distribution industry for holding and moving large quantities of case goods. Large foodservice operations may want to consider the design of store-room spaces to hold these large pallets, so that the double handling of hand goods is minimized. These pallets must be moved with either a hand-operated forklift device or a forklift truck.

Other Functions of the Receiving Area

The need for a separate receiving office, break-out area (a small space just inside the receiving doors for checking in and separating foods before putting them into storage), washdown room, or garbage room will depend on the size and complexity of the foodservice operation. These functions are usually carried out in the receiving area, and if space is not provided, they may encroach on other space. Office space should be small (50 square feet), and the washdown area and garbage room should also be limited in size: a range of 50 to 80 square feet should be sufficient. A small area just inside the receiving door can be allotted for break-out space. The following chart can be used as a guideline in deciding whether or not special rooms are needed.

| NUMBER OF SEATS | SPACE NEEDED | | |
	OFFICE	WASHDOWN	GARBAGE
Under 50 or fast-food	no	no	small
50–100	no	small	small
100–175	no	yes	yes
175–250	yes	yes	yes
250–500	yes	yes	yes
More than 500	yes	large	large

Storage

GENERAL DESCRIPTION OF THE SPACE

The amount of storage in a foodservice facility is primarily influenced by the number of meals per day served, the number of items that appear on the menu, the frequency of delivery, and the operating policies of the management staff. It is considered good management practice to turn the inventory over twelve times per year (once a month). Turnover for perishable products should, of course, be at least twice per week, and turnover for such items as paper and cleaning supplies may be infrequent. The attitude of management toward inventory turnover should always be discussed prior to beginning the design. The construction of a large canned goods storeroom, for instance, might be viewed by one manager as too small, because he likes the idea of keeping a large par stock of inventory on hand. Other management people might prefer to keep the par stock very low so that cash is not tied up in inventories. The use of computers in the foodservice industry has greatly enhanced the ability of manag-

ers to forecast the precise amount of food needed for each meal and, therefore, decrease the amount of food that must be kept on hand at any one time. Computers, more efficient distribution of food products by vendors, and high interest rates have all contributed to a trend toward smaller storage spaces.

The four categories of storage that must be available in all food facilities are:

· dry storage
· paper and cleaning supplies storage
· refrigerated storage
· utensil and cleaning equipment storage

RELATIONSHIP TO OTHER AREAS

Storage areas should be well ventilated, dry, and constructed of easy-to-clean surfaces. Concrete or tile floors, cement block walls with epoxy paint, and acoustic ceilings are common for all storage areas except those that are refrigerated. Large access doors and a high level of security must be included as part of the design. The most important relationship in the design is easy access from the storage area to both food production and receiving. The number of trips that will be made to the production area from the storage area will far exceed the number made from the receiving dock. It is therefore important to be sure that the staff in food production areas have short distances to travel to refrigerated storage and canned goods storage spaces. It is often possible to locate a produce walk-in refrigerator in the immediate vicinity of the cold food preparation department, so that few steps are necessary to procure salad materials and other frequently used perishable items.

Dry Storage

Standard weight and volume of cases of canned goods can be calculated easily. A case of 6 no. 10 cans weighs approximately 48 lbs. (21.8 kg) and occupies about 1 cubic foot (.028 cu. m) of volume. The maximum stack of cases of 6 no. 10 cans should be no more than 7 feet (2.1 m) in height.

Calculating a standard amount of dry storage space is difficult because of the many variables that affect the need. The method that is often used is to consider the many variables that cause fluctuations in the quantity of food to be stored and simply make an educated guess. It is usually better to estimate space needs on the basis of the industry's experience with different types of facilities. The following chart can be used as a rough guide for determining dry storage needs (assuming that deliveries are made twice per week, and that cleaning supplies and paper are stored separately).

| TYPE OF FOOD OPERATION | RANGE OF SIZE OF DRY STORAGE | |
	Sq. Ft.	(Sq. M.)
Fast-food	50–125	(4.65–11.63)
Small restaurant	100–150	(9.30–13.95)
Medium restaurant or small institution	200–300	(18.60–27.90)
Large restaurant or medium institution	400–1,000	(37.20–93.00)
Large institution with simple menu	1,000–2,500	(93.00–232.50)
Large hotel, restaurant, or institution with complex menu, catering facilities, snack bars	3,000 +	(279.00 +)

Paper and Cleaning Supplies Storage

The storage of paper supplies can be a very large space problem for food operations that use a large quantity of disposable cups, plates, napkins, and plastic ware. No standard space requirement is possible because the extent of the use of disposables and the frequency of delivery are different for each food operation. Paper supply companies and paper manufacturers tend to give significant price breaks for larger orders of paper goods, and the food operator is, therefore, forced to accept large quantities in order to purchase economically.

Cleaning supplies must be stored separately from food supplies to prevent contamination and accidental mixing of detergents with foods. A separate storeroom for cleaning supplies should be large enough to handle 55-gallon drums, cases of dishmachine detergents, and other cleaning items. A space 6 to 10 feet wide and 10 to 15 feet deep will handle the storage needs of most small- to medium-sized operations. A guide for cleaning supplies is as follows:

| TYPE OF FOOD OPERATION | SIZE OF STORAGE | |
	Sq. Ft.	(Sq. M.)
Fast-food	60–100	(5.58–9.3)
Small restaurant	75–120	(6.98–11.16)
Medium restaurant or small institution	120–175	(11.16–16.28)
Large restaurant or medium institution	175–250	(16.28–23.25)
Large institution with simple menu	250–300	(23.25–27.90)
Large hotel, restaurant, or institution with complex menu, catering facilities, snack bars	300 +	(27.90 +)

Refrigerated Storage

Space needed for bulk storage of frozen and refrigerated foods should be determined at this stage. (Estimates of the amount of reach-in storage needed are made in planning the layout of the kitchen itself. Reach-in refrigeration and walk-in refrigerators are discussed in detail in chapter 4.)

A bulk freezer should be selected on the basis of the menu and frequency of delivery. For instance, if the menu contains a large number of food items prepared from frozen food products, the need for freezer space will obviously increase. A fast-food restaurant or college cafeteria will usually use a large number of frozen french fries, and the college may also use large quantities of frozen vegetables. A seafood restaurant may use large quantities of frozen fish, french fries, onion rings, and perhaps no frozen vegetables at all. A hotel or large catering operation may use smaller quantities, but might stock a large variety of frozen foods.

Frozen foods are usually shipped in rectangular cartons that are easily stacked, and the height of the freezer is therefore an important part of the calculation. The size of a freezer should be determined on the basis of cubic feet of space needed. The following is an example of freezer size calculations based on the following assumptions:

· The facility is a small restaurant with delivery of frozen foods once per week.
· Frozen hamburgers, french fries, and onion rings are a significant part of the volume of the business.

- The menu contains five or six additional items that are purchased frozen.
- Ice cream, in six flavors, is a popular dessert.

FOOD ITEM	PURCHASE UNIT	CUBIC FEET/ (METERS)	TOTAL PER WEEK	CUBIC FEET/ (METERS)
French fries	case	1.8 (.050)	25	45 (1.260)
Hamburgers	case	1.2 (.033)	30	36 (1.008)
Onion rings	case	2.0 (.056)	20	40 (1.120)
Vegetables	case	1.5 (.042)	15	22.5 (0.630)
Hot dogs	package	.2 (.006)	35	7.0 (0.196)
Roast beef	12 to 15 lbs.	1.0 (.028)	30	30.0 (0.840)
Ice cream	3 gal.	1.5 (.042)	45	67.5 (1.890)
Miscellaneous	case	1.0 (.028)	35	35 (0.980)
		TOTAL cubic feet		283 (7.924 cu. m.)

Walk-in refrigerated storage space is very expensive because of the amount of building space that walk-ins occupy, and because of the high cost of the equipment. A careful calculation of the amount of space needed is therefore strongly recommended.

Assuming a 7-foot, 4-inch high standard walk-in is used, it can only be filled to a height of 6 feet. In fact, less than 50 percent of the space in the walk-in is usable, as shown in figure 3-10. Therefore, the total cubic feet of storage, per linear feet of walk-in freezer is: 6 feet (height) times 2-foot shelves times 2 (one on each side) equals 24 cubic feet per linear foot. To determine the necessary length, divide the total cubic feet needed by 24 cubic feet. In the example shown, the length of the walk-in would be:

$$\frac{283 \text{ cu. ft.}}{24} = 11.79 \text{ feet}$$

3-10. USABLE SPACE IN WALK-IN COOLER.

The walk-in should be 12 feet long by 9 feet wide in this example. The 9-foot width provides space on both sides for shelving and an aisle space of 3½ to 4 feet.

The size of a walk-in refrigerator is determined in a similar manner, but is more difficult to calculate because the products stored are not in rectangular boxes. The bulk cartons of milk, produce, fresh meats, foods that have been prepared, and other miscellaneous items that need to be stored under refrigeration are difficult to measure in cubic footage.

Small fast-food operations or restaurants with very limited menus may only need one walk-in refrigerator. Medium-sized operations may wish to separate meat produce and dairy products. Large hotels, restaurants, or institutions may need three or four large walk-in refrigerators, located in different sections of the kitchen. The following chart may be used as a general guide for determining the amount of space needed for walk-in refrigeration.

TYPE OF FOOD OPERATION	NUMBER OF WALK-INS	TOTAL SQUARE FEET/	(SQ. M.)
Fast-food	1	90–120	(8.4–11.2)
Small restaurant	1	120–150	(11.2–14.0)
Medium restaurant or small institution	2	180–240	(16.7–22.3)
Large restaurant or medium institution	3	240–400	(22.3–37.2)
Large institution with simple menu	3	400–600	(37.2–55.8)
Large hotel, restaurant, or institution with complex menu, catering facilities, snack bars	4	600–900	(55.8–83.7)

Utensil and Cleaning Equipment Storage

Food facilities that do not include a storage space for infrequently used utensils, backup utensil supplies such as knives and serving spoons, and cleaning equipment such as buffing machines and steam cleaners often are plagued with a considerable amount of clutter in the work areas. For instance, a restaurant that occasionally serves buffets for private parties may want to keep chafing dishes, punch bowls, and serving platters in a utensil storage room.

The amount of space needed is so variable that a standard cannot be easily established. For the small- to medium-sized foodservice facility, a closet with built-in shelving that can be easily secured provides a sufficient amount of space. Country clubs that hold private functions, buffets, and receptions and that need to store substantial quantities of Christmas decorations and other special events materials may require an extremely large storeroom with movable metal shelving. For the large food facility, the separation of cleaning equipment storage from utensil storage is recommended for reasons of security.

Office

GENERAL DESCRIPTION OF THE SPACE

Offices are needed for the manager, assistant managers, chef or food production manager, and clerical staff. The justification for these spaces is to provide a private environment for talking with employees, vendors, and other business people and to be sure that the management staff has a reasonably quiet place to work.

RELATIONSHIP TO OTHER AREAS

The offices of the general manager and catering manager need to be accessible to the public without the necessity of having customers walk through the kitchen. Office space for managers and assistant managers who have infrequent contact with the public in the office area should be located in a highly visible and easily accessible part of the food facility. Small foodservice operations often have the office located near the receiving area so that the movement of employees and of food in and out of storage areas and the building can be observed. Office space for receiving clerks, store room supervisors, and service supervisors should obviously be located in their respective work areas. Often these office areas are simple enclosures or spaces set aside without doors or four walls.

AMOUNT OF SPACE NEEDED

Small office areas are usually in a range of 60 to 80 square feet (5.58 to 7.44 sq. m.) and can be increased from this size as space and funds permit. Combination offices in which the clerical staff are adjacent to a manager's office and separated by a partition require additional space to accommodate door swings and extra office equipment such as computers, copy machines, and word processors.

The number of office spaces that may be needed for supervisory and management personnel will depend on the complexity of the organization. For instance, in a fairly complex operation, office space may be needed for:

- accounting and payroll personnel
- catering manager
- sales manager
- executive chef
- production manager
- dietitian
- assistant manager
- purchasing manager
- receiving supervisor
- maître d' hôtel

SPECIAL DESIGN FEATURES

Carpeted floors, light-colored walls with chair rails, and acoustical ceilings with fluorescent lighting are desirable surfaces in an office. The location of telephone and electrical outlets on all four walls will permit maximum flexibility as personnel and space needs change. Management and supervisory personnel often prefer an office with many windows for purposes of supervisory control. Clerical employees, on the other hand, often dislike windows that create distractions from their work or that do not provide a sufficient amount of privacy.

Preparation Areas

GENERAL DESCRIPTION OF THE SPACE

In a well-designed kitchen, the food preparation area is divided into four general areas. Although in a small kitchen these areas are often combined, recognition of each of the areas is an important part of the design. The four working areas of a kitchen are:

- prepreparation
- hot food preparation
- cold food preparation
- final preparation

Prepreparation

The prepreparation area of the kitchen is where foods are processed, mixed, combined, held, cleaned, or otherwise worked with before the meal period begins. Chopping celery, mixing meatloaf, simmering broth, peeling potatoes, and making salad dressing are all prepreparation activities. Sinks, large work surfaces, and all of the equipment necessary to accomplish food prepreparation tasks are a part of this area of the kitchen.

The prepreparation area usually includes all of the equipment needed to process foods before the meal begins. Typical equipment located in the prepreparation area includes:

- choppers
- work tables
- ovens
- utensil storage
- mixers
- kettles
- vertical cutter/mixer
- racks
- ranges
- tilting fry pan
- sinks

The amount of equipment in this area, and especially the amount of table surface needed, will be determined by the amount of hand preparation that is dictated by the menu and by the volume of food being processed. The layout and dimensions of a prepreparation area for a small restaurant are illustrated in figure 3-11. Note in the figure that the total space for prepreparation is 13 feet by 17 feet, 6 inches, or 227.5 square feet. The addition of an aisle on two sides of this would increase the needed space by approximately 90 square feet, to a total of 317.5 square feet (rounded to 320).

Hot Food Preparation

The "range" section of a kitchen is usually considered the hot food preparation area. Since

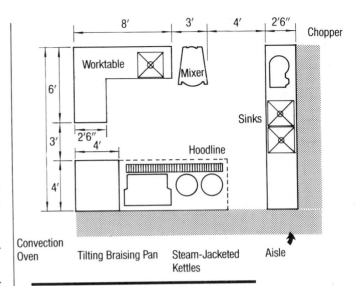

3-11. PREPREPARATION AREA FOR A SMALL RESTAURANT.

this is where heat is applied to the food product, the space must be extremely resistant to soiling from grease and high levels of heat. Also necessary are elaborate (and expensive) ventilation systems above the cooking surfaces. The area must be designed to meet the demands of the menu, and equipment should be selected accordingly. The most frequent design error in the kitchen is to select "generic" equipment that is manufactured to cook all foods under all circumstances rather than pieces best suited to preparing the foods served in the particular facility.

Cold Food Preparation

In small and medium-sized kitchens this area is the "pantry," where salads are assembled, desserts dished up, and appetizers made ready for service. For a large restaurant or hotel, a separate *garde mange* department may be required for the preparation of cold food appetizers, entrees, and beautifully decorated items for buffets. Typically most of the prepreparation and final preparation for cold foods will occur in the same general area. Worktables and refrigerated storage should be accessible to all food preparation personnel located in this area. A pickup station designed as part of cold food preparation gives easy access to the waiters and waitresses. In European kitchens, the traditional layout included a cold kitchen as a separate area. (An example of the typical European layout is contained in the appendix.)

Final Preparation

The final preparation area is the space in which foods are prepared very close to and during the meal period. It is important in the design to define this space carefully and to be sure that all equipment located within it has to do with final preparation. Foods usually cooked in this area include french fries, fried eggs, toast, hamburgers, frozen vegetables, and other similar items that can be prepared quickly and that will deteriorate rapidly if cooked ahead of time. In a successful restaurant the final food preparation area is the most carefully attended and supervised part of the entire kitchen. Foods prepared in this area must be held a very short period of time before being presented to the guest. Successful fast-food chains have designed elaborate means to be sure that foods are not held more than 5 to 6 minutes in the final preparation area before being served. The final preparation area typically includes a range, grills, fryers, steamers, and broilers. Obviously, some small amount of preparation also occurs in this area, but in an efficient operation, it is kept to a minimum.

RELATIONSHIP TO OTHER AREAS

The flow of people and materials from storage to preparation to final preparation can best be illustrated by a simple diagram (fig. 3-12). Although this diagram seems very simplistic, the concept that it illustrates is extremely important if good kitchen design is to be achieved. Frequently kitchens are laid out with steam jacketed kettles (a preparation piece of equipment) in the final preparation area or fryers (a final preparation piece of equipment) located in the preparation area. Although these arrangements may save some dupli-

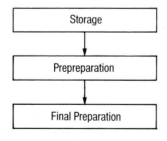

3-12. RELATIONSHIP OF FINAL PREPARATION AREA TO PREPREPARATION AND STORAGE.

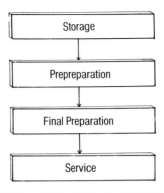

3-13. RELATIONSHIP OF PREP SPACES TO OTHER PARTS OF FOOD FACILITY.

cation in equipment, they tend to cause congestion in the flow of materials and personnel.

Figure 3-13 shows how preparation spaces relate to the service components of a food facility. The reader should also bear in mind the comprehensive picture of a facility, with the kitchen at the center of all the functional spaces (see fig. 2-2). The design should always reflect these relationships and facilitate the movement of employees and food between functionally related areas. For instance, the distance between the final preparation area and the customer should be short because the time that it takes to move the food is critical. On the other hand, the relationship of the preparation area to the employee locker room is not critical and these spaces could be a considerable distance away from each other.

Vertical as well as horizontal space relationships must be considered. As a general guideline, when spaces must be located on different floors, the following functional areas may be at a different level from the kitchen:

- bulk dry storage
- bulk frozen storage
- paper and utensil storage
- employee locker rooms
- receiving

The following functional areas must never be located at another level from the kitchen:

- warewashing
- dining room
- service areas

This guideline is often violated in large hotels and institutional kitchens, where it is quite common to see dishwashing located at a different level from the dining room. Architectural limitations at times make it necessary to violate this rule, but there is always a cost in labor, efficiency, and effectiveness of supervision.

AMOUNT OF SPACE NEEDED

The size of the different preparation areas will be determined by the menu, volume of food produced, and cookery methods used. A common method of establishing the space requirement is to list the needed equipment and make templates of each piece, using a scale of ¼ inch = 1 foot. The templates are shifted on a drawing board to arrive at a satisfactory arrangement, and the overall space is measured. In developing an equipment list, the food facilities design consultant will discuss the menu and equipment preferences with the owner, manager, or chef (or all three). A checklist for final preparation equipment is as follows:

ITEM	QUANTITY	CAPACITY OR SIZE
[ ] Convection oven		
[ ] Fryers		
[ ] Grill		
[ ] Kettles, table top		
[ ] High-pressure steamer		
[ ] Broiler		
[ ] Reach-in refrigerator		
[ ] Reach-in freezer		
[ ] Hot top range		
[ ] Open top range		
[ ] Pickup table		
[ ] Steam table		
[ ] Worktable		
[ ] Spreader plates		
[ ] Beverage pickup		
[ ] Plate storage		
[ ] Other		

The most frequently asked question concerning the kitchen by the client or architect at the beginning of a project is "What is the ratio of space for the kitchen to space for the dining room?" The food facilities design consultant will usually answer "It depends." First of all, no clear standards for a ratio between dining and kitchen exist, and secondly, different types of operations have different requirements. Space needs depend on:

· The size of the menu (number of items)
· The use of convenience foods versus cookery from scratch
· The complexity of the preparation required (fast-food versus expensive table service)
· The foodservice functions provided by a single kitchen (which may include banquet service, coffee shop service, and main dining room foodservice)

Arthur Dana, a highly respected foodservice consultant who practiced in the New York City area during the 1940s, wrote one of the first books on food facilities design (*Kitchen Planning*, published by Harper & Brothers in 1945). Concerning the relative size of dining and food preparation areas, Dana had this to say:

Because of the many variations within each type of restaurant design, a particular restaurant may not necessarily conform to a fixed percentage relationship between the seating and service areas.

About 20 years ago, designers allotted kitchen space for table service dining rooms equivalent to one-third to one-half of the dining area. As time went on it became apparent that more space for kitchen purposes was necessary to provide efficient service.

Recently, a well-known kitchen equipment engineer cited an example in which the kitchen (exclusive of storage and employee facilities) was equivalent to two-thirds of the dining area. Expressed in terms of 100% street level area available, the dining room took 60% of the space and the kitchen, 40%. Other facilities were located in the basement. Every expression of opinion, however (when it is possible to get one), is qualified by references to physical differences, varying needs and a myriad of operating ideas from the owners.

Comparisons of different types of facilities designed by Birchfield Foodsystems may be helpful in establishing guidelines for the size of the kitchen as it relates to the dining room. A comparison of kitchen sizes and dining room capacity can be made from the following chart:

TYPE OF FOOD OPERATION	MEALS PER DAY	DINING ROOM SIZE Sq. Ft.	(Sq. M.)	PREPARATION AREA SIZE[a] Sq. Ft.	(Sq. M.)
Restaurant, table service—100 seats	1,000	1,400	(130.20)	1,300	(120.90)
Restaurant, table service—175 seats	1,800	2,625	(244.13)	2,000	(186.00)
Country club—200 seats	600	3,400	(316.20)	1,288	(119.78)
Hospital, cafeteria, and 200-bed tray service	1,400	2,250	(209.25)	2,300	(213.90)
College cafeteria—350 seats	2,400	4,200	(390.60)	1,500	(139.50)
University cafeteria and catering department	4,000	5,625	(523.13)	2,530	(235.29)
Coffee shop—100 seats	800	1,225	(113.96)	850	(79.05)

[a]Does not include bakery, storage, and dishwashing.

The chart indicates the range of space requirements in different types of food facilities. Because of the extreme variability in space needs, the owner or manager should look to the design consultant for professional advice before deciding on the amount of space to allot to the food production area.

SPECIAL DESIGN FEATURES

Since food production areas are continually subjected to heat as well as soiling from grease and spilled foods, damage-resistant, easy-to-clean surfaces are essential. Equipment surfaces of stainless steel are the most practical. Floor finishes of Carborundum chips in quarry tile will provide a slip-resistant, easy-to-clean surface. When made of ceramic tile or structural glazed tile, walls behind the equipment will withstand the combination of heat and grease. Epoxy paint on cement block is not recommended, because the high heat will discolor and/or darken the painted surface. To avoid sanitation problems, careful attention should be given to eliminating cracks and spaces around equipment.

Mechanical engineers and architects working on a food facilities project are encouraged to give special attention to room air supply and exhaust because of the increased use in recent years of compensating hoods that bring a large percentage of makeup air (air that replaces exhausted air) into the hood itself. The kitchen must be well ventilated without complete dependence on the hood system to exhaust the air. (Lighting, ventilation, and aisle space are discussed in detail in chapters 3 and 6.)

Bakery

GENERAL DESCRIPTION OF THE SPACE

The bakery remains a popular production area in the foodservice facility in spite of the availability of a wide variety of fresh and frozen bakery products. The foodservice manager or owner must give the food facilities design consultant complete details concerning the extent and volume of baking that is to be prepared on the premises.

A small or medium-sized restaurant (under 150 seats) that plans to make only rolls, cobblers, sheet cakes from a mix, and a few specialty desserts may only require a small worktable, ingredient bins, a mixer, and access to an oven. On the other hand, a large institution planning to bake pies, cakes, rolls, loaf breads, danish pastries, doughnuts, and extensive specialty products may require a very large space and a sizable equipment budget. The long-range plans for the food facility need to be carefully considered. In planning for a bake shop, the following questions need to be answered by the owner:

1. Do you plan to bake on the premises or to buy bakery products from outside vendors?
2. If you plan to have baking capabilities, what will you bake on the premises?

   - rolls
   - biscuits
   - pies
   - cakes (round or sheet)
   - danish pastries
   - doughnuts (cake or yeast)
   - cobblers
   - bread for sandwiches
   - hamburger buns, hoagies, or specialty rolls

3. Will most of your bakery products be made from "scratch" or will you use mixes?
4. Will you deliver bakery products fresh from the bake shop to the service area, or will you freeze a large number of your products?
5. Will you sell bakery products retail in addition to supplying all bakery products to the foodservice area?

RELATIONSHIP TO OTHER AREAS

The bakery is one food production area that can be separate from the main activity of the foodservice facility. If sufficient space exists, however, the bakery should be near the main food production areas so that supervision is easier, equipment can be occasionally shared, and common storage spaces can be used. If the bakery is located at a remote point in the food facility, it should have easy access to receiving, and depending on size, may need its own separate dry storage and walk-in refrigerator/freezer.

The movement of finished bakery products to the kitchen or service area should be accomplished in rolling closed cabinets. Ramping or the use of elevators should be planned if the bakery is not on the same level as the area where the product will be served or sold. The planning of central bakeries serving multiple dining facilities must include well-thought-out food transportation systems to assure that the product is not damaged in transit and that the proper temperature (hot, cold, or room temperature) is maintained.

AMOUNT OF SPACE NEEDED

The following chart can be used to make a rough estimate of the amount of space needed in a bakery, keeping in mind the many variables that can affect this determination.

NUMBER OF SEATS IN THE FACILITY	LIMITED BAKING[a]		EXTENSIVE BAKING[a]	
	Sq. Ft.	(Sq. M.)	Sq. Ft.	(Sq. M.)
Under 50	40	(3.72)	80	(7.44)
50–100	100	(9.30)	150	(13.95)
100–175	250	(23.25)	400	(37.20)
175–250	300	(27.90)	600	(55.80)
250–500	400	(37.20)	800	(74.40)
More than 500	600	(55.80)	1,400	(130.20)

[a]Storage not included.

SPECIAL DESIGN FEATURES

The floors of most bakeries quickly become covered with flour and other dry ingredients that are used in large quantities in the baking process. The flour sticks to the floor of the work area, especially when the area becomes damp, and is difficult to remove at the end of the work day. The floor should be constructed of quarry tile or other smooth masonry material (marble, tile, or terrazzo) that will not be damaged by frequent scrubbing and occasional scraping.

The mechanical engineers will need to provide an air supply and exhaust for the bakery, usually in the form of simple oven vents. From 30 to 45 air changes per hour should be sufficient for this space, exclusive of the air ventilated by the oven exhaust.

Employee Locker Room/Toilet

GENERAL DESCRIPTION OF THE SPACE

The employee locker room and restrooms are too often given minimal consideration by those who are involved in the total design of a food facility. These facilities deserve careful attention because they affect sanitation, security, and employee attitude. The space, if properly planned, can be clean, orderly, and have a bright appearance that sets the tone for management's expectations of cleanliness and orderliness in other areas of the building.

RELATIONSHIP TO OTHER AREAS

The locker rooms and restrooms can be designed together (see fig. 4-17) so that space is efficiently used and control over uniforms is maintained. The area can be remote from the main food production areas, but the entrance and exit to the space should be arranged so that employees can be observed as they move from the work area to the locker room. Locker rooms can create food and utensil control problems if they are located near exits or are in remote locations that are difficult to supervise.

AMOUNT OF SPACE NEEDED

The space needed for a combined locker room/restroom area is estimated in the chart below.

Space requirements for restroom facilities should be checked with local codes to be sure that they comply with requirements for the handicapped and for the minimum number of employee toilet facilities.

NUMBER OF EMPLOYEES[a]	SIZE OF THE SPACE	
	Sq. Ft.	(Sq. M.)
5 or under	60	(5.58)
5–10	100	(9.30)
10–20	150	(13.95)
20–40	225	(20.93)
40–75	250	(23.25)
75–100	350	(32.55)

[a]Peak number of employees on duty at one time, not the total number of employees on the payroll.

SPECIAL DESIGN FEATURES

An employee locker room/restroom can easily be made too large, which encourages loitering. The purpose of the space is to provide a place for changing clothes, using the toilet, and washing the hands before reporting for work. It should not be used for coffee breaks, card games, eating and so on. The design should include locker room benches, double stacked lockers to save space, and for the larger food facility, a linen control system for exchanging soiled uniforms for clean uniforms.

Foodservice managers disagree about whether an employee dining room or coffee area is necessary. Some managers feel that these employee rooms encourage long breaks and that employees should eat in the main dining room before the meal period for customers. Large hotels and food operations, on the other hand, usually provide an employee lounge.

Service Areas

GENERAL DESCRIPTION OF THE SPACE

There are as many different types of service areas as there are types of foodservice establishments. Each of the following types of food operations has a different kind of service area, and the list is certainly not complete:

- table service restaurant
- snack bar
- lunch counter
- fast-food restaurant
- diner
- drive-in
- grill
- wine bar
- cafeteria—straight line
- cafeteria—free flow or "scramble"
- night club
- delicatessen
- cafe
- tea room
- pancake house
- buffet

The service area and the type of service planned for a food facility will be among the first decisions made during the concept development phase of the design process. For a small table service restaurant, the service area might be very small because only a pickup station at the hot and cold food areas in the kitchen and a waiter/waitress station in the dining room are needed. (Chapter 4 provides information on waiter/waitress stations in table service restaurants.) A large institutional food facility using the scramble form of cafeteria service may need extremely large service areas in the range of 2,000 to 3,000 square feet (186 to 279 sq. m.). The service area in a table service restaurant provides an efficient means for the food production staff to get the food to the service staff, while the service area in self-service food operations offers a means for the food production staff to get the food to the customer. In both of these circumstances the time that it takes for the food to be delivered to the customer is critical and obviously should be as short as possible. The method for accomplishing this task is often referred to as a "food delivery system."

The simplest food delivery system may involve holding a short order meal for a few moments under a quartz heater at the waiter/waitress pickup station. A complex food delivery system in a large hospital might involve numerous employees and hundreds of thousands of dollars in equipment. Regardless of the size of the food operation or its method of service, the importance of planning an efficient food delivery system cannot be overemphasized.

As an illustration of the typical delivery systems used in foodservices facilities, the following chart is a partial list of several types of service areas.

TYPE OF OPERATION	TYPE OF DELIVERY SYSTEM
Table service restaurant	Kitchen pickup station
Snack bar	Service counter direct to customer
Fast-food	Service counter direct to customer
Cafeteria	Straight line cafeteria
Delicatessen	Deli counter
Buffet	Buffet line
Scramble	Separate food stations
Food court	Separate food locations around a common dining area

RELATIONSHIP TO OTHER AREAS

The most important connection of the service area is to the hot and cold food production part of the food services. A small distance between these two functional areas will provide a reduced labor cost and a higher quality food product. Conversely, a long distance between these two areas will increase the cost of labor and equipment significantly and make it much more difficult to keep foods at the proper serving temperature. Service areas also have a primary relationship to the following spaces in the food facility:

· warewashing
· dining room
· private dining rooms
· customer entrances and exits
· cashiers or other control systems

Other facilities that must be accessible to service areas are:

· store rooms
· refrigeration
· bakery
· office areas
· cleaning supplies

AMOUNT OF SPACE NEEDED

Variations in the size and type of foodservice facility make it extremely difficult to develop a standard space requirement. As a guideline to the foodservice planning team, several types of service areas are listed in the charts below together with a range of sizes.

SERVICE AREA SPACE REQUIREMENTS FOR TABLE SERVICE RESTAURANTS—LIMITED MENU

NUMBER OF SEATS	MEALS PER DAY[a]	SERVICE AREA[b] Sq. Ft.	(Sq. M.)
Under 50	300	75	(6.9)
50–100	500	100	(9.2)
100–175	750	140	(12.9)
175–250	1,000	160	(14.7)
250–500	1,600	175	(16.1)
More than 500	2,400	200	(18.4)

[a]Breakfast not included.
[b]The chef's pickup station (excluding range and aisle space) and a waiter/waitress station.

SERVICE AREA SPACE REQUIREMENTS FOR LUXURY TABLE SERVICE RESTAURANTS—EXTENSIVE MENU

NUMBER OF SEATS	MEALS PER DAY[a]	SERVICE AREA[b] Sq. Ft.	(Sq. M.)
Under 50	200	100	(9.2)
50–100	300	120	(11.0)
100–175	600	160	(14.7)
175–250	700	200	(18.4)
250–500	1,000	250	(23.0)
More than 500	1,500	300	(27.6)

[a]Breakfast not included.
[b]Waiter/waitress stations, hot and cold food pickup stations, and separate beverage stations.

SERVICE AREA SPACE REQUIREMENTS FOR CAFETERIAS—STRAIGHT CAFETERIA LINE

NUMBER OF SEATS	MEALS PER DAY[a]	SERVICE AREA[b] Sq. Ft.	(Sq. M.)
100–175	800	350	(32.2)
175–250			
One Line	1,250	475	(43.7)
Two Lines	1,500	900	(82.8)
250–500	2,000	1600	(147.2)
More than 500	5,000	2000	(184.0)

[a]Breakfast not included.
[b]Size of the cafeteria line and aisle space in front of and behind the line.

SERVICE AREA SPACE REQUIREMENTS FOR SCRAMBLE OR FREE FLOW CAFETERIAS

NUMBER OF SEATS	MEALS PER DAY[a]	SERVICE AREA[b]	
		Sq. Ft.	(Sq. M.)
175–250	1,500	1,800	(165.6)
250–300	1,800	2,000	(184.0)
350–500	2,250	2,400	(220.8)
More than 500	5,000	3,000	(276.0)

[a]Breakfast not included.
[b]The service area of the scramble including interior circulation space. Condiment and beverage stations located outside of the service area are not included.

The charts for service area space needed indicate that as the level of service changes from table service to self-service scramble, the amount of space needed increases dramatically. The scramble cafeteria requires the greatest amount of space of any of the forms of service because of the need for good circulation within the space. It is assumed that the cost of constructing the scramble will be more than offset by the potential volume of customers who can be served, and by an increase in the speed of service. The scramble cafeteria also allows a wide range of menu items to be merchandised to the customer.

SPECIAL DESIGN FEATURES

Figures 3-14 through 3-19 show typical service area design features of the most common types of foodservice facilities: a table service restaurant, a family style restaurant, a snack bar or fast-food counter, a straight line cafeteria, a scramble free-flow cafeteria, and a health-care tray-makeup system.

Dining Rooms

GENERAL DESCRIPTION OF THE SPACE

The architect and interior designer give the appearance of the dining space the highest priority.

Obviously, an environment that is pleasant for the guests and that lends itself to an enjoyable dining experience should be a goal in designing the facility. The ease of cleaning floors, walls, and furnishings as well as the potential for food spillage must also be considered. Coverings such as carpeting, for example, are popular in table service restaurants but are inappropriate for dining rooms with a higher risk of soil from spilled foods and debris. Other factors in dining room planning include:

· ventilation
· heating and air conditioning
· view
· sound control
· seating arrangement
· waiter/waitress stations
· sanitation
· lighting
· cashier or other control systems

The owner or manager of a food facility is encouraged to visit a variety of food operations during the early planning stage of a project and to consult some of the illustrated trade journals and reference volumes that are available. Gaining familiarity with the design of a variety of dining room interiors will aid in the selection of mood, color, texture, lighting, and other interior features. (For further information on the interior design of this area, see chapter 6 below.)

As the number of meals consumed at foodservice chain facilities and franchise operations has grown, hotel corporations, restaurant chains, and fast-food companies have become more sophisticated in their interior design plans. The restaurant owner who succumbs to "do-it-yourself" decorating or who spends insufficient funds to create an attractive dining room will lose business to the more attractive and sophisticated chain operations. Similarly, the institutional cafeteria owner or manager who installs vinyl tile floors and "institutional" chairs and tables will experience a loss of customers to dining facilities that offer a more pleasant setting.

RELATIONSHIP TO OTHER AREAS

The dining room must be directly connected to service areas and to the kitchen. Remote dining rooms, such as hotel banqueting rooms or private meeting rooms that are located away from the kitchen, may require special equipment for food delivery. One solution for the remote banquet dining room is the use of specially designed service kitchens. (Information regarding the layout and equipment needed for service kitchens is included in chapter 4.)

Vertical space relationships can be solved in part by the use of elevators or dumb waiters. In one London eating establishment, an entire building of banquet rooms is serviced by a bank of dumb waiters from a central kitchen on the first floor. The building is seven stories high and the communication system is controlled by a series of hollow pipes that permit the staff to shout their needs back and forth through the pipes. The system is over 100 years old and continues to operate smoothly without the need for an electronic speaker. In spite of the success of this English banqueting hall, dumb waiters are usually not a good solution for the vertical movement of food. Dumb waiters do not transport people, and they must be attended by two persons. They are also difficult to clean and can cause excessive breakage of dishes and create communication problems. Budget and space considerations permitting, service elevators are much preferred to dumb waiters.

AMOUNT OF SPACE NEEDED

The proper size of the dining room can be calculated once it is decided how many customers the food facility will seat. Determining the proper number of seats is easy in an institutional foodservice if the number of persons to be fed is known. For a restaurant or commercial cafeteria project, however, where the number of customers is uncertain, determining the number of seats needed can be quite difficult. Forecasting the volume of business that might be anticipated for a commercial restaurant is often no more than an educated guess. In other instances, the number of seats planned into a restaurant is decided on the basis of the available space or funds. Deciding on the number of seats to be included in the design is a basic investment question, which should be given careful consideration. Dining room size, kitchen size, restroom capacities, parking

---

3-14. LAYOUT FOR A TABLE SERVICE RESTAURANT.

KITCHEN

RESTROOM

RAD.

Servers Station

RAD.

NORTH

STONE MANSION I

Seating Diagram

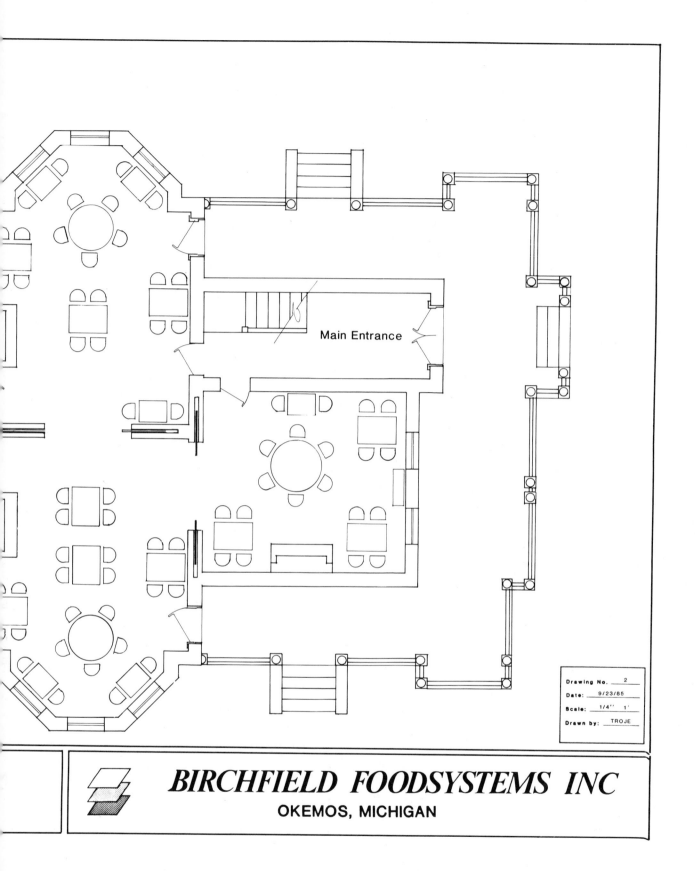

Main Entrance

Drawing No.	2
Date:	9/23/85
Scale:	1/4'' 1'
Drawn by:	TROJE

BIRCHFIELD FOODSYSTEMS INC

OKEMOS, MICHIGAN

lot size, and many other features of the building are affected by seating capacity.

The number of persons who can be accommodated during a meal period is determined by the space occupied by the chair and table, and by the seat turnover rate. Each type of service requires a different amount of space for tables and chairs. For instance, a snack bar with paper or disposable china can be designed with very small tables and utilitarian chairs without arms. On the other hand, a luxury table service restaurant would require a large dining room table with sufficient space for flowers, condiments, a variety of crystal glasses, and side dishes to accompany the main course. Chairs in luxury restaurants are often large because they are padded and have arms. Space in the aisles of such a restaurant needs to be large enough to accommodate iced wine buckets and the waiter's tray stand. The following space requirements are generally accepted industry standards for the various forms of service in the industry.

FORM OF SERVICE	SUPPORT AREA PER 100 SEATS[a]	SPACE REQUIREMENTS (SQ. FT./CHAIR)[b]
Table service, moderate price	100 sq. ft. of waiter station	12–14
Table service, high price	150 sq. ft. of waiter station	13–16
Table service, luxury	200 sq. ft of waiter station	16–20
Cafeteria service	500 sq. ft. of straight line cafeteria	11–13
Scramble	600 sq. ft. of waiter station	12–14
Booth service	100 sq. ft. of waiter station	12–14
Banquet (private dining)	25 sq. ft. of storage and service area	10–12
Fast-food	50 sq. ft. of counter area	9–11

[a]This is a separate area, not a part of dining room size.
[b]Includes space for aisles and general circulation.

3-14. CONTINUED.

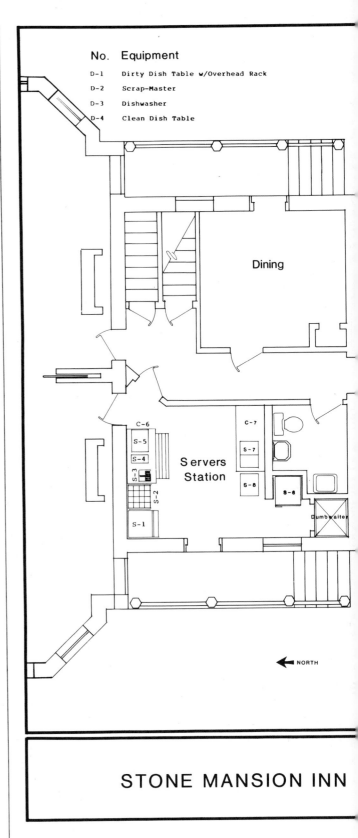

No.	Equipment
D-1	Dirty Dish Table w/Overhead Rack
D-2	Scrap-Master
D-3	Dishwasher
D-4	Clean Dish Table

Dining

Servers Station

Dumbwaiter

← NORTH

STONE MANSION INN

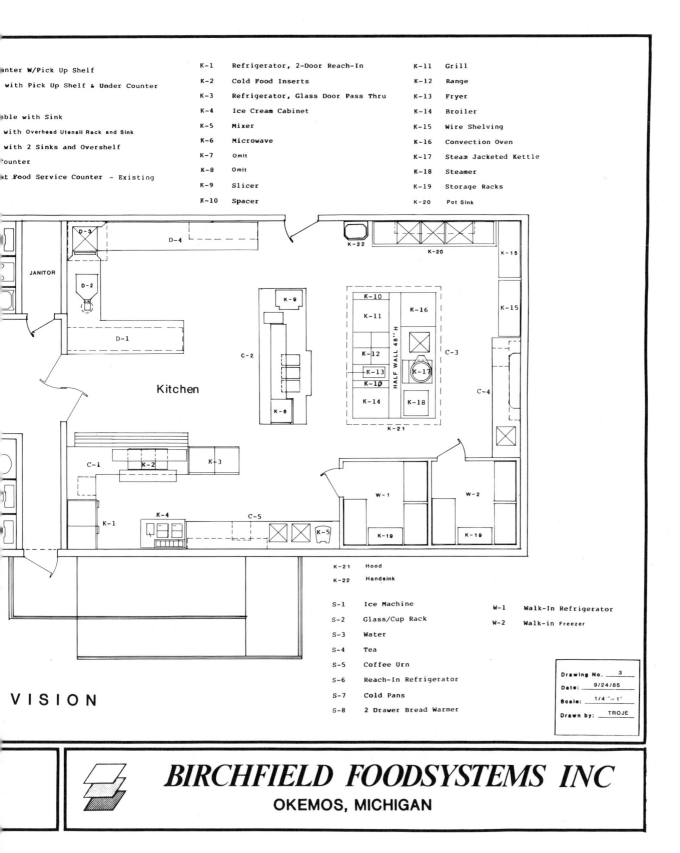

nter W/Pick Up Shelf	K-1	Refrigerator, 2-Door Reach-In	K-11	Grill
with Pick Up Shelf & Under Counter	K-2	Cold Food Inserts	K-12	Range
	K-3	Refrigerator, Glass Door Pass Thru	K-13	Fryer
ble with Sink	K-4	Ice Cream Cabinet	K-14	Broiler
with Overhead Utensil Rack and Sink	K-5	Mixer	K-15	Wire Shelving
with 2 Sinks and Overshelf	K-6	Microwave	K-16	Convection Oven
ounter	K-7	Omit	K-17	Steam Jacketed Kettle
t Food Service Counter - Existing	K-8	Omit	K-18	Steamer
	K-9	Slicer	K-19	Storage Racks
	K-10	Spacer	K-20	Pot Sink

Kitchen

VISION

| K-21 | Hood |
| K-22 | Handsink |

S-1	Ice Machine	W-1	Walk-In Refrigerator
S-2	Glass/Cup Rack	W-2	Walk-in Freezer
S-3	Water
S-4	Tea
S-5	Coffee Urn
S-6	Reach-In Refrigerator
S-7	Cold Pans
S-8	2 Drawer Bread Warmer

Drawing No. ___3___
Date: __9/24/85__
Scale: __1/4"=1'__
Drawn by: ___TROJE___

BIRCHFIELD FOODSYSTEMS INC
OKEMOS, MICHIGAN

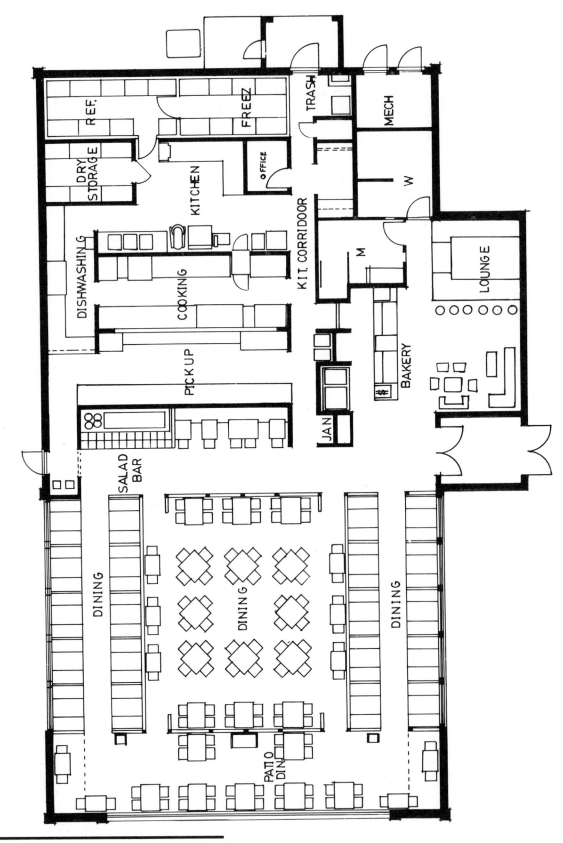

3-15. LAYOUT FOR A FAMILY STYLE SERVICE DINING FACILITY.

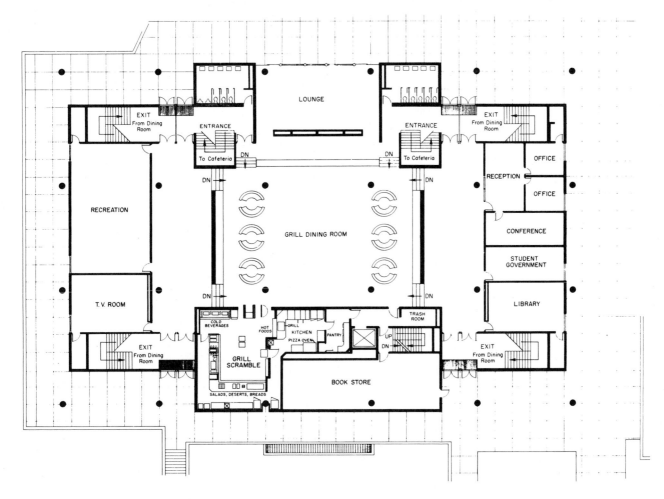

PRESIDENTIAL HALL
(First Floor)

3-16. LAYOUT FOR A SNACK BAR SERVICE AREA.

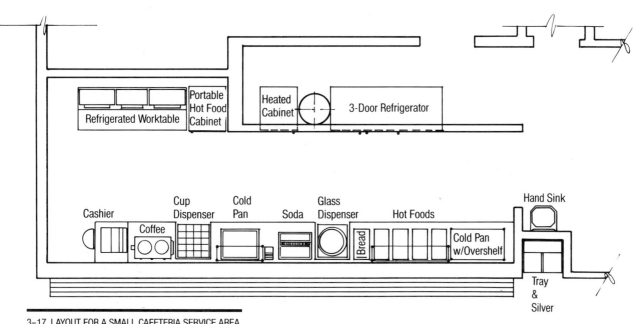

3-17. LAYOUT FOR A SMALL CAFETERIA SERVICE AREA.

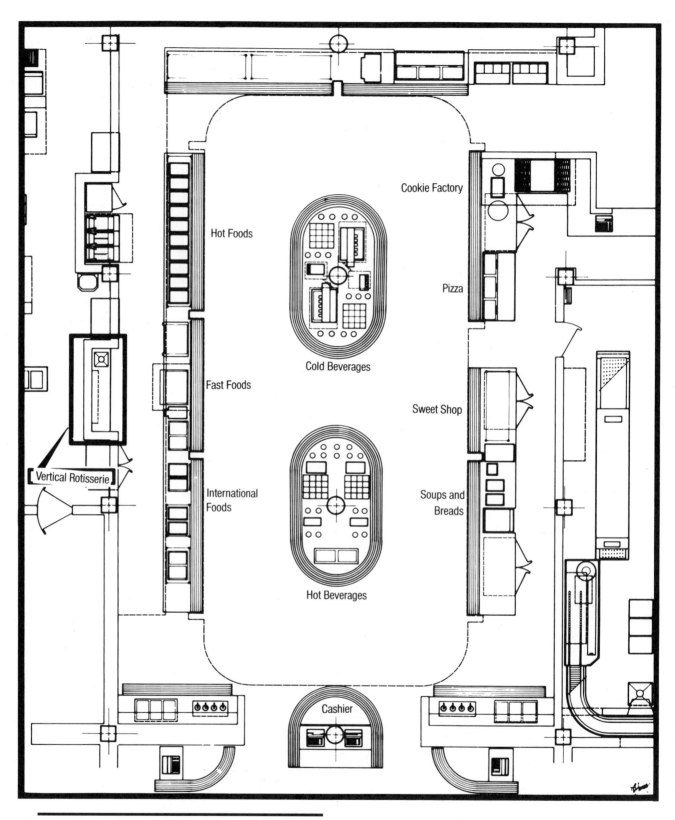

Hot Foods

Cookie Factory

Cold Beverages

Pizza

Fast Foods

Sweet Shop

Vertical Rotisserie

International Foods

Soups and Breads

Hot Beverages

Cashier

3-18. LAYOUT FOR SCRAMBLE SERVICE AREA (UNIVERSITY OF SYRACUSE).

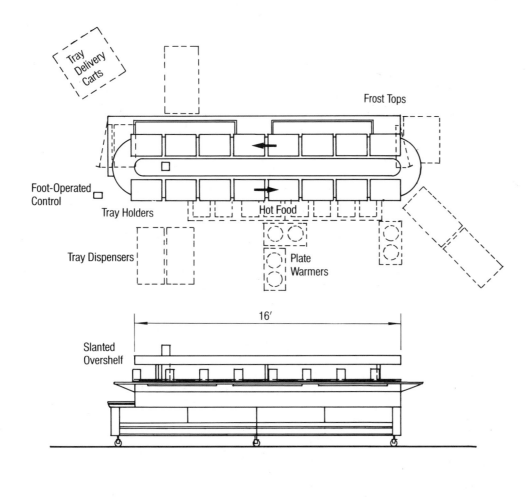

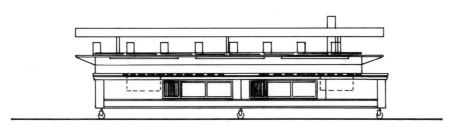

3–19. HEALTH CARE CIRCULAR TRAY MAKEUP SYSTEM.

The amount of space needed in a dining area is also influenced by the number of seats turned over per hour. For example, in a luxurious restaurant, the seats may turn over once every two hours, a turnover rate of 0.5 times. A snack bar or fast-food restaurant may experience a turnover of three times per hour. The following estimates of seat turnover for different segments of the foodservice industry should be used as a guide:

FORM OF SERVICE	SEAT TURNOVER
Table service, moderate price	1.0–2.0
Table service, high price	0.75–1.0
Table service, luxury	0.5–0.75
Cafeteria service	2.2–3.0
Counter service	2.0–3.0
Booth service	2.0–3.0
Fast-food	2.5–3.5

The following is a typical calculation to determine the size of a dining area and support service area for a restaurant serving a moderately priced menu with 200 seats:

1. Determine the size of the support area from the chart: a 200-seat restaurant would need 200 square feet of waiter/waitress station space.
2. Determine the size of the dining room: 200 seats times 13 square feet per chair equals 2600 square feet.
3. Calculate the number of persons who could be served in one hour in this restaurant: 200 seats times 1.5 turns equals 300 persons per hour.

In this example the restaurant would make maximum use of the waiter/waitress station by keeping in the station as many of the accompaniments to the meal as possible. For instance, the waiter/waitress station might contain:

- silverware
- linen (napkins)
- condiments
- coffee
- soft drinks
- ice
- glasses
- trash container
- crackers
- cups and saucers
- bread
- butter
- cream
- hot tea
- cold tea
- milk
- precheck machine
- soup

After determining the type of service, the amount of support space needed, and the seat turnover, the final consideration is the shape and size of the table. A dining room table in a fine restaurant might be shaped as shown in figure 3-20. This shape permits the service personnel to place side dishes, wine glasses, condiments, and other accompaniments to the meal on the table without crowding. This same shape for a cafeteria dining room would waste space and make it impossible for four people to place rectangular cafeteria trays on the table (fig. 3-21). The wasted space in the example could be quite significant for a large cafeteria dining room. An estimate of the wasted space for a 400-seat cafeteria would be: 4 square feet of wasted space per table times 100 tables equals 400 square feet. The extra amount spent in construction would come to 400 square feet times costs of $100 per foot equals $40,000 wasted. One solution to the problem is to choose a rectangular table on which four trays fit properly, arranged so that a natural aisle is created on the two short sides of the table, as shown in figure 3-22.

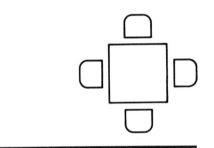

3-20. SQUARE TABLE—FULL SERVICE RESTAURANT.

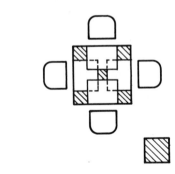

3-21. SAME TABLE—CAFETERIA DINING.

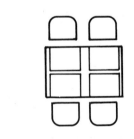

3-22. RECTANGULAR TABLE—CAFETERIA DINING.

SPECIAL DESIGN FEATURES

Two popular dining room styles that have been developed as alternatives to traditional table arrangements are fast-food or snack bar seating and booth seating.

Fast-food or snack bar seating: The special design features developed by the fast-food industry can be incorporated into any food operation in which space efficiency, ease of cleaning, and resistance to soiling is desirable. In these dining areas, table legs have been largely eliminated and seats are suspended from a table pedestal. The ease of sweeping and mopping the floors that this feature permits is important because of the large amount of food spillage and paper debris common in fast-food facilities. Another distinctive feature is the bevel or space that is often designed into the tabletop to encourage the sharing of the table with strangers. The division creates the impression of two tables when in fact it is only one.

Booth Seating: The use of booths in foodservice establishments, which creates a visual break from traditional seating, is popular because of the sense of privacy that it provides. Early American and Victorian decor often featured booths with extremely high backs and side panels that almost completely enclosed the diners. Although booths are more expensive than traditional chairs and tables, they are extremely space efficient—their higher cost is more than offset by a reduction in the size of the dining room. Space efficiency results from adjoining booths being placed back to back. Figure 3-23 illustrates a typical booth arrangement with standard dimensions.

Warewashing

GENERAL DESCRIPTION OF THE SPACE

The one word that best describes the environment in the warewashing area is "wet." With the exception of the hot food preparation area, warewashing equipment and surrounding areas receive more wear and abuse than any other section of the food facility. Water on the floor, spilled food, steam and high humidity, and the striking of carts and utensils against the walls and equipment are

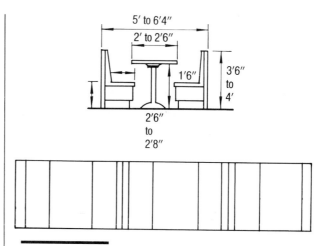

3-23. BOOTH SEATING.

often a common part of the warewashing environment. Food facilities designers, architects, and engineers should make every effort to eliminate the wet conditions while recognizing that the floor, walls, and ceiling must be constructed to withstand a large amount of moisture.

Health department standards for the equipment and interior of warewashing rooms have become increasingly stringent because of the potential for spreading food-borne diseases. In designing the warewashing area so that it is easy to sanitize and will withstand the wet conditions, the use of slip-resistant quarry tile floors, ceramic or structural glaze tile walls, and moisture-resistant acoustic ceiling is recommended.

RELATIONSHIP TO OTHER AREAS

The most important relationship of the warewashing space is to the dining room. The design should facilitate the movement of soiled dishes from the dining room to the warewashing area. In many institutions where self-bussing of dishes is encouraged, the warewashing space must be located adjacent to the exit from the dining room. Without this convenient feature, customers are unlikely to cooperate in bussing their own dishes.

The primary problem with the close proximity of warewashing to the dining area is the noisiness of the former. Conveyor belts for soiled dishes, screening with masonry walls, or the use of double sets of doors to isolate the warewashing area are all common solutions to the noise problem.

Warewashing must also have a close working relationship with the main kitchen, especially if pots, pans, and utensils are washed in the warewashing area. The warewashing room may be designed with three-compartment pot sinks, potwashing machines, or it may be the practice of management to have most small and medium-sized utensils washed by the standard dish machine. If pots and utensils are to be washed in this area, the distance between the primary food production spaces and the warewashing unit should be reasonably close. The diagrams in figures 3-24 through 3-27 show various warewashing layout alternatives.

AMOUNT OF SPACE NEEDED

Warewashing machine ratings are usually based on the number of standard 20-by-20-inch racks or the number of dishes per hour that can be processed through the machine. Since neither the machine or the machine operator can operate at 100 percent efficiency, an efficiency factor of 70 percent is normally used. The following chart provides a range of square footage requirements for several different styles of dishwashing systems. The data was determined under the assumption that a three-compartment pot sink with drain boards is included in the warewashing space.

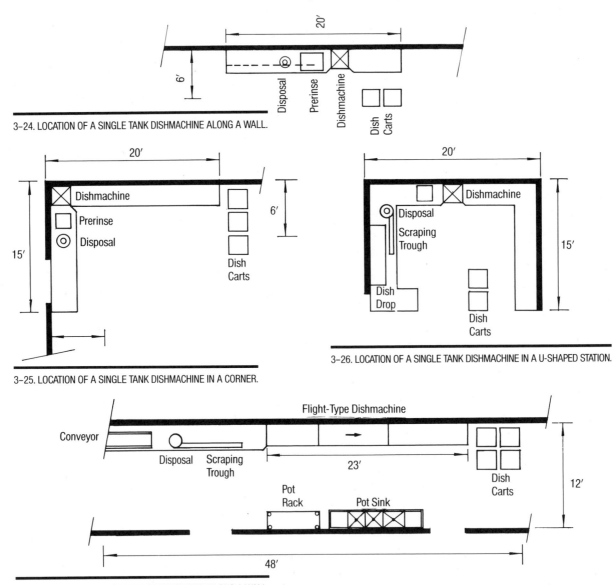

3-24. LOCATION OF A SINGLE TANK DISHMACHINE ALONG A WALL.

3-25. LOCATION OF A SINGLE TANK DISHMACHINE IN A CORNER.

3-26. LOCATION OF A SINGLE TANK DISHMACHINE IN A U-SHAPED STATION.

3-27. LOCATION OF A FLIGHT-TYPE DISHMACHINE ALONG A WALL.

TYPE OF DISH SYSTEM	DISHES PER HOUR	SIZE OF THE SPACE[a]	
		Sq. Ft.	(Sq. M.)
Single tank dishwasher	1,500	250	(23.25)
Single tank conveyor	4,000	400	(37.20)
Two-tank conveyor	6,000	500	(46.50)
Flight-type conveyor	12,000	700	(65.10)

[a]Including space for dish carts, empty racks, and pot washing. The size of the space will vary significantly on the basis of the layout of the soiled and clean dish tables. For instance, a single tank dishwasher located along a flat wall in a small restaurant might only occupy 125 sq. ft. (11.63 sq. m.).

SPECIAL DESIGN FEATURES

Nowhere in the design of a foodservice facility is an understanding of time and motion in the work environment more important than in warewashing. A dishwasher usually works in a restricted area with a minimum amount of walking. Good warewashing design must include a study of each move that the dishwasher makes so that the dishes can be handled in the most efficient means possible. The basic steps that are normally taken in washing dishes are:

1. separation of dishes from paper, trays, and so on
2. scraping (prerinsing may be done in step 2)
3. stacking or accumulating
4. racking
5. prerinsing (if not done in step 2)
6. washing
7. air drying
8. removing clean dishes

The design principle of simplicity discussed earlier is important to keep in mind when designing warewashing systems. Elaborate conveyor and "bridge" systems for soiled dish tables often add to the clutter and expense of the warewashing area and create barriers that are difficult to move around. At the other extreme, designs that do not provide sufficient space for soiled dish accumulation or warewashing rooms that have insufficient cart storage space for clean dishes are to be avoided.

Sound-absorbing materials on the ceiling, a high level of lighting (80 to 100 ft. candles), and the use of bright colors on the walls and ceiling are desirable design features. One frequent mistake in the engineering of warewashing areas is to provide inadequate circulation of air. The vents and small hoods required by the health department on dishmachines are not sufficient for the removal of moist air from the space. Supply and exhaust equipment that will accomplish 60 air changes per hour is recommended.

SUMMARY

A general description of the primary spaces of a foodservice facility has been included to provide the food facilities planner with general guidelines concerning the spaces needed. Each of the spaces should work in harmony with other functional areas so that a high level of efficiency is achieved. The penalty for ignoring space relationships is an increase in labor and other operating costs. Food facilities owners and managers are encouraged to visit existing operations to familiarize themselves with a variety of design alternatives and to see how others have dealt with spatial relationships.

The amount of space needed for each area will vary. Some spaces may be "squeezed" and others made larger, depending on the special circumstances of the design or the desires of the owner or manager. The special design features presented for each of the spaces reflect solutions to problems that are frequently encountered by the author in the process of planning and designing foodservice operations.

CHAPTER 4

EQUIPMENT LAYOUT

THIS CHAPTER WILL:

▶ Describe the desirable relationships between the component parts of a work area in a food facility

▶ Develop the methods for analyzing a layout and list the desirable features that should be included in each work area

▶ Illustrate typical layouts for each functional area of a foodservice operation

---

THE LAYOUT OF A WORK AREA

Although the space allocation for each area in a food facility may be deemed adequate, the number of square feet is not the designer's only concern. The work area must also lend itself to a logical arrangement of equipment that will eliminate unnecessary effort in the performance of assigned tasks.

This type of arrangement is a central concern of "ergonomics," which deals with the measurement of energy use. If the work spaces are logically arranged and the equipment is carefully selected to fit into the arrangement, the space has the potential to yield a high level of worker productivity.

DESIGN CONSIDERATIONS

A desirable layout must be established for each work area. Factors to be considered in these layouts are:

- access to raw materials
- flow
- relationship to other departments
- access to utensils and needed equipment

Access to Raw Materials

In a typical factory setting, materials move down an assembly line, so that each employee can work in a small area, while the manufactured product moves past the employee's work station. This is an ideal arrangement because the worker is not required to walk great distances, the raw materials are readily available, and the speed of the process (productivity) can be established by management. Often raw materials or parts are delivered to the factory at several points along the assembly line to eliminate double handling. A typical arrangement of a factory is illustrated in figure 4-1.

The idea of applying this model to a foodservice operation has not had wide acceptance except in hospitals, where a conveyor belt is often used to move the food product down an assembly line. While a conveyor belt would have limited usefulness for other types of foodservice facilities, the principles underlying the factory layout concept can be

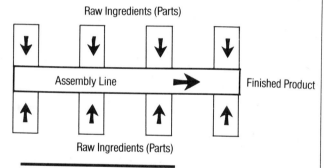

Raw Ingredients (Parts)

Assembly Line → Finished Product

Raw Ingredients (Parts)

4-1. TYPICAL FACTORY ASSEMBLY LINE.

adapted to the needs of any foodservice design. The first guideline that needs to be considered is worker access to raw materials.

Raw or unprocessed materials in a foodservice operation are usually stored in walk-in refrigerators and freezers or in the dry goods store room. The materials for the final assembly of the meal are usually found in or on:

- walk-in refrigerators
- reach-in refrigerators
- dish storage cabinets or carts
- steam tables
- slicing machines
- food-holding cabinets
- portable food racks
- beverage containers and dispensers
- utility or receiving carts

The raw materials must be available to each work area so that a minimum number of steps are required for the worker to obtain the ingredients, process them, and transfer them to the next work area or to storage.

Figure 4-2 illustrates a cold food preparation area with the raw ingredients stored in a convenient place. Notice that the walk-in refrigerator is available for storage of both raw ingredients and the finished product, thus serving a dual need. Designers frequently make the mistake of placing the walk-in refrigerators in a row, with little consideration of the worker's need for easy access to raw materials.

In the range section of a restaurant, it is customary to place a small refrigerator and freezer near the fryer, so that breaded seafood or french fries can be moved quickly and easily from refrigerator into the fryer. Spreader plates beside a grill permit raw ingredients such as steak or hamburger to be stored nearby for a short period before being placed on the grill for last minute preparation. Another spreader

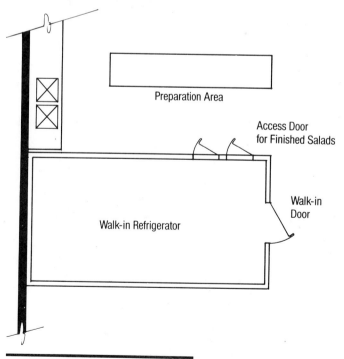

Preparation Area

Access Door for Finished Salads

Walk-in Door

Walk-in Refrigerator

4-2. LAYOUT OF COLD FOOD PREPARATION AREA.

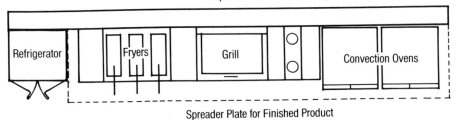

Spreader Plates for Raw Ingredients

Refrigerator | Fryers | Grill | Convection Ovens

Spreader Plate for Finished Product

4-3. LAYOUT OF RANGE SECTION.

plate gives the cook a place to put finished foods. This is illustrated in figure 4-3.

Flow

In discussing the design sequence (chapter 3), it was stressed that the layout of each part of the food operation should follow a logical progression. If the raw ingredients and/or the finished parts of the meal are arranged in the order they will be used (as on a factory assembly line; see fig. 4-1), the food operation will probably be more efficient.

The flow relationship in each work area is most efficient if the movement is in a straight line or L shape. If the worker is frequently required to move materials across an aisle, or to work around another person, inefficiency and worker fatigue will result. An example of poor flow is a situation in which the cook must work back and forth between range section and a cook's table to prepare a meal. In the range layout illustrated in figure 4-3, if the spreader plates were not available, and the cook were forced to place raw ingredients on a cook's table in front of the grill, much effort would be wasted in preparing each meal.

Relationship to Other Departments

Each part of a foodservice operation is closely related to the other parts. In design, the word "system" is often used to describe a functional part of the facility—a regularly interacting group of elements that form a whole. Dishwashing, for example, is described as a system, because each part of the process relates to each other part (see figure 4-4). At the same time, dishwashing relates to other functions or systems within the facility. For instance, in a cafeteria the dishes might be moved in small dish carts from the dishwashing area to the cafeteria line. A good layout in the cafeteria area would permit the dish carts to roll under the hot food steam tables, for use by the person who is dishing up the food. This feature of the service system eliminates double handling of dishes, and decreases labor and dish breakage.

The layout of one department must be care-

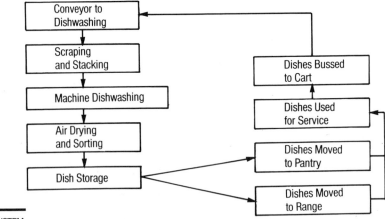

Conveyor to Dishwashing → Scraping and Stacking → Machine Dishwashing → Air Drying and Sorting → Dish Storage

Dishes Bussed to Cart → Dishes Used for Service → Dishes Moved to Pantry → Dishes Moved to Range

4-4. DISHWASHING SYSTEM.

fully considered to make sure that it works well with other departments. A helpful tool in understanding how the departments interact is the "bubble" diagram in chapter 2, under "Programming" (fig. 2-2), illustrating departmental relationships. The interaction of dishwashing to other departments is illustrated in figure 4-5. Notice in the illustration that some functions have simple relationships with one or two other activities while others have complex relationships with three or more departments.

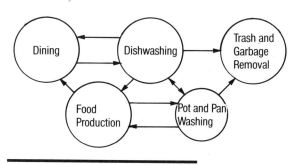

4-5. THE RELATIONSHIPS AMONG DEPARTMENTS.

Access to Utensils and Equipment

Certain pieces of equipment are needed in each work area of a food facility. For instance, all food preparation and service areas should have a sink with hot and cold water and a utensil storage area. Pieces of equipment that are infrequently used or too expensive to duplicate, or both, cannot be located in each work area. A slicing machine, for example, is often placed on a portable stand so that it can easily be moved from one department to another to avoid unnecessary duplication. A mixer may be needed by the salad preparation area workers for two hours a day, and for three hours per day by the cooks in hot food preparation. A single mixer could be located between the two departments, or each department could have its own small, high-speed food processor, since it is a small, inexpensive item, only one hour per day.

Another factor that needs to be considered in the duplication of equipment is the availability of "parking" space, which is often a problem in small kitchens. Two parking areas are needed in the food

production area: a place to temporarily place carts containing raw ingredients, and space for holding the finished product.

A space 3 feet deep by 4 feet wide will accommodate most portable carts. Parking spaces in a typical salad preparation area are shown in figure 4-6. Utensil storage is provided for frequently used tools adjacent to the work space (fig. 4-7).

Often the difference between an excellent layout and a mediocre one is the amount of attention given to detail in each work area. The checklist of utensil storage ideas on page 82 should be used in analyzing the quality of the layout.

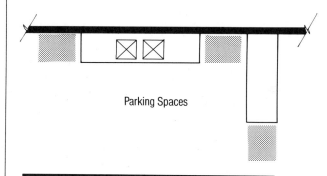

Parking Spaces

4-6. "PARKING SPACES" IN A TYPICAL SALAD PREPARATION AREA.

Utensil Storage

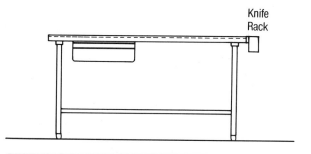

Knife Rack

4-7. UTENSIL STORAGE ADJACENT TO THE WORK SPACE.

PHYSICAL CHARACTERISTICS OF EQUIPMENT LAYOUT

The ability to judge a well-thought-out layout comes from experience as a food facility designer or from working for many years in a food operation. A layout can be planned in part on the basis of space allocation and desirable layout relationships, as already discussed in this text. There are other characteristics in equipment layout that are desirable if an efficient overall design is to be achieved. These characteristics are:

· configuration (shape) of the layout
· method for mounting the equipment
· utility connection methods

Configuration or Shape of the Layout

The three most common shapes for work area layout are the straight line, the L and the U. Each shape has advantages and disadvantages, but the straight line is usually considered the best arrangement from a time and motion efficiency standpoint. Although warewashing layouts have been designed using every imaginable shape for the clean or soiled dish table, more elaborate and expensive layouts tend to be inefficient. A straight line layout, in which the dishes are unloaded, scraped, stacked, and placed directly into the dish machine, is usually the most efficient one. An example of such a layout is illustrated in figure 4-8. The disadvantage of this layout for a high-volume food operation would be the limited dish dropoff area. It might, therefore, be desirable to create an L in this instance, as shown in figure 4-9.

These and similar layouts, each with its particular advantages, can be used for food preparation areas. Several examples are shown in figures 4-10 and 4-11. The L-shaped arrangement uses a limited

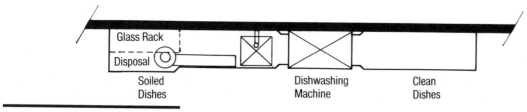

Soiled
Dishes

Dishwashing
Machine

Clean
Dishes

4–8. A STRAIGHT LINE DISHWASHING LAYOUT.

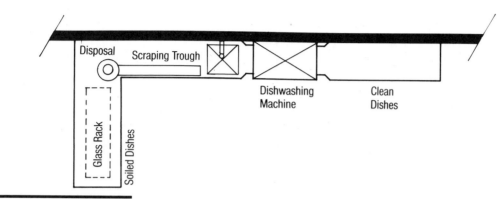

Disposal   Scraping Trough

Dishwashing
Machine

Clean
Dishes

Glass Rack

Soiled Dishes

4–9. AN L-SHAPED DISHWASHING LAYOUT.

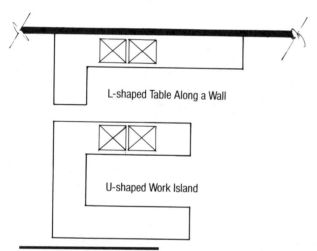

L-shaped Table Along a Wall

U-shaped Work Island

4–10. FOOD PREPARATION LAYOUTS.

amount of space and provides a very convenient work surface. This arrangement also creates a work station that is out of the traffic aisle, which is a desirable feature if other equipment is likely to be parked in the work area. The U-shaped layout offers a large amount of table surface area, but walking in and out of the U may add many steps to the employee's workday. The parallel and back-to-back parallel tables are very efficient as work areas and for this reason are frequently used in food production layouts. The tables shown are of a standard 2 foot 6 inch

width, but as can be seen in the illustrations, each shape uses a different amount of floor space.

Methods for Mounting Equipment

To design the area for efficiency, the layout of a work space must be considered from a three-dimensional perspective. The effective use of space above and below the table surface must be carefully considered by the food facilities consultant. Below the table surface, the most important consideration is

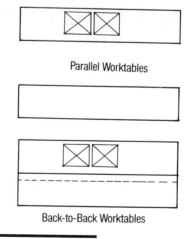

Parallel Worktables

Back-to-Back Worktables

4–11. FOOD PREPARATION LAYOUTS.

the method for mounting the equipment. The most common mounting arrangements are:

- concrete bases
- small steel legs
- equipment stands
- wheels
- wall hanging
- pedestals

CONCRETE BASES

Concrete bases are typically used under large pieces of equipment, such as refrigerators or broilers, as a means of eliminating difficult-to-clean areas under the equipment. Because of the inflexibility that a large concrete base creates in a kitchen, this mounting method is now used less frequently than in the past.

SMALL STEEL LEGS

The standard leg for kitchen equipment is 6 inches high. This height permits cleaning under the equipment, but does not allow thorough cleaning. Small 6-inch legs on large pieces of equipment such as ranges or broilers are especially difficult to clean under because of the distance from the front to the back of the equipment.

EQUIPMENT STANDS

The range section of a foodservice facility is traditionally mounted in a "bank" or row of equipment, one piece beside the other. This arrangement creates several problems:

- The grease that flows into cracks between pieces of equipment cannot be easily removed.
- The short legs on which the equipment is mounted make cleaning underneath difficult.
- Utilities are connected from behind the equipment, making cleaning and repair difficult.
- Ovens are located close to the floor in many pieces of equipment, making it difficult to load and unload food being cooked.

A good design solution to these problems is to place this equipment on an equipment stand. Since equipment stands are sized to accommodate modular equipment in the range sections, the designer can specify the proper stand to fit each piece. Figure 4-12 shows a typical range section mounted on an equipment stand.

EQUIPMENT WITH WHEELS

The use of wheels is a popular option in mounting foodservice equipment. Portability is often a desirable feature because the equipment can be easily moved for cleaning or shifted from one part of the food operation to another, permitting better utilization.

Wheels can be used on almost any piece of equipment that is electrically operated and occasionally on equipment connected to gas or water. If gas or water connections are necessary, a quick disconnect device can be specified that makes the connection simple for the employee to use. One disadvantage of portable equipment is the damage that often occurs when the equipment is moved without first disconnecting the power source. Damaged power cords and wall outlets are expensive to replace.

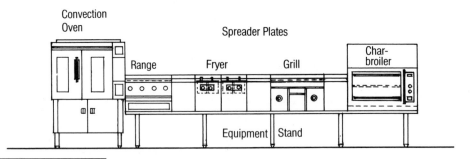

4-12. RANGE SECTION ON EQUIPMENT STAND.

WALL-HUNG EQUIPMENT

The best and most expensive means for mounting equipment is a wall connection that prevents the equipment from touching the floor. The advantage of this method of installing equipment is ease of sanitation. An example of a piece of wall-hung equipment is shown in figure 4-13. Notice that the wall mounting bracket is connected to a chair carrier, which has been built into the wall. The chair carrier transfers the weight of the kettle to the floor. Because the carrier must be built into the wall during the construction phase of the project, full coordination is necessary between the general contractor, kitchen equipment contractor, and the design consultant to make the installation go smoothly.

The cost of a wall-hung kettle is more than double the cost of the same size kettle mounted on legs. Most owners of a food facility cannot afford the luxury of wall-hanging large, heavy pieces of equipment. However, many tables, shelves, and other smaller pieces of equipment can be wall hung using brackets attached securely to the wall.

PEDESTALS

The mounting of equipment on tables supported by a pedestal base is a good method of solving a sanitation problem, and at the same time providing a space for undercounter portable equipment. Figure 4-14 illustrates a cafeteria steam table mounted on two pedestals, with undercounter "parking." Pedestals have the added advantage of providing a sanitary and convenient means of connecting the equipment to the appropriate utility. Water, gas, electric, steam, and drain lines can all be run through the pedestal, avoiding conduit that protrudes through the floor or walls. The disadvantage of pedestals is that the equipment is difficult to move in the event of a change in layout.

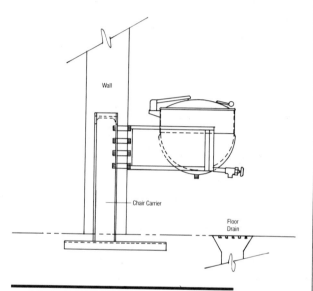

4-13. WALL-HUNG TRUNNION: STEAM-JACKETED KETTLE.

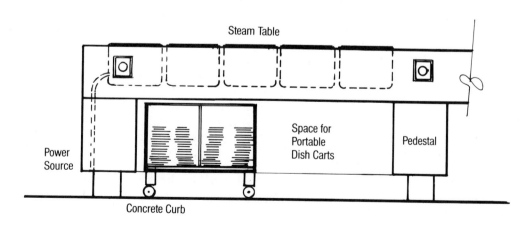

4-14. STEAM TABLE ON PEDESTALS.

FUNCTIONAL LAYOUT

To create a good layout, each area of the food facility must be considered according to its function. The functional areas discussed in this section are:

- storage
- prepreparation
- final preparation
- service and dining areas
- warewashing
- support areas, such as
    - washdown room
    - linen room
    - locker room
    - service kitchens

Storage

Refrigerated walk-ins have been considered in chapter 3 and will be further discussed in chapter 5. Dry storage usually consists of:

- canned foods
- pasta
- spices
- flour, sugar, and salt
- dehydrated foods
- condiments
- other foods not requiring refrigeration

A dry storage area might also include nonfood items such as:

- cleaning supplies
- paper supplies
- linens
- uniforms
- utensils, china, glassware

In laying out the storage area for dry goods, the designer should remember that the separation of cleaning supplies from food products is a health requirement in the United States. The reason for this requirement is to diminish the chances of accidentally mixing cleaning supplies with food.

The separation of food products from paper supplies or uniforms is desirable in order to increase control over those products and to prevent employee pilferage.

If a decision is made to issue partial cases of food to the kitchen, leaving the rest in the storeroom, then those partial cases would probably be sorted in a separate section than the unbroken cases. Opened cases of foods require different types of shelving than whole cases and they also invite pilferage. The separation of spices and broken cases into a special area of the storeroom equipped with solid shelving and secured by a special "caged" fence is a common solution.

SHELVING AND AISLE SPACE

The aisle space in a storeroom can be determined after deciding upon the method to be used for moving the food and supplies. For instance, if large wooden pallets are used in a dry storeroom, then the aisles must be at least 6 feet wide. The pallets, which are between 4 and 5 feet wide, must be moved with either a hand-operated fork or a forklift truck. A forklift truck requires a very wide aisle and is usually used in warehouse operations.

SANITATION STANDARDS FOR SHELVING

Metal three- or four-level shelving is the most common type used for storerooms in food facilities. Metal shelving can be purchased with the shelves either louvered, solid, or embossed. Health departments usually prefer solid or embossed shelving in refrigerators so that food or dirt will not fall from one shelf to another. Louvered shelves seem to be preferred in dry storerooms because they permit air circulation around the boxes, keeping them dry. Health codes are inconsistent on the types of shelving that should be used, but all health codes do specify that the cases of food should not be placed directly on the floor or against the wall. Since shelving can be purchased in a variety of widths and lengths, the designer will be able to select the size that will give the maximum storage in the smallest possible space.

For stacking case goods, it is best to use the small storage shelves called "dunnage racks." These racks have largely replaced the homemade wooden racks that once were used to keep case goods off the floor.

Prepreparation and Final Preparation

The layout of the food production area should be done so that the prepreparation area is near the storage area, and final preparation is near the place where food is to be served (fig. 4-15). The distance

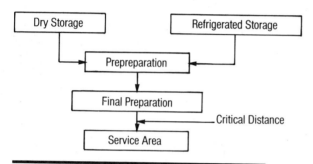

4-15. THE RELATIONSHIP OF FINAL PREPARATION AREA TO OTHER DEPARTMENTS.

between the final preparation area and the service area is critical, if an efficient design is to be created. For instance, in many fast-food operations, the distance between the final preparation area and the customer is just a few feet. This arrangement is extremely efficient. By contrast, the distance between the kitchen and the patient in a hospital room can be several hundred feet (vertical and horizontal), making the service of food extremely difficult and inefficient. The foodservice design consultant must seek every means possible to keep this critical distance short, so that food is served as soon as possible after it is prepared.

Cafeteria operations should be designed so that vegetable preparation grills and fryers are located as near as possible to the steam tables. Some cafeterias are designed with final preparation equipment in the service area or immediately behind it. Grills can be located directly on the service counters, so that the food is handed to the customer by the cook. Hotel banquet service areas are often equipped with broilers and fryers that can be used to prepare foods at the last minute to assure the best quality possible.

Service and Dining Areas

The complexities of service areas in the dining room can range from a simple side stand to an elaborate waiter/waitress station. In a restaurant the labor cost will be directly affected by the distance between the final preparation and the service area. This distance can be altered significantly by the use of well-designed waiter/waitress stations. The importance of the waiter/waitress station for quick, efficient service cannot be overemphasized. If the service personnel must walk to the kitchen to pick up the typical table set up, this might result in the following trips:

First trip: Pick up linen, glasses, silverware and condiments.
Second trip: Pick up water, ice, butter, crackers, bread.

After the order is taken, the following additional trips might be necessary:

Third trip: Pick up cocktail or wine order from the service bar.
Fourth trip: Place appetizer order and salad order.
Fifth trip: Pick up appetizer and salad.

After the cocktail and appetizers are served, the following trips might occur:

Sixth trip: Place the entree order.
Seventh trip: Pick up the entree.
Eighth trip: Clear appetizer and cocktail (or combine this with the seventh trip).
Ninth trip: Clear entree and place dessert order.
Tenth trip: Clear dessert, soiled linen, and all glassware and silverware.

Three or four of these trips to the kitchen can be avoided with a well-designed and properly located waiter/waitress station. The following is a list of thirty items that may be kept at the waiter/waitress station:

- bread
- butter
- butter plates
- baskets for bread
- coffee machine
- coffee and filters
- coffee cups and saucers
- cream
- cream pitchers
- sugar
- silverware
- water and water pitcher
- glasses
- ice
- cold tea
- hot tea and sanka
- boiling water
- linen napkins and tablecloths
- soiled linen
- milk
- crackers
- tray stand or shelf for trays
- condiments (salad dressings, sauces, seasonings)
- sour cream
- soup
- precheck machine and/or space for writing out checks
- microwave oven
- soft drinks
- trash container
- pickup control board

Eliminating four trips to the kitchen will provide the following advantages:

- an increase in the speed of service
- a possible reduction in service personnel
- a less-crowded kitchen
- more attention to guests by the service personnel

One disadvantage of the use of well-designed waiter/waitress stations is some loss of control over the products that are located in the station. For this reason, the items listed are generally inexpensive and are not the kind of food items that service personnel would steal or eat on the job. It would not be a good idea to place desserts, alcoholic beverages, or expensive appetizers on the waiter/waitress station. These expensive items should be picked up from the cold food area after being listed on the guest check.

An example of a redesigned kitchen in a country club, with a waiter/waitress station located near the dining area, can be seen in the "before" and "after" drawings of figure 4-16.

The interior design and layout of the dining room are discussed in detail in chapter 7.

Warewashing

The layout of warewashing areas has been discussed in chapter 3; washing equipment will be described in more detail in chapter 5.

Support Areas

WASHDOWN ROOM

The washdown room is a space, usually located in the vicinity of the receiving dock, used for cleaning carts and trash cans. For a small or medium-sized food operation, the room needs to be large enough to accommodate a hose reel, a large floor drain, and one or two parked carts. A space 6 feet wide by 10 feet long would be adequate. Large hotel or hospital foodservice facilities would need a larger washdown room because of the extensive use of carts. Washdown rooms may be equipped with steam cleaners and foot-operated can washers, but these are usually not necessary.

LINEN AND LOCKER ROOM

Table linen is usually stored in a special storage space that is protected from moisture and convenient to the service personnel. Uniforms are usually issued to the employees on an exchange basis (the employee turns in a dirty uniform for a clean one). The use of a combination linen room/locker room/toilet is a good space-saving design for handling uniform exchange (fig. 4-17). Notice in the drawing that linen is placed in the back side of the employee

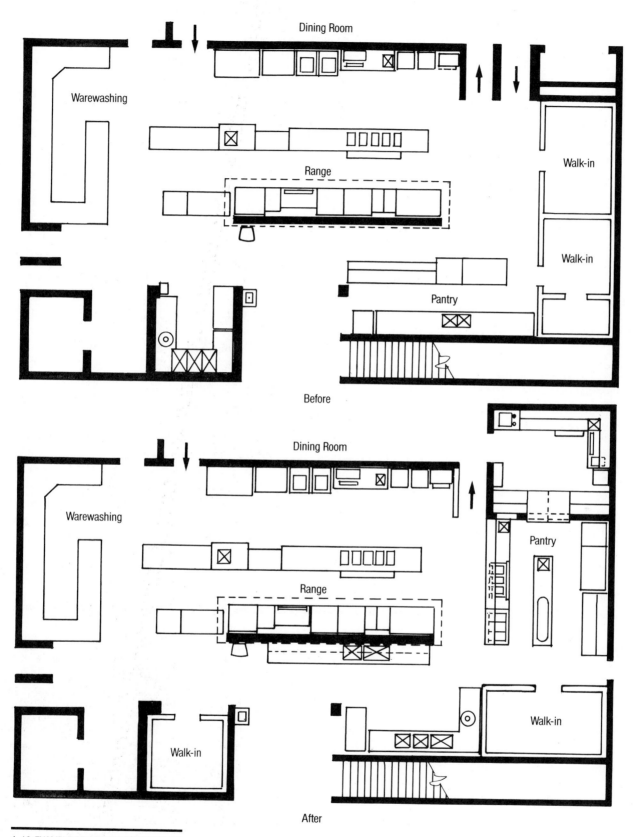

Dining Room

Warewashing

Walk-in

Walk-in

Range

Pantry

Before

Dining Room

Warewashing

Range

Pantry

Walk-in

Walk-in

After

4–16. EXAMPLE OF A REDESIGNED KITCHEN.

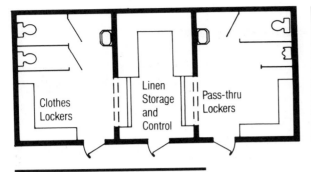

4-17. LINEN STORAGE BETWEEN LOCKER ROOMS.

locker by the linen rental company or the person responsible for linen. The employee places his or her soiled uniform into the locker in exchange for a clean uniform. Separate lockers are provided for coats and street clothes.

SERVICE KITCHENS

Banquet halls and private dining rooms can best be served if a space is provided for holding the food prior to service. Service kitchens are not usually needed, however, if the banquet hall or private dining room is near the kitchen.

Service kitchens can be equipped with support cooking equipment and elaborate hot and cold holding cabinets. An empty room that can accommodate portable equipment will serve the same function. A simple service kitchen with a minimum amount of equipment is preferred by most food facility design consultants. The following equipment should be considered for the service kitchens:

NECESSARY	MAY BE DESIRABLE
Sink with hot and cold water	Dishwashing machine
Ice machine	Refrigeration
Storage for china	Fryers, grills, or broilers
Table for holding service equipment	Steam table
Coffee urn	Storage for catering equipment
Electrical outlets for portable equipment	Heated cabinets
	Convection oven
	Three-compartment sink

The amount of space needed for a service kitchen will vary with the number of seats being served. As a guideline, the square footage requirements for a service kitchen should be approximately:

50- 100 seats	75-100 square feet
100- 250 seats	100-150 square feet
250- 500 seats	150-300 square feet
500-1000 seats	300-500 square feet

If space is needed for the storage of tables and chairs, this should be added to the above space requirement figures. A formula that can be used as a guideline in calculating the space for storage of tables and chairs is to add 0.6 of a square foot per seat.

SUMMARY

A foodservice facility must be designed with both space and function in mind. The work space will function best if attention in design is given to the interface between the employee and the foodservice equipment. The equipment must be laid out with due consideration given to access to raw materials, the flow of raw materials and people, the relationship to other departments in the facility, and access to needed utensils and equipment.

There are certain physical characteristics that are desirable in all work areas. To determine the best physical arrangement, the designer must consider the shape of the layout, the best method for mounting the equipment, and the best means for connecting the utilities to each piece of equipment.

Design considerations are different for each area of the food facility, and each area must therefore be considered according to its function. Storage, preparation, service areas in the dining room, and special support areas must have special design features if they are to be efficient.

CHAPTER 5

FOODSERVICE EQUIPMENT

THIS CHAPTER WILL:

▶ Describe the basis for selecting foodservice equipment

▶ Outline the standards of workmanship and common materials for constructing foodservice equipment

▶ Describe the major pieces of equipment that are likely to be included in a food facility design

▶ Provide an overview of the primary uses of each major piece of equipment and describe the method of determining the proper size and capacity to fit a particular food operation

▶ Recommend energy-efficient foodservice equipment

EQUIPMENT SELECTION

The purchase of a major piece of equipment is an important event for the manager or owner of a foodservice operation. The purchase is important because not only might the initial cost be high, but the cost of operating the equipment over the years will probably exceed the original cost by two or three times the purchase price. In addition to the purchase and operating costs, buying the equipment will involve the following cost considerations:

- the amount of floor space occupied by the equipment
- the amount of labor expended to operate and clean the equipment
- the useful life of the equipment

The owner must carefully consider all of the costs of the equipment before making a selection.

Cost Justification

A new piece of equipment may be selected for any of the following reasons:

- The equipment is a part of a new food facility.
- Existing equipment needs to be replaced.
- Changes in the menu or variations in volume of business require an addition to the food facility.
- The equipment will reduce labor costs.
- The equipment will reduce maintenance costs.
- The equipment will produce savings in energy.

Trade journals and equipment shows in the foodservice industry offer a smorgasbord of interesting equipment that can be tempting to a prospective buyer. A careful evaluation of available alternatives is important in order to select the correct piece of equipment at the lowest possible cost. The form on page 93 may be helpful in arriving at a decision to purchase or not to purchase. This form does not contain a formula for calculating the exact cost of the equipment, but it does summarize the data needed for making a reasonable decision.

If the yearly cost of the equipment will be returned to the food operation through higher productivity and a better quality food product, then the equipment cost is justifiable.

Useful Life

How long will a piece of equipment last? When should an old piece of equipment be taken out in favor of a new piece? The answer to these questions depends mostly on the amount of maintenance care given to the equipment and how heavily the equipment was used in the food operation. A steam-jacketed kettle that is well cared for and that does not have deep dents or scratches should last twenty-five years or more. The valves and piping to the kettle may need replacement before the useful life of this piece of equipment is over. On the other hand, a poorly maintained convection oven that is used continuously during the day for baking, roasting, and grilling might have a useful life of only five years. The chart on page 94 shows guidelines for the useful lives of major pieces of equipment.

EQUIPMENT STANDARDS

National Sanitation Foundation (NSF)

The NSF seal of approval is a recognized standard of acceptance for many pieces of equipment. This seal assures the buyer that the equipment meets certain construction standards of sanitation and safety.

NSF is an independent, nonprofit organization dedicated to the improvement of public health. Equipment manufacturers can write to the NSF testing laboratory to describe the equipment that is being developed and can learn whether or not it will meet NSF standards of construction. The manufacturer pays a fee to NSF to arrange for a representative to visit the manufacturing plant to inspect and test the equipment. (In some cases the equipment is shipped to the NSF testing laboratories for inspection.) If the equipment passes the inspection and tests, the manufacturer is given permission to display the NSF seal of approval. The continued use of the NSF seal requires an ongoing communication between the manufacturer and NSF to assure that changes in the equipment continue to meet the organization's standards.

Questions concerning equipment and the approved list of manufacturers can be obtained by writing to:

NSF Testing Laboratory, Inc.
P.O. Box 1468
Ann Arbor, Michigan 48106

▼
EQUIPMENT NEED ANALYSIS

Name of equipment:
Replacement or new?

If replacement, what is the condition of the existing equipment?

_____ Old and worn out
_____ Energy hog
_____ Capacity too small
_____ Cannot get replacement parts
_____ Produces an inferior product
_____ High repairs and maintenance costs

Costs to fix the existing piece of equipment: $_____
Useful life if the equipment is repaired:

If equipment is new:
Capacity needed:

Features wanted:

Costs

1. List price:
   Budget price:
2. Cost to install:
3. Annual operating costs (energy):
4. Annual maintenance costs:
5. Labor costs
   A. Estimate of additional labor costs to operate the equipment
   B. Estimate of actual labor costs saved as a result of buying the equipment (subtract from A):
6. Annual interest expense on investment:
   Useful life of the equipment in years:
7. Divide purchase price and installation cost by the useful life to determine annual costs.
   Total annual cost (add items 3 through 7):

▼
PROBABLE USEFUL LIFE OF KITCHEN EQUIPMENT

ITEM	USEFUL LIFE (YEARS)
Convection oven*	7–10
Deck oven	10–15
Rotary oven	12–20
Mixers	15–25
Ranges*	10–15
Steam-jacketed kettles	15–25
Food choppers	10–15
Vertical cutter mixer	12–15
Tilting fry pans	12–20
Grills	8–12
Fryers*	8–12
Broilers	8–12
Steamers—high pressure*	10–15
Steamers—low pressure	12–15
Steamers—no pressure*	8–12
Refrigerator/freezer—walk-in	12–20
Refrigerators/freezers—reach-in	12–20
Carts and cabinets	8–12
Coffee urns	8–12
Dishwashing machines*	10–15
Stainless steel tables, sinks, and counters with stainless steel legs	Unlimited
Galvanized tables and sinks	8–12
Stainless steel shelving	Unlimited
Galvanized shelving	6–10
Hoods and ventilation systems*	8–12

*These pieces of equipment have been improved in recent years so that they are much more energy efficient than in the past. The decision to replace these items might be made on the basis of energy efficiency, even though existing equipment may still be useful and in good operating condition.

The NSF carries on a variety of activities in pursuit of its objectives, including:

· Providing liaison services to strengthen communications between industry, the public health professions, and the general public
· Conducting basic research and establishing standards on health-related equipment, processes, products, and services
· Disseminating research results to educate industry, regulatory agencies, and the general public regarding health hazards and means of eliminating them

Issuing official NSF seals for display on equipment and products tested and found to meet NSF standards

The NSF seal of approval and the food facilities design consultant's specifications containing the statement "equipment must be constructed to NSF standards" imply two different things. In the instance where the specifications state that the equipment must bear the NSF seal of approval, it is assumed that only those pieces of manufactured equipment that have been inspected and approved by NSF may bear this seal. For fabricated equipment, the consultant and fabricator follow the NSF handbooks containing the construction methods and standards that have been approved by NSF. In this case, the equipment will not bear the NSF seal, but will be constructed in compliance with NSF standards.

Specifications

Chapter 3 of this text contains information on the types of specifications and some examples of both fabricated and manufactured equipment specifications. The standards for the purchase of equipment will come from five primary sources:

·   NSF, UL (Underwriters Laboratory), and other regulatory agencies
·   The standards of the manufacturer
·   The specifications desired by the buyer
·   The specifications written by the food facilities design consultant
·   American Society of Mechanical Engineers (ASME) for pressure vessels (such as steam-jacketed kettles)

FABRICATED EQUIPMENT

The buyer must write a complete and comprehensive specification for a piece of equipment that will be fabricated. Fabricated equipment, such as a soiled dish table, must be described in complete detail so that the kitchen equipment contractor and the fabrication shop will know exactly how to build it. To assist the dealer and fabricator in understanding the appearance and general construction quality of the equipment, the food facilities consultant will prepare plan and elevation drawings. These drawings may also include detailed sections of the equipment so that the quality of the equipment and the way that it is constructed will be clearly understood. The fabrication shop will read the specification very carefully and prepare shop drawings, in large scale, showing all of the details of construction. The owner and/or foodservice design consultant will have an opportunity to approve the shop drawing before the equipment is actually built.

MANUFACTURED EQUIPMENT

The specifications for equipment that is selected from a catalog are less complex than for fabricated equipment. The specifier should look at the catalogs of all of the major manufacturers of the type of equipment desired, and based on the desires of the client, make an equipment choice (many other factors, as discussed in this text, are also involved in the selection process). The specification should be written in general terms, so that bids are encouraged from several manufacturers. On the other hand, the specification must be specific as to the quality and special features desired by the owner or manager. The following are typical variations found when choosing equipment from a catalog:

·   Electrical characteristics
·   Door swing, windows in doors, and locks on doors
·   Portable or stationary
·   Rubber, aluminum, or stainless steel bumpers
·   Finish (stainless steel, aluminum, galvanized steel, or baked enamel on galvanized steel)
·   Color
·   Steam, electric, or gas operated
·   NSF standards of construction
·   Lids or back covers
·   Gauge of steel
·   Automatic timers, signals, valves, gauges, or thermostats
·   A wide selection of accessories

Obviously there can be a considerable cost variation for each piece of equipment depending upon the quality of the finish selected and the number of accessories added to the product.

EQUIPMENT CONSTRUCTION MATERIALS

The most common materials for constructing a piece of foodservice equipment are:

·   stainless steel
·   aluminum
·   galvanized iron
·   plastic
·   wood

Stainless Steel

Specifications for stainless steel in foodservice facilities are usually type 302 or 304, with a U.S. Standard 18.8 composition (18 percent chromium and 8 percent nickel). The stainless is polished to a number 4 finish, and the thickness is specified by gauge. The gauge (or thickness) has a great impact on cost, and the specifier should use the minimum thickness needed for each part of the equipment. The following chart can be used as a guideline for gauge selection.

GAUGE	TYPICAL USE
8 and 10	For support elements for heavy equipment or at stress points
12	Heavily used table tops, pot sinks, or other surfaces that will receive a great amount of wear
14	Table tops, sinks, overshelves, and brackets that will receive frequent use or that will carry heavy weights
16	Equipment tops and sides that are small and that will carry light weight; shelves under equipment and heavily used side panels
18	Side panels that are not exposed to wear, equipment doors, hoods, and partitions
20	Covers for supported or insulated panels, such as refrigerators or insulated doors

Stainless steel is usually shaped under pressure at a fabrication shop and then welded and polished. The weld should be of the same metal as the material being welded; usually spot welding, soldering, or bolting equipment is not acceptable. If equipment pieces are to be attached to each other, bolting is acceptable, and the pieces should be tight enough to form a hairline seam. The seam should be sealed with silicone to prevent grease or moisture from flowing through the crack.

Galvanized Iron

Galvanized iron and galvanized sheet metal containing other rust-resistant materials are frequently used in foodservice equipment construction. The obvious advantage of this material is that it has a significantly lower cost than stainless steel. A typical use of galvanized iron is a structure or underbracing for equipment. The iron is welded to the underside of tables and cafeteria lines and stainless steel is then welded to the exterior.

Galvanized sheet material is used for the construction of sinks, tables, and interior shelves in food facilities that have limited funds for kitchen equipment. Galvanized iron piping is frequently used for legs as an economy measure rather than stainless steel piping. Again, the advantage is lower cost, but the disadvantage is that a painted surface chips in a short period of time, and the legs and undershelving are difficult to clean and are not attractive.

Galvanized steel gauges and recommended usages are as follows:

GAUGE	RECOMMENDED USE
12	Support channels and bracing
14	Under shelves and partitions
16	Under shelves and side panels
18	Utensil drawers, hoods, body panels, interior partitions

Plastics

Thermoplastic cutting boards and tops have been NSF approved because they do not warp or crack. Traditional maple cutting boards crack and separate in a short period of time, and the cracks harbor bacteria and soil. Thermoplastic tops and cutting boards should be used where cutting, chopping, or carving will occur. Typically, sandwich and salad makeup tables and occasionally the entire top surface of a worktable will be covered with this plastic material.

Plastic is now being used for the construction of carts and enclosed cabinets because of its strength, light weight, and ease of cleaning. Fiberglas, laminate tops and cutting boards have also been used in place of wooden cutting surfaces. Plastic laminates, which have been used for many years for dining room tables, are beginning to be used in food preparation areas. Cafeteria counters, waiter/waitress stations, snack bars, condiment stands, dish enclosures, and some worktables are all pieces of equipment that can be successfully covered with plastic laminates. In addition to the cost advantage over stainless steel, the use of plastic laminates permits inexpensive changes to be made to the equipment.

Wood

Hard rock maple and pecan cutting tops are frequently used for dining room tables and bakery production tables in food operations. Many bakers prefer the maple top because the surface is easy to clean and dough and flour do not stick to it. Separation of the wooden top does not normally occur in a bakery because the fats from the dough keep the wood from being saturated with water. A well-cared for maple table or countertop in a bakery should last for many years.

Wood finishes in service areas and on cafeteria counters are used primarily for decorative purposes. Wood may not be used in places where it can come in direct contact with the food, but is appropriate for cafeteria slides, decorative sneeze guards, edging for display shelves, and enclosures for dining room service stations.

Other Materials Used in Equipment Construction

Many different types of materials are used to build foodservice equipment. No list of materials can be considered complete, because imaginative designers are continually developing and experimenting with new surfaces and textures. The surfaces that need the most careful scrutiny, if they are to be built to NSF standards are those that come in contact with the food or the food handler. These surfaces should be smooth, nonporous, and resist chipping or wear under frequent use. They should also be resistant to the corrosive effect of salt, food acids, and oils. Some alternative materials used in construction include:

- glass
- chip board
- composition paper board
- tile
- Fiberglas
- rubber
- copper
- brass
- cast iron

FABRICATED EQUIPMENT CONSTRUCTION METHODS

The food facilities design consultant usually prepares a set of general specifications for fabricated equipment. The specifications describe the quality of workmanship expected for all the equipment in a particular project. The following sections provide a partial list of items, together with specifications, that might appear in the general specification section of a set of contract documents.

Qualification

The manufacturer of this equipment must be able to show that he is now, and has been for the past ten years, engaged in the installation of equipment, as required under the contract, as his principal product.

Upon demand, the kitchen equipment contractor being considered for possible negotiation shall submit to the architect and owner evidence of having executed contracts of a size comparable to this contract and of his experience and ample financial resources to enable him to handle the work in a satisfactory manner and to deliver the required items of equipment, so as not to delay the progress of the work.

The kitchen equipment contractor shall be a recognized distributor for the items of equipment specified herein, if of other manufacture than his own. The contractor shall guarantee such equipment for a period of one year and shall be in a position to furnish service or replacement parts when required to do so.

Shop Drawings

The kitchen equipment contractor shall submit shop drawings of all work included in his contract. He shall prepare drawings, indicating sizes, heights, and so forth, of all mechanical services required in items of equipment and send sets of said drawings to the owner for approval and subsequent distribution to other contractors.

The kitchen equipment contractor shall furnish four (4) copies of brochures showing machinery and items not specially fabricated. Cuts sheets, line drawings, measurements, and information with regard to utility and plumbing connections are required.

Verifying Conditions

The contractor, before beginning his work, shall examine the space and existing conditions and shall report to the owner any work performed by others that prevents him from executing his work as required under the contract.

Material and Workmanship

Unless otherwise specified or shown on drawings, all material shall be new, of best quality, perfect, and without flaws. It shall be of the best of their respective kind, equal to the standards of manufacture used by the Southern Equipment Company of St. Louis, Missouri; S. Blickman & Company, Weehawken, New Jersey; or Ruslander & Son, Inc., Buffalo, New York. All labor shall be performed in a thorough workmanlike manner by qualified, efficient, and skilled mechanics of the trades involved.

Sanitary Construction

All fabricated equipment is to be constructed in strict compliance with the standards of the National Sanitation Foundation as outlined in their bulletin on foodservice equipment entitled "Standard No. 2," dated September 1978, and in full compliance with the public health regulations of the locality in which the installation is to be made. All fabricated equipment shall be constructed to the standards of the National Sanitation Foundation.

Responsibility and Insurance

The kitchen equipment contractor entering into a contract under these specifications thereby agrees to be held wholly responsible for the faithful execution of the same and for all damages occurring from a failure to do so; and no expense or trouble through oversight, concealment, or otherwise shall relieve the contractor from such responsibility.

Inspection and Condemnation

The architect, or his duly authorized representative, shall have free access to the kitchen equipment contractor's shop or shops during the construction of this equipment for the purpose of making inspections to see that plans, specifications, and detail drawings are being adhered to carefully. The kitchen equipment contractor shall correct any errors found during these inspections to the extent and within the scope of the plans, specifications, and detail drawings.

Materials

All materials shall be new, of first grade; no seconds will be acceptable.

Gauges herein specified shall refer to United States Standard Gauge for sheet steel and plate.

Stainless steel shall be U.S. Standard Gauge A.I.S.I. Type no. 304 as produced by "Armco," "Republic," or other approved firms, with a content of 17 to 19½ percent chromium, 8 to 11 percent nickel, and maximum carbon content of 0.08 percent.

Stainless steel sheets shall be stretcher leveled and of cold rolled stock.

Welded tubing shall be thoroughly heat treated and properly quenched to eliminate carbide precipitation. All exposed tubing shall be given a final grind of not less than 180 grit emery. All exposed stainless steel surfaces shall have a number 4 finish unless otherwise specified.

Workmanship

All workmanship shall be done with welded rod of the same composition as the sheets or parts welded. Welds shall be strong, ductile, with excess metal ground off, and finished smooth to match the adjacent surface. Welds are to be free of imperfections such as pits, runs, spatter, cracks, and so on, and shall have the same color as adjacent sheet surfaces. All joints in the top of fixtures, tables, drainboards, exposed shelving, sinks, and the like shall be electrically welded, but welds made of spot welding straps under seams and filled in with solder will not be acceptable. It is the intention of these specifications that all welded joints shall be homogeneous with the sheet metal itself. Where sheet sizes necessitate a joint, such joints shall be welded. Tops of fixtures shall be fabricated in the factory with welded joints to reduce field joints to a minimum. Where field joints are necessary, the tops shall be continuous. All body joints made in the field shall be closely butted together, pulled together in the field, and tightly belted on the inside or in a concealed location.

Drainboards

Drainboards, unless otherwise specified, shall be constructed of 14-gauge stainless steel, having edges and splashback as specified in the item specification. Drains shall be pitched to the sink compartments.

Channel rim on the front of the sink shall continue level along the front and ends of the drainboard except where they contact building walls. There they shall be turned up and finished in the same manner specified for "Sinks." All interior and exterior horizontal and vertical bonds and corners shall be rounded on a ¾-inch radius with all joints welded.

Metal Table Tops

All tables of the sizes and shape designed are to be furnished and installed as specified herein. Tops of tables, unless otherwise specified, shall be constructed of 14-gauge stainless steel with sanitary edge extending around the perimeter of the top, as specified in item specification with corners bullnosed or rounded,

and all joints welded. Where specified with a splashback, it shall have an edge at the top furnished as specified for "Sinks."

The height of the splashback shall be covered as in the itemized specifications with ends closed in and all joints welded. The end of the splashback shall finish off with the end of and even with the rim of the top. The top shall be reinforced with 14-gauge steel channel-shaped battens not more than 30 inches in any direction to prevent deflections. Battens are to be 4½ inches wide and are to be secured to the underside of the top by means of welded stainless steel studs and stainless steel nuts.

Sound Deadening

A coat of cork base sound-deadening mastic is to be applied to the underside of all sink bowls, drainboards, table tops, dish tables, and undershelves, and the sound-deadening material is to be finished with aluminum lacquer. Sound-deadening may only be applied to tables that do not have an undershelf. For tables with undershelves, sound-deadening shall be applied between the channels and/or angle supports.

Table and Sink Legs

All legs for open-base tables, sinks, and the like shall be constructed of stainless steel, 14 gauge, seam welded and polished to a number 4 finish. Legs shall be of square or round design, fitted at the floor with 1¼-inch diameter stainless steel bullet-shaped adjustors providing not less than 1½-inch adjustment before the threads show. Legs around adjusters are to have welded stainless steel closed bottom, making them vermin proof.

Tops of legs shall be welded to a 14-gauge stainless steel section of channel, closing the top of the leg. This channel section shall be sized to nest inside table-reinforcing channel and then bolted in place with stainless steel bolts and lock washers through both vertical channel legs and gusset—for an open-leg type table. Wherever there are threads of bolts and screws on the inside of fixtures, which are either visible or might come in contact with the hand or wiping cloth, such bolts and screw threads shall be capped with suitable lock washers and chrome-plated brass or bronze acorn nuts. Where screw threads are not visible or readily accessible, they may be capped with a standard lock washer and steel nut threaded to prevent rusting or corroding.

Cabinets — Base Units

All cabinet units shall be 18-gauge stainless steel, electrically welded, streamlined construction, with all vertical corners rounded on a ¾-inch radius. Bodies shall be reinforced across the top and bottom with 1½-inch stainless steel shapes or angles, all welded. Additional angle and channel cross members shall be supported on legs as specified or shown on drawings.

Drawers

All drawers shall have an 18-gauge stainless steel body measuring 20 by 20 by 5 inches deep, or be of a size called for in item specifications. Drawers shall be die stamped with bottom corners rolled on a 1-inch radius and vertical corners rounded on a 2-inch radius. Pulls shall be formed as part of the front.

Drawers shall operate on ball bearing rollers to slides, firmly attached to the fixture and fitted with stops. Slides are to be of framed stainless steel welded to the front and to have a cross-brace at the rear, forming a cradle or frame. The drawer body is to fit into this frame and be removable for cleaning. The frame shall also be removable by tilting slightly upward while pulling the drawer out.

Elevated Shelves

Elevated or overhead shelves shall be constructed of stainless steel, of the size and gauge called for in item specifications, with edges turned down 1¼ inch on a 90-degree angle and then back under ½ inch on a 75-degree angle from vertical. Where shelf edges are along walls, they shall be turned up 1½ inches, resultant corners rounded and coved with joints welded, ground, and polished.

Faucets

The kitchen equipment contractor will furnish all the faucets, including spray rinse at soiled dish table, and will provide drilling for faucets. The faucets will be installed by the plumbing contractor.

Wall Anchors

Wherever it is necessary to mount fixtures that are supported from the wall, the fixtures shall be securely attached thereto by means of stainless steel tapped screws into stainless steel face and anchor type grounds that are built into the walls. The successful kitchen equipment contractor is to furnish these grounds to the general contractor, with dimensioned drawings, at the proper time so the general contractor can build them into the walls as work progresses, as his part of the work. Itemized specifications note the fixtures requiring such grounds.

Table Tops

The metal top edge of tables and counters in food facilities can be specified in many different shapes, depending on the intended use of the table top or the counter. For instance, a "marine" edge is a raised table used in a kitchen where water or other liquids are likely to be spilled. The purpose of the raised edge is to prevent liquids from draining off the table onto the floor or the shelving under the table. Tables with sinks that are to be used for cleaning fresh produce should have a raised edge specified.

Dishtables are typically constructed with a 2 or 3-inch high edge on the side where the employee would work and a backsplash on the edge located along the wall. Six typical table edge profiles are illustrated in figures 5-1 through 5-6.

5-1. DISH TABLE EDGE.

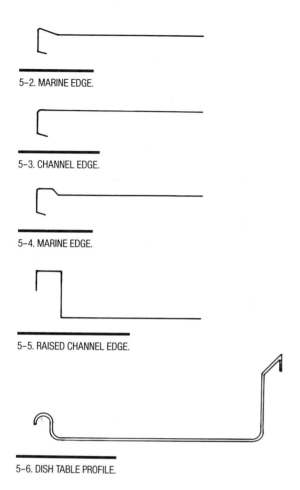

5-2. MARINE EDGE.

5-3. CHANNEL EDGE.

5-4. MARINE EDGE.

5-5. RAISED CHANNEL EDGE.

5-6. DISH TABLE PROFILE.

Table Legs and Bases

Equipment legs must include the following features:

- rust-proof construction (stainless steel top)
- adjustability
- vermin proof construction
- strength and rigidity
- adaptability for replacement with casters

The legs of kitchen equipment are subjected to much abuse through kicking, being struck by other equipment, and being subjected to cleaning solutions and water. A table leg constructed of stainless steel or galvanized steel that would support a table, dishtable, or lightweight cabinet would measure 1⅝ inch O.D. (outside diameter). Crossrails to give added strength to these legs would be constructed of 1¼-inch O.D. stainless steel. Heavier pieces of

equipment, such as cafeteria serving equipment, would be fabricated with 2-inch O.D. stainless steel or galvanized legs. To make the table strong and rigid, it is important to construct the table leg with connecting rails (crossbracing) and 45-degree-angle pieces where the leg connects to the table.

Enclosed Cabinets and Tops

To make the best use of available space, table tops often have storage cabinets placed beneath them. The cabinet frame is usually constructed of galvanized angle iron or 14-gauge stainless steel, to provide strength and rigidity for the cabinet. Figure 5-7 shows a typical cabinet base in section view.

The outside of the cabinet is usually covered with 18- or 20-gauge stainless steel or plywood with plastic laminate. Shelving inside of cabinets should be constructed with coved corners, so that crumbs and soil are easy to remove. Figure 5-8 illustrates a coved corner that is typically used in an enclosed cabinet.

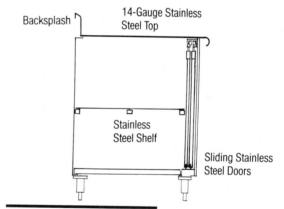

5-7. TYPICAL CABINET CONSTRUCTION.

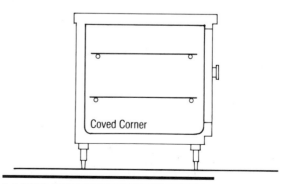

5-8. COVED CORNER USED IN CABINET CONSTRUCTION.

Sinks

Sinks can be constructed as part of a worktable or as a free-standing unit with drainboards. There are many variations in size and use (fig. 5-9 is one example), and no attempt is made here to list them all. Two of the most frequently used sink applications, pot-and-pan sink construction and worktable sink installation, are discussed below.

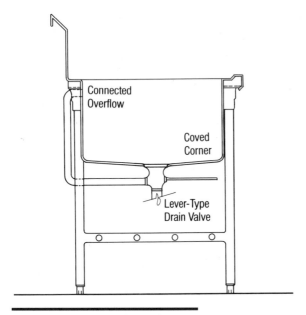

5-9. SINK WITH COVED CORNER CONSTRUCTION.

POT-AND-PAN SINK CONSTRUCTION

The health codes in most states require a minimum of three compartments (in some states four) for pot, pan, and utensil sinks. The sinks should be constructed of 12- or 14-gauge stainless steel because of the wear and tear that will occur from heavy utensils striking its surface. A well-designed sink will have the following components:

- drainboard for soiled utensils
- a garbage disposal
- a prerinse hose
- a detergent dispenser
- a drainboard for clean utensils
- storage rack for clean utensils (a separate piece of equipment)

At least one compartment in the sink should be of a size to accommodate the largest pans for soaking, which is the easiest way to remove materials encrusted as a result of roasting or baking. A standard sheet pan is 18 by 26 inches in size. Roasting pans can be purchased in 18 by 26-inch size, but many other sizes are commonly used. Frequently, the first compartment of a pot sink will not permit the standard 18 by 26-inch pan to be fully immersed in water. The design consultant will need to specify that the first compartment be at least 20 by 30 inches to permit soaking (fig. 5-10).

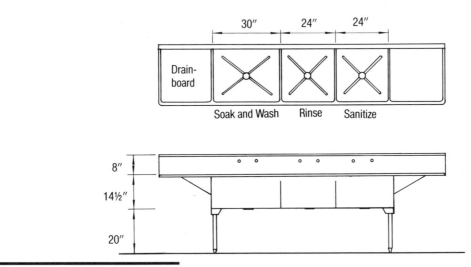

5-10. POT SINK WITH LARGE SOAK COMPARTMENT.

The backsplash on a pot sink should be at least 10 inches high because of the splattering and wet conditions that occur during potwashing. The top edge of the backsplash should be at a 45-degree angle to the wall so that water will not drip behind the sink. Other useful features are:

- lever handle waste disposal
- strainer assembly for drains
- power pot-washing devices
- circulating sink heaters

WORKTABLE SINK INSTALLATION

Sinks that are fabricated into worktables can be constructed in any dimension and typically are 12 by 14 inches deep. Deeper sinks are used for areas where fresh produce is washed in large quantities.

Sink construction should be of 14-gauge stainless steel, and all vertical and horizontal corners should be coved to a ¾-inch radius. The sink should be welded and smoothed to the table top; plumbing is normally mounted to the table top surface. Swivel faucets should be specified that would not permit water to drain on the table surface itself. A sink to be used on a cook's worktable would typically be 20 by 20 by 12 inches (deep) (508 by 508 by 305 mm).

Sinks that are to be used for cleaning fresh produce or washing other food products may be larger than the cook's worktable sink. The following sizes are typical:

24 by 20 inches (610 by 508 mm)
24 by 24 inches (610 by 610 mm)
24 by 30 inches (610 by 762 mm)

Typical depths might be 14 inches (356 mm), 16 inches (406 mm), or 18 inches (457 mm).

MANUFACTURED EQUIPMENT

The major kinds of foodservice equipment are discussed below under six functional categories:

- receiving and storage
- prepreparation
- final preparation
- service
- warewashing
- waste removal

Receiving and Storage Equipment

RECEIVING CARTS

Many foodservice operations use utility carts to transport foods from receiving to storage areas. Because utility carts are made of relatively light-gauge materials, using them to transport heavy cases of food causes the top shelf to bow and buckle. As a result, the utility cart loses its utility. A receiving cart made of heavy-gauge materials and designed to support heavy items is a good investment in a foodservice operation.

SHELVING: FREE STANDING AND PORTABLE

Shelving systems can be purchased to solve almost any food storage problem or to fit almost all types of spaces. The efficiency of a storage space is influenced by the efficiency of the storage shelves used in the space. The wooden "homemade" shelves that are often used in dry storerooms are difficult to clean and are not allowed by many health departments in the United States. The cost of heavy-duty (14- or 16-gauge) stainless steel shelves with wheels is very high, but the great durability of the equipment, its ease of cleaning, and portability may offset the initial investment.

Types of shelves include

- embossed, louvered, or flat
- portable, free standing, or wall hung (cantilever)
- modular

- one to five shelves high (one shelf high may be called a "dunnage rack")
- metal
    - stainless steel
    - galvanized steel
    - chrome-plated wire (fig. 5-11)
    - epoxy-coated steel
    - aluminum
    - trade-name alloys

The accessories that can be added are almost limitless, but the most common ones are:

- casters
- stainless steel posts (uprights)

- rotating bumpers
- strip or wrap-around bumpers
- extra bracing
- wall-mounting clamps
- wire enclosures (for security)
- name and labeling clip-ons

The sizes that are most often used in food-service are:

Width: 14 inches (35.6 cm), 18 inches (45.7 cm), 21 inches (53.0 cm), 24 inches (61.0 cm), and 27 inches (68.6 cm) are the most common widths for use in dry store rooms, walk-in refrigerators and freezers, and for general kitchen utensil storage.

5-11. WIRE SHELVING UNIT. (COURTESY OF METRO)

Length: 36 inches (91.4 cm), 42 inches (106.7 cm), 48 inches (120 cm), 54 inches (135 cm), and 60 inches (150 cm) are the most popular sizes. These lengths should not be exceeded because of the loss of strength and rigidity beyond the 60-inch length.

Height: The posts (uprights) can be purchased in many different heights. The most common are: 36 inches (91.4 cm), 42 inches (106.7 cm), 72 inches (182.9 cm), 78 inches (198.1 cm), and 86 inches (218.4 cm).

General guidelines for shelving selection are as follows:

Walk-in refrigerators: The 27-inch width (68.6 cm) shelf with the maximum height possible is a good selection to maximize storage capacity. Narrow walk-in refrigeration (less than 7 feet 6 inches—229 cm) will require narrow shelving.

Walk-in freezers: Frozen foods are often shipped in boxes that are easily stacked. A combination of dunnage racks for case goods that can be stacked and four-shelf portable shelving units for odd-shaped items or small frozen packages would be a good choice.

Dry storage: Four- or five-shelf portable shelving units work well for spices, broken cases, or small food operations that elect to remove number 10 cans from the cases. For many larger foodservice facilities, the use of wooden pallets that are moved by forklift trucks may be appropriate, in combination with the standard shelving.

SHELVING: FIXED AND ATTACHED TO EQUIPMENT

There are three kinds of attached shelving typically found in a foodservice facility, elevated shelving, under-table shelving, and cabinet shelving.

Elevated shelving is attached either to a wall above the equipment or to the piece of equipment by stainless steel tubular uprights attached directly. Wall-mounted shelving is preferable because of the elimination of the uprights from the table surface of the equipment. For equipment that is placed away from the wall, however, the elevated shelving must be mounted onto the table. The most sanitary means for accomplishing this is to mount the uprights into

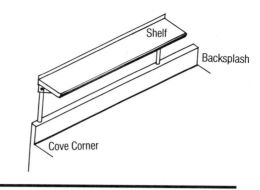

5-12. ELEVATED SHELF MOUNTED ON BACKSPLASH OF TABLE.

the backsplash of the table. An example of this mounting method is illustrated in figure 5-12.

REFRIGERATION

The cooling of foods to reduce the rate of deterioration and spoiling has been practiced for thousands of years. The use of ice blocks and cold water from natural springs or streams for cooling foods is still common on farms in many parts of the world. Mechanical refrigeration has been available since the latter part of the nineteenth century, becoming widespread only around the beginning of the present century.

Refrigeration is used to slow down molecular movement within the food product, which in turn, reduces its heat. Heat reduction diminishes enzyme action and bacterial growth and prolongs the fresh appearance and taste of the food. Heat removal also helps to decrease the poisons that are produced from bacterial growth that can cause illness. Refrigeration is also useful for making ice, changing the form of foods such as gelatin and ice cream, and enhancing the texture and crispness of foods. Many food products simply taste better if they are cold! The refrigeration equipment found in the modern foodservice facility may include:

- reach-in refrigerators and freezers
- walk-in refrigerators and freezers
- under-counter refrigerators and freezers
- roll-in refrigerators and freezers
- pass-through refrigerators and freezers
- refrigerated cold pans

- soft serve machines and ice cream cabinets
- display refrigerators, such as deli counters, refrigerated grocery display cases, and other merchandising devices.

The special features available for the many different types of refrigeration equipment are too varied to cover in this volume. This information can be found in any of the excellent reference books on foodservice equipment and refrigeration that are available. The four most commonly used refrigeration systems are:

- walk-in refrigerators and freezers
- reach-in refrigerators and freezers
- ice machines
- display refrigerators

WALK-IN REFRIGERATORS AND FREEZERS

Currently, the two primary methods for specifying and installing walk-in refrigerators and freezers are pre-engineered or prefabricated, and built-in. The prefabricated walk-in is usually constructed from a series of 4-inch (10 cm) thick manufactured modular panels. Each panel is constructed with urethane insulation material that is foamed into place between two sheets of metal. The kinds of metal that can be specified for prefabricated walk-ins include:

- galvanized steel
- painted galvanized steel
- aluminum (embossed or plain)
- painted aluminum
- 18-, 20-, or 22-gauge stainless steel

5–13. WALK-IN REFRIGERATOR. (COURTESY OF VOLLRATH)

These panels are attached to each other (with a variety of latches and bolts) to form the outer walls, ceiling, partitions, and floor (optional) of the refrigerator. They can be purchased in many combinations of heights, lengths, and widths (see discussion on sizes and space needs in chapter 3).

The specification of a prefabricated walk-in using the manufacturer's standard modular panels produces a refrigerator that is "nominal" in size. The standard widths, lengths, and heights are determined by each manufacturer. A typical nominal sized walk-in might be 8 feet 4 inches wide by 19 feet 6 inches deep. Custom or "full-size" walk-in refrigerators are available and can be purchased, at an additional cost, in almost any size including even foot lengths and widths. For example, a typical full-size walk-in might be 8 feet wide by 20 feet deep. The primary difference between nominal and full-size walk-ins is cost. Nominal size units, because they use standard size panels, are less expensive to manufacture than full-size units requiring custom sizing of the panels.

A built-in refrigerator or freezer, which is more expensive than a prefab, is constructed of styrofoam walls, floors, and ceiling that are protected with structural glazed tile walls, quarry tile floors, and aluminum or stainless steel ceilings. Large built-in refrigerators may also be constructed of Fiberglas panels laid over the insulation. The built-in refrigerator has the advantage of lasting many years under conditions of heavy use, but the disadvantage of being more expensive and more difficult to enlarge or move.

Walk-in refrigerators and freezers are usually specified with either self-contained (top or side mounted) or remote refrigeration systems. The self-contained units are usually hidden on top of the walk-ins by closure panels, but sufficient air space must be available for keeping air cooling units from building up heat in the space above the walk-in. If the large air mass in the space above the false ceiling is insufficient for removing the heat of the compressor, additional ventilation will be necessary. Remote refrigeration systems can be located some distance away, but the further the distance, the greater the heat (efficiency) loss. Remote refrigeration has the advantage of keeping noise and heat away from the food production area. Refrigeration systems can be either air cooled or water cooled depending on environmental conditions and utility availability. Heat recovery equipment from refrigeration systems is an important accessory because of high energy costs, and can be effective for preheating water or heating space in the building. Common accessories and features that may be added to the walk-in specifications are:

· Outdoor, protected refrigeration systems
· Freezer alarm system—activates at 15° F (−9.4° C)
· Extra interior vapor-proof lights
· Roof caps for walk-ins located outdoors
· Wall protectors to prevent damage from carts (interior or exterior)
· Ramps for walk-ins not level with the floor
· Locks for doors
· Windows for doors
· Closure panels and trim strips for improving the outside appearance
· Thermoplastic strip curtains to reduce loss of refrigeration when door is open
· Foot treadle openers for doors
· Air vent to relieve pressure when doors are opened or closed
· Glass access doors for placing foods in the walk-in without the necessity of walking in

REACH-IN REFRIGERATORS AND FREEZERS

The word "refrigeration" refers to mechanically cooled refrigerators and freezers, and "refrigerators" means a refrigeration unit that cools from 38° F (3.5° C) to 42° F (5.6° C). The most frequently used refrigerators in all types and sizes of food facilities are the reach-ins. The versatility, reasonable cost, and storage efficiency explain why this kind of refrigeration is popular.

Reach-in refrigerators can be purchased in one, two, or three compartments (sections), and are available with many different options and accessories. In selecting this type of equipment, the questions to consider are the following:

Will space and budget permit the installation of one, two, or three compartments?

5-14. REACH-IN REFRIGERATOR. (COURTESY OF TRAULSEN CO.)

Will the refrigerator be used for general storage or for special products that would fit better on interior tray slides?

Should the refrigerator be adapted for roll-in carts, which eliminate all interior shelving?

What capacities of storage are needed for reach-in refrigerators and freezers in the food production area?

Is this refrigeration the primary cold storage capacity for the food facility, or is the refrigeration being used to augment walk-in refrigerators and freezers?

What special features would the owner like to have specified for this refrigeration?

Typical specifications might include:

· Automatic condensate evaporator, which eliminates the need for a floor drain
· Adjustable shelving or tray slides to accommo-

date trays that are standard in the foodservice industry, such as an 18-by-26-inch sheet pan or a 12-by-20-inch steam table pan
- Cam lift on spring loaded hinges that cause the doors to close automatically
- Stainless steel interior, exterior, or a combination of anodized aluminum and stainless steel, or anodized aluminum on the outside and inside
- Exterior thermometer
- Interior lighting
- Full-sized door or half doors
- Doors with glass windows
- Pass-through (doors on both sides)

In summary, there are many options available to the food facilities planner in choosing refrigeration for a food operation. An excellent source of information is the equipment catalog from one of the leading refrigeration manufacturers. These can be seen in the offices of the food facilities consultant or at the dealer's showroom or can be obtained directly from the manufacturer.

Primary Use in the Food Operation

Reach-in and walk-in refrigeration must be provided within easy access of the primary food production areas. Many restaurants, hotel dining facilities, and institutions use a combination of walk-ins and reach-in refrigerators. Walk-ins are usually used to store bulk foods, while reach-ins provide convenient cold storage near the production area.

Determining Capacity and Size

The method of calculating the capacity of walk-in refrigeration is included in chapter 3. Reach-in refrigeration capacities are usually listed as "net capacity" in cubic feet (cubic meters). This designation should mean that the available interior space for storage is the net cubic feet. However, in many instances, the interior space is not totally available for storage because of evaporators, lights, tray slides, and so on, and the net cubic feet may be somewhat less. Typical interior capacities are:

one compartment (section):
21.5 cubic feet (.6 cu.m.)
two compartment (section):
46.5 cubic feet (1.3 cu.m.)
three compartment (section):
70.0 cubic feet (2 cu.m.)

One interesting variation on refrigeration is the "refrigerator" that heats rather than cools. These heated cabinet units are used to hold hot foods, and are an excellent application in food operations that need a large holding capacity.

The following chart of capacities may be useful in estimating the needed refrigeration:

SIZE OF FOOD FACILITY (SEATS)	WALK-IN REFRIGERATION				REACH-IN REFRIGERATION			
	FREEZER		REFRIGERATOR		FREEZER		REFRIGERATOR	
	Number	Size[a]	Number	Size[a]	Number	Size[b]	Number	Size[b]
Under 50	None	–	None	–	1	B	2	B
50–100	1	X	1	X	1	C	3	B
100–175	1	Y	2	X	2	B	3	C
175–250	1	Z	2	Y	2	B	3	C
250–500	1	Z	3	Y	2	C	4	C
500–750	2	Y	3	Z	2	C	5	C
More than 750	2	Z	4	Z	3	C	5	C

[a]Walk-in size key:
X: 9 by 12 ft. (10 sq.m.)
Y: 9 by 15 ft. (12.6 sq. m.)
Z: 9 by 20 ft. (16.7 sq.m.)
[b]Reach-in size key:
A: one compartment (section)
B: two compartment (section)
C: three compartment (section)

SOURCE: Sandra Ley, Foodservice Refrigeration (New York: Van Nostrand Reinhold, 1980).

Energy Usage and Utility Requirements

The efficiency of the refrigeration equipment will be determined in part by:

- The amount of insulation
- The number of doors and the frequency of opening
- The efficiency of the air flow within the cavity
- The distance between the compressor and the evaporator
- The level of humidity
- The degree of cleanliness of the compressor (air cooled)
- The temperature of the incoming water to the compressor (water cooled)
- Refrigerant level in the refrigeration system
- The condition and method of sealing the doors

The refrigeration system is usually rated by the horsepower of the motor and the BTUH (British Thermal Units per hour). Most reach-in refrigeration is connected to a 115-volt, 60-cycle, 1-phase power source. Walk-in refrigeration systems are also rated by horsepower (HP) and BTUH, and may be connected to a 115-volt, 208-volt, 240-volt, or 460/480-volt power source.

Because the refrigeration equipment in a foodservice facility will be operating twenty-four hours a day, it is wise to do everything possible to reduce the loss of energy through the purchase of the best equipment possible. Refrigeration is not the place to cut corners or to omit energy-saving accessories. Heat recovery from water-cooled refrigeration systems is easy to engineer and will bring a quick return on the investment.

Prepreparation Equipment

Prepreparation is the area in a food facility where food is processed before the meal is finally prepared and served. Typically, foods are mixed, seasoned, chopped, roasted, or cleaned in this part of the kitchen. The designer must group only the equipment that will be used for prepreparation in this area so that the highest level of efficiency can be achieved. The mixing of prepreparation equipment with final preparation equipment is a frequent layout mistake made by inexperienced designers.

A well-laid out prepreparation area must always include pieces of equipment that enable the worker to achieve a high level of productivity. Desirable features of the prepreparation area are sinks, work tables, utensil storage, access to refrigeration, and access to warewashing, as well as various kinds of food production equipment. The most commonly required equipment is discussed in some detail below.

MIXERS

Specifications

The mixer is a very versatile piece of preparation equipment that is found in nearly all kitchens. The specifier has many choices of sizes and accessories. Mixers are sized by bowl capacity, which ranges from 5 to 140 quarts. The mixer bowl normally is stationary, and the mixer head rotates inside the bowl with a dual circular motion, so that all edges of the bowl are covered in the mixing process. The mixer beaters usually furnished with the machine include a flat beater for general mixing, a wire whip for light products such as whipped cream, and a dough hook for heavy yeast doughs. Large mixers (80 quarts or larger) are usually constructed with power lifts to raise the heavy mixer bowls to the proper position. Most mixers are equipped with a power takeoff for attaching optional equipment.

Primary Use in the Food Operation

Mixers are used where large quantities of food are being mixed, where a variety of attachments are required, and where food processing is done.

Determining Capacity and Size

The chart on page 111 should be used as a guide to determine the proper mixer size.

Energy Usage and Utility Requirements

Mixers operate with an electric motor ranging in size from $1/3$ to 5 horsepower, and are available in any electrical characteristic (110-, 208-, 240-, or 460/480-volt, single or three phase). They use very little power, compared with the heat-producing equip-

5–15. MIXER. (COURTESY OF HOBART CORPORATION)

NUMBER OF MEALS PER DAY	RECOMMENDED MIXERS, BAKERY NOT INCLUDED		RECOMMENDED MIXERS, BAKERY INCLUDED	
	Quantity	Size	Quantity	Size
Less than 100	1	5 quart	1	10 quart
100–200	1	10 quart	1	10 quart
			1	20 quart
200–400	1	10 quart	1	20 quart
	1	30 quart	1	30 quart
400–600	1	20 quart	1	30 quart
	1	60 quart	1	60 quart
600–1,000	2	60 quart	1	60 quart
			1	80 quart
1,000–1,500	1	60 quart	2	60 quart
	1	80 quart	1	80 quart
More than 1,500	2	60 quart	1	60 quart
	1	80 quart	2	80 quart
			1	140 quart

ment in the kitchen. Mixers are usually well constructed and should last many years if they are reasonably well maintained.

Accessories

Vegetable slicers, meat grinders, bowl dollies, and special dough mixer attachments are typical of the desirable accessories that can be purchased for a mixer.

FOOD PROCESSORS

Specifications

Recently, high-speed food processors, similar to the popular French-made models designed for

5–16. HIGH-SPEED FOOD PROCESSOR. (COURTESY OF HALLDE)

home use, have been introduced to the commercial foodservice industry. Prior to this, the most common food processors were the "buffalo chopper," VCM (vertical cutter mixer), and the Qualheim. These three processors are still very much in use in large commercial kitchens, and each has its advantages.

BUFFALO CHOPPER

The buffalo chopper (not designed for chopping buffalos!) is illustrated in figure 5-17. The food is chopped by a semicircular blade that rotates rapidly under a protective cover. As the food moves around the outside edge of the revolving bowl, it is chopped hundreds of times. The more often the food travels around the bowl, the finer the product is chopped. Typical foods that can be chopped include the following:

VEGETABLES	MEATS	OTHER
Onions	Beef	Bread crumbs
Carrots	Pork	Hard-boiled eggs
Celery	Chicken	
Radishes	Lamb	
Parsley	Turkey	
Peppers	Fish	

VCM (VERTICAL CUTTER MIXER)

Similar to a blender except that it is much larger and more expensive, the VCM will cut, mix, and blend foods in seconds, and is used primarily for chopping meats and vegetables (see fig. 5-18). It is also an excellent piece of equipment for the bakery and will blend most doughs and frostings in two or three minutes. The VCM uses a high-speed stainless steel curved knife that rotates on the inside of the bowl. It should be located in the kitchen beside a floor drain and near a hot and cold water

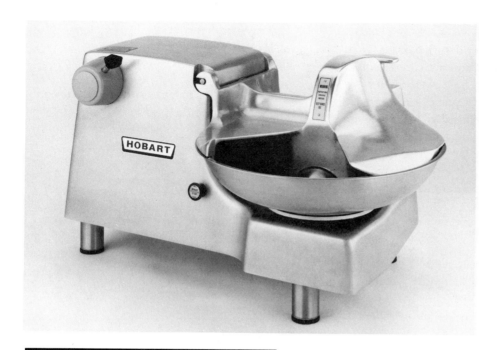

5-17. BUFFALO CHOPPER. (COURTESY OF HOBART CORPORATION)

5-18. VERTICAL CUTTER MIXER. (COURTESY OF HOBART CORPORATION)

outlet for ease in cleaning. The most common VCM bowl sizes range from 30 to 45 quarts. Typical capacities used for frequently processed foods are:

| | TIME | VOLUME | |
		30 Quarts (28.4 l.)	45 Quarts (42.6 l.)
Bread crumbs	2 min.	2–4 lbs. (.9–1.8 kg)	4–6 lbs. (1.8–2.7 kg)
Pie dough	1½–2½ min.	2–6 lbs. (.9–2.7 kg)	3–8 lbs. (1.4–3.6 kg)
Hamburger	1–2 min.	12–24 lbs. (5.4–10.9 kg)	18–36 lbs. (8.1–16.3 kg)
Lettuce	2–3 jogs	4–6 heads	6–10 heads
Meat loaf	1–1½ min.	12–25 lbs. (5.4–11.3 kg)	20–30 lbs. (9.1–13.6 kg)
Cake batter	2½–4 min.	15–30 lbs. (6.8–13.6 kg)	25–60 lbs. (5.4–27.2 kg)

SOURCE: Hobart Corporation.

QUALHEIM

A Qualheim is a large rectangular food processor that provides many different methods of chopping or slicing foods. (Qualheim is the only company that manufactures this type of large processor.)

The variety of food-processing machines available is far too great to list or describe in this text. The manager or owner might want to see a demonstration before choosing any kind of processor. The new, smaller high-speed food processors are made by several companies, offering a wide number of choices. The use of a small model in combination with a buffalo chopper, VCM, or Qualheim might be a wise choice for the large food operation, especially if a wide variety of salads is included in the menu.

OVENS

There are many different types of ovens, and each has special advantages that must be carefully considered by the foodservice consultant or the owner. The most popular ovens are classified as follows:

- standard (under the range)
- convection
- deck (conventional) or pizza
- rotary
- conveyor
- microwave (see "Final Preparation Equipment," below)
- slow roasting

STANDARD OVENS

Specifications

The most widely used oven in the food service industry is the standard oven built into a hot top, open top, grill top, or other heavy-duty piece of range equipment. These ovens are popular because they are inexpensive and they are conveniently located in the range (hot food preparation area) section of the kitchen.

Standard ovens have some disadvantages that have caused specifiers of equipment to look for better types of ovens. The primary disadvantages are the following:

- The location under the range makes it difficult for the cook to see or reach into the oven.
- The ovens are energy inefficient.
- Under conditions of heavy usage, the ovens are often a maintenance problem—especially the

thermostat that controls the oven temperature. Cleaning under standard ovens is extremely difficult.

Several leading manufacturers of range equipment have improved the traditional standard oven, and it is now possible to specify a convection oven in the same location under the range top.

Primary Use in a Food Operation

Standard ovens are used for roasting and baking in the small- to medium-sized foodservice operation. This type of oven should not be specified for a foodservice facility unless space and/or funds are severely limited. Other types of ovens discussed in this chapter offer superior choices for most foodservice operations.

Energy Usage and Utility Requirements

Standard ovens are available using either gas or electricity. They lose much of their heat when the door is opened and are therefore very energy inefficient.

CONVECTION OVENS

Specifications

The convection oven is the most efficient oven available in the foodservice industry because of its effective use of energy and the fact that it occupies a small amount of space in the kitchen. Convection ovens can be purchased in either single- or double-cavity units. A double convection oven would measure approximately 36 inches wide by 40 inches deep.

In the convection oven, a fan circulates the heated air through the cooking cavity at a high rate. As the heat flows rapidly over the food product, heat transfer occurs more quickly than in a conventional oven, and cooking time is reduced. Because the rapidly moving air reaches all parts of the oven chamber, the food can be placed in the convection oven on closely spaced shelves.

The energy and space efficiency of the convection oven is primarily a result of rapid cooking and the utilization of almost all of the interior space of the oven. Typical convection ovens will hold five full sheet pans of product in each of the oven chambers. Accessories for convection ovens include

removable liners for ease of cleaning, automatic timing devices, and a variety of exterior finishes.

Primary Use in the Food Operation

Convection ovens are excellent for cooking many products that will fit on a standard 18-by-26-inch sheet pan. Meats, baked potatoes, bakery products, and small roasts are products that can be easily prepared in this oven. The roasting of large pieces of meat such as a whole turkey or ribs of beef can be done in a convection oven, but the space utilization is not as effective, because the size of the meat does not permit the use of all five closely spaced shelves.

Determining Capacity and Size

The oven capacity selected will depend on the number of items on the menu that are normally cooked in an oven and whether or not there is a bakery in the operation. The following chart illustrates typical oven capacity needs for foodservice operations.

NUMBER OF MEALS PER DAY	SINGLE OVEN	DOUBLE OVEN
Under 100	One	None
100–200	One	None
200–400	One	One
400–600	None	Two
600–1000	None	Three
1000–1800	None	Four
1800–3000	None	Five

DECK OVENS

Specifications

Often called a pizza oven because of its widespread use for making pizza, the deck oven is con-structed of one, two, or three levels of oven space and can be either gas or electrically heated. For many years, this was the most common oven in large restaurants or institutions for doing all types of baking and roasting. Because of the variety of foods that were cooked in these devices, the manu-facturers developed different sizes and capacities to handle different food products. One variation of the deck oven is the roasting oven. This is the same as a conventional deck oven, except that the cavity is higher to accommodate large standing rib roasts, whole turkeys, or steamship rounds of beef. The typical specifications for these ovens include:

- Gas or electric energy power
- Exterior finish of stainless steel or galvanized steel with black lacquer finish
- Number of decks
- Height of the cavity
- Steel or brick hearth (baker may prefer a brick hearth for French bread)
- High heat levels for pizza baking

5-21. DECK OVEN. (COURTESY OF BLODGETT)

Primary Use in the Food Operation

The deck oven is a general purpose piece of equipment that will handle a variety of roasting and baking needs. The equipment may be considered too large for the small food operation, because it does use a large floor space compared with the space and capacity of a convection oven. Many bakers continue to prefer the deck oven for the small- to medium-sized bakery, however. Deck ovens are excellent for pizza because the interior cavity is large, permitting easy peeling (removal of pizza with a large spatula), and the oven can be heated to high temperatures.

Determining Capacity and Size

A standard 42-by-32-inch deck in a deck oven would hold two standard roasting pans, two 18-by-26-inch sheet (bun) pans, or twelve 10-inch pies. Stacking the oven to three decks will increase these capacities accordingly.

Energy Usage and Utility Requirements

Gas-fired deck ovens will usually consume between 20,000 and 50,000 Btu/hour per section, and a three-deck oven may have a 150,000 Btu/hour consumption. Electrically heated deck ovens use approximately 10 kwh per section and are connected to a 208-, 240-, or 440/480-volt source. A three-deck oven would draw 30 kwh of electricity.

Deck ovens are usually not well insulated, and when the door is opened, a large amount of the heat flows out. These ovens are not energy efficient when compared with a well-insulated convection or rotary oven.

ROTARY OVENS

Specifications

Rotary or revolving tray ovens operate on the principle of a ferris wheel. The food is cooked while it moves around in a circular motion in a large,

5–22. ROTARY OVEN. (COURTESY OF MIDDLEBURG-MARSHALL)

heated chamber. This method of roasting or baking is excellent because the heated chamber can be well insulated, and is therefore energy efficient. Moreover, the food can be cooked more evenly as a result of the air flow (convection) that is created when the food is in motion.

The primary disadvantage of a rotary oven is its size. These ovens occupy a considerable amount of floor space as well as ceiling height. The small rotary ovens of one leading manufacturer measure 81 inches wide by 44 inches from front to back and 82 inches high (2060 by 1120 by 2089 mm). Baking rotary ovens are much larger and are built on the site by the manufacturer.

Specifications that are typically used when purchasing this equipment include:

- Exterior finish (stainless steel or baked enamel on galvanized steel)
- Number of trays (capacity)
- Heating method (gas, electricity, or oil)
- Method of opening the door
- Insulation
- Adjustable revolving shelves
- Method of venting the oven cavity
- Temperature ranges
- Stem injection (for hard crust breads)

A similar type of equipment that is now gaining popularity in baking operations is the revolving rack oven. Primarily manufactured in Western Europe, this oven uses a turning rack that can be rolled inside the heated chamber. The baker loads the rack with items ready for baking and wheels it into the oven. The rack is lifted and rotated during the baking period and then wheeled from the oven to cool. The advantage of this kind of oven is that the baker does not have to remove the bun pans from the rack, simply rolling the entire rack into the oven.

Primary Use in the Food Operation

Rotary ovens are very popular with bakers because of the large capacity and even baking characteristics. These ovens often last many years under conditions of constant use, with only an occasional need for realignment or repair. Small rotary ovens are also excellent pieces of equipment

for the production kitchen for roasting and are often used in conjunction with convection ovens.

Energy Usage and Utility Requirements

The oven doors for rotary ovens are small, and each shelf is loaded or unloaded through the small opening. The small oven door, together with its well-insulated walls and ceiling, make this piece of equipment extremely energy efficient. Either gas- or electrically-fired models can be purchased.

CONVEYOR OVENS

Specifications

The conveying of foods through a heated chamber is becoming more and more popular, especially in food operations that employ semiskilled and unskilled labor. A conveyor oven permits the food product to flow through the heated cavity at a predetermined speed while insuring the same cooking time for each product prepared. Conveyor ovens are not in common usage (except in large-volume pizza operations), but will probably become more popular as equipment improvements are made.

There are two techniques for heating the product. In one method, the heating elements are located above and below the metal conveyor belt, so that the product can be cooked on both sides at once as it passes through the oven cavity. The second cooking method involves the transfer of heat from a heating chamber, which is then blown through small outlets, located above and below the conveyor belt. This second method "blows away" the cold barrier that surrounds the food product and cooks it more evenly, without the danger of scorching or overcooking the surface of the food product.

Primary Use in the Food Operation

The conveyor ovens are best used in foodservice operations that have a high-volume production need. Once the conveyor speed is set, the products can be cooked in rapid succession with consistent results. Pizza, cookies, muffins, hamburgers, and other products that are not too thick (dense) cook uniformly in the conveyor oven. These are excellent merchandising ovens, because they can be located where the customer can watch and smell food such as pizza or cookies being prepared.

5-23. CONVEYOR OVEN. (COURTESY OF LINCOLN/WEAREVER)

Determining Capacity and Size

Conveyor ovens are sized by length, width of the conveyor belt, and speed of the belt. The length will in part determine the amount of heat that is applied to the food product as it passes through the cavity of the oven. The width of the belt will determine the amount of food that can be placed on the conveyor at one time, and the speed of the belt will determine the degree of doneness and amount of heat applied. These factors, plus other engineering features, determine the capacity of the oven. A typical conveyor oven has the following production capacity:

BAKING AREA (SQ. FT.)	BELT WIDTH (IN.)	PIZZAS PER HOUR	UTILITY REQUIREMENTS (BTU/HR)
8	24	30	135,000
10.7	32	60	135,000
21.4	32	120	270,000

SLOW-ROASTING OVENS

Specifications

Experimentation with low temperature roasting has been in progress for many years. High heat applied to protein creates a hardening of the surface, removal of excessive moisture, removal of fat, carmelization of the sugar content of the product, and shrinkage. Low-temperature roasting of meats roast meats. Some operators have claimed a savings large enough to pay for equipment in only one year.

Specifications for slow-roasting ovens might include low power requirements, double stacked ovens, portability, and the "hold" feature on the time. The "hold" timer will automatically drop the temperature to approximately 140° F (60° C), so that the meat will remain at a proper serving temperature, but will no longer cook. This is an important feature for foodservice operators who make a practice of cooking in the oven all night. (Ovens should not be set below 140° F because of the danger of bacterial growth.)

Primary Use in the Food Operation

The slow-roasting oven is primarily used for roasting meats. However, the oven can be very effective as a warming cabinet for holding hot foods and as a proof box for bakery products.

Determining Capacity and Size

A slow-roasting oven will hold between 80 and 120 pounds (36–54 kg) of raw meat per cavity. Where large food operations require additional capacity, these ovens can be double stacked. The ovens are very space efficient. For example, one leading manufacturer's slow-roasting oven takes up only 23 by 28 inches (56 by 75 cm) of floor space.

The capacity of slow-roasting ovens is relatively less than similarly sized convection ovens because they require a long roasting period—typically between 3½ and 6 hours, depending on the size of the meat and the degree of doneness (internal temperature) desired. In the same period, a convection or conventional oven could roast several times the amount of food.

Energy Usage and Utility Requirements

The energy savings using slow roasting ovens is dramatic, for several reasons. First, even though the slow-roasting oven cooks over a longer period of time, a relatively small amount of energy is required to hold it at 220° F (104° C). For example, one manufacturer of these ovens requires a connected load of only 3 kilowatts, using a 110-volt power source. A convection oven, by comparison, may require 16 to 17 kilowatts and a 220- or 240-volt

5–24. DOUBLE-STACKED SLOW-ROASTING OVEN. (COURTESY OF ALTO-SHAAM)

reduces the shrinkage and decreases the browning effect on the outside of the product. Ovens that are specifically designed to cook at temperatures of approximately 200° F (104° C) to 240° F (116° C) and that hold the moisture from the meat within the oven cavity are classified as slow-roasting ovens. Manufacturers claim a 30 to 40 percent reduction in shrinkage, which translates into significant savings for food operators who serve large amounts of power source. Since electrical energy is charged to the customer by the utility company on the basis of connected load (demand) and usage, the low-temperature roasting oven scores exceedingly well. Second, energy savings are realized because of the excellent insulation that encloses the entire cooking cavity. Third, energy savings are achieved because the oven does not need to be placed under a ventilation hood. Very little heat or smoke is added to the food production area as a result of installing these ovens.

TILTING FRY PANS (BRAISING PANS)

Specifications

The tilting fry pan is also called a tilting skillet or a tilting braising pan. The advantage of this piece of equipment is versatility. Tilting fry pans can be used for grilling, steaming, braising, sautéing, or stewing. The piece of equipment has a long rectangular shape, with sides that are usually 6 to 10 inches (15.2 to 25.4 cm) high. The large, flat, inside surface is good for grilling, and the tall sides give the added advantage of holding a large volume of food. Typical sizes range from 20 to 40 gallons (76 to 152 l), and measure from approximately 36 inches wide by 30 inches deep (91 cm wide by 76 cm deep) up to 56 inches wide by 34 inches deep (142 cm wide by 86 cm deep). The fry pan tilts, as the name suggests, so that the liquids can be poured into a container. The tilting feature also permits easy cleaning, if the pan is located over a floor drain. Accessories that are usually purchased with the equipment include a hot and cold filler faucet and/or spray rinse hose, as well as spreader plates for each side of the pan.

Primary Use in the Food Operation

The tilting fry pan can be used as:

- a bain marie for holding foods in a hot water bath
- a grill
- a braising pan

5-25. TILTING SKILLET. (COURTESY OF GROEN)

- a kettle for simmering or stewing
- a steamer with the lid in a closed position
- a fryer for foods cooked in small amounts of fat
- a poacher

Determining Capacity and Size

The tilting fry pan should be purchased in the largest size that space and funds permit. The smaller fry pans are difficult to use for grilling because of the high sides. The equipment is most useful when it is installed beside a steam-jacketed kettle or grill. This arrangement permits the cooks to have a choice of equipment to use, depending on the menu and/or volume of food that must be prepared.

Energy Usage and Utility Requirements

The fry pan can be purchased with either gas or electricity as a source of energy. The electric fry pan with the open unobstructed stand is simple and easy to clean and might therefore be preferred. Energy efficiency is a strong selling point for the fry pan. The direct contact of the heated surface with the food, plus the large lid, contribute to the energy efficiency.

STEAM-JACKETED KETTLES

The kettle is often described as the workhorse of the kitchen because of its versatility and popularity among cooks and chefs. The steam-jacketed kettle is heated from an inner jacket that contains the steam. This double-walled construction is very effi-cient because the heat from the steam is transferred directly into the food product through the stainless steel wall of the kettle.

Specifications

The American Society of Mechanical Engineers (ASME) has established safety codes that must be followed by the manufacturer of steam equipment that is operated under pressure. The ASME requires that the inner jacket be able to handle from 5 to 50 pounds per square inch (psi) and that the kettle be constructed of heavy-gauge stainless steel. Steam-jacketed kettles should last many years in a kitchen, unless they are dented or scratched through rough treatment. Most kettles use a simple steam valve that is opened slightly for simmering foods, and more fully for cooking at higher temperatures.

Steam-jacketed kettles are usually furnished with a lid, and a large number of options are available to the equipment specifier. The most important of these is the selection of the method of mounting. Kettles can be mounted in a number of different ways:

- on legs
- on a pedestal base
- on a yoke (trunnion) for tilting
- wall hung
- wall hung-tilting
- on a table top

5-26. STEAM-JACKETED KETTLE. (COURTESY OF GROEN)

The price of the kettle increases dramatically as the mounting method becomes more complex. For example, a 40-gallon kettle mounted on legs will cost approximately one third the price of the same kettle wall mounted. The comparative advantages of the different mounting methods relate primarily to ease of cleaning and the convenience of pouring liquids from a tilting kettle.

Other accessories that are often specified to accompany a steam-jacketed kettle are the following:

- Hot and cold water flexible hoses for filling the kettles
- Spray rinse device for cleaning
- Water-metering device for measuring exact quantities to be added to the kettle
- Mixer attachments (these are very expensive)
- Cold water attachments for rapid cooling of the product
- Large draw-off spigot
- Etched numbers on the inside of the kettle indicating the volume of liquid
- Self-contained gas or electrical heaters that eliminate the necessity for a steam line

Primary Use in the Food Operation

The steam-jacketed kettle is most often used for bringing any liquid product up to a boiling temperature. Soups, stews, vegetables, stocks, sauces, boiled meats—any food product cooked in a liquid—can be efficiently handled in a steam-jacketed kettle.

Determining Capacity and Size

The menu and cooking procedures will have a direct influence on the number and type of kettles needed. The table-mounted kettles are small in capacity, ranging between 6 and 40 quarts, while floor models range in size from 20 to 150 gallons. When considering the kettle capacity, allowance must be made for boilover or foaming on top of the product. The following chart may be used as a guideline for selecting kettles that will meet the needs of different types of food facilities.

Energy Usage and Utility Requirements

Steam-jacketed kettles are very energy efficient and operate best when they are directly con-

NUMBER OF MEALS PER DAY	QUANTITY	SIZE
Under 100	1	10 quart, table mounted
100–200	1	20 quart, table mounted
200–400	1	20 quart
	1	20 gallon
400–600	1	20 gallon
	1	40 gallon
600–1,000	1	20 gallon
	2	40 gallon
1,000–1,500	1	20 gallon
	1	40 gallon
	1	60 gallon
1,500–2,500	1	20 gallon
	2	40 gallon
	1	60 gallon
2,500 or more	1	20 gallon
	2	40 gallon
	2	60 gallon
	1	80 gallon

nected to a source of steam. If a steam source is not available to the building, the kettle can be connected to smaller steam generators located in the kitchen. Steam cookers and other pieces of kitchen equipment are often hooked up to a small steam boiler that can supply the kettles as well. If it is impractical to provide a steam line, electrically operated table-mounted kettles can be purchased.

Steam-jacketed kettles that are self-contained with either gas or electricity as a source of energy are large and expensive. Self-contained kettles are in common use, although the heating source increases the height and thickness of the kettle walls, making access to the inside awkward for the cook.

Final Preparation Equipment

The final preparation area is physically located between preparation and the service area of a food facility. The definition of final preparation is the area where foods are prepared immediately before and during the meal period. It should not contain preparation equipment such as large kettles or food processors, which create confusion and many unnecessary steps for the kitchen personnel.

The final preparation area should include refrigeration for storing foods that have been processed and are ready to be prepared. Final preparation equipment such as grills and fryers produces a large quantity of grease and soil and therefore should be installed in a manner that will permit easy cleaning. The final preparation area should be adjacent to the warewashing area for easy access to the pot and pan sink and a supply of clean dishes. The final preparation area should always include the following equipment for storing and handling:

· work tables or spreader plates
· utensil racks and storage drawers
· sinks
· a pickup station
· hot and cold food holding equipment
· a storage place for raw ingredients

The food preparation equipment for this area consists of:

· low- and no-pressure steamers
· high-pressure steamers
· bain maries
· broilers
· microwave ovens
· fryers
· ranges
· grills
· grooved griddles

LOW- AND NO-PRESSURE STEAMERS

Specifications

Steaming is an extremely efficient cooking method because of the quick heat transfer between the steam and food product. Steamers can be purchased in high-, low-, and no-pressure models. The low- and no-pressure models may also be considered prepreparation equipment because they can be used to prepare large quantities of food before the meal period begins. High-pressure steam cookers are used to prepare foods just before and during the meal period.

Low-pressure steamers, which have been in use in commercial kitchens for many years, operate under a pressure of 5 pounds per square inch. One-, two-, and three-compartment models are available. Each compartment has a large capacity, and can be

specified to hold two large (12 by 20 inches) perforated pans for cooking such items as boiled potatoes. The compartments can also be fitted to accommodate six full-size steam table pans. The capacity of this equipment makes it most suited to large institutions or restaurants.

No-pressure "convection" steamers have become popular in recent years because they are compact, will handle a large quantity of food, and are well-liked by cooks and chefs. Since all steamers operate on the basis of convected heat, the term "convection" steamer is primarily a marketing device.

All steamers can be purchased with automatic timing devices, interior fittings to accommodate different sized pans, and special exterior finishes. Floor-mounted, wall-mounted, and modular units are available. The methods of producing steam and transferring the steam to the cooking cavity varies considerably from one model to the next. Many steamers are available with steam boilers located in a compartment under the cooker.

Primary Use in the Food Operation

Low- and no-pressure steamers are used in the preparation of vegetables, starch products, seafood, and eggs. They cook these items quickly, and thus support the batch cookery concept.

Determining Capacity and Size

The standard for judging the size of a steamer is the cooking time and the steam table pan capacity. Low- and no-pressure steamers will cook most vegetables in 8 to 15 minutes. Rice, spaghetti, and potatoes will cook in 20 to 30 minutes. Typical capacities for low- and no-pressure steamers are as follows.

FOOD ITEM	COOKING TIME (MINS.)	
	Fresh	Frozen
Chicken, 5–8 oz bread pieces	18–20	
Ribs, 3 lb and under	20–26	
Halibut, 6–8 oz portions	4–6	6–8
Asparagus, spears	4	6
Broccoli, spears	3	2–3

SOURCE: Cleveland Range Co., Division of Alco Foodservice Equipment Company.

Energy Usage and Utility Requirements

The best way to operate these steamers is through a direct connection to a steam source. Care must be taken to be sure that the direct source of steam is clean. Often steam boilers have chemicals added for reducing rust and foaming, which can contaminate the steam. If the steam is not clean, a steam-fired boiler can be used to produce a clean steam source. If direct steam is not available, gas or electric boilers located under the steam cooker can be used. Low- and no-pressure steamers are high in steam consumption, and the volume of steam provided must be carefully engineered in the food facility. In spite of the high steam consumption, however, steam cooking is more energy efficient than electric or gas cooking.

HIGH-PRESSURE STEAMERS

Specifications

A high-pressure steamer cooks at approximately 15 pounds per square inch, and because of this pressure, cooks at a higher temperature than low- or no-pressure steamers. The higher temperature cooks the food quickly and therefore permits the foodservice staff to prepare batches of food as the meal progresses. "Batch cookery" is a widely accepted technique that assures a freshly prepared product, keeps leftovers to a minimum, and improves the appearance and maintains the nutritive value of the food. High-pressure steamers are usually designed so that vegetables can be cooked in a steam table pan, which eliminates double handling of the cooked product and the washing of an extra pot.

5-27. HIGH-PRESSURE STEAMER. (COURTESY OF MARKET FORGE)

Accessories that can be specified with the high-pressure steamer are:

· a steamer base with a self-contained boiler
· automatic timing devices
· floor or table mounting
· freezer bases for holding small amounts of vegetables

Primary Use in the Food Operation

Vegetables, starch products, seafood, and eggs are the primary food items that are quickly and easily prepared in high-pressure steamers. The large capacity of these pieces of equipment permits the design consultant to place the steamer near the service pickup area to assure a hot, high-quality product.

Determining Capacity and Size

High-pressure steamers will prepare many vegetables from the frozen state in 2½ to 3 minutes. The steamers are designed for third-, half-, or full-sized (12-by-20 inch) steam table pans. The capac-ity rating for these steamers is listed by the number of portions per hour. Typical output for steamers would be within a range of 500 to 2,000 portions of vegetables per hour. Capacities for starch products would be less than vegetables because of the longer cooking time.

Energy Usage and Utility Requirements

High-pressure steamers are at the top of the list of energy-saving equipment. The closed cavity of the steamer keeps most of the steam in contact with the food, and very little of the heat escapes into the air of the kitchen. The speed of the cooking process and the use of automatic timers means that the steamer uses energy for short periods and only as needed.

BAIN MARIES

Specifications

The bain marie is a hot water bath usually located in the cook's table or in the range area. For many years, bain maries were very popular in large

5-28. BAIN MARIE. (COURTESY OF HATCO)

hotel and institutional kitchens as a place to hold sauces, soups, and gravies at boiling temperature. The bain maries were usually heated by a coil at the bottom of the bain marie sink. As equipment manufacturers developed modern holding equipment, food facilities designers stopped specifying the bain marie. In recent years, small bain maries have become popular again because cooks find a "double boiler" effect very convenient for making sauces without fear of scorching or burning.

Bain maries can now be specified with small, attached water-circulating heating elements that connect to the side of the bain marie sink. These heating devices maintain the water at 200° to 210° F (93.3° to 98.9° C).

Primary Use in the Food Operation

The bain marie is used for holding sauces, soups, and stock at near-boiling temperatures.

Determining Capacity and Size

Electrically heated stainless steel tables and holding cabinets with humidity control are both excellent pieces of equipment for keeping foods at the proper temperature. Kitchens, therefore, do not need large bain maries. A bain marie sink approximately 2 feet by 2 feet would be sufficient for most kitchens.

Energy Usage and Utility Requirements

Steam and electricity are the primary energy sources available for the bain marie. If steam is available in the building, it is usually less expensive to use than electricity. Bain maries are energy efficient unless they are allowed to boil rapidly for long periods of time unnecessarily.

BROILERS

Specifications

A broiler is a final preparation piece of equipment that cooks rapidly from radiant or infrared heat. Most broilers cook either the top or the bottom of the food product, although some models cook the top and bottom at the same time. Broilers can be purchased as large free-standing pieces of equipment or can be table mounted. There are five

types that are typically used in the foodservice facility:

· free-standing top burner broilers
· charbroilers
· salamanders
· conveyor broilers
· rotisseries

In broiling, the cooking time is usually controlled by the distance between the food and the

5-29. BROILER. (COURTESY OF SOUTH BEND)

5–30. CHARBROILER. (COURTESY OF VULCAN-HART)

source of heat. When using the heavy-duty, overfired broiler (with heating elements above) the food is placed on a steel grate that can be adjusted up and down to control the temperature. The grate slides in and out also, so that food can be placed in or removed from the broiler. The distance from heat source to food product is usually fixed in char-broilers; the time the food is exposed to the heat controls cooking.

Conveyor broilers and rotisseries are excellent cooking devices because they can be operated by semiskilled personnel. One well-known hamburger chain uses a conveyor broiler to cook the hamburger on both sides at once at a predetermined speed. In this application, the employee does not need to judge the cooking time for preparing the hamburger.

Salamanders are small overfired broilers located above the range. This type of broiler is used by

cooks and chefs for last-minute heating, browning, or broiling of food products such as fish and other seafood and food items that are topped with cheese or breadcrumbs.

Accessories for broilers are limited to the type of exterior finish and the inclusion of ovens under the broiler opening.

Primary Use in the Food Operation

Dry heat cookery is used for steaks, chops, hamburgers, and other meat products. Foods that have been broiled are popular because the fat content is reduced and the carmelization of the food is appealing to the public taste.

Determining Capacity and Size

Broilers are often rated for performance on the basis of the number of hamburgers or steaks that can be prepared in one hour. One well-known manufacturer of overfired broilers lists a range of production capacities from 100 12-ounce T-bone steaks per hour for a small model to 200 12-ounce T-bone steaks per hour for a large double-section broiler. Determination of the correct size and number of broilers needed will be based on estimates of the number of portions of each broiled item on the menu sold in a one-hour period.

Energy Usage and Utility Requirements

Broilers use either gas or electricity as a source of energy. Gas broilers are often preferred, especially in food operations where the broiler can be seen by the public. A broiler with an open flame adds a touch of showmanship.

Both the charbroiler and heavy-duty broiler generate large amounts of smoke and airborne grease, and both of these pieces of equipment use large quantities of energy. Unfortunately, most of the energy is removed from the kitchen through the hood. The energy waste associated with these pieces of equipment is further aggravated by the fact that cooks tend to leave the equipment turned on when food is not being prepared.

MICROWAVE OVENS

Specifications

Raytheon Corporation first manufactured the microwave oven in the early 1940s. The name of

this oven is derived from the short wavelength of the energy that radiates from the oven into the food. Microwaves are a part of the electromagnetic spectrum and are similar to radio waves. The microwave oven converts 110 volts of electricity from an energy form with long wavelengths to one of short wavelengths, and transmits this energy through the cooking cavity. This energy source causes water and fat particles (molecules) to vibrate at very high speeds, thus generating heat. The food product heats most rapidly where moisture occurs and where the density or thickness is minimal. Thus a product that is thick in the middle will not cook as uniformly as a flat or thin food product, and a liquid will heat more quickly than a solid of the same dimensions. Uniform cooking is accomplished when small amounts of foods are cooked at one time and the oven is equipped with two emitters (magnetrons). The greater the amount of power from each magnetron, the faster the foods will cook. Oven ratings of over 1,000 watts are recommended for commercial use; home-style microwave ovens rated between 400 and 800 watts are not recommended for commercial use.

Primary Use in the Food Operation

Microwave ovens are widely used in restaurants to thaw and/or quickly cook small quantities of food. The chef can hold foods in the frozen or uncooked state until they are ordered and then

5-31. MICROWAVE OVEN. (COURTESY OF LITTON)

prepare them rapidly. The oven has not been widely accepted for institutional use because it does not perform well for quantity cooking. As larger amounts of food are placed in the oven, cooking time increases.

Factors that affect cooking time are:

- temperatures of the food placed in the oven
- amount of moisture in the food
- density or thickness of the product
- amount of food placed at one time in the oven
- rated wattage of the oven

Typical uses of the microwave oven and the cooking times that can be expected from a 1,400-watt unit are as follows:

FOOD ITEM	WEIGHT OF SERVING		COOKING TIME
	Ounces	*(Grams)*	
Roast beef	6	(170.0)	25 seconds
Steak (to be thawed)	12	(340.0)	20 seconds (each side)
Bowl of soup	8	(226.4)	45 seconds
Precooked bacon	2	(56.6)	15 seconds
Ham, sliced	3	(85.0)	30 seconds
Turkey, sliced	5	(141.5)	50 seconds
Meatloaf	5	(141.5)	50 seconds
Hot dog (2)	5	(340.0)	1 minute, 10 seconds
Stuffed lobster (thawed)	12	(340.0)	1 minute, 30 seconds
Fish fillet	5	(141.5)	30 seconds

FRYERS

Specifications

The fryer cooks the food product by immersing the food into hot fat. Frying temperatures range between 300° and 450° F (148.9° and 232.2° C). Fryers can be purchased either free-standing, table mounted, modular, or as a drop-in. If the free-standing fryer is selected, gas can be used as an energy source. If the modular or drop-in method for mounting the fryer is chosen, electricity must be used. The design of the gas-operated fryer requires a greater amount of depth under the fat container, which must be enclosed in the floor-mounted cabinet.

Gas fryers are heated by a ring or straight "ribbon" burner located under the fat container. Electrical fryers are heated by resistance heaters

enclosed in metal and immersed in the fat around the outside edges. Electric fryers are easy to clean because the immersion heaters can be raised out of the fat and the container can be removed and scrubbed in the pot sink. Gas fryers usually have a "cold" zone at the bottom of the fat container where crumbs and burnt food particles can accumulate. Both types of fryers are popular and neither type is recommended as more desirable than the other.

All fryers represent a safety hazard because the fat is kept at a very high temperature and can easily catch fire. Fire codes require that a fire extinguishing nozzle capable of automatically extinguishing a flash fire be located over each fryer. Fire codes also require a disconnect device that will cut off the source of energy from the device in the event that a fire does occur. Accessories that are available for fryers include:

- automatic fryer basket lifters
- covers
- solid state controls
- self-contained automatic fat filtering device

Because of the heavy amount of grease that spills around fryers, sanitation is a major concern for the food facilities design consultant. Fryers that are portable or that are mounted in a modular bank and wall hung are an excellent means of simplifying the sanitation problem. Both of these mounting methods permit mopping under the fryer on a frequent basis so that grease is not allowed to accumulate.

PRESSURE FRYERS

Pressure fryers seal the cooking cavity and introduce pressure. Pressurized frying results in a quicker cooking time. It takes more time, however, to load and seal products in a pressurized fryer than in a standard model.

Primary Use in the Food Operation

Fryers are popular pieces of equipment because the public demands foods that are cooked in hot fat to a golden brown appearance. French fries, breaded meats, batter-dipped meats and vegetables, and french toast are common foods typically cooked in the deep fat fryer.

Determining Capacity and Size

Fryers are rated by the capacity of the fat container. Typical sizes range from 15 to 75 pounds of shortening or fat. Specifications are also often used in which pounds of french fries per hour are the standard of performance. A typical range of french fries that could be prepared is 30 to 100 pounds per hour. The number of fryers needed would depend on the variety of fried items on the menu and the volume of food to be prepared.

Energy Usage and Utility Requirements

Electric and gas are the only sources of energy for deep fat fryers. Fryers are energy efficient unless they are left on needlessly. The number of BTUs required or the kilowatt electrical load is determined by the size of the fryer and the speed of recovery. Fryers that have a quick recovery when the fat temperature drops are more expensive but are preferable because of the shorter cooking time. Fryers that permit the temperature of the fat to drop to a low level will produce a greasy, unpleasant food product.

5-32. GAS FRYER. (COURTESY OF FRYMASTER)

RANGES

The range section of a foodservice facility is the most heavily used and often the most poorly designed section of the kitchen. Open top and hot (closed) top ranges are not energy efficient to begin with, and they are usually turned on by the cooks when the food operation opens and left on until it closes. Most food facilities would be better designed if the kitchen did not include open top or hot top ranges. The exception to this is the restaurant or club that includes a large number of sautéed foods or omelets on its menu. The open top range is preferable for sautéing because the flame can be seen and adjusted to accommodate the amount of heat needed for the sauté pan.

Specifications

The types of ranges most often used in foodservice facilities are:

- radial fin top
- open top
- grill top
- hot top
- combination grill top and open top

5–33. RANGE SECTION. (COURTESY OF U.S. RANGE)

The ranges are often placed in the hot food section of the kitchen in a "bank" or line of equipment to form a continuous range section. Spreader plates can be placed between the equipment pieces to create convenient spaces for holding raw or cooked foods. The equipment can be specified with ovens under each piece, or modular with the equipment mounted on a stainless steel stand. The modular version is much easier to clean, but less space efficient.

Ranges can be purchased that are only one foot wide with two hot plate burners. These are very handy for small-volume range needs in a foodservice facility that does not have sautéed food items on the menu.

Primary Use in the Food Operation

The small kitchen with a limited budget would probably include a range with an oven below it, and an assortment of pots and pans for handling all of the cooking. The difficulty of cleaning, the inefficiency in energy usage, and the high labor costs in using and cleaning the pots and pans make the range an undesirable choice for a well-designed kitchen. The food facility that does a large amount of sautéing should include only one or two open-top ranges in combination with other more efficient cooking equipment.

Energy Usage and Utility Requirements

The range ranks as one of the worst energy hogs in the entire kitchen equipment field. In a hot top range, 91 to 94 percent of the energy is lost up the hood, with only 6 to 8 percent absorbed by the pot or pan; in an open top range, 84 to 86 percent of the energy is lost up the hood, with 14 to 16 percent absorbed by the pot or pan.

Utility connections for ranges include both electricity and natural gas. Gas open top ranges are usually preferred by cooks. The gas consumption by these pieces of equipment is typically between 40,000 and 120,000 BTU/hour.

GRILLS

Specifications

A grill (often called a "griddle") has a flat, heated surface that is used to cook foods quickly in short-order, institutional, and restaurant food facilities. Grills can be purchased as a free-standing

5–34. GRILL. (COURTESY OF KEATING OF CHICAGO, INC.)

unit, as a part of a range top, as a table model, or in a modular unit for mounting on an equipment stand. Recently, grills have been manufactured that can be dropped into a stainless steel table, creating a smooth, easy-to-clean cooking area.

In institutions, grills are used to prepare a wide variety of food products, including steaks, chops, scrambled eggs, pancakes, or sautéed vegetables. The fast-food industry often uses a grill and a fryer for all of the hot food preparation. Grills can be purchased for mounting on a stand with casters, permitting ease of cleaning after the grill is turned off at the end of the day. Fire regulations require automatic extinguishing devices because of the high temperature and the presence of inflammable grease.

Accessories for grills are limited to the various methods for mounting the equipment, as discussed above. Grills that are purchased as part of a range section should be specified with spreader plates on each side, so that raw ingredients and cooked products can be easily handled by the cook. Chrome-plated grills are popular because of the ease of cleaning the surface after the grill is turned off.

Primary Use in the Food Operation

In the short-order restaurant, the grill should be used for almost all breakfast menu items. At lunch, hamburgers, hot dogs, steaks, grilled sandwiches, and many other fast-food items are cooked quickly and efficiently on the grill. In all types of food facilities, the grill is an extremely valuable piece of equipment that can prepare many different types of food.

Determining Capacity and Size

Grills are usually purchased in widths of 2, 3, 4, 5, or 6 feet (61, 92, 122, 153, or 183 cm). The depth of the grill top is usually between 21 and 34 inches (53 and 86 cm), less the narrow trough that is located along the front or back edge for collecting grease. Grills are rated by the number of hamburgers per hour that can be prepared. This cooking performance standard usually falls within a range of 400 hamburgers per hour for a 24-inch (61-cm) grill to 2,400 hamburgers per hour for a 6-foot (183-cm) grill. Large grills usually have one control dial and thermostat for each 12 inches (30 cm) of

grill surface. This heating feature permits the cook to prepare several different types of food product at the same time. For instance, fried eggs, sausage, and pancakes could all be cooked at the same time on a 4- or 6-foot (122 or 183 cm) grill.

Energy Usage and Utility Requirements

The grill is energy efficient only if it is turned off when not in use. The common practice of keeping the grill on for many hours though it is not being fully utilized makes this piece of equipment a high energy user. Grills can be preheated in 6 to 8 minutes and should be either turned off or set at a very low temperature during the slow periods of the day. Gas and electric grills are both popular, and neither seems to have any advantage over the other. Special grills that significantly decrease the cooking time are now manufactured by a few equipment companies. These grills use a hinged device that is placed over the food with infrared heaters that cook the product on the top while the grill surface cooks the bottom.

GROOVED GRIDDLE

Specifications

The grooved griddle (grill) is a relatively new piece of equipment that is constructed much in the same way as a conventional grill. Deep grooves are molded into the cooking surface of the grill, which give a dark, striped appearance to the meat as it is cooked. The grooved griddle is an excellent alternative to the overfired or underfired broiler for several reasons:

- The energy consumption is less.
- The amount of smoke produced is greatly reduced.
- Grease from the product is easily collected.
- The quality of the food product is more easily controlled.
- Meat products are marked attractively and the carmelizing effect is pleasant to see and to taste.

Primary Use in the Food Operation

This type of grill is an excellent substitute for the conventional broiler. In addition, grooved griddles can be used for almost all the same foods that are normally prepared on a grill, except for eggs and pancakes.

Energy Usage and Utility Requirements

Grooved griddles consume significantly less energy than broilers and approximately the same amount of energy as grills. Gas and electricity are the two available sources of energy for this piece of equipment.

Service and Cafeteria Equipment

A wide variety of choices exists for the food facilities design consultant in developing the plans for service and cafeteria equipment. Service equipment usually includes those items that are located in or near the place where the food is presented to the customer. Typical kinds of equipment in these areas are:

- Food warmers
- Coffee urns
- Ice machines and dispensers
- Refrigerators for holding dressings, butter, cream, and other perishables

Shelves for holding small items used by the service staff, such as condiments, silverware, linen, paper supplies, and crackers

Information on some of these service items is included in other sections of this book. Certain kinds of equipment—cold beverage dispensers, for example—are furnished by vending companies and therefore not included in this text. Service equipment that should be carefully considered by the food facilities planner are food warmers, coffee urns, and ice machines and dispensers.

FOOD WARMERS

Specifications

As the name "warmer" suggests, this piece of equipment heats and/or holds foods to a temperature that is just below the cooking temperature with a minimum loss of moisture. The thermostat setting for this equipment is usually between 100° F and 300° F (38° to 149° C).

Because a wide variety of bread and food warmers are available, the capacities of this equipment can best be determined by reading the information available in the equipment catalog.

One common type of food warmer is the "steam

5-35. FOOD WARMER, DROP-IN INSERT. (COURTESY OF WELLS)

table." In the early part of the nineteenth century, steam tables were large steam-heated, water-filled compartments that kept foods hot in deep pans from either a hot water bath or the evaporating steam. A modern steam table usually has no steam at all, instead featuring electrically heated wells that hold standard 12-by-20-inch pans. The heat level is controlled by a thermostat. The capacity of this food warmer is a function of the number of heated wells in the counter and the depth of the pans inserted into the wells.

The most popular bread warmers are constructed of one, two, or three stainless steel drawers mounted in a cabinet. These warmers can be purchased as a "built-in" or a free-standing unit. Capacities of the warmers vary with the height and width of the drawers and the number of drawers specified. Often, these bread warmers are located in the waiter/waitress service area of a restaurant so that the service staff can serve rolls without making a trip to the kitchen.

Other food warmers include heated pass-through cabinets that are constructed to hold the standard 12-by-20-inch pan and full height pass-through warmers that are similar in appearance to a single compartment refrigerator.

The food facility design consultant should be conservative in specifying the number and capacity of food warmers because of the tendency of cooks to prepare food too early and then to store it away in the food warmer well before the meal begins. To encourage "last-minute" and "batch" cookery, there should be enough food warmers to hold only a small proportion of the total food needed for the meal.

Energy Usage and Utility Requirements

Thermostats and well-insulated bottoms, sides, and backs of warming cabinets have dramatically increased the energy efficiency of bread and food warmers. Utility connections are usually 115 volts or 208/220 volts. Most hot food inserts for steam tables are wired as a single bank of warmers. These food wells may be purchased with or without drains for wet or dry steam table operations.

COFFEE URNS

Although coffee urns have been improved significantly over the chuckwagon style of throwing a handful of grounds into a boiling pot of water, the basic method of brewing urn coffee has been the

5-36. COFFEE URN. (COURTESY OF CURTIS)

same for many years. Boiling water is sprayed or poured over coffee grounds for a precise period of time so that the coffee flavor and aroma are deposited in the holding container of the urn. The coffee grounds are held in a cloth or stainless steel basket, and the grounds are removed after the brewing process ends. This is done so that the bitter substance from the grounds does not continue to drip into the coffee. The formula for good coffee includes a clean urn, a good blend of coffee, and a fresh supply of water. The equipment is designed to hold the coffee at just below the boiling point by surrounding the coffee container with boiling water. This outer jacket of boiling water is used as the source of boiling water for the next batch of coffee and for making hot tea or other beverages.

Specifications

The most popular urns have a capacity of 3 gallons, twin 3 gallon (6 gallons), 6 gallons, or twin 6 gallons (12 gallons). Automatic coffee urns do not require the operator to pour the boiling water over the grounds or to measure the water. These urns usually are provided with a mixing device that forces a small amount of steam through the brewed coffee to prevent "layering."

Determining Capacity and Size

The standard cup of coffee is 5 to 6 ounces, and the amount of coffee produced from one pound is usually 2½ to 3 gallons. For this reason, coffee urns are sized in multiples of 3 gallons. Typically, production capacities of coffee urns are:

SIZE OF URN	GALLONS PER HOUR	CUPS PER HOUR
3 gal. (11.4 l)	18	432
6 gal. (22.7 l)	25	600
12 gal. (45.4 l)	30	720
18 gal. (68.1 l)	45	1,080

5-37. COFFEEMAKERS USING DECANTERS. (COURTESY OF BUNN-O-MATIC)

Energy Usage and Utility Requirements

Coffee urns may be heated with gas, electricity, or steam. Gas-heated urns are economical but need a method for removing the gas fumes. Steam urns are energy efficient and do not tend to "burn out," because they provide a more even supply of heat than gas or electrically heated urns. Electric urns are popular because they are less expensive to purchase, easy to install, and can easily be relocated.

Although the coffee urn is frequently used in medium and large capacity foodservice facilities, one of the most popular coffee machines for restaurants, hotels, and small institutions is the automatic coffee brewer that deposits the coffee directly into a decanter. The principle of this coffee maker is that the water is heated as it flows through the device (rather than being stored) and is sprayed over a premeasured amount of coffee held in a paper filter. The coffee immediately pours in a small stream into a glass or stainless steel container. The container or decanter can then be used by the waiter or waitress to pour coffee for the guests in the dining room. These units are less expensive than urns and produce an excellent quality of coffee. They are heated by electricity and most can be plugged directly into a wall outlet.

ICE MACHINES AND DISPENSERS

Specifications

Ice machines and dispensers have become commonplace in the United States because of the high

5-38. ICE MACHINE. (COURTESY OF KOLD-DRAFT)

demand by American consumers for ice in almost all beverages. In the United States, unlike other parts of the world, ice is considered essential in beverages. It helps maintain carbonation in soft drinks and cools foods and holds them at low temperatures, preventing bacterial growth. Ice adds aesthetic appeal to salad bars and other food displays. Automatic icemakers and dispensers facilitate the use of ice in institutional and commercial foodservice operations.

In the early days of automatic ice making, the machine and storage bin were housed in one cabinet. That concept, however, was not adequate to the large variety of production and storage requirements across the industry. Manufacturers then separated the icemaker and the storage bin, allowing operators greater flexibility in sizing their equipment. With separate production and storage units, an operation can have the production capacity it needs to store ice for peak demand periods, rather than

5-39. ICE DISPENSER. (COURTESY OF FOLLETT)

producing it all at once. Today, the separate production and storage concept is the industry standard.

Another major trend has been toward increased customer self-service. Higher labor costs, more stringent sanitation requirements, and the overall convenience of self-service have made ice dispensers standard equipment in a growing number of food-service operations.

Ice dispensers are total systems comprised of three major components: production, storage, and a dispensing mechanism. With respect to production, icemakers can be divided into two general types: flakers and cubers. Cubers produce clear, solid forms of ice that melt more slowly than flakes. However, the equipment required to produce cubes in high volume is more complex and expensive than flake-producing machines. Flakers produce ice on a continuous basis and require fewer moving parts and less energy than cubers. Their major disadvantages are that the quality of the ice is difficult to control and it melts much faster than cubes.

Storage bins are available with varying capacities; 400 to 800 pounds is typical of one major manufacturer's line of dispensers. The bins can be refilled manually or automatically and are designed to stand on the floor or countertop or to be integrated into the service counter. Bins are insulated, equipped with a drain, and constructed of plastic, aluminum, galvanized steel, or stainless steel.

Dispensers with storage bins located above the counter generally give a more consistent quality of ice dispensed than those with storage compartments below and are mechanically simpler in design. However, when large quantities of ice must be stored, it is generally preferable to build the storage compartment into the serving counter and out of the customers' view.

Dispensing mechanisms consist of all the components necessary to move the ice from the storage bin into the customer's glass. The most common (and least expensive) dispensers are gravity fed, with the ice stored above the dispensing device. Such dispensers may combine production, storage, and dispensing functions into a single unit, or they may only store and dispense. In other systems suitable for large volume operations, the icemaker is located below the service counter and fills a storage bin located adjacent to it. Ice is mechanically drawn up from the bin, by means of a rotating "sweep" arm or auger, and dispensed into the customer's glass.

Primary Use in the Food Operation

The ice machine or ice dispensing system is used to produce, store, and dispense ice for the various needs of the operation.

Determining Capacity and Size

In choosing equipment to meet the requirements for ice in a foodservice operation, a number of factors need to be taken into consideration. Ice requirements include the amount needed for beverages and for other cooling/holding purposes such as salad bars and seafood displays.

Beverage ice requirements can be determined using a rule of thumb based on the capacity of the glass. A glass typically requires one half its capacity in beverage volume (fluid ounces) and one half in the weight of the ice. For example, a 10-ounce glass filled to capacity will have approximately 5 ounces (fluid) of beverage and 5 ounces (by weight) of ice. If it is typical in the operation to fill the glass only half-way with ice, then the weight of the ice required would be 25 percent of the capacity of the glass.

The main problem in determining the total ice required for beverage service is the varying demand for beverages experienced in almost all foodservice operations. During peak business hours, especially in the warmer months, the demand for ice is high; it drops off precipitously at other times.

Ice machines are rated according to the amount of ice they can produce in a 24-hour period; ice storage bins, by the amount that can be contained. Although an ice machine may have the rated capacity to produce, for example, 384 pounds of ice per day, this does not necessarily mean that this amount of ice will be produced. If the storage bin holds 200 pounds of ice, the machine will shut itself off when the bin is full. When the peak demand hits, the 200 pounds of ice in the storage bin plus the amount of ice that the machine can produce during the peak period is the total amount of ice available. To obtain the full amount that the icemaker can produce, a storage bin must be selected that is slightly larger than the machine's rated production capacity. With a very large bin, however, there is the risk of ice melting at the bottom.

The following chart may be helpful in determining the capacity needed in ice production and storage to meet requirements for beverage service. For the sake of illustration, it is assumed that one peak period of demand occurs during the day and that the glasses contain 25 percent ice by weight.

| | SIZE OF GLASS | | | |
NUMBER OF GLASSES	4 OUNCE	6 OUNCE	8 OUNCE	10 OUNCE
200	25 lbs.	37 lbs.	50 lbs.	62 lbs.
400	50 lbs.	75 lbs.	100 lbs.	125 lbs.
600	75 lbs.	112 lbs.	150 lbs.	187 lbs.
800	100 lbs.	150 lbs.	200 lbs.	250 lbs.
1,000	125 lbs.	187 lbs.	250 lbs.	312 lbs.
2,000	250 lbs.	375 lbs.	500 lbs.	625 lbs.

The production and storage capacity of the ice machine selected should exceed the amounts indicated on the chart by 25 percent or more, depending upon the operation, for the following reasons:

- Ice is used for other purposes, such as salad bars.
- Ice is wasted.
- The production capacity of the ice-making unit may decrease during the summer months, when the air (or water) used to cool the refrigeration system is warmer.
- Employees may take ice out of the bin because they assume it is "free."

Energy Usage and Utility Requirements

Motors on ice machine compressors, which usually fall in the range of $1/3$ to 1 horsepower, consume small amounts of electricity. They are connected to a 110-volt or 208/240-volt power source, depending on motor size. Air-cooled ice machines do not use large amounts of water. If the icemaker is water cooled, however, it uses a large amount of water because the machine typically operates for longer periods during the day. In a well-ventilated area where the heat released by the ice machine is not objectionable, air-cooled machines are preferable. In areas where ventilation is restricted or the release

of heat into the environment is undesirable, then water-cooled ice-making equipment may be advisable.

Warewashing Equipment

The warewashing machine in a foodservice facility usually represents the largest single cost of any piece of equipment. The purchase price of the machine plus the cost of the dishtables represents a substantial investment. In addition to the purchase price, the operating costs of the machine will include:

- water
- electricity for machine motors
- electricity, steam, or gas for the tank and water booster heater
- ventilation
- sewer charges
- detergents
- drying agents
- labor
- maintenance

Because of these costs, warewashing equipment is among the most expensive to operate in the foodservice facility. The dishmachine must therefore be carefully selected, with consideration given both to the initial (capital) cost and to the ongoing cost of operation.

One common misconception is that the larger the warewashing machine, the higher the operating costs. In some instances the opposite is true. The smaller single-tank dishmachine requires an employee to lift the doors and push the racks through manually, and it uses hot water and detergent less efficiently. And since the low speed and small capacity require longer working hours, the cost per dish washed indeed might be higher.

The machine selected should wash the dishes at the lowest possible cost per dish, assuming that the needed funds and space are available. For purposes of comparison, a university foodservice dining hall will be used as an example. The hall serves 800 students 3 meals per day with 1½-hour dining periods. The number of dishes to be washed per meal is estimated as follows:

800 persons × 6 dishes (includes glasses) =
4,800 dishes and glasses per meal

A small single-tank machine (rated capacity 1,500 dishes per hour with a 70 percent efficiency factor) would wash these dishes in 4½ hours. A single-tank conveyor machine (rated capacity 4,000 dishes per hour but assuming only a 70 percent efficiency factor) would wash them in 2 hours. With the same efficiency factor, a three-tank conveyor machine (rated capacity of 6,500 dishes per hour) would complete the job in one hour. If one full-time professional employee were assigned to dishwashing, and students working part-time were used for the one-hour period, then the economy of the largest machine is clear. In other words, by oversizing the machine, a significant labor savings is realized. If one full-time dishwasher were eliminated,

then the investment on the more expensive machine would be quickly returned to to the university.

Warewashing machines all operate on the same principle. A spray of water is pumped over dishes and other utensils so that the soil is washed off by hot water and a detergent. The final rinse sanitizes the dishes by spraying either water at 180° F (82° C) or by using a chemical sanitizer. The dishes should be hot enough to dry without toweling when exposed to the air. The major types of dishmachines and some suggested layouts for the warewashing area are described in chapter 3.

SINGLE-TANK DOOR DISHMACHINE

Single-tank door machines consist of a tank containing hot wash water and a detergent dispenser. The machine is provided with stainless steel doors.

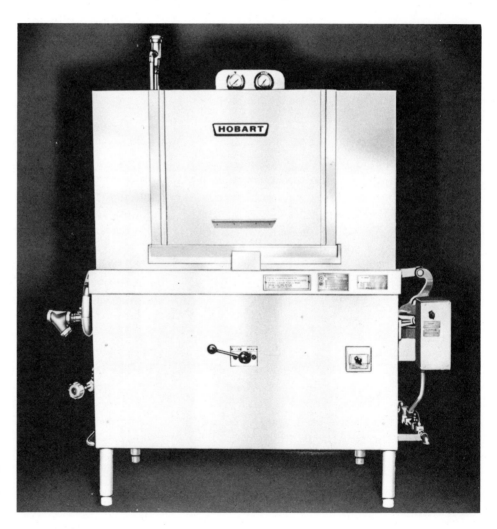

5–40. SINGLE-TANK DOOR DISH-MACHINE. (COURTESY OF HOBART CORPORATION)

Water and detergent are recirculated by an electric motor-driven pump that pushes water through spray arms or nozzles above and below the rack of dishes. The fresh water final rinse is sprayed onto the dishes at 180° F (82° C) after the wash cycle is complete. Scraping, loading, and unloading are done manually.

SINGLE-TANK CONVEYOR DISHMACHINE

A single-tank conveyor machine consists of a tank of hot wash water held at a temperature of 140° F (60° C) mixed with a detergent. The water and detergent are circulated by a motor-driven pump through spray arms above and below the dishes.

5–41. SINGLE-TANK CONVEYOR DISHMACHINE. (COURTESY OF BLAKESLEE)

After the dishes are manually racked and prescraped, the conveyor carries them through the dishwasher at a preset speed. The dishes pass through a final rinse at 180° F (82° C) and air dry on a clean dish table as they emerge from the machine.

TWO-TANK CONVEYOR DISHMACHINE

Two-tank conveyor type dishwashing machines are also available. The first tank contains hot wash water and detergent, and the second, recirculated rinse water. The dishes go through a final rinse at 180° F. Motor-driven pumps circulate the wash water and spray rinse water over the dishes while they are carried through the machine by a conveyor. The addition of the extra rinse water tank permits dishes to be conveyed through the machine faster and results in a cleaner dish or utensil.

FLIGHT, RACKLESS, OR PEG-TYPE DISHMACHINE

A flight-type machine typically has two or three tanks. The two-tank machine consists of a wash tank and a rinse tank; the three-tank model has tanks for prewash, wash, and rinse. Both types provide a sanitizing final rinse. The flight machine uses a conveyor designed to hold most dishes and

5–42. TWO-TANK CONVEYOR DISHMACHINE. (COURTESY OF VULCAN-HART)

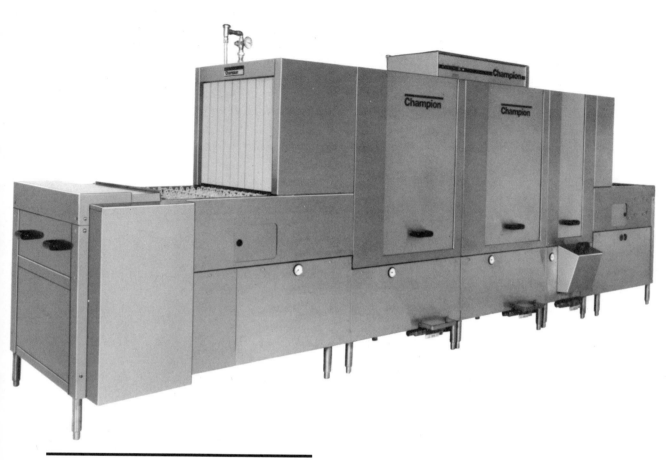

5–43(a). FLIGHT-TYPE DISHMACHINE. (COURTESY OF CHAMPION IND.)

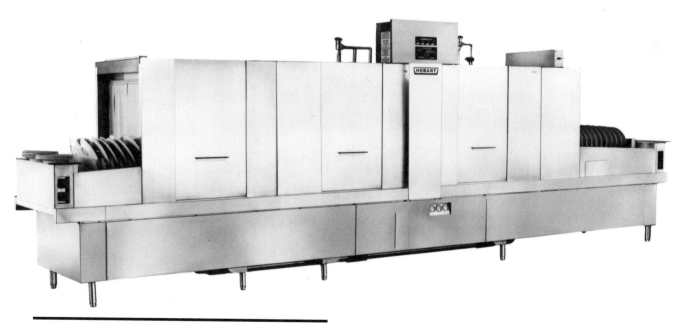

5–43(b). FLIGHT-TYPE DISHMACHINE. (COURTESY OF HOBART CORPORATION)

utensils without the need for racks. Items such as cups, glasses, and silverware, however, must be racked in order to be conveyed through the machine. Dishes and trays are loaded directly onto the conveyor, which is equipped with rows of pegs approximately 4 inches high to hold trays and plates upright for proper washing, rinsing, and draining. The conveyor may be made of plastic and/or heavy-gauge stainless steel.

Flight machines are frequently used in operations that wash dishes for 1,000 persons or more per meal. Smaller flight machines with two tanks may be economical for food facilities serving 600 to 900 persons per meal.

CIRCULAR, CAROUSEL, OR CONTINUOUS CONVEYOR DISHMACHINE

A circular dishmachine is a two- or three-tank machine attached to an oval-shaped dish table. The system uses a series of standard 20-by-20-inch dish racks that are conveyed around the oval. The circu-

lar dishwashing system is labor efficient because the dishes are loaded directly onto the moving dish racks without first being stacked or accumulated. The second primary advantage is that the machine will continue to operate if left unattended for a few moments. (A flight-type machine will stop if a dish blocks the end of the conveyor without being removed.) The circular conveyor machine is especially labor efficient in food operations that serve continuously over a long period of time or in high-volume foodservice operations.

Accessories

Many accessories and options are available for all types of warewashing machines and of course add to their cost. Some of the options are:

· Blower dryer for rapid air drying of dishes and utensils
· Chemical sanitizing
· Steam coils for heating water storage tanks
· Vent hoods for each end of the machine

5-44. CAROUSEL OR CIRCULAR DISHMACHINE. (COURTESY OF ADAMATION)

- Stainless steel legs and frames (standard on some machines)
- Stainless steel enclosure panels to cover the motors and plumbing
- Automatic fill
- Energy-saving features such as automatic shut-off after dishes (or racks) pass through the machine

Primary Use in the Food Operation

In addition to washing dishes, warewashing machines may be used to wash pots, pans, utensils, trays, sheet pans, and a variety of other items from the production areas. Unusual uses may include washing grease filters and ceiling tiles.

Determining Capacity and Size

Dishmachines are rated by the number of dishes or racks per hour (at about 20 dishes per rack) that can be washed. The following chart and calculations illustrate the method for determining the dish machine size, assuming the standard efficiency factor of 70 percent. Remember, it is always wise to err in selecting a machine that is too large rather than too small.

TYPE OF FOOD FACILITY	NUMBER OF DISHES AND GLASSES PER PERSON*
Limited menu restaurant	5–8
Extensive menu restaurant	12–14
Cafeteria	7–10
Luxury hotel dining room	12–16

*Does not include silverware or stainless eating utensils.

The volume of dishes for a 100-seat restaurant with an extensive menu that turns over the dining room 1.5 times in one hour would be:

100 seats $\times$ 1.5 = 150 persons per hour
150 persons $\times$ 13 pieces of dinnerware =
   1,950 dishes per hour

The following are typical capacities, taken from the catalog of a leading manufacturer of dish-machines:

	DISHES PER HOUR	RACKS PER HOUR
Single-tank door	1,550	62
Two-tank conveyor	5,850	234
Three-tank conveyor	6,650	265
Flight-type	12,000	–

In the example, 1,950 dishes per hour at 70 percent efficiency would require a machine that would handle:

$$\frac{1,950}{.70} = 2,786 \text{ dishes per hour}$$

A two-tank conveyor machine would be an excellent choice in this operation.

Energy Usage and Utility Requirements

To qualify for the NSF seal of approval, ware-washing machines must have a preset time and volume of water for the dish to pass through the wash spray. The required volume of water for the final rinse for a single-tank machine is 74 gallons per hour, while for a flight machine the flow is 342 gallons per hour. This amount of water heated to 180° F (82° C) obviously consumes a large amount of energy. Added to this is the energy consumed by:

- electric motors
- tank heaters
- electric controls
- ventilation fans
- heat for the blower dryer (if specified)
- hot water that is used to fill the tanks

Electrical connections are usually 208 volt, 220 volt, or 460/480 volt, and motors can be operated at 1 or 3 phase. Since the energy and water bill for washing dishes is a very significant part of the total utility cost of operating the food facility, energy-saving accessories are certainly worth considering when purchasing a warewashing machine.

POTWASHING MACHINES

Specifications

There are two primary differences between a potwashing machine and a conventional dishwashing machine. First, the motor that pumps water under high pressure onto the pots and pans is larger than that normally installed on a dishmachine. Dishwashing machines usually are manufactured with 2- or 3-horsepower motors, while potwashing machines are built with 5- to 10-horsepower motors that create a high-velocity water stream to strip off encrusted foods. Second, the internal size of the potwashing machine is large enough to accommodate large pots and standard 18-by-26-inch sheet pans.

The specifications of a pot (heavy-duty utensil) machine will be determined primarily on the basis of the volume of pots and pans to be washed. Many large foodservice facilities do not use that equipment at all. Managers often feel that a standard three-compartment sink with a garbage disposal and hand operated prerinse is sufficient for washing pots, pans, and utensils. Extremely large institutions and large restaurants with complex menus can justify the expense of these machines.

The construction of potwashing machines is usually extremely rugged, with frequent use of 12-gauge stainless steel. Some of the larger machines employ a complete self-contained system in which the pots and pans are washed and rinsed on a large carousel. Smaller machines are designed to fit between soiled and clean tables in a simple layout similar to that used for a single-tank dishwasher.

Primary Use in the Food Operation

The use of pot and pan machines is very much a matter of personal preference among foodservice

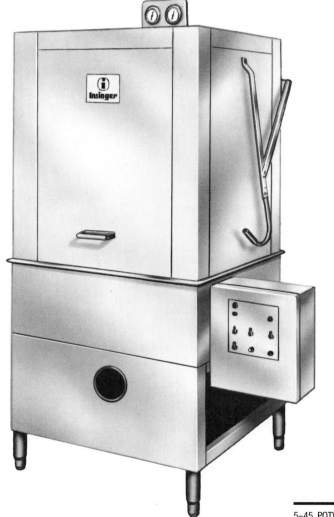

5–45. POTWASHING MACHINE. (COURTESY OF INSINGER)

managers. Most management people feel that the pans must be washed before being placed in the machine and that the only purpose of the machine is to sanitize and remove any greasy film that might remain. Other managers feel that the machine does an excellent job if encrusted materials are prewashed or scraped off before putting the pots into the machine. Many steam table pans and sheet pans do not have hard, encrusted food particles and therefore are easily washed by the machine.

The primary use in a food operation, and the decision to use this type of warewashing machine, may be based on:

· The number of persons being fed
· The complexity of the menu
· The type of equipment used in food prepara-

tion (for instance, a steam-jacketed kettle eliminates the need for pots from a food preparation area)

The amount of money and/or space available for equipment

Determining Capacity and Size

Only a few companies manufacture pot and pan machines, and the types of machines that are available do not fall into any standard classification. Because each of the machines is very different in construction and design, the best way to determine the size and capacity is to determine the number of 24-by-28-inch racks or standard bun pans per hour that can be washed. These numbers should then be compared to the volume of such pans used each day in the food operation.

5–46. POTWASHING MACHINE WITH ROTATING RACK WASHING SYSTEM. (COURTESY OF METALWASH)

Energy Usage and Utility Requirements

The amount of hot water, electricity, and steam used by this equipment is significant when compared with the amount of energy used in a three-compartment sink. For instance, the energy consumption of one medium-sized machine from a manufacturer in the United States is specified as follows:

Capacity: twenty-four 24-by-28-inch racks per hour
Motor: 5 horsepower, 208 volts, 3 phase
Steam: 65 pounds per hour
Water: 11 gallons per minute (rinse only), 26-gallon water tank

Waste Removal Equipment

The garbage can has been the primary piece of equipment for removing waste from food production areas for thousands of years. It continues to be used in modern kitchens, in spite of the development of sophisticated machines that have improved waste removal methods.

Waste removal through the use of garbage disposals, compactors, and pulper/extractors has several advantages over the garbage can:

- The liquid portion of the garbage is flushed into the sewer system, thus reducing the weight and volume of the garbage.
- The odors and vermin associated with garbage are greatly reduced.
- The waste material is transported through a soil pipe, eliminating the necessity of carrying a heavy can to a larger waste disposal container.

The advantage of the garbage can is that it can handle metal and glass objects while the mechanical systems cannot.

GARBAGE DISPOSALS

Specifications

Commercial disposals are specified primarily by motor size (See below, "Determining Capacity and Size"). The following accessories and features are frequently specified for disposals:

- Prerinse sprays
- Cones to direct the water and garbage into the disposal
- Electrical control panels for switching the disposal and water on and off
- Electrical overload and reversing mechanisms
- Silverware saver devices to prevent metal objects from entering the disposal
- Stainless steel covers

5-47. SECTION VIEW OF A GARBAGE DISPOSAL. (COURTESY OF IN-SINK-GRATOR)

Primary Use in the Food Operation

Disposals grind food wastes and mix them with water so that they can be piped from the operation into the sewer system.

Determining Capacity and Size

Garbage disposals are usually specified by horsepower with typical ranges being between ½ and 5 horsepower. Many food facilities designers are of the opinion that the small horsepower disposals are not a good buy. They do not have sufficient power to handle large quantities of refuse at one time, and they therefore often will cause clogging in the drain lines. Larger disposals in the range of 1.5 to 3 horsepower are recommended for general kitchen use. For dishwashing operations, particularly those that will require the disposal of both garbage and small quantities of paper, a 5-horsepower disposal is recommended. The installation of any type of disposal should provide adequate water intake to mix with solid particles, forming an easily handled slurry.

Energy Usage and Utility Requirements

The primary cost of utilities for garbage disposals is water. The use of electricity to operate the motors and controls consumes a relatively small amount of energy, and therefore is not an important purchasing consideration.

PULPER AND EXTRACTOR SYSTEMS

Specifications

The need for a waste disposal system that will not place large amounts of food or paper solids into the sewer system has increased dramatically. Many municipalities have ordinances against the use of commercial disposers because of the heavy load that they place upon the sewer system. A pulping and extracting waste system is one of several alternatives available.

In a pulper, water and wastes are mixed together and ground into very small particles. The grinding process is very similar to that of the conventional disposal, but the pulper does not wash the ground wastes into the sewer system. Instead, the water and waste slurry are piped to the extractor, where the solids are separated from the water. The water is returned to the pulper, mixed with fresh water, and reused in the grinding process. The solids from the extractor are conveyed to a conventional trash container. This material, which resembles wet sawdust or ground paper, is virtually odor free.

Since much of the weight of garbage is the liquid, and the bulk of the garbage is reduced by grinding, the pulping and extracting process results in significantly less waste for a foodservice operation. However, the system costs considerably more than the conventional disposer and garbage can. The high initial cost of the pulper/extractor is offset by savings from:

- a reduction in waste handling resulting from a smaller volume of waste
- reduced water consumption
- labor simplification, as the garbage does not need to be physically carried from the kitchen

An additional, important advantage of the pulper/extractor system is the reduction in odor in the kitchen and around the trash container. The specifications for the equipment options and accessories are limited because only a few manufacturers make the equipment. Systems can be specified that will:

- Operate under a soiled dishtable
- Operate with the extractor connected to a remote location (the slurry is piped from the pulper to the extractor)
- Connect directly to the waste trough on a soiled dish table

A foodservice facility with the kitchen and warewashing area located on the second floor is an ideal application for a pulper/extractor system. The pulper can be located on the second floor, the extractor on the first floor near the garbage containers, and the slurry piped from the pulper to the extractor downstairs. The need to carry heavy, smelly garbage down the stairs is eliminated.

Primary Use in the Food Operation

The primary use of the pulper/extractor system is as an alternative method of garbage and paper disposal that does not place these waste materials into the sewer system.

Determining Capacity and Size

Pulper/extractor systems handle from 600 to 1,000 pounds of typical food waste per hour; higher capacity is available if multiple pulpers and extractors are installed. A facility considering a pulper/extractor system will need to estimate the quantity of waste produced. This type of waste system, unlike a garbage disposal, requires a significant quantity of pulp—that is, paper products—to work effectively. Ideal applications are in large-volume facil-

5–48. PULPER/EXTRACTOR SYSTEM. (COURTESY OF SOMAT)

ities using Styrofoam and paper plates, cups, and other containers.

Energy Usage and Utility Requirements

The pulper/extractor systems use large motors (5, 7 and 10 horsepower) to grind the garbage and paper, and smaller motors to extract the solids. The engineering of these systems is complex because it involves plumbing for the slurry lines to the extractor and lines to return water to the pulper. The ideal time to install this equipment is when a building is new or is being renovated. If the distance from the warewashing area to the trash containers is not too great, plumbing lines can frequently be run in existing buildings.

The energy usage for the pulper/extractor is modest, particularly in view of the savings in water use.

Pulping and extracting systems are not cost justified in the small restaurant or institution. A restaurant or institution serving under 500 meals per day would probably not have the funds necessary to purchase this equipment, and would probably not have adequate space to house it. For larger foodservice operations, municipal codes, the amount of paper used in the operation, and the relative costs of using a conventional disposer and trash removal system are important considerations in determining whether to adopt the pulper/extractor system.

TRASH COMPACTORS

Specifications

Trash compactors are mechanical devices that compress waste materials so that the volume is greatly reduced. Compactors also permit wastes to be more easily transported out of the food production areas in portable carts or containers.

In recent years, the sale of compactors has dropped off considerably because their cost is high, and they are difficult to clean and thus often create sanitation and odor problems. In addition, many of the early designs had poor repair and maintenance records. The advantages of compactors in certain applications may outweigh the disadvantages, however. Large compactors may be installed at the back dock of large foodservice facilities, from which the garbage can be removed by trucks especially designed to lift and empty the compacted garbage from waste containers. Smaller compactors are often used in facilities that have a large accumulation of glass, boxes, and other types of trash.

SUMMARY

Foodservice equipment should be selected based on necessity, the condition of present equipment, and the possibility of reducing energy and operating costs.

The NSF (National Sanitation Foundation), which establishes sanitation and safety standards for equipment construction, is a good source of information. The NSF seal of approval is a recognized standard in the foodservice industry.

The types of equipment included in this chapter are the major pieces that foodservice consultants and their clients will consider purchasing. Comprehensive information about this equipment can be obtained from equipment catalogs, manufacturers' representatives, or at any of the large equipment shows, such as the NRA or NAFEM. The foodservice consultant should be well versed in the many types of equipment available so that he or she can help the client make the best choices.

CHAPTER 6

FOODSERVICE FACILITIES ENGINEERING

THIS CHAPTER WILL:

▶ Describe the primary considerations to be addressed by facilities planners to assure the most economical use of energy in foodservice operations

▶ Provide a basic understanding of the primary utilities used in foodservice

▶ Describe the construction of hoods and ventilation systems in kitchens, dishwashing rooms, and service areas

▶ List the most commonly used finishes for floors, ceilings, and walls in foodservice operations

▶ Describe the methods for reducing sound in both public spaces and employee work areas

---

FOODSERVICE FACILITIES ENGINEERING

The engineering of a hotel dining facility, a complex restaurant, or a large institutional foodservice requires the expertise of both architects and professional engineers. The facility owner or manager who attempts to design and install electrical, plumbing, or heating, ventilation, and air-conditioning (HVAC) systems without professional assistance is courting disaster. Even the seemingly simple instal-

lation of a new warewashing system in a restaurant involves:

- hot and cold water
- floor drains
- dishmachine drains
- electricity
- steam or natural gas

- special ventilation to remove moist air
- special floor, wall, and ceiling finishes
- special lighting
- hoods

The material in this chapter is not intended to be a do-it-yourself guide to complex engineering systems in foodservice facilities but to offer a general overview and some useful ideas for resolving problems peculiar to the foodservice industry. For both students and foodservice planners, it will serve as a basic guide to the most accepted methods of engineering a foodservice construction or renovation project, as well as providing an understanding of the basic language of the technical trades involved in electrical, plumbing, and HVAC systems.

OVERVIEW OF ENERGY MANAGEMENT

Foodservice operators traditionally directed their attention to the cost of food and labor, because these two expenses represented the largest part of the expense of operations. Prior to 1970 energy was a minor item compared with other operating costs. Since the energy cost increases of the 1970s, however, utilities have ranked as the third most significant expense on the profit and loss statement. This has caused foodservice operators to look for better methods of energy control and conservation.

The costs of number 2 oil, electricity, and natural gas have been increasing at a rate of approximately 10 percent per year over the past ten-year period. Energy costs for the typical food facility in Annapolis, Maryland, as of January 1988 were:

Electricity: $.056/kwh
Natural Gas: $.660/therm
#2 Heating Oil: $.730/gal

The impact of these increases on commercial foodservice establishments is severe because of the large amount of energy needed to store, cook, and serve food. An example of this problem can be seen in the table below, developed in the *Energy Conservation Manual for Wisconsin Hotels, Motels and Resorts.*

As this table shows, restaurants, especially table-service facilities, use the greatest percentage of their energy in the food preparation and refriger-

▼
ENERGY PROFILE: PERCENT OF ENERGY USAGE

	TABLE-SERVICE RESTAURANTS	FAST-FOOD RESTAURANTS
HVAC[a]	32.1	36.0
Kitchen and refrigeration	47.1	37.0
Lighting	8.2	26.0
Hot water	12.6	1.0
Total	100.0	100.0

[a]Heating, Ventilating, and Air Conditioning

ation areas. The reason for this high consumption can be illustrated as follows. Assume:

Ten 100 watt bulbs burn for 8 hours
8 hours $\times$ 10 100-watt bulbs = 8,000 watts

8,000 watts/1,000 = 8 kwh (kilowatt hours)

Compare this to:

24-kw hot top range with oven operating for 8 hours
24,000 watts $\times$ 8 hours = 192,000 watts

192,000/1,000 = 192 kwh

In this typical illustration, one range with an oven uses twenty four times more electrical energy than ten 100-watt light bulbs during an eight-hour period. All heat-producing appliances use far more energy than illumination or motor-connected appliances. A fan, refrigeration motor, light, mixer, or slicer uses very small amounts of energy when compared with fryers, grills, ovens, or ranges.

This is not to suggest that the cost of HVAC should receive less attention. Heating and air conditioning can be especially expensive in the food facility because of:

· Long operating hours
· The large amount of heated or cooled air that is vented through the kitchen hood
· The odors from food and customer smoking that must be removed
· The large number of people per square foot occupying the dining area

Developing an Energy Management Program

Many government and private agencies and other organizations have published studies and guides relating to energy usage by the commercial food industry because of its high consumption rates and the increasing number of meals being eaten outside the home each year.* Overwhelmed by the amount of information available, many foodservice operators feel that it takes an engineer to understand how to proceed. The following material, which presents a simplified approach to the subject, is intended to help the manager and his or her staff develop an energy management program without becoming bogged down in technicalities. The foodservice planner should be able to write realistic goals for establishing an energy management program, while leaving the engineering complexities to professionals. Outside experts should be consulted for advice on implementation and any other technical aspects of the energy program that may be difficult to understand. Foodservice managers and their employees will need to become familiar with the terminology associated with energy usage, however, in order to carry out the program effectively.

Three Phases of Investment in Energy Improvement

Energy conservation investments must meet the return-on-investment criteria fundamental to any capital expenditure decision. Building renovation expenditures are no exception to this principle. Fortunately, the rates of return on such expenditures are extremely attractive when measured against the cost savings and cost avoidance potential. Investment payouts within three to five years are the rule rather than the exception for intelligently planned conservation rehabilitation programs.

Review of commercial conservation case histories discloses a three-phase pattern of building investment programs that affords energy consumption reduction opportunities at varying levels of expenditure.† The three phases may be outlined as follows:

*For detailed information on energy consumption, see *Guide to Energy Conservation for Food Service*, prepared by the Federal Energy Administration, Office of Industrial Programs, Washington, D.C.

†From Energy Task Force, Energy Conservation, "The Capital Investment Needs for Building Rehabilitation for Non-Profit Educational Institutions," paper no. 2 (Washington, D.C.: Energy Task Force, 1985).

PHASE	CONSUMPTION REDUCTION	EXPENDITURE PER SQUARE FOOT
1. Quick fix	10%	$.00
2. Refit	20–25% (including quick fix)	$.40–1.40
3. Systems convert	30–40% (including refit)	$1.20–3.00

PHASE 1: QUICK FIX

Definition and Cost

This initial phase involves basic and important energy savings that are easily attainable at negligible cost. Nontechnical energy conservation measures, such as lowered temperatures and regular preventive maintenance, will quickly eliminate obvious energy waste and result in energy consumption reductions of at least 10 percent for most institutions. Minimal lead time is required for the implementation of a quick fix program, especially if in-house cooperation can be elicited for achieving such vital consumption reductions.

Examples

- Specific temperature ranges and thermostat settings: 65°-68° F in the winter, 75°-80° F in the summer
- Reduction in illumination levels and lamp wattage
- Scheduling of vacations or shutdowns during energy-intensive periods
- Closely managed appliance and air-conditioning usage
- Reduction of hot water temperature
- Reduction of building heat leakage using blinds and drapes
- Maintenance review of the existing energy system
  - Appoint a staff energy committee
  - Appoint building energy monitors
  - Conduct briefing sessions with employees

PHASE 2: REFIT

Definition and Cost

This second phase goes beyond the simple steps taken in the quick fix stage. The expected consump-

tion reduction of 20 to 25 percent requires a capital investment of approximately $.40 to $1.40 per gross square foot. Greater attention in this phase must be devoted to the development of technical studies in an effort to diagnose the differing types and levels of energy consumption within an operation, prior to committing capital to a specific investment option.

Examples

- Review of existing mechanical systems and controls to identify capital investment options
- Infrared aerial photographic survey to identify heat loss
- Review of electrical rate structures, power factors, load profiles, and demand peaks
- Development of energy-efficient space allocation practices
- Conversion from incandescent to fluorescent fixtures
- Utilization of time clocks on lighting systems
- Revision of light switch circuitry to reduce overlighting
- Increased steam line insulation
- Installation of roof and wall insulation
- Installation of weatherstripping, storm windows, caulking, sun screens, and blinds
- Installation of timers on exhaust and air handling systems
- Reduction of fresh air makeup

PHASE 3: SYSTEMS CONVERT

Definition and Cost

Systems conversion, the third and most sophisticated level of conservation investment, requires capital expenditure for engineering and other technical studies and substantial conservation of building systems in order to achieve a dramatic consumption reduction. An additional 10 to 15 percent reduction can be achieved after the first and second phases, at an incremental cost of approximately $1.00 per gross square foot.

The cumulative impact of the three phases results in a consumption reduction ranging from

30 to 40 percent at a total cost that would not exceed $3.00 per gross square foot. It is important to recognize that the third phase is not appropriate for all buildings. Significant savings of energy as a result of systems conversion investments would accrue to most operations, however, particularly those constructed before the energy crisis of 1975 to 1979.

Examples
- Installation of central computerized controls and building monitoring system
- Installation of waste heat recovery systems
- Conversion of building systems
  - Solar energy systems
  - Independently zoned environment controls
  - Rewiring of major electrical systems to minimize demand changes and avoid establishing new peaks

A break-even analysis for energy investment and equipment replacement should be computed after prices are obtained on the conversion.

The owner or manager has a complex set of alternatives in choosing the appropriate energy sources for the foodservice facility. In many instances, no alternatives are available for heating because the facility has already been designed and constructed to use the least expensive heating fuel. When the cost of energy seems to be unusually high, however, as shown in the energy audit, or when new building or equipment decisions are being made, an alternative energy source should be given careful consideration.

External Considerations

The foodservice professional must be aware of the global energy problem before making a decision on energy to be used within the food operation. The use of one fuel source to create a second source may be an extremely poor use of energy; the direct use of an energy source in the heating of a building or in food preparation is usually more efficient. The American Gas Association claims that from the natural gas well to the user's meter, 81 percent of the energy is delivered with only 19 percent transportation and pipeline loss. On the other hand, it has been established that 28 to 32 percent of the energy is lost when natural gas heats a boiler, which turns a generator to produce electricity. The local utility company is usually an excellent source for obtaining information on the relative cost of one fuel source against another.

A second concern in choosing a fuel source is availability. In the early 1970s, as the public became aware of the energy crisis, the expansion of the use of natural gas in commercial foodservice operations was stopped in many sections of the country. In the late 1970s and early 1980s, new gas sources were found and now the supply seems to be quite adequate. This type of change in availability makes intelligent fuel source decisions difficult. It would seem that price consideration is the most reliable gauge in choosing the correct fuel. The efficiency of the energy source within the food operation can easily be monitored by the manager or maintenance supervisor. Although fossil fuels, such as oil and natural gas, are now readily available and in good supply, these fuels will deplete in the not too distant future. The foodservice manager who is planning for the future must be aware of the high cost and scarcity of fossil fuels.

Internal Considerations

This section provides an overview of energy source alternatives. (For information on the selection for energy-efficient kitchen equipment see chapter 5.) The following simple, step-by-step system can be used by any foodservice manager to determine the most economical fuel for heating, cooling, or cooking:

1. Look on the plate on the piece of equipment for the following: kw rating for electricity, cubic feet or Btu capacity for gas, gallon or Btu capacity for oil, and pounds per hour for steam. (This information can be obtained from the local equipment dealer or equipment catalog.)
2. Convert the energy capacity (usage) to Btu's, using the following values:

Electricity: kwh × 3,413 = number of Btu's per hour

Gas: cubic feet × 1,000 = number of Btu's

Oil: gallons × 140,000 = number of Btu's

Steam: pounds × 1,000 = number of Btu's

Compare the Btu consumption of each piece of equipment presently in use or under consideration for the foodservice facility.

3. Determine the cooking time for several typical products that would be prepared by a piece of equipment. For instance, a 3-pound box of green peas cooked on an open top range might take 12 minutes to prepare, but this product would only take three minutes to cook in a high-pressure steamer. A roast of beef might take 4 hours to cook in a conventional deck oven, but only 3 hours and 14 minutes in a convection oven. Multiply the Btu consumption by the number of hours of preparation.

4. Gather all utility bills for gas, electricity, oil, and purchased steam. Find out from the local utility company (or the utility bill) the cost of each fuel source, to determine the cost of operating any piece of equipment for one hour. Multiply this cost by the consumption per hour. The following example will illustrate this method for determining the cost of operating an electric grill for one hour:

A 3-foot electric grill consumes 12 kwh

12 kwh × 3,413 = 40,956 Btu's per hour

Typical charge for electricity (excludes demand charges and step rate increases) = \$.046/kw

\$.046 × 12kw = \$.552/hour

The grill operates at breakfast and lunch for 6 hours.

\$.552/hour × 6 hours = \$3.31/day for the grill

Cost per 1,000 Btu's \$3.31/245,735 = .0135

The grill consumes 40,956 × 6 hours = 245,736 Btu's per day.

It is assumed that this grill replaced a hot top range consuming 120,000 Btu's per hour. If this range were left on for most of the day (for example, from 7 A.M. until 2 P.M., and from 5 P.M. until 8 P.M.), the consumption of Btu's would be:

120,000 × 10 hours of operation = 1,200,000 Btu's

11,200,000 × .0135 (cost/1,000 Btu's) = \$16.20/day for the hot top range

This example assumes that the grill will cook all of the foods that are normally prepared on the range. The difference in operating cost of \$3.31 per day for the grill against the \$16.20 per day for the range is clear, and the appropriate decision is obvious.

Employee Awareness

Scheduled energy awareness meetings at least every three months with all employees will yield a reduction in energy consumption. Insulation of walls and ceilings or an expensive refit approach will make the physical plant more efficient, but the equipment that consumes large amounts of energy, such as air-conditioning, heating, or cooking equipment, is controlled ultimately by the employee. A cook who turns on a fryer, a hot top range, an oven, and a grill when he or she comes on duty has used more energy in one hour in the kitchen area than any other employee in the entire facility will use in an eight-hour period. Consider the amount of energy consumed, if the above kitchen equipment is electric:

Fryer, 220 volt: 18 kw

Hot top range: 15 kw

Small oven: 8 kw

Grill, 3 foot: 12 kw

In the hour the equipment was turned on— one hour before the equipment was really needed— 53 kwh of electricity would have been consumed. That amount of electricity would burn a 100-watt light bulb for 22 days (100 watts × 53 kwh × 24 hours).

Training the employee to avoid the waste of energy involves three important steps:

1. Awareness of the amount of energy being consumed by the equipment. This would include information on the number of Btu's per hour consumed, and the speed of recovery of the

piece of equipment. Recovery speed information is available from the equipment dealer or manufacturer. The recovery for a typical fryer to a temperature of 350° F from room temperature is six minutes. The common practice of turning on fryers, grills, and ranges one hour or more before being used results in an enormous waste of energy.

2. The employee must feel that the conservation of energy will benefit him and the company. "What's in it for me?" is an important part of motivating the employee to change work habits.

Profit sharing, bonus systems, posted progress charts, and praise for keeping costs down are all good motivating methods.

3. Supervision of the employee with reinforcement of those ideas that have been presented in training sessions is necessary. Vocal reminders to turn off a range or fryer after the meal period and supervision of the thermostat that controls the air-conditioning system are examples of techniques that make the energy management program work.

UTILITIES IN FOODSERVICE OPERATIONS

Water

Dishwashing, utensil sanitation and floor, wall, and ceiling cleaning are all dependent on a source of clean hot water. The preparation of food and the consumption of water in the dining room are also dependent on a clean source of hot or cold water. Hot water consumes about 13 percent of a restaurant's energy budget. Food facilities consultants and foodservice managers are interested in the way water is used in a food facility because of the high cost of:

- *Supply:* the metered cost of cold water
- *Heating:* the energy to heat water
- *Waste disposal:* the sewage costs of disposing of water

Water is usually supplied through a municipal water system. Under most circumstances, these water sources are frequently checked and carefully monitored to keep out pathogenic bacteria or other harmful materials. The cost of this water is computed on the basis of gallons of consumption during a one-month to three-month period. When the water meter is read, the cost is then computed and a bill sent to the end user.

WATER HEATING

Water-heating systems heat water to temperatures appropriate for dishwashing, food preparation, and lavatories. A water heater provides hot water to faucets in one of two ways: water can be heated to the temperature at which it will be used at the faucet; or it can be heated to a higher temperature, stored, and then tempered with cold water before it reaches the faucet. Some foodservice establishments maintain separate water-heating systems for kitchen and lavatory use. One system generates very hot water to be piped to the kitchen, where it is needed; the other warms water for the lavatories, where moderate temperatures are adequate.

All forms of energy can be used to heat water. Most foodservice establishments use electric or gas water heaters, although a few use oil or steam. Electric water heaters are efficient at converting electrical energy to hot water. However, they generally heat water more slowly than do other kinds of heaters and require a larger tank to keep an adequate supply of water available.

Even while maintaining the necessary high standards of sanitation, energy can be saved in water heating and dishwashing. Energy-saving procedures can be simple or exotic. Foodservice operations now use rooftop solar collectors. The captured solar energy is used to provide partial heating of the water before it enters the water heater, thus significantly reducing the energy expended by the water-heating system. Another popular idea is to use the waste heat from refrigeration cooling systems to heat dishwashing water. The concept of heat recovery is discussed in greater detail later in this chapter.

Significant energy and dollar savings can be made by keeping two basic objectives in mind. The first is to reduce the amount of hot water used. Every time water is used, some of it is wasted. The lower the temperature of the wasted water, the lower the energy loss. The second goal is to reduce the temperature of the water to the lowest temperature appropriate for the use. The reason for this is that heat losses from distribution pipes are related directly to the difference between the temperature of the water in the pipes and that of the surrounding air. When the water temperature is reduced from 180° to 125° F, heat loss from the pipes in a 70° F room is reduced by half. The procedures described below are based on these principles.

- Use hot tap water for cooking, whenever possible, except in localities where water contains heavy concentrations of minerals. Use cold water only when required by the cooking method. A water heater uses less energy than a range top to heat the same amount of water.
- Heat water only to the temperature needed. Only the rinse water for the dishwasher needs to be heated to 180° F. Most dishwashing boosters require entering water to be 140° F in order to provide 180° F water to the dishwasher for rinsing. Water for the restrooms should be heated only to a temperature comfortable for hand washing (approximately 110° F); hot water should not have to be mixed with cold to achieve a comfortable temperature. Ask the service representative to adjust the automatic tempering valve on the water heater or, if necessary, to install such a valve.
- Hot water boosters should be located within 5 feet of a dishwasher to avoid heat loss in the pipes.
- Install a spring-operated valve on the kitchen and restroom faucets to save water. One type is

attached to hand levers and another operates with a foot treadle. For kitchen sinks, spring-operated foot treadles are most effective because they leave the operator's hands free for other tasks. For lavatory faucets, a 15-second delay-action valve is required to satisfy health standards.

The hot water consumption tables on page 162 are provided as a general guideline for those involved in estimating hot water use in a foodservice facility.

Hot water usage can easily be determined for dishwashers, glass washers, pot and pan washers, and silverware washers, as calculated in gallons per hour established by the National Sanitation Foundation (NSF), and the manufacturer of the particular piece of equipment.

WATER SOFTENERS

Hard water contains mineral deposits in solution that subsequently precipitate in water heaters, boilers, and water lines. These deposits can decrease energy efficiency, clog the water supply pipes, and cause valves and other controls to malfunction. In addition, mineral deposits can leave unattractive spots on glasses and silverware, giving the impression of an unsanitary condition. Hard water increases the amount of detergent needed for proper cleaning and degreasing in dishwashers and pot sinks.

The hardness in water is usually measured by the grains of hardness, expressed as a quantity contained per million of calcium carbonate and other minerals. One grain of hardness is equal to approximately 17 parts per million (ppm). If water contains less than 4 grains of hardness it may not need to be softened. Water containing between 4 grains and 6 grains will leave deposits on pipes and on the walls of water heaters, unless the water is treated by a water softener. Water softeners most commonly use a zeolite process in which a chemical reaction occurs between salt and a catalyst in the water softener. These systems are effective, but are occasionally objectionable because of the small amount of sodium that remains in the water.

An alternative to the zeolite process is the use of magnetic water treatment. These systems keep the minerals in water in suspension by passing the

▼
WATER CONSUMPTION TABLES

	GALLONS PER HOUR	
ITEM	High[a]	Low[b]
Vegetable sink	15	15
Single pot sink	20	15
Double pot sink	40	30
Triple pot sink	60	45
Prerinse for dishes—shower head type (hand operated)	45	45 (0 if cold
Prescraper for dishes (Salvajor type)	180	H₂O piping
Prescraper for dishes (conveyor type)	250	only)
Bar sink (three-compartment)	20	–
Bar sink (four-compartment)	25	–
Lavatory	5	3
Service sink	10	6
Cook sink	10	6
Hot water filling faucet	15	10
Bain Marie	10	6
Coffee urn	5	3
Kettle filler	5	5
Back bar sink	5	3
Garbage can washer	50	30
Single compartment dishwasher	45	50
Sixteen pound clothes washer	60	30
Employee shower	20	15

SOURCE: The State of Michigan, "Guidelines for Hot Water Generating System for Food Service Establishment," Lansing, Michigan, 1984.

[a]For food operation utilizing multiuse eating utensils.
[b]For carry-out food operations where single service eating utensils are utilized.

water through a multifield magnet, which helps prevent crystallization of the mineral substance.

Steam

LATENT HEAT

One of the important factors in holding our earth's surface temperature within the rather narrow bounds in which man can exist is that while it takes just about 1 Btu to change the temperature of a pound of liquid water by 1° F, it takes 144 Btu's to freeze one pound of water (latent heat of fusion) and about 1,000 Btu's to convert 1 pound of water to steam (latent heat of evaporation). The relatively large amount of heat change required to convert water into either ice or steam acts to keep our earth's temperature moderate.

Heating water from 70° F (21° C) to its boiling point, 212° F (100° C), at sea level, requires about 142 Btu's per pound (one Btu per degree F). Converting the water at 212° F to steam at the same temperature requires about 1,000 Btu's per pound. This is the heat applied in the steam boiler. Conversely, when the latent heat is extracted from the steam, the 1,000 Btu's per pound are given up by the steam without any change in temperature, and the steam changes back to water.

Figure 6-1 shows how the temperature of one pound of water would vary with time if subjected to a constant rate of Btu input. Notice that it would stay at 32° F (0° C) and 212° F (100° C) at sea level until, in each case, the latent heat conversions had taken place for the entire pound of water.

SATURATION

If a container of water is heated sufficiently at a constant pressure, the water temperature will rise until the boiling point is reached. While boiling, the temperature will remain constant until all the water has been converted to steam. Then the temperature will rise again as the steam is further heated (see fig. 6-1). Steam at the temperature at which it coexists with water is called "saturated steam," and the temperature is called the "saturation temperature." The saturation temperature varies with the pressure. An increase in pressure increases the temperature at which the latent heat transfer takes place. The pressure at which the latent heat transfer takes place at a given temperature is called the "saturation pressure."

PRESSURES

In the English-speaking world, steam pressures are measured in pounds per square inch (psi). There are, necessarily, two reference levels. One is the pressure above atmospheric. This is the boiler's pressure, commonly called the "gage pressure" and abbreviated psi or psig. Because of the variable nature of atmospheric pressure, steam pressures are more accurately described in terms of their "absolute pressure," which is the total amount of their pressure above a perfect vacuum.

SUPERHEAT

Steam is a gas. As in the case of any gas, it can be heated above the boiling point. Once it is past the saturation temperature, it requires only about

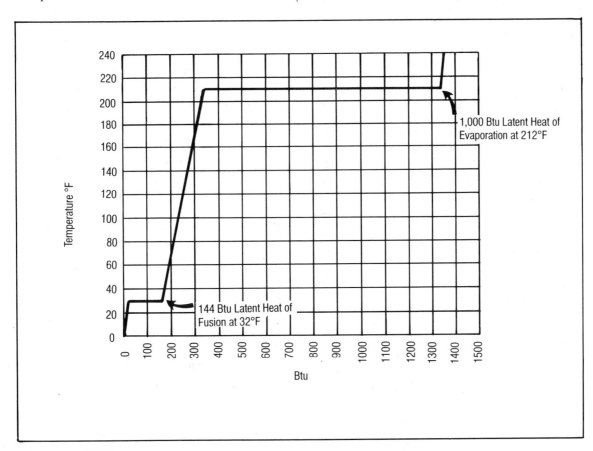

6-1. LATENT HEAT OF WATER.

½ Btu per pound to increase its temperature 1° F.

The increase in temperature above the saturation temperature is called "superheat." Steam that has a small amount of superheat is called "dry steam." If heated more than a few degrees above the saturation temperature, it is referred to as "superheated steam." Obviously, neither dry nor superheated steam can coexist with liquid water. Since steam is a gas, it tends to expand in direct relation to increased temperature. The increased volume and small amount of extra heat value makes superheat a relatively worthless factor in steam heating. Its only real value is to ensure that there will be dry steam at the point where the steam is to be used. In other words, a few degrees of superheat at the boiler will minimize condensation in the supply lines to the steam coils.

CONDENSATION

When steam gives up its latent heat and changes from saturated steam to water at the same temperature, it "condenses." The water is spoken of as "condensate."

HEAT TRANSFER

Heat transfer usually occurs through a steam coil. The heat produced by the condensation of the steam travels through the boundary layer of steam, through the condensation that forms on the inside of the tube, through the tube itself, out into the fins, through the boundary layer of air on the fins' surfaces, and into the passing stream of moving air.

All steam coils are 100 percent efficient in the sense that the heat released by condensing steam within the coil has nowhere to go but into the air surrounding the coil. Tube and fin material, fin spacing, air velocity, and several other factors affect the rate at which the heat transfer (and therefore the condensation) takes place, but they cannot alter the fact that the steam's latent heat has only one place to go: into the air stream.

Reduced to its barest elements, a steam-heating system consists of a means of converting water to steam (the boiler or converter), piping to conduct the steam to where it is to be used, a coil or other surface for condensing the steam and transferring the latent heat from the steam to the air, a "trap" to prevent the steam from passing through the coil before it is condensed, and return piping to conduct the condensate back to the boiler.*

COOKING WITH STEAM

Steam cooking is highly efficient for several reasons:

- Because steam always remains at 212° F (100° C) when not under pressure, and at up to 250° F (121° C) under pressure of 15 pounds per square inch, it is a moderate, uniform cooking medium.
- Steam transfers its heat to food rapidly.
- Steam equipment requires little or no warmup time; thus preheat time losses are minimal.
- Cooking times are usually much shorter than for range top cooking or boiling.

SOURCES OF STEAM

Steam is generated for use in foodservice in several ways. It can be:

- Piped in and purchased from a utility owned by a municipality or commercial company
- Generated inside in a building boiler room and piped to the kitchen
- Generated in the kitchen by small boilers located under or near the equipment
- Generated in the kitchen by a small boiler that is part of the foodservice equipment

Of the four sources of steam, the installation of small boilers for each piece of equipment is the least satisfactory because of the high maintenance costs and additional kitchen heat that they create.

The food facilities consultant must provide data to the building engineers regarding the amount of steam required for each piece of equipment. Steam is measured by flow (pounds per hour) and pressure (pounds per square inch). One common designation used in equipment catalogs for rating steam equipment is boiler horsepower (BHP), which is calculated as follows: The generator firing rate

*C. J. Trickler, "Fundamentals of Steam and Application of Steam to Industrial Heating," in *Engineering Letter No. A-1*, The New York Blower Company, Willowbrook, IL.

(Btu/hr) is first multiplied by the operating efficiency to learn the effective output of the generator. The output of the generator is then divided by 34,000 Btu's to determine the effective bhp. As a general guideline, 34.5 pounds of steam per hour equal 1 BHP.

The following table may be helpful in estimating the BHP for commonly used kitchen equipment. The equipment specifier should not rely on the table, but should instead get the correct BHP from the manufacturer for each piece of equipment.

EQUIPMENT	BHP
Steam-jacketed kettle—10 gal.	½
Steam-jacketed kettle—20 gal.	1
Low-pressure steamer	¾–1
Coffee Urn—twin 10 gal.	⅕–¼
Single-tank dishmachine with steam booster and steam heat in tank	3

In foodservice facilities, steam is an economical energy source, especially under the following circumstances:

· The facility already has a source of steam.
· Several pieces of equipment are selected that are steam heated. This helps to justify the cost of installing steam supply lines and condensate return lines.
· The steam source is "clean." Clean steam does not have unsafe impurities from rust inhibitors and antifoaming chemicals. Many hospitals must have a clean source of steam because of the frequent use of steam in autoclaves for sterilizing equipment. These clean steam systems use chemicals that are approved by the United States Department of Agriculture and are also safe for direct injection on food products.

Typical uses of steam in the kitchen are:

· steam-jacketed kettles
· vegetable steamers
· steam-cleaning systems
· booster heaters for dishwashing machines
· hot water tanks for dishwashing machines
· plate warmers
· bain maries
· steam coils in makeup air systems
· final rinse for pot sinks
· steam injection for bakery ovens

Electricity

Electrical energy for the foodservice facility represents a large part of the total energy consumed. Lighting, motor power, cooking, food preparation, air circulation, and air conditioning are necessary parts of the total energy usage system, and this usage must be controlled.

Understanding the method of purchasing electrical energy requires an understanding of the electric kilowatt meter. Of the several types of electric meters, the most common type consists of dials that record the amount of electrical energy passing through the meter. Reading the dials on a regular basis permits a careful monitoring of consumption and allows the foodservice manager to check the bill received from the utility company. The dials are read from left to right (see fig. 6-2). Notice the arrows for the direction of movement of the hands.

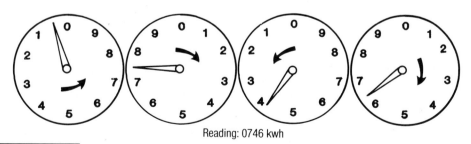

Reading: 0746 kwh

6-2. TYPICAL ELECTRIC METER DIALS.

All hands on the dials move in the direction of the numbers 1 through 9. When reading the meter, start with the dial on the left and put down the last number the hand has passed. The dials in figure 6-2 read 0 7 4 6. At the end of the billing period (usually one month), read the meter again and subtract the difference to find the kilowatt hours used during the preceding month. Some meters do not have dials, but instead use a series of indicators similar to the odometer on a car. These meters are not used in small restaurants or homes.

STEP RATE

Utility rates are often based on a reduction in the cost per kilowatt hour as the consumption increases. Recently, objections have been raised to this method of billing because it rewards the customer for excessive usage. However, the idea of getting a discount for the purchase of large quantities still exists in the business community, and electricity is usually no exception.

The step rate schedule is often controlled by a local or state regulatory agency and may change as the cost of energy rises. A typical step rate schedule is illustrated below:

KILOWATT HOURS	RATE PER KILOWATT HOUR
1–50	$0.15
51–100	0.10
101–200	0.05
201–300	0.04
301–500	0.03
Over 500	0.025

If the meter reading for a one-month period indicated that 750 kilowatt hours were used, the cost would be:

50 kwh at 0.150 =	$ 7.50
50 kwh at 0.100 =	5.00
100 kwh at 0.050 =	5.00
100 kwh at 0.040 =	4.00
200 kwh at 0.030 =	6.00
250 kwh at 0.025 =	6.25
TOTAL	$33.75

DEMAND CHARGE

A relatively large consumer of energy will probably have two charges on the electric bill—one charge for energy used and one for demand. While the energy billing represents the number of kilowatt hours actually used, the demand charge reflects the cost to the utility of maintaining sufficient generating capacity to supply large, short-term energy demands put on the utility lines by consumers. The charge is based on the maximum kilowatt demand imposed on the utility lines during a short interval, generally a fifteen-minute period, during the billing period. The maximum demand is measured by a demand meter and the bill is based on the maximum demand (kilowatts) times that demand charge (cost per kilowatt) for the billing period. If the peak usage for a given billing period is 50 kilowatts and the demand charge is $5 per kilowatt, the demand charge for that period will be $250, even if this peak is reached for only one fifteen minute period during the month.

Demand charges may constitute a large percentage of the total electric utility bill. A serious energy management program needs to focus on demand as well as energy use because significant savings can be realized by lowering the peak demand. The food facilities consultant must be aware of the kilowatt rating of each piece of equipment and give consideration to the total electrical demand created as a result of the kitchen design.

TYPICAL ELECTRICAL CHARACTERISTICS OF FOODSERVICE EQUIPMENT

General guidelines for selecting the electrical characteristics of a piece of equipment are as follows:

1. Ask the architect or engineer for the electrical characteristics of the building. The answer will typically be 120/240 volts, 120/208 volts, or 120/240/460/480 volts.
2. Select the piece of equipment desired and use the largest electrical voltage possible. This will usually reduce the size of the copper wires that are used in the building and will reduce the cost.
3. If electrical motors are involved, use the highest electrical voltage possible and use the designa-

tion "3 phase." (Motors can operate at 1 or 3 phase, but 3 phase is more efficient.)

4. Select the method for connecting the electrical equipment to the power source. Equipment that will be permanently installed should be direct wired. A male and female adapter (plug) can be used for equipment that will be moved or frequently disconnected.

5. Be sure that the electrical characteristics and the type of connector appear:
   - on the mechanical drawing
   - in the equipment specification
   - on the order for the equipment

Gas

GAS VERSUS ELECTRICITY

The efficient use of energy is important to the manager of a foodservice operation not only because everyone has a responsibility to conserve energy, but also because conservation can save money and increase profits. The average cost of energy for a restaurant now equals 5 percent of the total sales. Food and labor are the only costs that exceed the cost of energy.

For those engaged in planning food facilities, the selection of the most economical fuel is a complex matter. The use of steam, for instance, has previously been mentioned as an economical cooking source under certain circumstances of availability, because of its ability to transfer heat efficiently to food. The American Gas Association has published the following chart, from which a strong case can be made for the use of natural gas based on the efficiency of this fuel in cooking.

TYPICAL APPLIANCE	TOTAL BTU'S REQUIRED FOR ELECTRICAL APPLIANCE	TOTAL BTU'S REQUIRED FOR GAS APPLIANCE
Deck oven	243,786	181,292
Fryer	243,786	151,200
Convection oven	243,786	151,200
Broiler	243,786	117,437
Steamer	243,786	117,437
Range	243,786	91,747
Griddle	243,786	91,747

SOURCE: American Gas Association, *Energy Conservation and Economy.*

The problem with the above chart is that it does not take into account two important considerations when comparing the cost and efficiency of natural gas versus electricity. First, the electrical appliance would vary significantly from one piece of equipment to another in connected load and energy usage. Secondly, the chart does not consider the amount of energy that is actually transferred to the food. Studies done by the author at Michigan State University indicate that the type of equipment selected is often more important in energy savings than the source of the energy. For instance, a 3-pound package of frozen vegetables cooked on a hot top range (gas or electric) will require much more energy than the same amount of vegetables cooked in a pressure steamer. The reason for the difference is obvious. With stove top cookery, most of the energy goes up into the hood and is wasted, while the closed container holds the energy inside the steamer and allows it to be absorbed into the product being cooked.

Most of the energy used in a typical restaurant is used to prepare and store food. Cooking equipment is the greatest consumer of energy for the following reasons:

- Heat-producing appliances require the highest consumption (flow of electricity or rate of use of gas).
- Cooking equipment is turned on for many hours during the day (often unnecessarily).
- Most of the heat produced is lost to the hood and is not recovered.
- The conversion of electricity or gas to heat is inefficient.

The answer to conservation is not easily found, but there are certain things that the foodservice operator can do to reduce cooking energy loss:

1. Select equipment that is enclosed and insulated, so that the energy stays within the cooking vessel and is absorbed by the food (rotary ovens, convection ovens, convection steamers, steam-jacketed kettles with lids, and microwave ovens are good examples).

2. Cook foods in the largest quantity possible. This cannot be done for vegetables and other

foods that are cooked in small batches as the meal progresses. However, energy savings can be realized when certain foods (chili, soups, and casseroles) are cooked in large quantities all at once.

3. Cook at the lowest temperature possible. The savings in shrinkage for low-temperature roasting of meats has been known to the foodservice industry for years. However, cooks continue to roast meats at high temperatures (300° to 400° F) to "seal in the juices," which serves only to dry out the product. Slow cooking means lower energy consumption even though the cooking time is longer.

4. Carefully monitor preheating time for each piece of equipment. It is all too common for cooks to turn on the main battery of cooking equipment first thing in the morning and allow the ranges, fryers, and ovens to go full blast all day long. Most modern cooking appliances have a quick recovery time and can be brought up to proper cooking temperature in only a few minutes.

5. Monitor the demand curve for electricity. Electricity is sold in part on the basis of peak demand for the day. Be sure that the equipment is not turned on all at once during the opening hours of the food facility.

Lighting

Well over 80 percent of our impressions are visual. Rapid hand and eye coordination are essential to many elements of the restaurant business, such as preparation, service, and cash handling. Failure to see accurately causes the signals our brain receives to be distorted, resulting in errors and delays. Productivity is then seriously affected. Consider also the many reasons people go to restaurants. Not only to eat, but also because of the quality of the physical and mental environment. The difference between "eating" and "dining" depends upon the ambience of the restaurant and the total experience—conscious and subconscious—of the customer. People want their food delivered promptly and in such a way that their nerves are soothed after a hectic day. Properly directed light can help dissolve negative

feelings and tensions. The goal is to provide guests with pleasant sensations designed by the restaurateur to fit together into a complete dining experience.

To create consistently positive experiences, control must be exerted over where the light goes, what its true color will be, what effects it will have on the guests and workers, as well as the effects on the overall appearance of the interior design elements of the restaurant.

Each part of the eye sees a specific type of light. The cones of the retina allow one to see colors and details in bright sunlight. Studies have shown that cone color vision is improved by the stimulus of sound waves. The normal hustle and activity in a lunchroom therefore stimulate a keener perception of color. This may require the alignment of the color decor elements with the light levels and their direction to avoid assaulting the mind with a barrage of tension-producing stimuli. The effects work both ways. During evening dining the sound waves from service activity will appear to warm up the colors in the room. This is an advantage, as the colors are otherwise perceived as being duller under the lower evening light levels. However, the efficiency of the retina rods, which allow one to see black and white under dim lighting conditions, is reduced by the stimulation of sound waves. Therefore, the patron will experience greater difficulty in reading the black and white print of the menu, promotion cards, wine lists, charge slips, or guest checks. The room may have appeared to be well lighted to the manager when he or she set the light levels during the quiet early evening hours. What happens is that the menu becomes harder to read as the sound in the dining room increases with more arriving guests. Ironically, when people are waiting to be seated, and the restaurateur wishes to turn the tables faster, the patrons need more time to make a selection due to unbalanced light levels.

While the eye is strong and can adapt to a wide range of lighting conditions, it doesn't always function with the same degree of efficiency. In order to establish light levels that can assist the eye in seeing more efficiently, five factors must be considered: time, size, contrast, brightness, and sound. The following sections consider these five factors and how they relate to lighting efficiency.

TIME

One's level of comfort or discomfort, and therefore one's perception of time, are affected by the level and the tone of light. Waiting to be served and waiting for a check can be very tense experiences for a customer in a hurry. The degree of environmental comfort can mean the difference between the customer's being irritated or satisfied. Reading a menu under poor lighting conditions could take up too much prime time during a lunch or dinner rush and slow the turnover unnecessarily. Or if the customer is rushed into making a selection, he or she may not have had time to read the entire menu.

SIZE

Light also affects space perception. Proper lighting can make a small room seem open and can make a large room feel cozy. In a darkened room, people seated 3 feet apart feel much closer together than they would in a room with more light. On the menu, the size of the print has a direct relationship to the customer's ability to see efficiently at various light levels.

CONTRAST

The perceived difference between the detail of an object and its background is referred to as contrast. Spot lighting, which shines directly on a specific area, offers high contrast. The contrast between a coffee stain and a brown rug is low contrast. Good contrast between the color of the ink and paper can make a menu easier to read at any light level. In the kitchen, contrast comes into play when cooks work on highly reflective stainless steel tables.

BRIGHTNESS

The amount of light the eye sees on an object's surface is the brightness. This is the last controllable element of lighting since time, size, contrast, and sound are often fixed before the acceptability of the light levels is evaluated. Putting more light (brightness) on an object will improve the visibility of the object despite its small size, poor contrast, or the shortness of time allotted in which to distinguish the object.

SOUND

As was mentioned earlier, light levels should be readjusted as the sound levels vary in the room. This can be done quite effectively with a light dimmer switch.

HOW MUCH LIGHT IS ENOUGH?

If you were in a dark cave with only a book of matches to light your way, you would be amazed at how efficient such a small amount of light can be. There is a rapid increase in the efficiency of light when moving from darkness into light, using as little as 3 footcandles of light. In fact, when a task is illuminated, the available light may be as much as 90 percent efficient at a very low level. However, to move to 95 percent efficiency may require three times as much light, and to be 100 percent efficient may require 10 to 100 times as much light. Close work involving very small objects, such as microcomputer chips, may require as high as 1,500 footcandles of light, but only at the working surface.

Another factor in efficiency, similar in concept to contrast, is the reflective difference level of the task and the surrounding area. The comparative brightness of the light reflected off the object and off the background determines how easily the eye can distinguish the former. Ideal reflective levels would range from 40 to 60 percent at 40 footcandles of light illuminating the task and the surrounding area. The surrounding area should reflect back 40-50 percent of the light, while the task should reflect back 50-60 percent. Except in a case such as reading, which normally requires a brighter background, there should be at least 10 percent more light reflected back from the task than from the surroundings. For instance, as the illumination of a cash register keyboard is kept constant and the surrounding brightness of the counter top is raised gradually, the ability to see the keyboard improves. This improvement will be gradual and constant and will be at its maximum when the brightness of the surrounding counter is equal to or slightly less than the brightness of the keyboard. When the brightness of the surrounding counter exceeds the brightness of the keyboard, there is a radical falling off in the ability to see the keyboard without making computation errors.

Another example of reflectance difference would be a menu board on a bright wall. The bright wall would be improper as it competes for the eye's attention and would reduce the efficiency of reading the menu board.

One solution to this problem is found in the use of brightness ratios that mathematically compare the brightness of the task with the surrounding brightness. A 3 to 1 ratio is normal, 10 to 1 the high limit. However, brightness ratios can be misleading. A work area could have a favorable brightness ratio, but abnormally high levels of reflected glare from the task. If the menu board to wall brightness ratio, for example, were 3 to 1 and the light on the menu board were the 1,000 watts required to compete with the stainless steel wall brightness, the excessive task light would reflect glare back into the customers' eyes and reduce their ability to see the board.

Glare is a common problem in poorly designed lighting systems. To reduce glare, one can eliminate the reflected light by reducing the reflectance of the surface or by moving the light out of the direct line of vision. Another solution is to build up a balanced intensity of brightness that absorbs and distributes the glare. For example, if the windows of the restaurant perimeter lighting reflect glare back into the eyes of the customer, shades may be hung in the windows to reduce reflectance, thus moving the light perpendicular to the customer, or the over-all lighting level in the room may be increased so as to build a balanced intensity, which could be reduced as the sun sets.

LIGHT AND PRODUCTIVITY

Light is one of the many inputs that affect productivity. Its impact shows up most obviously in problems that can be traced to poor visibility. For example, low productivity may be revealed in sales figures that are not correctly transcribed, or by a waitress's check that cannot be read under kitchen illumination, resulting in the preparation of the wrong item. But light has less noticeable effects. The level and kind of light can influence the way we function, both physically and psychologically. How motivated do we feel, for instance, when the weather

is gray and cloudy, or when lighting is subdued rather than bright and warm?

Providing more illumination, however, is not the whole answer. In fact, reduced productivity often occurs in operations with high light levels that are merely running up utility costs unnecessarily. Better lighting and higher productivity are the result of knowledgeable planning, not merely adding wattage.

Studies show that a small increase in light levels can raise productivity significantly. Increases of 5 to 33 percent in productivity have been achieved by the proper placing of as little as 25 footcandles of light. Better lighting reduces time required to see and act on the task to be done. When speed increases, confidence grows, which further increases speed. Too little light or an unbalanced distribution increases the rate of error and reduces output.

The reduction of error is as important as increasing output. In a Federal Energy Administration test conducted at Ohio State University, a 12 percent reduction in errors in handwritten numbers was revealed when light levels were properly adjusted. A 12 percent reduction in handwritten errors could be significant for restaurateurs—at the cash register!

Motivation is influenced by the way people perceive their environment. Workers seldom consciously consider the light falling on their tasks until strain, a headache, or fatigue sets in, but it affects them none the less. With better task visibility, work can be accomplished and high standards achieved with less effort. The right lighting also helps to create the impression of a comfortable work environment, in which employees are likely to approach their day with a more consistently positive attitude.

LIGHTING DESIGN

People tend to orient themselves and their activities according to the brightness levels of their environment. And this visual aesthetic sense has a significant effect on what activities people consider proper in different levels of light. Overall brightness is appropriate for spaces in which physical activity takes place, such as washing areas, receiving areas, stock rooms, assembly areas, and refrigerators. Lower light levels would be suitable for accounting, cash handling, counter sales, waiting areas, expediting stations, and access corridors. In either case, light levels should remain within a moderate range. When areas are too bright, colors and shapes appear jarring or distorted, and workers' concentration is affected.

Brightness also influences the mind's perception of the apparent weight of objects. Tote boxes, cases, trash cans, and trays will seem easier to lift if they are white or painted a bright color. It is a pity that most cardboard cartons remain a standard dull brown. If more manufacturers bleached or painted their containers white, as Sexton does, the handling of cases of food off the truck and into storerooms would be perceived as an easier task than it is now. In any event, to achieve a good level of reflectance, light levels should be high in areas where lifting and handling must be done.

The color of uniforms is another factor in lighting design, because of its visual impact and the sensitivity of human skin to light. Even people who are totally blind respond to light by perceiving radiant energy through their skin. Since color also is energy in various wavelengths, uniforms for physical work should be bright.

Bacterial strains, especially those that cause odors and food poisoning, respond to light as well. Research has shown that streptococci of various strains (the kind usually found in food poisoning cases traced to poor employee hygiene) are killed by natural daylight, either direct or filtered through glass. The possibility of killing or preventing the growth of bacteria during food preparation, or of destroying odors without having to cover them up with equally obnoxious fumes, should interest any foodservice manager. Ultraviolet light also benefits employee health directly. It has been found to increase the level of working capacity and resistance to infections, improve the stability of clear vision, and reduce respiratory infections. Although the wavelengths of ultraviolet light that proved effective have not yet been produced in standard fluorescent lamps for use in the kitchen, high-powered ultraviolet lamps are now commonly used in walk-ins and meat-aging rooms to slow the growth of bacteria, in conjunction with standard lighting. Harmful overexposure to ultraviolet rays is avoided by turning off the lamps before entering the cooler. Lamps such as Vita-Lite by Duro Test produce light in the necessary range below 500 nanometers at the same time as producing visible white light. In fact, the variety of specific light bulb capabilities has grown to meet our every need.

Another lighting consideration in many food facilities is the need to maintain live plants economically. Good results can be obtained with standard fluorescent fixtures at considerable savings over costly grow lamps. Fluorescent light should be blended in a 3-to-1-watt ratio with incandescent light to supply the infrared missing in all fluorescent lamps. (For example, 75 watts of fluorescent should be blended with 25 of incandescent.) Architects' lamps house fittings to supply power for both lamps in one fixture. Your plant specialist can tell you how long to operate plant lights and how bright they should be.

The role of color and quality of light, a related consideration in food facilities design, is discussed in chapter 7. The chart on page 47 lists recommended light levels for various foodservice applications.

Heat Recovery Systems

Refrigeration, air-conditioning, ice-making, and heat pump systems all generate heat, which needs to be removed from the area. Three common ways to remove heat are by means of air-cooling, water-cooling, and cooling-tower systems. In all three methods, the heat is wasted unless it can be transported back to the food facility to be used for purposes such as heating water for kitchen or dishwashing use.

The cost of hot water is one of the biggest items on the foodservice energy bill. Hot water is used almost constantly during the normal operating hours of the facility, with peak usage when dishes are washed at breakfast, lunch, and dinner. Likewise, refrigeration equipment operates continuously during the normal operating hours of the foodservice facility. One way to save energy is to take the heat lost during refrigeration and use it for partial heating of dishwashing water.

With technology that has been in use for many years, heat from refrigeration can be easily transferred to water. Heat recovery systems were not widely used in the past only because fossil fuels were so cheap and abundant that such systems did not make sense economically.

The systems that are used to heat water from refrigeration all operate on the same principle. Cold water that normally enters the hot water heater first passes through the heat exchanger and removes the heat from the refrigeration system (water cooling of condensers). The cold water is now slightly warm water as it enters the water heater and the cost of increasing the temperature of the water to acceptable levels (120°-140° F, or 49°-60° C) is reduced. The equipment to accomplish the transfer of heat looks like a large domestic water heater. Figure 6-3 illustrates how this type of heat recovery system works.

Heat recovery systems can be designed either to cool the water from an air-cooled heat exchanger, as described above, or to connect directly to a water-cooled refrigeration system and cool the superheated refrigerant as it leaves the compressor. Each manufacturer claims that its own system will:

· Capture the most heat
· Reduce scale buildup in the hot water system (for more efficient operation)
· Bring a rapid return on investment through energy cost savings
· Reduce wear and maintenance costs of the refrigeration equipment

All of the systems accomplish the good results claimed, with varying degrees of success. The main point is that water-preheating heat recovery systems definitely reduce energy costs, and the return on investment can be very dramatic. Important factors to consider before purchasing a heat recovery system are:

· the hot water needs of your operation
· energy costs in your area
· hot water storage needs
· the location and condition of existing refrigeration equipment
· the amount of refrigeration in use

The most logical application for heat recovery systems in foodservice facilities is the large refrigeration system used for walk-in coolers and freezers. The compressors for these units are by themselves large enough to justify the cost for many heat recovery systems. Lesser, though significant, energy cost savings may be realized by connecting compressors for smaller pieces of equipment to the recovery system. Typically, reach-in refrigerators, display coolers, ice machines, and beverage dispensers are installed with "self-contained" refrigeration systems.

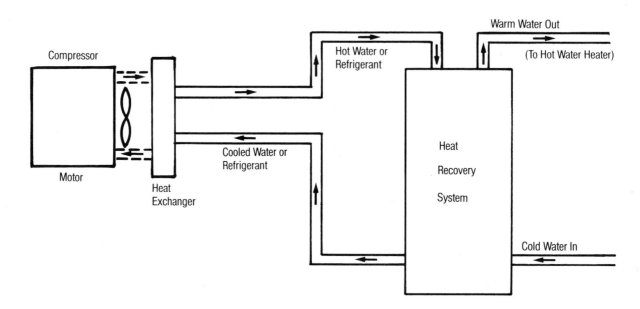

6-3. HEAT RECOVERY SYSTEM.

The compressors on these pieces are usually air cooled, which means that the heat is dissipated into the kitchen, serving area, or dining room. If these areas are air conditioned, each refrigeration unit adds to the air-conditioning load. Imagine the combined water-heating and air-conditioning savings that could be accrued by tying these smaller compressors into the heat recovery system. This is an excellent opportunity for energy savings that should not be overlooked when planning a new facility or facilities renovation.

Other forms of heat recovery include solar heating and exhaust systems with heat exchangers. Systems for recovering heat from kitchen exhausts are designed to pull heat out of very hot air (from hoods over range sections and ovens) and recycle it into the water-heating system. Without some method of heat recovery, a tremendous amount of heat is lost "up the flue"; however, the air-to-water transfer that is used in these systems is much less efficient than other methods and requires a very large volume of hot exhaust air to justify the investment.

AIR AND HUMIDITY CONTROL

Hoods

The successful removal of heat and air that is ladened with grease particles and food odors requires a well-designed hood exhaust system. Many "energy-saving" hoods are now available, and each hood manufacturer claims to have come up with the most effective design. The buyer cannot hope to make an intelligent choice without understanding the principles of hood exhaust operation, including both the action of thermal air currents and the functions of the component parts of a hood system. Because of the high initial cost of the hood and the high ongoing costs of operation for the life of the entire system, time spent in acquiring such knowledge is a worthwhile investment.

Hoods remove air, water vapor, grease, and food odors from the kitchen range area and air and water vapor from dishwashing rooms. Ovens and steam-jacketed kettles require hoods that remove only air, heat, and water vapor. If large quantities of grease from a broiler, charbroiler, fryer, or grill are present, the hood system must extract this pollutant before the air is drawn by fans to the outside. To understand the most effective and energy-efficient means of removing airborne grease, it is necessary to look at the parts and functions of a

simple hood system; following are a few definitions and explanations.

Cubic feet per minute (CFM): This standard measurement is used for all hoods and ventilation systems to indicate the volume of air flowing through the system. The flow is usually produced by a combination of supply (makeup) air and air from fans. Depending on their design, the fans either "push" or "pull" the air through filters and ducts into the open air.

Makeup air: This is the term for air that is supplied to the kitchen from the dining room (an energy-wasteful source), from ducts installed in the walls of the kitchen, or from ducts built into the hood system. If insufficient makeup air is supplied to replace the air exhausted by the hood, a negative pressure will be created in the kitchen. This pressure will in turn draw from other parts of the building—heated air during the winter and air-conditioned air in the summer. In either instance, large quantities of energy will be wasted.

Filters and extractors: For many years, filters of wire mesh were used to collect grease and dust from the air as it moved through the hood system. The accumulated grease and dust, in contact with the high heat from the kitchen cooking equipment, caused fires and destroyed many food operations. A more modern development is the "extractor," a stainless steel mechanism located in the hood. The device is constructed so that the air flowing through it must rapidly change direction, and the grease particles are flung against the sides of stainless steel baffles. The grease collects into a trough, from which it can easily be removed. In more expensive extractors, the grease is cooled by a continuous spray of water and flushed down the drain, or a spray of water mixed with a detergent is periodically turned on to wash away accumulated grease.

Compensating or short-circuiting hoods: In this design, a special duct is installed to bring air to the hood, so that the amount of air exhausted from the building is reduced. Some manufacturers believe that the compensating hood improves the "capture" capacity by increasing the volume of air that curls under the bottom edge of the hood. The amount of air supply needed to make such a system effective is a matter of debate in the industry. The author's experience is that a reasonable quantity of air and food odor must be drawn from the kitchen, but that systems that use as much as 90 percent makeup air are not satisfactory. A hood system using 80 percent or less makeup air seems to create a good balance between energy savings and a reasonable amount of air removal from the kitchen.

The following information will help to clarify the principles underlying hood design.*

To start with, it is not the hood, but rather the cooking equipment, which determines the basic exhaust requirement; different types of cooking have different needs for exhaust. Certainly the hood design and dimensions are important, but they also are essentially dictated by the cooking equipment.

Exhausting over hot cooking equipment is like handling most other hot processes—you must at least match the thermal air currents. Heated surfaces of cooking equipment generate thermal air currents, and just like any other heated surface, the temperature, area, and configuration of the surface are major factors in determining the extent of those currents. Variable as they may be, they establish the minimum exhaust volume.

Consider a single item of cooking equipment as shown in [figure 6-4]. When heated to operating temperature it generates a thermal air flow, let's say 1,000 CFM (cubic feet per minute). There is no hood or fan involved at this time, as a hood has no control over the thermal currents generated. As heated air rises from the cooking surface, the resulting low pressure at the surface causes room air to pull in to replace it. Thus, a pattern is established. Note that air is drawn in at the cooking surface level to sustain the cooking process.

When an exhaust hood is applied, as shown in [figure 6-5], the exhaust volume must at least equal the thermal air currents being received by the hood—otherwise the hood will overflow and eject some of the smoke and heated vapors into the kitchen.

Equal flow will work under ideal conditions but leaves no capture velocity at the front lip of the hood since all the air is coming from the cooking surface and entering the hood from below. Theoretically, no capture velocity is needed at that point since thermal and exhaust flows are in equilibrium. However, in the real world it is necessary to add safety factors, as shown in [figure 6-6], to counteract cross currents, turbulence and surges in thermal currents. These safety factors are derived from a combination of calculation, experience and good judgment. They vary according to application, hood type and manufacturer. In this case we applied a 20% safety factor and thus increased the exhaust volume to 1,200 CFM.

The additional 200 CFM enters the hood at the front lip and thus establishes the "upper level" capture velocity. It does not change the "lower level" capture velocity significantly since nothing has changed at the cooking surface. In the event of a thermal surge, the extra air is drawn in at the "lower level" and subtracts from the "upper level" safety margin.

Figure [6-6] illustrates a system which should perform adequately at a minimum practical exhaust volume. This would surely be the most expedient and logical way to go.

But, the local code official may claim that this hood, at this size, must exhaust 2,400 CFM to comply with code. One popular response

---

*From a paper by David Black, presented to the American Society of Heating, Refrigerating, and Air-Conditioning Engineers, February 1984, in Atlanta, Georgia.

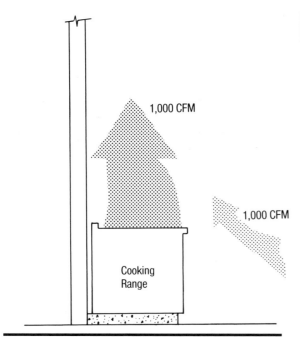

6–4. RANGE ONLY, NO HOOD. THERMAL AIR CURRENTS COMING OFF THE COOKING RANGE, 1,000 CFM.

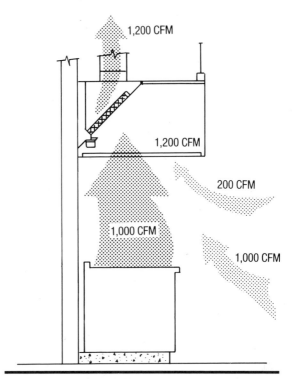

6–6. A 20 PERCENT SAFETY FACTOR ADDED TO COUNTER TURBULENCE, CROSS CURRENTS, THERMAL SURGES, ETC.

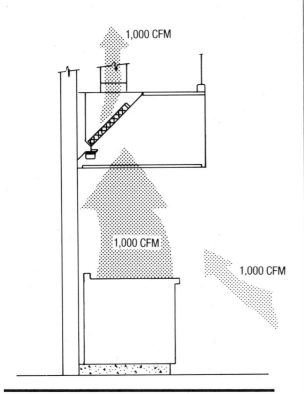

6–5. HOOD BALANCING OF THERMAL AIR CURRENTS COMING OFF THE COOKING SURFACE. NET EXHAUST FROM KITCHEN, 1,000 CFM.

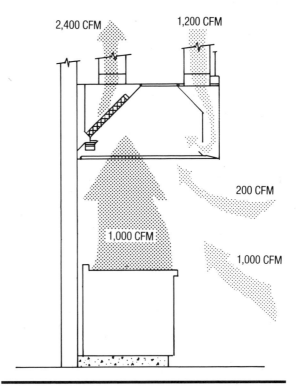

6–7. FIFTY PERCENT COMPENSATING HOOD. NET EXHAUST FROM KITCHEN, 1,200 CFM.

to that is to add a supply air plenum, as shown in [figure 6-7], and introduce untempered air directly into the hood interior, short circuiting it to the filters. Since we have already determined that a total of 1,200 CFM needs to come from the kitchen space, only 1,200 CFM can be introduced to satisfy the 2,400 CFM exhaust. We now have a balanced condition with the proper amount of air coming from the kitchen space—but at the expense of twice the exhaust volume, thus larger duct, shaft and fan, and the addition of the untempered air fan and ductwork—and the HVAC system sees no change in tempered air volume. This would be a 50% short circuit hood.

As another example, what if 4,800 CFM is called for, as shown in [figure 6-8]? Simply increase the short circuit to 3,600 CFM. The required 1,200 CFM is retained and there is now a 75% hood.

The 3,600 CFM literally compensates for the surplus exhaust and thus the term "compensating hood" which is often applied to that design. The 4,800 CFM exhaust permits the 3,600 CFM supply. Conversely, the 3,600 CFM supply literally compels the 4,800 CFM exhaust. By increasing the exhaust to 12,000 CFM we should have a 90% hood, but nothing has really been gained.

Air and Humidity Control for the Dishwashing Room

Since warm air will hold more moisture than cool air, when moist warm air is cooled, water vapor condenses. Cool air containing less moisture increases the amount of moisture that can evaporate from the skin, and therefore is more cooling and comfortable for customers and employees. In foodservice establishments, the concern for the customer is that the air seem fresh and that humidity be low enough for comfort while sitting quietly in the dining room. For the employees, who hopefully are more active, a work space is comfortable if the temperature and humidity are slightly lower than in the dining room and if the air is moving rapidly. Unfortunately, in the dishroom the air is often very moist and the temperature extremely high.

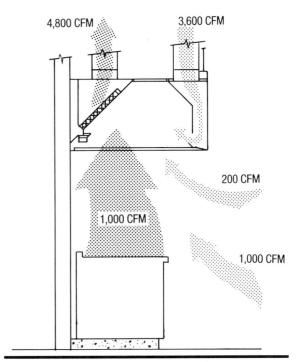

6–8. SEVENTY-FIVE PERCENT COMPENSATING HOOD. NET EXHAUST FROM KITCHEN, 1,200 CFM.

Food facilities planners must insist that architects and engineers design into the mechanical systems (HVAC) a sufficient amount of air supply and exhaust to keep the moisture level as low as possible in the dishwashing and potwashing areas. Failure to create this condition will result in low productivity and high employee turnover among the warewashing personnel. A second problem arising from poor ventilation in the dishroom is a decrease in the effectiveness of air drying as the dishes emerge from the washer. Wet dishes encourage bacterial growth and make a poor impression on customers.

HVAC Systems for Dining

The heating, ventilating, and air-conditioning systems for the dining room and other public spaces in a foodservice facility are beyond the scope of this text. The best heating source, the complexities of humidity and temperature control, and the environmental treatment of all spaces in both the front and back of the facility are technical matters that should be left in the hands of licensed and trained engineers.

CONVEYOR SYSTEMS

Conveyors have been used for many years in the industrial and manufacturing industries for moving materials from one place to another, at a maximum speed and with a minimum effort. In foodservice facilities, conveyors not only move objects but can also be designed to improve food quality (as in hospital tray makeup systems) and provide asthetically pleasing dish tray areas in cafeterias and other self-service operations.

Although many conveyor systems are fabricated especially for the needs of a particular food operation, conveyors designed for general use in a foodservice facility can be purchased by model number from the manufacturer's catalog. The general construction features of conveyors are:

- conveyor belt
- conveyor bed
- drive mechanism (if the belt is powered)
- drive enclosure
- return track for belt
- limit switch
- wash tank and belt-washing system
- drip pan
- removable skirt panels

These parts vary, depending on the complexity of the conveyor system and the features desired by the foodservice owner or manager. Five types of conveyors are manufactured: belt, slat, roller, pin, and link.

Belt: Flat, water-resistant conveyor belts were common during the early period of conveyor usage. Belts are still available, but are not as popular as slat conveyor because of their inability to "bend" around turns and corners.

Slat: These belts are usually made of Delrin or other hard, flexible plastics and are linked together to form a continuous chain. They are usually designed so that the belt can turn corners, and the slats overlap on the turns. Slat conveyor belts, with self-washing systems, are a clean and attractive solution for self-bussing dish drop-off areas in cafeterias.

Roller: The "skatewheel" or roller conveyor is frequently used for gravity conveyors, or at the termination of a powered conveyor system. Gravity conveyors are less expensive and require little maintenance. However, in self-service applications they are not as attractive and can cause accidents or dish breakage.

Pin: Pin conveyors are constructed of metal links with small pins protruding upward. The pins insure that the tray or container being conveyed does not slip.

Link: Conveyor belts constucted of a series of Delrin or other hard, flexible plastic links are an excellent solution for conveying cafeteria trays. Installed in parallel pairs, these conveyors can be designed to move trays around sharp turns (fig. 6-9). The links are very strong and have been successful in self-service applications because they are attractive and do not break easily.

FLOORS, CEILINGS, AND WALLS

The specification and construction of building surfaces are usually the responsibility of the architect in new or renovated foodservice facilities. However, the foodservice consultant and/or the owner are often asked by the architect for recommendations on the types of finishes that are desirable. The decision on the type of finish to be used may be based on budgetary limitations rather than the desirability of the surface. Ideally, the finishes that are recommended, especially for floors and walls, are chosen on the basis of ease in cleaning and resistance to damage or wear as well as aesthetics.

6–9. LINK CONVEYOR BELT. (COURTESY OF ADAMATION CORPORATION)

Floors

The floor surface in the kitchen and service areas should be easy to maintain, wear resistant, slip resistant, and nonporous. The most universally accepted floor material is quarry tile, which has the qualities suggested. Quarry tile has an excellent record in the foodservice industry for not being slippery and for resisting grease absorption. The grout between the tile is slightly porous, but quickly becomes sealed from the dirt and grease of the typical food operations. Grout can also be coated with commercial floor sealers before use. These sealers need to be reapplied at appropriate intervals. The use of a colored or tinted grout creates a better appearance and eliminates the need for bleaching or cleaning the grout joint. Quarry tile with embedded carborundum chips has greater slip resistance and is recommended for use in wet or high-grease conditions such as are found in range areas and potwashing and dishwashing rooms.

Floor finishes in dining rooms and public places can be of any material that is wear resistant and that can be easily cleaned. Carpeting in dining rooms is popular because it is sound absorbing and provides a feeling of luxury. Carpeting is not recommended in high soil areas such as:

- service areas for waiters and waitresses
- tray and dish drop-off areas
- beverage stations
- condiment stations
- major traffic aisles
- cashier stations

Ceramic tile is an excellent floor finish for public restrooms or high soil areas. Unglazed tiles are the best selection because of their slip resistant qualities.

Vinyl tile is not recommended in dining rooms or public areas because it usually requires a high level of maintenance, especially waxing and frequent machine buffing. The amount of labor required over a few years will exceed the extra costs of an easy-to-care-for quarry or ceramic tile floor finish. A vinyl tile floor wears out quickly in a commercial kitchen, is slippery when wet, and is not grease resistant. Vinyl tile can be used as an inexpensive floor covering in employee dressing rooms, employee dining areas, or foodservice offices. The following chart is a list of suggested finishes for floors in foodservice facilities.

FOODSERVICE AREA	RECOMMENDED FLOOR FINISHES
Kitchen	Quarry tile
Dishwashing	Quarry tile with Carborundum
Storerooms—dry stores	Sealed concrete
Washdown room—carts and trash containers	Quarry tile with Carborundum; quarry tile; sealed concrete
Receiving	Quarry tile; sealed concrete
Offices	Quarry tile; vinyl tile; carpet; wood
Employee restrooms	Quarry tile; vinyl tile; unglazed ceramic tile; terrazzo
Corridors, back of the house	Vinyl tile; unglazed ceramic tile; sealed concrete; terrazzo
Corridors, public	Vinyl tile; unglazed ceramic tile; carpet; terrazzo
Dining rooms	Quarry tile; unglazed ceramic tile; carpet; terrazzo
Public restrooms	Quarry tile; unglazed ceramic tile; terrazzo
Service areas—waiter area or cafeteria	Quarry tile; unglazed ceramic tile; terrazzo

Walls

The following chart illustrates acceptable wall finishes for different areas in a foodservice facility. Budget limitations may dictate the less expensive finish over the more desirable ones. One mistake frequently made is to use cement blocks covered with epoxy paint behind the equipment in the range section of a kitchen. The problem with this approach to cost savings is that the paint will turn brown and eventually flake off under conditions of high heat and grease. The best wall finish in cooking areas is structural glazed tile or ceramic tile, either of which will resist damage from heat, grease, and frequent cleaning. The structural glazed tile has an additional quality of being highly resistant to impact when struck by a cart or other portable equipment. The following chart lists suggested finishes for walk-in foodservice facilities.

FOODSERVICE AREA	RECOMMENDED WALL FINISHES
Kitchen—range section	Structural glazed tile; glazed ceramic tile
Kitchen—cold food section	Structural glazed tile; glazed ceramic tile; cement block with epoxy paint
Dishwashing	Structural glazed tile; glazed ceramic tile
Storerooms—dry stores	Cement block with epoxy paint
Washdown Rooms—carts and trash containers	Structural glazed tile
Receiving	Cement block with epoxy paint
Offices	Painted dry wall
Employee restrooms	Glazed ceramic tile; cement block with epoxy paint
Corridors, back of the house	Cement block with epoxy paint
Corridors, public	Painted dry wall; decorative wall selected by interior designer
Dining rooms	Decorative wall selected by interior designer
Public restrooms	Glazed ceramic tile; decorative wall selected by interior designer
Service areas	Glazed ceramic tile; cement block with epoxy paint

Ceilings

Ceilings in a foodservice facility are of two types: the structural ceiling, which supports the floors above, and the "false ceiling," which may hide ducts and other architectural features or serve mainly to enhance the room's attractiveness.

CEILING MATERIALS

New materials for ceilings are introduced so frequently and ceiling materials vary so widely that any list would be outdated in a short period of time.

The most common ceiling materials are:

- acoustical tile
- dry wall, painted
- plaster, painted
- wood, sealed or painted
- exposed concrete
- Fiberglas
- aluminum or other metal

The acoustical ceiling is the most common of those listed, because of its low cost and excellent sound-absorbing qualities. Special acoustical tiles have been developed that do not easily absorb moisture or grease from the air. The health department or local building codes usually have specific recommendations for the type of ceiling material that is acceptable for foodservice operations. Aluminum panel ceilings with perforations are often used because they can be easily removed for cleaning. Some aluminum ceiling panels can actually be put through the dishwashing machine.

If the ceilings in work areas are sound absorbent and resistant to grease and moisture absorption, and have a light-reflective surface, they will probably be acceptable to health officials. Ceilings in dining rooms and other public areas can be constructed and/or covered with many types of materials, as long as they do not create either a fire safety problem or a health hazard.

SOUND

Sound pollution in the workplace is of concern to managers because excessive noise can cause fatigue, irritability, and low productivity among workers. Sound control in the dining room and public areas of a foodservice facility is a significant consideration in creating a pleasant dining experience. Stopping the transfer of sound from areas adjacent to a banquet hall or private dining room can mean the difference between a successful or unsuccessful meeting or convention.

Architects, engineers, and foodservice consultants spend a significant amount of time seeking methods of creating a quiet environment. One of the problems with sound control in a typical foodservice operation is the nature of the operation itself. The activity and movement of workers, the noise of equipment, conversations between guests at the table, waiters and waitresses taking food orders and communicating with the kitchen, the clatter of glasses and dishes, and background music (when present) add up to a very high sound level.

Sound level (loudness) is measured in decibels, which range from zero to 130 for the human ear. Decibels above this range are painful to the normal ear and would seldom be encountered in a foodservice operation. Another characteristic of sound is the number of vibrations per second created from the sound source. Those who are interested in stereo music equipment frequently will shop for amplifiers and speakers that will handle from 5 to 25,000 hertz. Since the average ear can only hear from 15 to 20,000 vibrations per second, vibrations below or above this range cannot be heard.

In the dining environment, it is desirable to keep the decibels low and to introduce background music in a low-frequency range. High-frequency music or sound is generally less pleasant to the ear, especially in an eating place where conversation is encouraged among the guests.

Sound-Absorbing Materials

Carpeting, the customers' clothing, and draperies are all soft materials that absorb sound and that can create a pleasant appearance in the dining room.

Glass and hard surface floors, walls, and ceilings reflect sound and create reverberations that make table conversation difficult.

A mixture of these materials in the public spaces of a foodservice establishment is the usual approach taken by the architect and interior designer to control sound. For example, glass, quarry tile, and terrazzo reflect 70 to 90 percent of the sound, while carpet or cloth reflect only 40 to 65 percent (depending on the density and characteristics of the material). A mixture of hard and sound-absorbing surfaces will decrease the reflective quality of sound. Generally, the use of some carpeting in the dining room and the selection of acoustical material for the ceiling will create the proper sound levels.

Loud sound in the kitchen and other support areas of a foodservice facility can be decreased but not eliminated. The use of quarry tile floors, ceramic tile, or other hard-surface walls and ceilings create a sound-reflecting environment. Noises made by the use of motors, metal pots and pans, stainless steel tables, and other metal utensils add a considerable amount of sound to the kitchen. The following list of sound reduction ideas should be considered in the planning of the kitchen and other support areas:

· Acoustical ceilings
· Sound deadening on the underside of tables (The following statement, added to the specification of any stainless steel table or cabinet will assure proper sound deadening: "Sound deaden underside of table (cabinet) with mastic, premium type that 'skins' on surface when dry. Surface of mastic coating shall be smooth, equal in smoothness to standard for hot rolled steel, and coated with a lead-free aluminum paint or coating to match color of the cabinet.")
· The use of remote compressors for reach-in and especially for walk-in refrigerators and freezers
· The transfer of food orders from the waiters and waitresses to the cooks electronically or with written checks, rather than by shouting
· The use of low-volume background music in the workplace; such music tends to discourage radio owners from playing their sets full blast in the kitchen
· The separation and/or enclosure of dishwashing and potwashing from other parts of the kitchen with walls; masonry walls constructed of cement blocks or structural glazed tile stop sound because of the density of these building materials

SUMMARY

The owner, architect, foodservice consultant, and engineer must become involved in the engineering decisions affecting the foodservice facility. The quality of interior lighting, the HVAC system used, the energy efficiency of kitchen equipment, and the final cost of the project are all outcomes of engineering decisions.

A basic understanding of the types of energy sources available and the methods for designing high-energy equipment such as hoods and dishwashing machines is helpful in arriving at sound decisions regarding utility usage. Because floor, ceiling, and wall finishes have a great impact on the final cost of the project, the foodservice consultant must understand which ones will perform best. Trade journals, manufacturers' representatives, and professional engineers are good sources of information on foodservice facilities engineering.

CHAPTER 7

FOODSERVICE INTERIOR DESIGN

THIS CHAPTER WILL:

▶ Describe the process of selecting and interviewing an interior designer for the foodservice facility

▶ Provide an understanding of the basic services offered by the interior designer

▶ Assist the reader in developing a working relationship with an interior design professional

▶ Describe the design process and the primary elements of the interior of a food facility

▶ Describe the primary coordinating considerations in designing a menu

▶ Illustrate some typical interior design projects

OVERVIEW

Interior architectural design is a business investment. More and more frequently, the quality of this interior investment is the arena where patrons will judge a restaurant's performance. Discerning foodservice operators are commissioning the most talented designers. The payback is a strong recognition factor; design's most salient value is a reputation for quality that works with food and service to produce a loyal clientele.

The clientele will evaluate how comfortable or uncomfortable they are, whether the restaurant is too noisy or too quiet, too bright or too dim, whether it is exciting, sophisticated, quaint, boring, or perhaps unpleasant. The design of the restaurant contributes significantly to productivity, employee attitude, operational efficiency, and enhanced community image. Restaurant patrons clearly support good design: they not only appreciate beautiful space—they are willing to pay for it. Thus, professional interior designers can make a significant contribution to the "bottom line."

A foodservice operator can provide creative

and competitive entertainment, and experimental and innovative decor; or the operator can provide a no-nonsense environment where food reigns supreme. In either case, the goal remains the same: to combine functional and efficient planning and layout with an aesthetic effect that makes the restaurant memorable. Function and aesthetics are essential in equal measure to ensure success.

SELECTING AN INTERIOR DESIGNER

In *A Guide to Business Principles and Practices for Interior Designers,* Harry Siegel gives a brief summary of the early development of the interior design profession.

> Throughout the recorded past, interiors had been designed and fabricated by people operating under innumerable guises and with many different relationships to the patron or client on one hand, and to the workmen, artisans, and suppliers on the other. Interiors have been produced by architects, builders, artists, sculptors, artist-craftsmen, artisans, upholsterers, drapers, cabinet makers, shopkeepers, antique dealers and after World War I, by imaginative, magnetic amateurs on the social scale. It was with the advent of the very last group that the term decorator became important and popular . . . but "decorator" is ambiguous; it can mean a painter or paperhanger; it can mean a housewife with spare time on her hands . . . .

The foodservice owner or planner should look for an interior designer, not a "decorator." Many amateur decorators operate solely by virtue of an easily obtainable tax license and/or occupational license. Before hiring a designer, the foodservice planner needs to check his or her credentials, portfolio, and membership in a professional organization such as the American Society of Interior Designers (ASID). Association with a professional organization usually implies at least a four-year degree program in interior architectural design from a university, college, or private design school. Membership in ASID, for example, requires accredited education, professional experience, and a comprehensive two-day NCIDQ exam (National Council for Interior Design Qualification). The exam is the last "rite of passage" into professional membership. High standards of ethical practice are also specified. It would be worthwhile to contact the nearest ASID chapter for information on the designer's credentials and membership status.

An experienced interior designer who has specialized in foodservice design will have a repertoire of tested approaches and ideas to bring to the task. A good designer, however, is always learning, and in many cases the designer and client can learn from each other. The designer must look at the space objectively with no emotional ties. In the designer's role of transforming the dream into a successful reality, he or she acts as a psychologist, space planner, coordinator, and technical problem solver all rolled into one. The following suggestions may aid in getting a good start and achieving a good product:

- Schedule enough time to find the right interior designer.
- Remember that the fee is being paid for the service of a *professional*, so be prepared to trust the designer's expertise.
- Detail all requirements of the project, explaining the menu, marketing, and concept. The initial meeting with the designer is of paramount importance. Detail items of concern—write them down. Something forgotten in that first meeting can make all the difference in the fee structure or design planning.
- Pay attention to the communication process. The designer and owner are two people who often do not speak the same language, so it is important to communicate both directly and in writing.

Interviewing a Designer

The major qualifications that should be considered during the surveying and interview stage of selecting an interior design professional are listed below:

1. Education—where, how long, degrees?
2. Past job experience—where, how long, doing what? How long has the designer been involved with restaurant design? What other types of design experience does he or she have? Does the designer have training or experience in:

   - space planning
   - graphics, signage
   - industrial, office—commercial design
   - furniture design
   - construction (knowledge of drafting, detailing)
   - lighting and circuitry
   - art history (history of interior architectural design, knowledge of architectural and design periods)
   - textiles, finishes, resources
   - selection and purchase of accessories
   - artistic skills
   - knowledge of building codes, health department requirements, and barrier-free regulations

3. Other restaurants that have used the designer's services
4. References

To work well with a designer, you must be able to establish an open, cooperative working relationship. While many of the criteria in evaluating any designer are relatively objective, some are personal. During the interview, keep in mind the following questions as a check on your personal impressions of the designer:

- Do you feel comfortable with the designer?
- Does the designer immediately understand the space, the project needs, your own desires and preferences?
- Does mutual open-mindedness exist between you and the designer?

Portfolio

The best way to get a sense of the designer's creative and professional skills is to examine his or her portfolio, which contains graphic presentations of examples of the designer's completed work. When reviewing portfolios, look for good communication skills, and check to see if the designer can verbally and graphically communicate visual ideas.

Services to Be Provided

The restaurant or foodservice owner must evaluate the scope of services to be rendered. Typical services that are available from the interior designer are:

- Design concept only
- Design concept and specifications
- Design concept and specifications, with materials and labor resources supplied
- Space planning
- Specifications of architectural alterations
- Supervision of the construction and installation on the job site
- Preparation of purchase specifications for client's direct bidding or procurement
- Purchasing, supervision, and follow-through on orders
- Custom design detailing and preparation of specifications
- Research and purchase time and/or market trips for special items
- Coordination of storage, warehousing, receiving, and delivery requirements

WORKING WITH THE DESIGNER

Early Planning Meetings

The essential first step is for the foodservice owner or manager to detail the requirements of the projected operation. Critical information that is needed at the first meeting with the designer includes:

- The design concept and menu
- The nature, size, and location of all the areas included in the design
- The budget
- Purchasing information: whether it is to be done by the designer, the design firm, or the owner
- Relationships between the interior designer and contractors, food facilities planners, and architects (accountability and division of responsibility)
- Installation timing and deadlines

This initial meeting is an exchange of necessary information acquainting the designer, the design firm, and the client with the nature of the job. The owner should not attempt at the first meeting to get definitive answers to questions he or she may have concerning particular design problems. To avoid misunderstanding or disappointment, the consideration of design options should await the designer's first preliminary presentation.

The Budget

Many foodservice operators or restaurant owners are not totally open with the interior designer regarding the budget. A typical conversation may go something like this:

> *Designer:* "What kind of budget has been set aside for interior design, construction, materials, furnishings, and so on?"
> *Owner:* "You tell me how much it's going to cost. Don't worry about money."
> *Designer:* "The interior budget is essential. It is relative to everything; the square footage,

menu, concept, marketing, clientele, maintenance, your entire business philosophy. Is the budget realistic or impossible for this space?"
> *Owner:* "Oh, it's realistic."
> *Designer:* "Would you say realistic is between $60,000 and $80,000 or, say, $80,000 and $100,000?"
> *Owner:* "Oh no! It's definitely in the first category."
> *Designer:* "Do you think between $60,000 and $70,000 or $70,000 and $80,000 would more accurately define the budget?"
> *Owner:* "$62,000 should cover it."

Notice the useless energy expended to discover a $62,000 budget! In the process of deciding upon the right person for the job, the restaurant owner will often keep the budget confidential. If the design person at this stage is expected to bid on the job, however, it is essential to be fair, direct, and realistic about the financial parameters.

Without a thorough understanding of the requirements and scope of the foodservice project, neither concepts, costs, nor fees can be ascertained. An estimate or design based on guesswork is worse than useless. Just as the business owner respects the designer who makes a comprehensive study estimate before quoting, the designer can work more effectively with the restaurant owner who has thoroughly analyzed the project requirements. To expect designers to develop a concept and reasonable budget to fit that concept without knowing how much financing is available can have disastrous results, as the following stories illustrate.

Two design firms were asked to develop a concept and budget for an extensive urban restaurant renovation. No budget was given, not even a hint. Both designers were asked to develop an elegant, sophisticated approach to the space. The difference in cost between the two proposed budgets was substantial, and the client gave the job to the lower bidder. Once the job was underway, however, the client complained bitterly about the lack of quality and workmanship in every aspect of the work. Here the client got what he paid for. His "secret budget," not the design firm, was the real culprit.

In another instance, two design firms were asked to develop a concept and budget for a restaurant. No budget limitation was specified. Without clues of any kind, the first firm took an elegant approach, while the second opted for simplicity. Again the difference was substantial and the client, unable to afford the first design, gave the job to the second firm. Later the client asked the second firm to develop the job in the elegant style proposed by the first firm, but to cut corners to lower cost. It is unnecessary to emphasize that the first firm was victimized by this unbusinesslike procedure. Professional designers are always on the alert for the "blind budget."

An example of a preliminary budget, prepared by a designer on the basis of the client's specifications, is presented on page 187.

In summary, the early planning with the interior designer should include:

- A realistic budget, openly discussed
- A description of the scope of services
- The establishment of the desired time frame for project completion

If the client and designer are not in complete agreement on these issues, the alternatives are for the designer to:

- Revise the design concept
- Advise the client that the concept must be changed or the budget must be changed
- Resign from the job and submit a bill for the work provided to that point

The Letter of Agreement

The letter of agreement, contract, or proposal spelling out the conditions of the job is an absolute necessity in all areas of business, including interior design. Each proposal should delineate:

1. Premises on which the work is to be done (a full description)

2. Exact definition of the designer's responsibility and specific areas involved
3. Services to be performed
4. Definition of the functional and sequential phases of the job
5. Budgetary guidelines
6. The responsibilities of the client's own contractors (if necessary)
7. Other conditions specific to the job (inclusions and/or exclusions)
8. Design payments and schedules
9. Termination option

On pages 188-89 is an example of an actual Letter of Agreement and statement of services. Many variations exist, but this will serve as a model for wording and organization.

Although many designers cover these in their flat fee, there may be reimbursements of expenses for areas such as:

- Travel
- Blueprint costs
- Long-distance telephone charges
- Preliminary concept sketches (if done before the signing of a Letter of Agreement)
- Color rendering
- Time charges for custom design items
- Financial liabilities such as:
  - Warehouse, storage, prep, receiving, inspection, and delivery
  - Sales tax
  - Additional services not covered in the Letter of Agreement
  - Changes made by the client after the designer's preliminary designs have been approved (in writing)
  - A service charge of a certain percentage for purchases made by the client through the designer

Design Fee Schedule

There are several possible methods of compensation for the interior design professional. Design payments must be clearly defined, both as to their

▼ EXAMPLE OF A PRELIMINARY BUDGET

Projected Budget: $92,000

Name of business: Friendly Restaurant
Location: Lansing, Michigan
Market: University staff and students; secondary market—young professional people
Type of restaurant:
   Style: Table service
   Mood: Informal
Square footage: total 6,000
Number of seats: 150
Objective: To develop an informal interior, designed to encourage young people to meet socially.

	HIGH	LOW
Design fees	$6,000	$4,000
Demolition (if necessary)	—	—
Interior construction	10,000	7,000
Façade construction	12,000	10,000
Carpet, flooring, hardsurface flooring	20,000	16,000
Wall material	8,000	7,000
Ceiling design or treatment	12,000	9,000
Electrical		
Rewire circuitry	6,000	5,000
Rework existing	—	—
New fixtures	2,000	1,500
Plumbing	3,000	2,000
Furniture and furnishings	10,000	8,000
Accessories, art, planting, and so on	3,000	2,800
TOTAL Projected Budget:	92,000	72,300

type and timing. An initial payment (or retainer) marks the beginning of the actual design commitment. Progress payments are usually scheduled to keep up with the designer's production cost. Some examples of methods of compensation include:

- Percentage of construction costs
- Flat fee (based on a projection of time to be spent on the project)
- Flat fee and percentage
- Square footage multiplier
- Hourly or per diem (a top-end "not-to-exceed" fee limit can be a part of the agreement)

▼
EXAMPLE OF A LETTER OF AGREEMENT

Dear [_____]:

It is our pleasure to be of service to you for your new project, "_____" located at [__address__]. [__design firm or designer__] will collaborate with you as the client, and [_lease firm_], by attendance of necessary conferences as required by you.

Listed below is a summary of our previous discussions, which form the basis of this proposal, outlining the specifics of design intent, scope of responsibility, design fees, methods of payment and installation.

[__design firm or designer__] agrees to perform the following services:

1. Research and develop an interior restaurant concept for the renovation of the existing space at [_location_].
2. Produce a design concept board and preliminary sketches for the client's approval.
3. Develop a preliminary budget based on the design concept.
4. Submit a preliminary design and budget for approval.
5. Prepare the following (after receiving approval of the preliminary design):
   · detailed floor plan
   · elevations
   · sections as necessary for construction
   · furnishings specifications
   · details of custom design
   · construction drawings
   · lighting and circuitry specifications

   In addition, if requested the interior designer will at additional cost:
   · make suggestions on uniform/costume design
   · assist with menu design
   · select accessories
   · supervise the installation

[__design firm__] is not responsible for services such as kitchen design, engineering, HVAC, electrical tabulation of loads, typesetting charges, or reproduction costs of plans. Upon request, [__design firm__] will provide client with sets of plans at cost. Original documents remain the property of [__design firm__].

The design fee for above services is [$_____] payable as follows:

$_____ on acceptance and signing of this proposal

$_____ at completion of design project drawings and specifications, submitted to [__client and leasing company__].

$_____ on installation day

The design fee does not include warehousing, receiving, delivery, or payments for merchandise, sales tax, or services.

Any changes incurred by client or contractor after preliminary designs have been approved by client will be based on an hourly cost of $_____/hour (portal to portal).

In the event that the client wishes [_design firm_] to act as a full or partial purchasing agent, we will handle such transactions at a service charge of _____ percent of that particular cost.

All orders require a 50 percent deposit; a proform (the full amount) may be required for custom design work or special vendors. Balances due on merchandise or services will be CBD (collected before delivery) or immediately upon invoice. These terms are firm. All payments are to be forthcoming from [_client_].

[_design firm_] has no responsibility for work or service people not directly employed by the design firm.

It is understood and agreed that either party may terminate this agreement upon formal written notification to the other. In the event of such termination, [_design firm_] is entitled to compensation for design work completed to that point. Special orders cannot be cancelled.

Any unresolved items will be handled expediently by legal arbitration at a shared cost if such situations occur.

If this agreement meets with your approval, kindly sign and return the enclosed copy of this letter, together with a check in the amount specified to initiate the design. Thank you kindly!

Sincerely,

[_designer name, appellation_]
[_design firm_]

Accepted by: _____
Date: _____

THE DESIGN PROCESS

The purpose of this section is not to explain how to design, but rather to help the reader understand the principles, requirements, restrictions, and attitudes that govern the interior design of food facilities.

Every food operation is the expression of an individual personality. The character, color, texture, furnishings, finishes, and accessories that are chosen are all based on the initial impression the owner imparts to the designer. The end result is the product of the designer's skills and experience meshed with the owner's personality ideas.

Space Planning

Space planning should achieve the optimum in food and beverage service capability as well as provide for the comfort and enjoyment of the customer. It is the most critical and thought-provoking stage for the interior designer.

The space of the facility must be broken down in the designer's mind and reassembled into a three-dimensional working configuration. Space planning is not just a visual picture on a plan, but has to relate to the facility's work requirements and to human scale and proportions. For example, adequate space must be allowed for traffic aisles and the moving of chairs in and out around tables; and service stations must be provided. Restroom doors must be placed away from public eyes; barrier-free standards must be adhered to; and the kitchen network must be hidden from the customers' view. The success of the space planning depends on hundreds of ideas generated and decisions made by the designer and client. A perfectly planned space functions so optimally that it will merely need to be "redecorated" occasionally! And a beautifully decorated space that doesn't function well will ultimately hurt the operation's profitability.

Finishes

Choice of finishes is influenced by the concept and style of interior design. Specific finishes are associated with certain design styles. For instance, a modern contemporary setting might utilize reflective metal finishings, sleek surfaces, and unconventional or trendy color schemes. A traditional interior might contain antique brass, rough-textured or dark stained wood, homespun weaves, and rich color schemes such as golds, deep greens, or burgundies.

The operation's design concept dictates the degree of practicality of the finish materials, and the materials used can influence the menu pricing of the restaurant. Fast-food or coffee shop facilities with high traffic volumes require hard flooring and table tops, vinyl upholstering and easily cleaned walls, while the fine dining restaurant with a higher check average is apt to have carpeting, more delicate wall coverings, upholstery fabrics, and table linens, which all require more maintenance and more frequent replacement. Health department regulations and flammability requirements must also be taken into consideration when selecting finishes. A mixture of textures and a variety of patterns and contrast will make the space more visually exciting.

Furnishings

The most suitable furnishings for foodservice use are those designed or built with commercial use in mind. Their construction is usually "beefed up" with stronger materials and additional fasteners or supports. Here again, the operation's concept (its style, design theme, mood, and price range) influences the type of furnishings selected—the kind of seating furniture, tables, serving carts, and specialty furnishings such as buffets or hutches.

The furnishings for a project constitute a fairly large percentage of the budget. Many restaurant owners and foodservice managers are too concerned with cost without adequate attention to quality. A small additional cost can often mean the difference between a durable line of furniture and items that will need to be replaced after a year or so. When poor quality furnishings are subjected to the heavy use that is normal in a food facility, they will deteriorate amazingly fast, leaving the restaurant owner faced with replacement costs. For example, a better quality furnishing might have initially cost $14,000.00 as against $11,000.00 for the inferior product. Replacing even a portion of it may amount to $7,000.00 or more, for a total investment of $18,000.00.

Accessories

Accessories are the final visual dressing. An awkward space or a very bland space can be brought to life with the innovative choice and placement of accessories. Selection of accessories should emphasize the essential elements of the concept and can often be a starting point for a theme. A healthy percentage of the preliminary budget should be allocated for accessories. Typical accessories may include:

- etched or stained glass
- metal sculptures or plaques
- ceramic vases
- plants and trees
- pictures and other artwork
- banners
- floral arrangements
- architectural elements
- decorative lighting

Lighting

A design approach in lighting any space, including restaurants, encompasses five principles:

1. space relationships
2. perspective
3. contour
4. special details of intrinsic beauty
5. imaginative and subtle qualities

These principles apply to the three general types of illumination found in a foodservice facility:

Overall general illumination: Even if a restaurant has the most intimate atmosphere, candlelight is just not enough! General lighting has to function for both day and night time activity, achieving a perfect balance. Otherwise "dark spots" and "dead spots" occur, creating misreading of space, which can produce disastrous results. For example, if a room is filled with dark mahogany wood tables, chairs, and woodwork, dark ceiling and deep-colored carpeting, sufficient general illumination is needed to see the materials and direct the traffic pattern.

Sparkle and excitement: A burst of color or light strategically placed can enhance an otherwise monotonous lighting plan. Once the general illumination level has been established, these bursts of light force certain areas to "pop out." This treatment is appropriate for reception areas, front windows, cathedral ceilings, partitions, special flooring or changes in flooring.

Specific focal points: The subtleties of light placement can direct the eye away from trouble spots and create an illusion of extra space. Special effect spots, uplights, indirect lights, and the like can accent a piece of sculpture, the table, the patrons, the bar, a stairway or stage, the menu, plants, or the food. Repetition of focal lighting creates a general illumination and can create a visual relationship between specific focal areas. The various methods of achieving these qualities within a restaurant space are listed below:

- *Silhouetting:* Emphasizes objects having interesting line and form
- *Grazing light:* Emphasizes textural qualities
- *Modeling:* Gives depth and three-dimensional character to objects
- *Highlighting:* Emphasizes special focal points
- *Shadow patterns:* Creates broken or solid patterns or introduces the excitement of movement
- *Tinted Light:* Emphasizes, exaggerates, or distorts

Special lighting effects can create mood and theme in a restaurant space. For example, to create high drama in the arched entry corridor of a large hotel, lighting consultants specified lavender and blue tinted spotlights to simulate moonlight and theatrical projectors to cast shadow palm leaves on the walls. Theatrical lighting is sometimes used in restaurant and bar settings. The technique is not as important as the attitude the lighting generates. Neon, lasers, and fiber optics have been around for years, although new design applications for them have recently been created. Colored neon combined with dimmed downlighting gives sparkling ambient light. A neon dimmer system is now available to aid in architectural impact. New baffles, gels, and filters correct or conceal harshness of glare and light. There are now twenty-two varieties of fluorescent light bulbs, including incandescent fluorescent. Low-voltage lighting, which has been developed in response to the need for energy efficiency, can be so sensitively attuned to the foodservice interior, the patron, and the food that it should be considered a significant element in creating the mood of the interior space. Knowing how to make people look and feel good is what really counts. Good lighting design flatters people as well as food and enriches the total dining experience.

Lighting options that are available to enhance the interior design include task lighting over table surfaces using:

- recessed downlights
- surface-mounted fixtures
- pendant lights (generally mounted 30 to 32 inches above the table top)

and lighting for areas surrounding table surfaces by means of:

- luminous ceilings
- luminous walls
- cornice or cove lighting for indirect effects
- wall sconces
- recessed luminaires
- ceiling-mounted luminaires
- pendants
- table lamps
- floor lamps or torcheres
- decorative chandeliers

LIGHT SOURCES AND COLOR

Color is one of the most difficult light source characteristics to evaluate. The colored appearance that a source gives an object or a space is subjective, strongly influenced by the viewer's experience, bias, color adaptation, color vision, and psychological characteristics as well as the setting of the object. When an object is moved into another setting, even under the same light source, the perception of it changes.

Because the terms used to describe the color characteristics of light sources have rather limited use outside scientific circles and are often highly technical, the planner may find it difficult to describe precisely what he or she wants, much less specify it. Color is therefore often disregarded or chosen on the basis of insufficient knowledge. The following general hints will help the planner in discussing the desired lighting atmosphere with the designer.

Where the proper appearance of people and food is concerned, there is a strong unconscious preference for white light sources that are rich in red light. These lamps impart a healthy sense of well-being to the skin and complexion. People prefer warm light in areas where low levels of illumination are involved, while cool light seems to be more acceptable for higher levels.

Where strong, saturated colors (such as deep claret, kelly green, or spectrum yellow) are prominent in the decor, people generally agree that warm colors appear to advance, while cool colors recede and help support a feeling of spaciousness. However, given the same colors, a competent designer can manipulate light so that cool colors advance and warm colors recede.

Changes in the color of light appear to alter the mood of a space. Through using different colors of light, a range of impressions can be achieved: warm sunlight and cool shadows, the pinks and purples of a sunset, the effect of sun through stained glass windows, the brilliance and glitter of moving carnival lights. People feel the psychological impact of light and color without realizing they do and without consciously associating color with moods.

Sound

Good quality sound is as important as the insulation of noises. The clientele can be soothed and entertained, or made jittery with sound-produced fatigue. Sound engineers are as highly specialized as interior architectural designers and architects. A sound specialist or sound production team may be brought in during the planning and layout stages. To design a sound background for dining, the specialist will need to know something about the restaurant's expected patrons—what they will wear, how old they will be, their cultural or ethnic heritage, their educational level, and their degree of sophistication. The following are some of the considerations a sound specialist will need to review with the owner:

- *"K" response* (measurement of sound frequencies heard by the human ear): An effective restaurant sound system should have a 15K response.
- *Proper speaker distribution:* Ceiling speakers can give the best possible sound distribution.
- *Speaker power:* A rule of thumb is always to have more speaker power than actually needed for the desired sound level.
- *Proper equalization:* Each space of a restaurant has different elements of sound absorption and/or reflectiveness. Each space is analyzed for excess sound and/or lack of sound. A calculation is then made for proper tuning of that space.
- *Programming:* It is wise to rent tapes from music suppliers to bring a continuous flow of new material into the food facility. The owner needs a license to operate copyright music in a commercial establishment. If the owner insists on taping his own material, a copyright attorney should be consulted (copyright infringement is a felony).

LOCATION OF SOUND

The bar: The length of time spent in the bar by patrons is affected by what they hear. A thorough understanding of design psychology is necessary for the perfect balance of mood, patron behavior, sociability, and type and quantity of beverages consumed.

The dining room: Volume should be monitored carefully and set conservatively low. Loud sound programming can upset patrons so much that they may never return to your restaurant.

Lounge and service areas: Kitchen, bathrooms, and other nonpublic areas should have appropriately measured background levels of sound.

The dance floor: The concentration of sound should be focused on the dance floor. Customers seated near the dance floor will not be bothered by a high sound level. However, those seated some distance away from the dance floor are probably seeking a quiet place away from the loud music.

The Menu

The menu aims at offering an attractive and tantalizing range of choices to the patrons of an eating establishment. A major element contributing to the restaurant's ambience, it is important advertising and must be conceived, designed, and executed with precision. Taking advantage of this creative opportunity, a skilled designer will be able to integrate the menu into the total interior design development of the restaurant. The menu can include graphic details relating to special features of the building, its history or location, famous people linked with it, or any other association that may help to define the restaurant's image. The design should take into account the firm's house colors, including interior design motifs and the style of lettering used.

While a menu should be in keeping with the style and design of the establishment, it must also appeal to customers, regardless of differences in background, interests, education, and so on. The menu instantly conveys a message to the customer, who may find it elegant, pretentious, "cute," stylish or boring, agreeable or irritating, straightforward or complicated, too big, too hard sell in tone, too syrupy, or difficult to read. It is up to the designer to promote the appropriate messages and avoid creating inadvertent impressions that work to the disadvantage of the restaurant.

It is impossible to overstate the importance of readability in creating a favorable impression on patrons. One of the most common customer complaints is a menu made illegible by a poorly chosen color combination, type style, or letter size. There are literally thousands of different typefaces, styles, weights, and sizes to choose from, and most are acceptable if selected with a concern for legibility. Stylishly hand-lettered or handwritten menus require brighter than average lighting and may still be difficult and time-consuming to read.

Choice of paper stock is critical. In handling

the menu, even if it is laminated, the weight and texture are consciously or subconsciously experienced as rough or smooth, grained, velvety, slick, or heavy. The material on which the menu is printed reflects on the quality of the food and the food facility.

Folding, punching, embossing, corner design, and cutting can be effectively used to call attention to "specials for the day." A menu design that offers a visual change of pace for your steady patron will increase sales. This is simple to do if coordinated with food preparation planning for the different seasons of the year. Summer and winter dishes—salads, entrées, even hamburgers—can be marketed creatively through changes in menu design.

A menu may serve as a souvenir and a valuable piece of advertising long after the meal is eaten. For a certain type of restaurant, an inexpensive mini-scale menu is printed so that interested customers can take home a copy. It is also a good idea to have a special menu printed for a particular occasion. A special form may be adopted for a convention group, meeting, or corporate party. The menu tends to go home with the patron and may be referred to again. Menus have been ingeniously printed on meat cleavers held by the waitperson, Chinese scrolls, blocks of lacquered tree cuts, and other novel items. By considering all the necessary elements, a menu can be created that pleases the patron, the designer, and the staff of the food facility.

EXAMPLES OF INTERIOR DESIGN FOR RESTAURANTS

Illustrated on the following pages are three types of restaurant setting. The elements considered in each example are the definition of space, the problem to be solved, basic requirements of the job, restrictions, and final design solutions.

EXAMPLE 1

Definition of Space Mall setting, 1,500 square feet; public seating area, serving hamburgers, sandwiches, and salads; nearby competition—fast food and deli.

Problem The original restaurant name, which was bland and hackneyed, needed to be changed to reflect a new environment. Poor space use and traffic flow problems were noted in the corner location of the bar, which deemphasized liquor service. The design and treatment of the existing bar created the appearance of an uninviting beer garden. The existing façade—a Tudor-style cottage, rough white stucco, with small residential type windows—was unassuming and no match for the competition.

Objective Restyle and update interior for the purpose of increasing business; change the name of the restaurant.

Requirement Redesign the space, rethink functions, play up the bar to increase bar business and subdivide the dining area.

Restrictions Very limited budget.

Solution Exterior façade was restructured into an open, airy café tearoom, in the Art Nouveau style. The former entry was changed from single to double doors, retaining the original recess. Windows were enlarged, creating an indoor-outdoor feeling, and an Art Nouveau graphic was conceived and etched on window surfaces to communicate style, mood, and theme. The rest of the exterior façade materials of bleached white oak were downplayed so the eye of passersby would be enticed to the interior by the use of color.

The bar became the main focal point, jutting out diagonally and thereby creating a divisional dining area. The bar creates a "see and be seen" space. The use of mirror panels psychologically accentuates an infinity reading. A deep, drop soffit defines the bar space and creates psychological intimacy. The use of moldings defines the traditional character and subdivides the flat ceiling surface.

The floor material change—from hexagonal

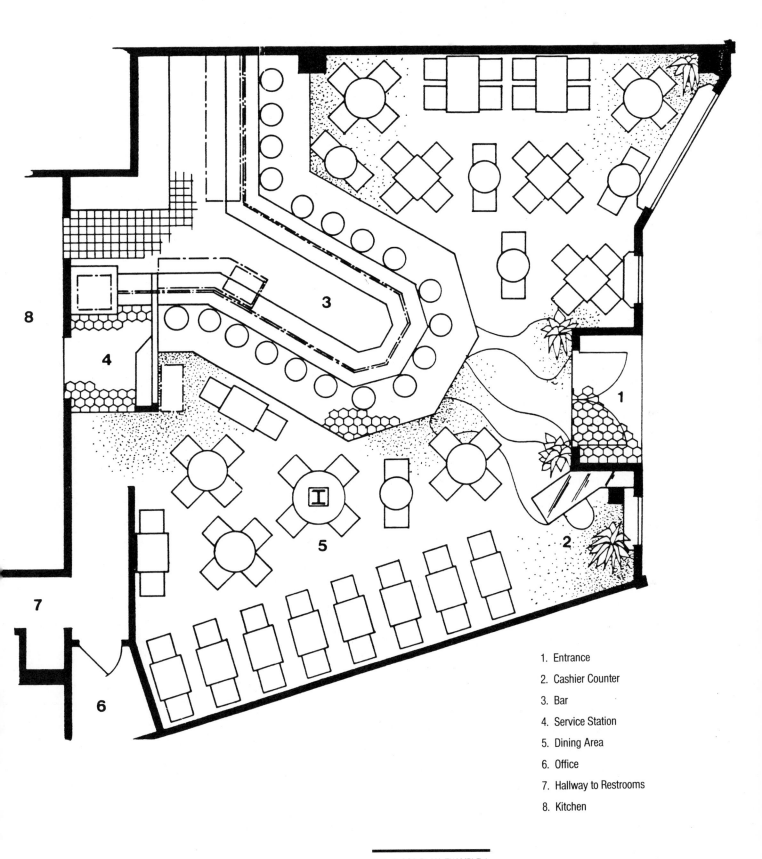

1. Entrance
2. Cashier Counter
3. Bar
4. Service Station
5. Dining Area
6. Office
7. Hallway to Restrooms
8. Kitchen

7-1. FLOOR PLAN, EXAMPLE 1.

7-2. INTERIOR VIEW, EXAMPLE 1.

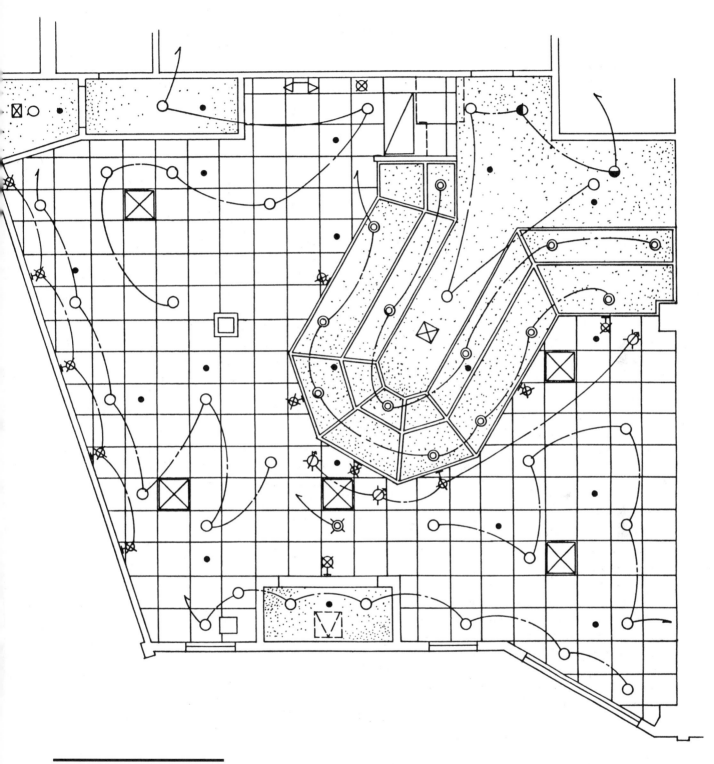

7-3. REFLECTED CEILING PLAN, EXAMPLE 1.

ceramic tile to carpet—articulates a division between the bar and dining area. Color carpet inlays at the front entryway provide interest. A textured anodized metal laminate for the bar surface with brass elbow and foot trim fills the need for sparkle, contrasting to other nonreflective matte materials. A sherbet color palette of plum, cantaloupe, and raspberry creates a "sunset" harmony and repetition. The use of 100 percent nylon textured fabrics, Scotchguarded, ensures durability.

Tables and chairs were chosen over booth design to cut cost and maximize the flexible use of space. Each dining area has a focal point of interest. One was handled with inexpensive framed art posters, with subject matter emphasizing the Art Nouveau period (1890-1910). Color prints were carefully selected to repeat the color theme, and a mix of metallic frames adds variety and contrast.

Two dining areas were created for alternate purposes. During less busy times patrons can be grouped in one area near the front windows to give the appearance of more activity. The other area can handle the additional patronage and also be arranged for larger groups of up to eighteen people. The second area offers a repeat view of the galleried wall through custom-designed mirrors. The design of the mirrors provides interest in itself. A custom-glazed color was used to meld with the color scheme.

EXAMPLE 2

Definition of Space Historical renovation of existing furrier warehouse, 7,800 square feet, in ethnic downtown restaurant district.

Problem Because of the incredible massiveness, in spatial volume, and hard textures (existing brick walls and wood support columns), the space needed softness and rescaling for human comfort.

Objective Completely renovate the interior, including plumbing, electrical, and HVAC. Develop a full-service restaurant, bar, and "psistaria" (open-front kitchen), to be the largest and most fashionable in the area.

Requirements Develop a large bar, two dining areas, and psistaria (front kitchen).

Restrictions Time deadlines.

Solutions The interior was designed to provide 278 seats, including an 88-foot bar. Some of the HVAC was housed in 426,587 square inches of latticework soffits. The latticework was placed directly over the booths to create an outdoor gazebo effect and visually rescale cubic space. The visual heights were articulated from high (the structural ceiling); medium (the niche boxes); to low (the underside of the lattice). To break the harsh geometry, 60,000 pieces of silk ivy were individually flameproofed and placed on the latticework. It looks as if it has been growing there naturally for many generations. Niche boxes were recessed into the latticework for decorative motifs, flowers, and lighting. A central hallway is the master divider between the bar/dining area and the front and back kitchens.

Dining room layout allows a patron to have a cozy private spot for lunch or dinner or for large groups to be together. The majority of seating is booth design, to give a visual solidness congruent with the structural interior. Booths also reduce the confusion of table and chair legs.

It was important to give the back dining area desirability, as many times back areas of restaurants appear neglected or out of the mainstream of activity. Utilizing two of the structural columns for backlighting, fabric-gathered capitals soften the strong structural geometry and push the color palette to an upper plane for balance. All aspects of barrier-free design were planned for (for example, ramps and bathrooms).

7-4. FLOOR PLAN, EXAMPLE 2.

1. Entrance
2. "Psistaria" (Open-Front Kitchen)
3. Ramp
4. Bar
5. Service Counters
6. Dining Areas
7. Stage
8. Restrooms
9. Downstairs/Offices & Storage
10. Kitchen

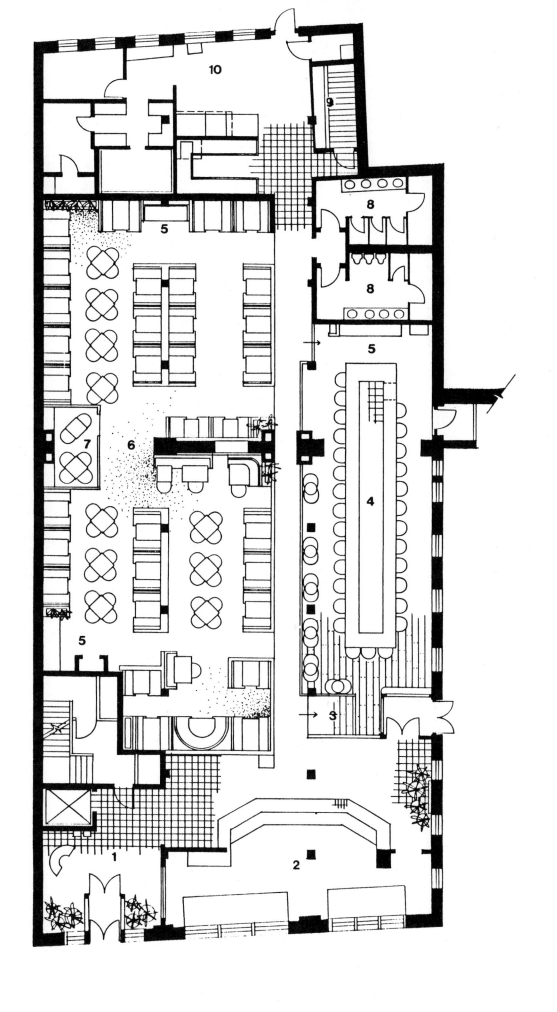

7–5. INTERIOR VIEW, EXAMPLE 2.

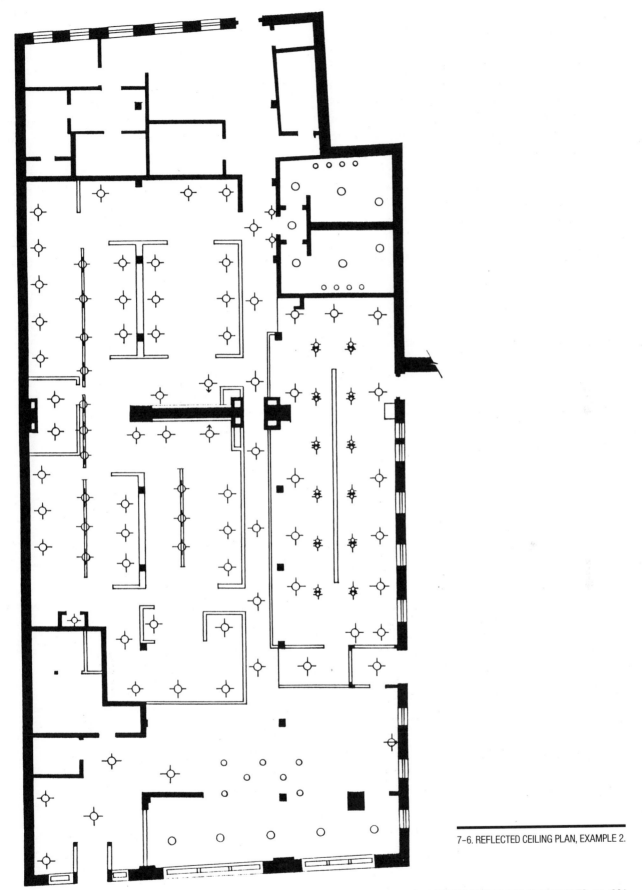

7-6. REFLECTED CEILING PLAN, EXAMPLE 2.

EXAMPLE 3

Definition of Space A mall setting, 980 square feet.

Problem An architect had been commissioned to design the space incorporating a mezzanine. Disastrous results included the following: a stairway in front of entry window panels; no handicap consideration; awkward steps into the dining area; too many useless walls taking away from dining space; ⅛-inch scale furniture template used on a ¼-inch drawing, giving the false illusion of ample headcount, creating major traffic flow problems, ruling out service stations, and so on.

Objective Develop a concept and functional design to correct these deficiencies.

Requirements Rework the existing space, maximizing seating, removing unnecessary mini walls, and salvaging the mezzanine level. Make one large step into lowered main level seating, line up structural supports for uniformity, maximize seating on both levels, and create an attractive contemporary Chinese ambience using a nonconventional color scheme. Redesign the façade to incorporate signage and to correspond with visual aesthetics of interior. Develop service stations on both levels as well as coffee and condiment setups for patrons.

Restrictions The existing spiral and straight stairway placement is to be maintained. The main floor dining must remain sunken in order to accommodate proper ceiling heights for the mezzanine.

Solutions By realignment of support walls and removal of unnecessary columns, seating arrangements were enlarged and made functional and space was saved. By placing steps to the dining area on the perpendicular rather than on an angle and spanning the entire length of the opening, traffic flow was better organized for patrons and employees.

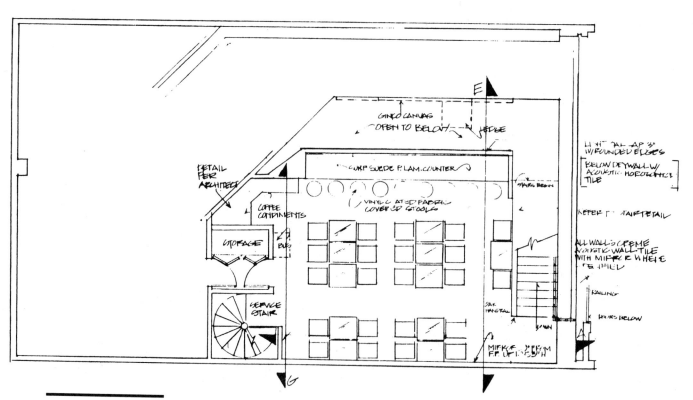

7-7. FLOOR PLAN, EXAMPLE 3.

The addition of banquettes along the side wall increased seating capacity and table flexibility. The use of a mirror wall enlarged the space visually.

The design of a counter centering around one side of an open three-panel archway allowed for single patrons to dine and enjoy an aesthetic view, yet have a sense of privacy from the cafeteria line. Japanese shoji screens on the front façade allowed for maximum visual lightness and openness on the interior.

Smoothing out the angled structural juts relieved the corner dirt maintenance problem and visual confusion, and directed traffic flow from the service line to dining areas.

A contemporary sophisticated design for a fast-food operation was created using black, white, blond oak, and camel color scheme mixed with a rough textural variety including ribbed acoustic wall covering, brass, glossy high-tech black plastic laminates, dark mirrors, and oak and caned cantilevered tubular chairs.

A custom graphic of a ginkgo tree on the second level wall opposite the mezzanine level gave the illusion of space and size beyond. A three-dimensional, architectural ornamental bracket holding a large Chinese vase, primitive in style, was applied in front of the ginkgo graphic. This is seen from the second level as well as the first and seems to be floating in space. There is no floor connected with this wall, so the relationship becomes ephemeral.

The darkness of color is balanced on the main level, utilizing all elements of line on the horizontal (including the front oak façade), and leads upstairs to a cream and white space, dramatizing the ginkgo graphic on the wall beyond.

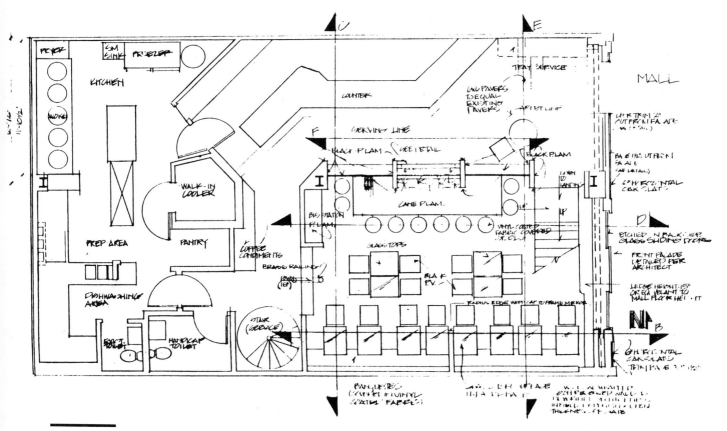

7-7. CONTINUED.

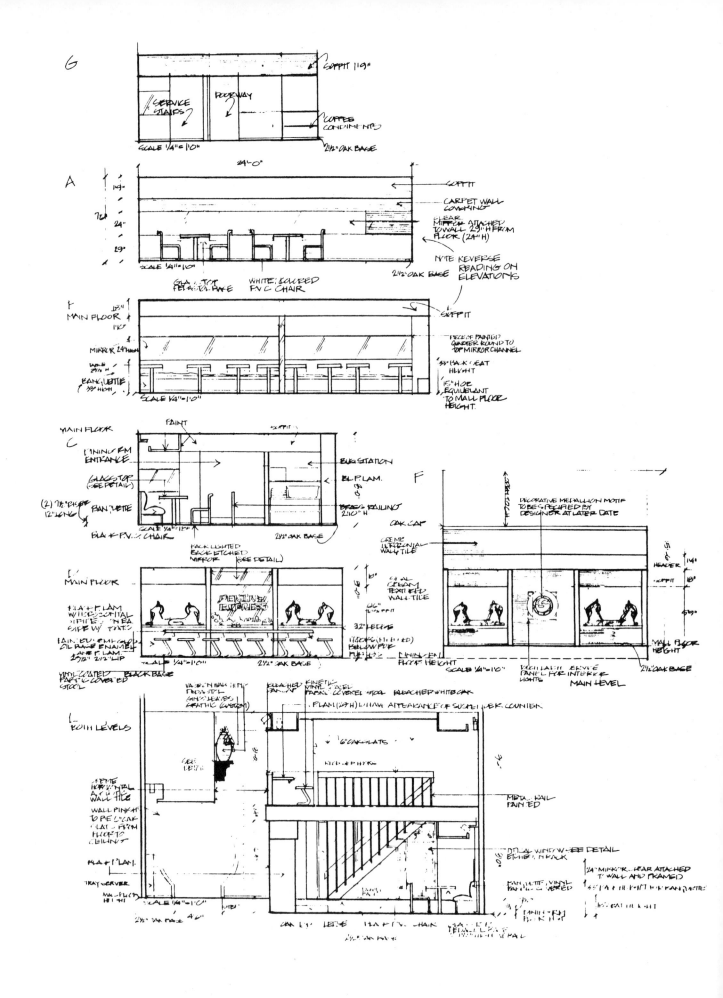

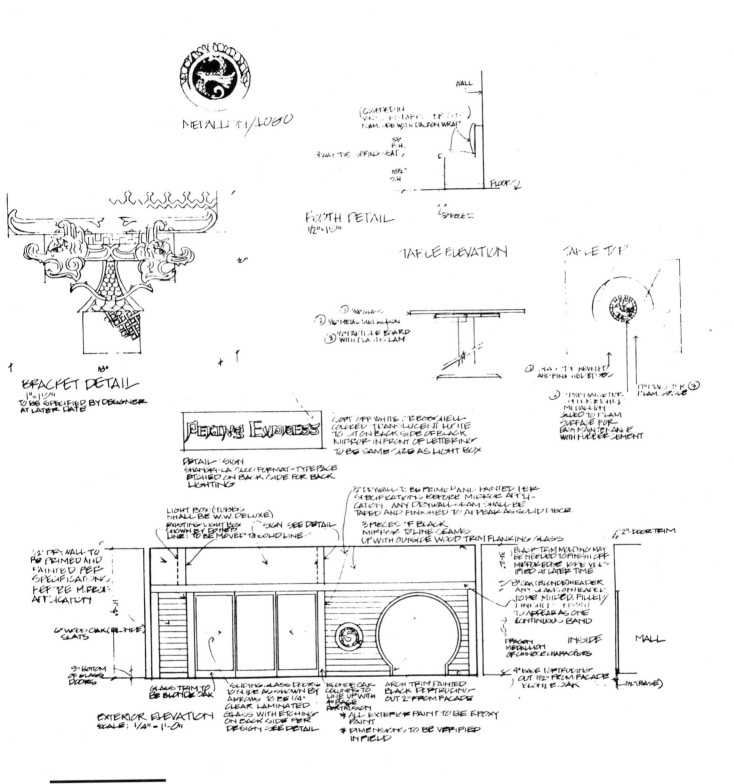

METAL LOGO

BRACKET DETAIL
1"=1½"
TO BE SPECIFIED BY DESIGNER AT LATER DATE

BOOTH DETAIL
½"=1'-0"

TABLE ELEVATION

TABLE TOP

DETAIL: SIGN
SHANGRI-LA 5000 FORMAT - TYPEFACE ETCHED ON BACK SIDE FOR BACK LIGHTING

EXTERIOR ELEVATION
SCALE: 1/4" = 1'-0"

7-8. ELEVATIONS, EXAMPLE 3.

7-9. INTERIOR/EXTERIOR DETAILS, EXAMPLE 3.

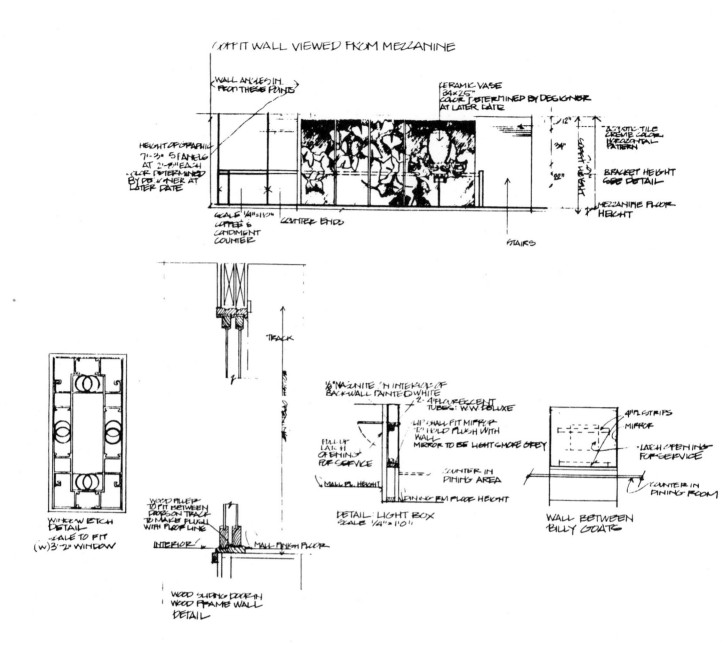

7-10. INTERIOR/EXTERIOR DETAILS, EXAMPLE 3.

SUMMARY

Foodservice facilities and theaters have much in common. Besides a food operation's function as a place to eat, a dining room or bar can be looked on as a showcase for its patrons. This philosophy allows the designer to orchestrate a full symphony of dramatic effects, which can be achieved in infinitely diverse ways. Historical recall can be vividly expressed in period furnishings creating a French Art Nouveau tearoom, a nineteenth-century Viennese cafe, an old English cottage-style pub, an Art Deco oceanliner, or a Tibetan mountaintop retreat. Style and effect can range from the most romantic to urbane, from real to surreal, traditional to modern, contemporary, futuristic, interpretative, or freewheeling combinations of any of these approaches.

Designer, kitchen consultant, architect, and owner should meet in the early planning stages to develop a concept based on the owner's needs and desires. The restaurant represents an investment and a livelihood for the owner, as well as a reflection of personal tastes and style. The task of the interior designer is to create an environment that not only expresses the owner's character but enhances the attractiveness and profitability of the operation as a whole.

APPENDIX 1

TYPICAL FOODSERVICE FACILITY DESIGNS

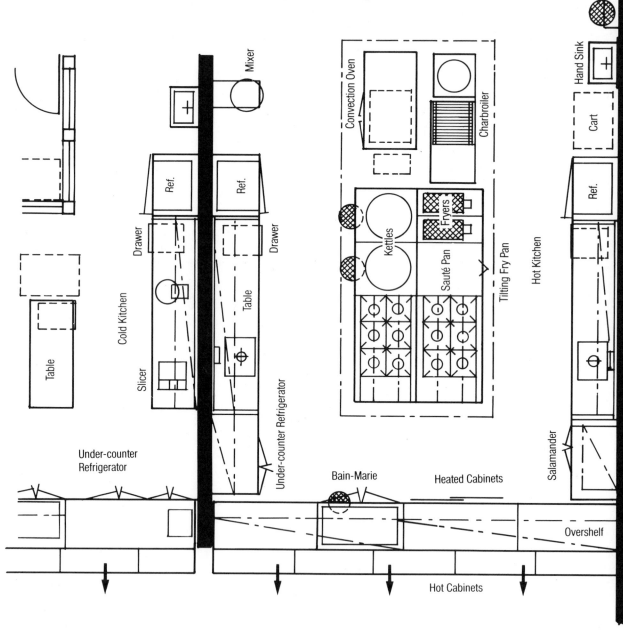

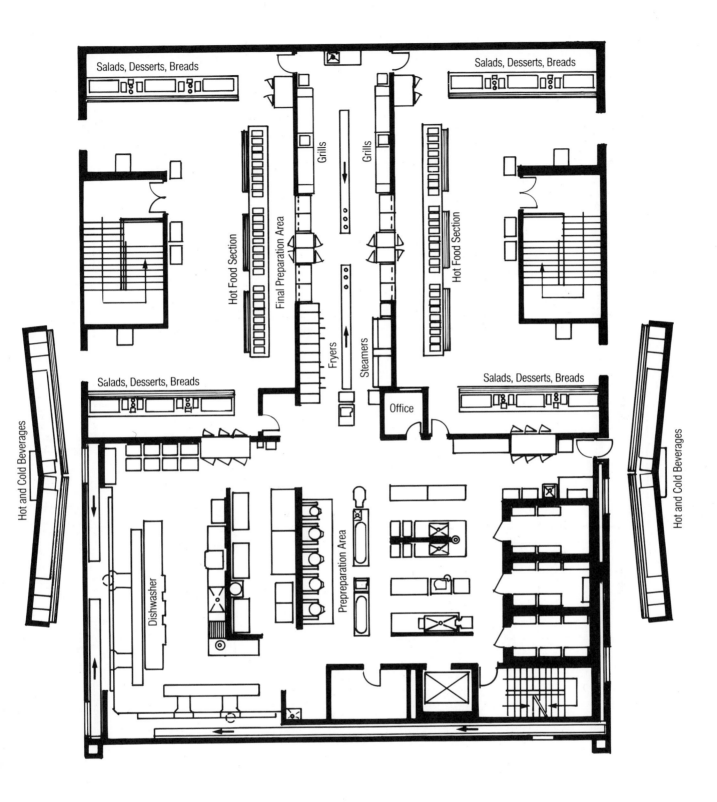

Salads, Desserts, Breads

Salads, Desserts, Breads

Grills

Grills

Hot Food Section

Final Preparation Area

Hot Food Section

Fryers

Steamers

Office

Salads, Desserts, Breads

Salads, Desserts, Breads

Hot and Cold Beverages

Hot and Cold Beverages

Dishwasher

Prepreparation Area

APP. 1
_____
LAYOUT OF TYPICAL EUROPEAN KITCHEN.

APP. 2
_____
DINING HALL SERVING 6,000 MEALS PER DAY (UNIVERSITY OF TENNESSEE).

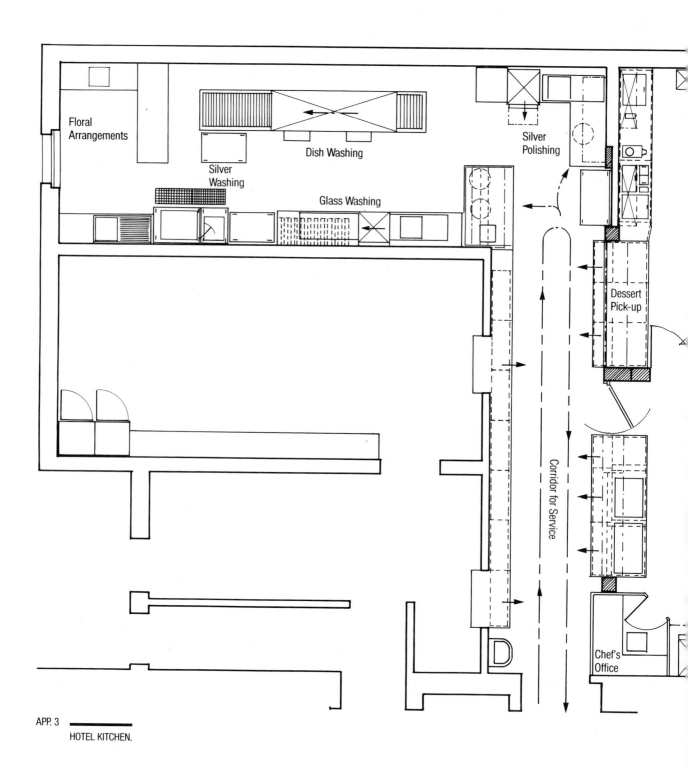

Floral
Arrangements

Dish Washing

Silver
Washing

Glass Washing

Silver
Polishing

Dessert
Pick-up

Corridor for Service

Chef's
Office

APP. 3

HOTEL KITCHEN.

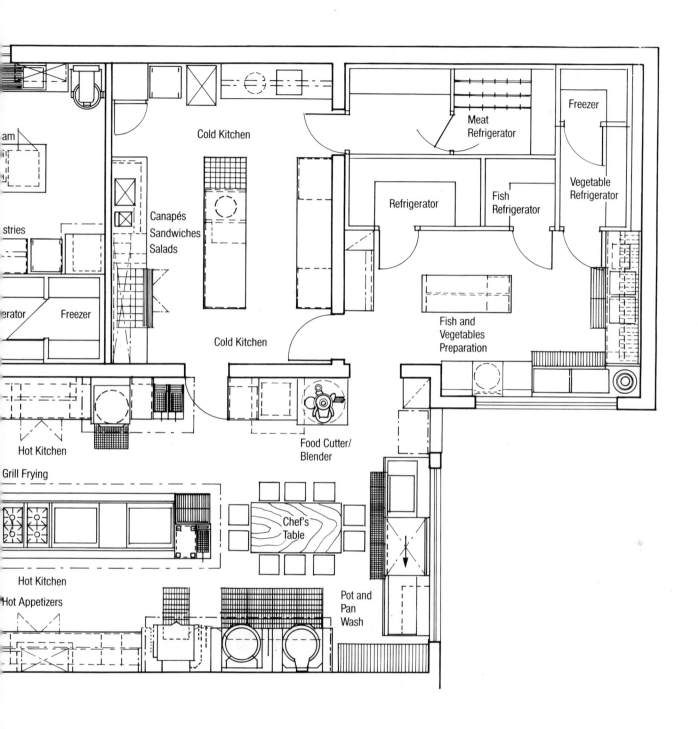

Cold Kitchen

Meat
Refrigerator

Freezer

Canapés
Sandwiches
Salads

Refrigerator

Fish
Refrigerator

Vegetable
Refrigerator

Cold Kitchen

Fish and
Vegetables
Preparation

Food Cutter/
Blender

Hot Kitchen

Grill Frying

Chef's
Table

Pot and
Pan
Wash

Hot Kitchen

Hot Appetizers

stries

erator

Freezer

am

APPENDIX 2

COMMON FOODSERVICE FACILITY DESIGN SYMBOLS

PLUMBING

Water rough-in ●

Water rough-in and connection ●○

Waste-water rough-in ○

Condensate drain or indirect waste ○--- IW

Waste-water rough-in and connection ○-○W

Gas-supply rough-in ✪

Gas-supply rough-in and connection ✪-○

Steam supply ■

Steam supply stub-out ▶

Steam return ◪

Steam return stub-out ▷

Floor sink—open ⬚ FS

Floor sink—angle grate ▤

Floor sink—funnel grate ▤

Floor drain ⬚ FD

Hose bib ⊤ HB

Hose rack ▭○ HB

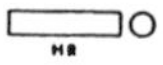

Hot-water tank ○ HWT

Lavatories: wall, corner ◗ L,1 L,2 etc. ▭ L,1 L,2 etc.

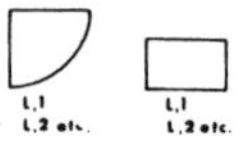

Grease trap ▭ GT

Can washer ○ CW

Clean out ⚇ CO

Dishwasher ▭ DW

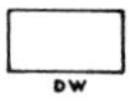

Sink ▭ S-1 S-2 etc.

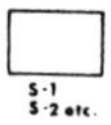

Water Heater ○ WH

PIPING

Above-grade soil or waste ————

Below-grade soil or waste — — —

Cold water —·——·—

Hot water —··——·—

Gas ——·——

ABBREVIATIONS

HW	Hot water
HSW	Hot soft water
CW	Cold water
PRV	Pressure reducer valve
AFF	Above finished floor
KEC	Kitchen equipment contractor
PC	Plumbing contractor
EC	Electrical contractor
C&P	Cord and plug
EF	Exhaust fan
AC	Air conditioning
FD	Floor drain
FS	Floor sink
D.S.	Dimmer switch
LV	Low voltage
V.A.	Vinyl asbestos tile
V.B.	4-inch vinyl base—cove type
E.C.	Exposed construction
E. PAINT	Epoxy paint

A.T.	Acoustical tile
C.T.	Ceramic tile (base to be coved)
P.L.	Plastic laminate
Q.T.[1]	6×6 quarry tile
Q.T.B.	6-inch coved bull-nose quarry-tile base
G.C.B.	Glazed concrete block
Q.T.[2]	Six-sided quarry
M.P.	Metal pan-ceiling system
ML	Marlite fiberglass
S.P.	Stucco paint on drywall
E.M.U.	Exposed masonry units
C.B.	Exposed concrete block
PT.	Paint
GL. BR.	Glazed brick base, recess ½-inch
PART. BD.	Particleboard

ELECTRIC SYMBOLS

Conduit stub flush couple with curb   ▲

Flex tubing feeder (36-inch minimum exposed)   ℧

Waterproof conduit stub   ●

Junction box, waterproof with final connection to equipment (36-inch minimum seal tight flex.)   ⓙwp

Junction box at ceiling   ⓙ

Junction box at wall   ⊸ⓙ

Junction box above floor   ℘

Junction box with final connection to equipment (36-inch minimum exposed)   ⟳

Junction box installed in equipment   ⟲

Single convenience outlet (wattage as shown)   ⊖

Duplex convenience outlet (wattage as shown)   ⊖

Single convenience outlet w/switch   ⊖⌐

Duplex convenience outlet (installed in equipment)   ⊖

Single purpose power outlet, 1 phase   ◕

Single purpose power outlet, 1 phase (installed in equipment)   ⊙

Single purpose power outlet, 3 phase   ⊗

Single purpose power outlet, 3 phase (installed in equipment)   ⊗

Floor outlet, flush or pedestal   ⊘

Floor junction box   ⊙

Recessed convenience outlet, single (wattage as shown)   ⊖.

120V Motor   ●

208-204 V 1-phase motor   ○

208-204 V 3-phase motor   ◕

Clock outlet   ©

Ground connection   ⟟

Buzzer   ⊏⟍

Infrared warmer   ▨

Heat lamp   ⊘

Incandescent light (number when scheduled)   ⊕

Pull box (installed in equipment)   ⊏⊐

Switch   s

3-way switch   s₃

4-way switch   s₄

Switch with neon pilot   sₚ

Vaporproof switch   sᵥₚ

Automatic door switch   s_D

Double-pole waterproof switch   s₂wₚ

Pull switch   Ⓟ

Push button switch   ⊡

LIGHTING

Incandescent strip (number when scheduled)   ⊶⊕⊷

Fluorescent fixture (number when scheduled)   ⊏⊙⊐

Fluorescent strip light (number when scheduled)   ⊶⊙⊷

Wall washer light (number when scheduled)   ⊙▷

Neon tubing   ---

Exit light   ⊗

Transformer   ⊞

Lighting panel   ⊏⊐

Power panel   ▧

REFRIGERATION

Thermostat   ⊶Ⓣ

High-temperature alarm relay with red light and bell   ⊟⊟

Safety alarm bell with red light

Vaporproof light, 100 watts

Evaporator (blower coil) with fan

Reprinted from *News and Views*, Food Equipment
Distributors Association, January, 1977.

Liquid line solenoid

Conduit run for refrigerant, CO_2, gas,
and carbonation lines

Pull box

SAMPLE
DOCUMENTS

EXHIBIT A

SAMPLE
CONSULTANT PROPOSAL AND COVER LETTER TO THE
CONSULTANT/CLIENT AGREEMENT

(Note: Because of potential legal complexities which could involve this document, consultation with an attorney is suggested.)

Date

Addressee

_____

_____

_____

Re: Project Name:
      Location:
      Proposal No.:

Dear:

Introductory Paragraph

1.   Pleased about the opportunity to submit a proposal for

     (services) for (project) located at _____ .

2.   Brief description of project

Statement of Objectives

A brief statement of the work to be done on the project by the consultant.

Recommendation of Specific Services (statement of scope of services pertinent to this project or requested by client)

Reference should be made to Exhibit B

Example: It is our opinion, based on your project objectives, that a phased proposal is the most prudent approach to accomplishing your goals. The phases are listed in the approximate chronological order they would be accomplished with a fee for each phase so that you can evaluate the overall project.

 FCSI DOCUMENT PCL-1. Consultant Proposal and Cover Letter to the Consultant/Client Agreement.
© 1987 Foodservice Consultants Society International.

		Not to Exceed
Phase I	- Programming and Preliminary Planning	$ _____
Phase II	- Design Development & Engineering	$ _____
Phase III	- Preparation of Bid Documents	$ _____
Phase IV	- Coordination and Approval of Shop Drawings	$ _____
Phase V	- Final Inspection and Training	$ _____
	TOTAL FEE	$ _____

This Proposal and cover letter defines each of the phases in detail; it is upon the amount of work included in this detail that the fee has been computed. In addition to the fees set forth above, we will invoice for all reimbursable expenses incurred in the interest of the project as set forth in the Consultant/Client Agreement (Exhibit B) to which this proposal has been attached and made reference.

Additional Services Option that can be provided by the Consultant (to be included unless <u>specifically</u> asked to omit)

Closing Paragraph (assures follow-up)

1. Schedule follow-up or next step or arrange to call client at a certain time.

2. Tickler follow-up for a certain date to find out what is happening to proposal.

3. Thank client for consideration of our firm.

Respectfully submitted

Writer's Name
Title

Initials:initials

- -
Attached to this proposal and letter is:

Exhibit B: Consultant/Client Agreement

 FCSI DOCUMENT PCL-1. Consultant Proposal and Cover Letter to the Consultant/Client Agreement.
© 1987 Foodservice Consultants Society International.

EXHIBIT B

SAMPLE
CONSULTANT/CLIENT AGREEMENT

(Note: Because of potential legal complexities which could involve this document, consultation with an attorney is suggested.)

CONSULTANT: (name and address of consultant)

hereinafter called the CONSULTANT

CLIENT: (name and address of the client)
(name of primary contact person, as designated by the client)

hereinafter called the CLIENT

PROJECT: (official name of project)

hereinafter called PROJECT.

REFERENCE DOCUMENTS:

Exhibit A.   Consultant Proposal and Cover Letter attached to the Consultant/Client Agreement

Exhibit B.   Consultant/Client Agreement

WHEREAS, the CLIENT desires, in connection therewith, to engage the Consultant and the Consultant desires to be retained by the CLIENT to perform consulting services as described in Exhibit A all upon the terms and subject to the conditions hereinafter stated;

NOW, THEREFORE, in consideration of the covenants herein contained, the parties agree as follows:

1.   AGREEMENT

The Consultant agrees to perform the basic services hereinafter set forth. Pursuant to the payment schedule, the CLIENT agrees to pay the Consultant for their services the fees as set forth in Exhibit A herein made a part of this Agreement.

2.   THE CONSULTANT'S SERVICES

The Consultant's basic services shall include all those services as set forth in Exhibit A.

FCSI DOCUMENT CCA-1. Consultant/Client Agreement.
© 1987 Foodservice Consultants Society International.

3. REIMBURSABLE EXPENSES

The CLIENT will reimburse monthly to the Consultant for all actual expenditures made in the interest of the PROJECT for the incidental expenses apart from the fee set forth in Exhibit A, including:

- expense of transportation
- traveling in connection with the PROJECT at actual cost for automobile rental and public transportation and the current U.S. Government approved allowance for automobile travel
- long distance telephone calls, telegrams, postage, delivery charges
- reproduction of drawings, specifications, programs, reports, and manuals
- other normal disbursements and obligations incurred on the CLIENT's account. The Consultant will request, in advance, the CLIENT's authorization and approval for any unusual or extraordinary expense

4. PAYMENT SCHEDULE OF FEES

The CLIENT will compensate the Consultant for services performed in accordance with the schedule set forth in Exhibit A. Invoices are due and payable upon presentation monthly and a late charge of _____% will be added to all balances unpaid _____ days after date of invoice and each month thereafter cumulatively. In addition, should it become necessary that an unpaid invoice be referred to our attorneys for collection, the CLIENT agrees to pay their reasonable fee for such work as well as any costs of suit which may be incurred.

Fee Retainer: The CLIENT shall pay to the Consultant upon execution of this Agreement a retainer in an amount equal to _____% of the Fee, either estimated or actual, unless specified otherwise in Exhibit A. Said retainer shall be held by the Consultant until the completion of the PROJECT, at which time it will be applied against the final invoice on the PROJECT.

(**Note:** Fees may be paid in several ways including, but not necessarily limited to, the following. CONSULTANT/CLIENT terms to determine which applies.)

a. Hourly Fee Basis: Invoices will be issued monthly for the total number of hours expended during the month in the interest of the PROJECT in accordance with the Hourly Rate Schedule that is a part of this Agreement. The current rate schedule will remain in effect for this Contract for _____ years after the date of this Agreement. After _____ years the then current rate schedule will be reviewed with the Client and will become the effective rate schedule.

b. Fixed Fee Basis: Invoices will be issued monthly in accordance with the schedule set forth in Exhibit A.

5. DEFERRAL OR TERMINATION

This Agreement may be terminated by either party upon _____ days written notice should the other party fail substantially to perform in accordance with its terms through no fault of the other.

In the event the PROJECT is deferred for a period of more than _____ months during any stage prior to completion of the Scope of Work outlined in Exhibit A or there is more than one delay or deferral of _____ months or more each during any stage prior to completion of the Scope of Work outlined in Exhibit A or the PROJECT is terminated or the CLIENT ceases to require services for any reason beyond the Consultant's control, the CLIENT agrees to pay the Consultant within _____ days, in addition to any amount which may have been paid pursuant to the terms of this Agreement the following:

a. all fees which may be payable to the Consultant as previously identified herein but are unpaid at the date the CLIENT notifies the Consultant in writing of such deferral or termination (the date of such notification being hereinafter referred to as the "deferral date" or the "termination date" — whichever shall apply);

b. all expenses due to the Consultant as previously identified herein for which the Consultant has not been reimbursed as at the|deferral or termination date;

c. all amounts representing compensation for extra services as identified hereinafter which have not been paid as at the deferral or termination date; or

---

d. in the case of deferral, all work necessary to reactivate the PROJECT and to make adjustments in design, equipment selection drawings, and all other data made necessary or desirable due to the deferral; in addition, the Consultant shall be compensated on the basis of the rate schedule in use at the time of the resumption of work, and all other fees shall be adjusted to suit the revised rate schedule and any other changes.

6. OWNERSHIP OF DOCUMENTS

Drawings, specifications, reports, manuals, and programs as instruments of service are the property of the Consultant whether the PROJECT for which they are made be executed or not and are not to be used on other projects except by agreement in writing with the Consultant.

(**Note:** The CLIENT and the CONSULTANT are free to agree to the above, or that the documents may become the property of the CLIENT. This is suggested language favoring the CONSULTANT.)

7. SUCCESSORS AND ASSIGNS

The CLIENT and the Consultant each binds himself, his partners, successors, assigns, and legal representatives to the other party to this Agreement and to the partners, successors, assigns, and legal representatives of such other party in respect to all covenants of this Agreement. Neither the CLIENT nor the Consultant shall assign, sublet, or transfer his interest in the agreement without the written consent of the other.

8. EXTRA SERVICES

If the Consultant is caused extra services or other expense due to change orders or revisions to documents previously approved by the CLIENT, the Consultant shall be paid for such extra expense or services in accordance with paragraph 4.a Hourly Fee Basis. Such extras or changes shall be requested or confirmed in writing.

For the purpose of carrying out any special project requested by the CLIENT, the Consultant agrees to prepare a written proposal covering the scope of the special project, which proposal shall be accepted or rejected in writing by the Client.

9. PROFESSIONAL RECOGNITION

The CLIENT agrees to acknowledge the professional services provided by the Consultant in detailed press releases, magazine articles, and the like where reference is made to the planning, design, or management consulting services performed by the Consultant relative to the Hospitality Facilities for the PROJECT.

10. INDEMNIFICATION

It is further agreed by the CLIENT that, except for breach of the terms of this Agreement by the Consultant, and for losses and damages due to the gross negligence or intentional torts of the Consultant, its officers, agents, and employees, the CLIENT shall defend, indemnify against, and save harmless the Consultant, its officers, agents, and employees from all losses, expenses, liabilities, demands, suits, and other actions of every nature and description (including attorneys' fees and any liability imposed by an applicable law, ordinance, code, rule, or regulation) to which any of the aforesaid may be subjected by reason of any act or omission of the Consultant or officers, agents employees, licensees, or invitees of the Consultant, where such loss, expense, liability, demand, suit, or other detriment directly or indirectly arises out of or in connection with the Consultant or its successors' and assigns' activities on the premises of CLIENT or with this proposed Agreement.

(**Note:** The above suggested language favors the Consultant, and may have to be modified under certain contractual conditions imposed by the CLIENT in order to obtain the project.)

11. Where the Consultant is requested by the Client to engage the services of other Subconsultant(s) in connection with the Project, or to select Subconsultant(s) to render services to the CLIENT, the Consultant shall obtain the Client's written approval of the selected Subconsultant(s). The Consultant shall not be responsible to the Client or other persons for any losses, damage, or other expenses incurred as a result of the errors, omissions, or negligent acts of the selected Subconsultant(s).

FCSI DOCUMENT CCA-1. Consultant/Client Agreement.
© 1987 Foodservice Consultants Society International.

12. This contract, by agreement of the parties, has been made in _____ (City, County, State) _____ and the laws of the State of _____ (State) _____ shall govern this contract. In any action by either party to enforce the terms of this agreement, at the option of _____ (Consultant firm) _____ the venue thereof shall be in _____ (City, County, State named above) _____ .

13. This Agreement shall not be binding upon either party hereto until the agreement is signed by the CLIENT and returned to and accepted by the Consultant within _____ days of date of proposal. Such acceptance by the Consultant shall be evidenced by the signature of the Consultant on this agreement.

IN WITNESS WHEREOF the parties hereto have made and executed this Agreement, the day and year indicated in the acceptance area below.

ATTEST   CLIENT: _____

_____

                                      By: _____

Date: _____

                                      Title: _____   Date: _____

- -

ACCEPTED AT (Location)   (Name of Consulting Firm)

ATTEST: _____

                                      By: _____

Date: _____

                                      Title: _____   Date: _____

GLOSSARY

Au Gratin Oven. Enclosure with hinged door mounted on top of a broiler. Also called finishing oven.

Bain Marie. Sinklike depression in a table top with a water bath heated by steam, gas, or electricity into which containers of food are placed to keep foods heated. Often used by chefs as a double boiler. Also called sandwich unit when used for refrigerated foods in sandwich preparation.

Bake Oven. *See* Oven.

Baker's Stove. *See* Pot Stove.

Baker's Table. Table whose top has 4- to 6-inch-high curbing along the rear and sides to minimize spillage of flour onto floor during preparation. Often furnished with mobile or tilt-out ingredient bins under the top.

Banquet Cart. Insulated or noninsulated mobile cabinet with a series of interior shelves and/or racks to hold plates and/or platters of food. Usually equipped with an electric heating unit or refrigeration device.

Barbecue Grill. A live charcoal or gas-fired open-hearth horizontal grill having spits set across the top of the unit with rotisserie-type drive mechanism along the front working side.

Barbecue Machine. *See* Rotisserie.

Bar Workboard. Equipment below the top of a bar containing sinks, drainboards, cocktail mix stations, ice storage chests, beverage coolers, glass washers, etc. Also called sink workboard.

Beef Cart. Mobile unit, with or without bottled gas, alcohol, or electric heating unit. Used for display and slicing of roast beef in the dining room.

Beer Cooler. Cooler in which kegs, cans, or bottles of beer are refrigerated. The direct-draw cooler is a low-counter type with self-contained tapping equipment and dispensing head(s).

Beer Dispenser or **Tapping Cabinet.** Refrigerated or ice-cooled insulated cabinet with beer-, or soda-, and/or water-dispensing heads, drainer plate, and pan recessed flush with the bar top and a drain trough under. Usually built into a liquor bar top, between workboards.

Beer System. A method for tapping beer from remotely located refrigerated kegs and transporting it through pressurized, refrigerated, and insulated lines to dispensing heads located at one or more stations in the bar and/or backbar.

Beverage Carrier. *See* Carrier.

Bin. Semienclosed rectangular or round container, open on top, with or without lift-off, sliding, or hinged cover. Floor-type bins are usually mobile, of height to roll under a table top. Bins under a baker's table may be mobile or built in to tilt out. An ingredient bin may be used for flour, sugar, salt, beans, dry peas, etc. A vegetable storage bin has a perforated or screened body. An ice storage bin is fully enclosed and insulated with hinged or sliding insulated door(s) at the front; it is normally stationary and set under an ice-making machine (head). A silverware (flatware) or cutlery bin is small and mounted in a holder set on or under counter top with other bins.

Blender. Vertical mixing machine with removable cup or jar, having mixing and stirring blades in the bottom and mounted on a base with a drive motor. Normally set on a table or counter top. Used in preparing special diets in hospitals, mixing cocktails in bars, as well as to whip or purée food generally at home.

Blower-Dryer. Motor-driven attachment with a blower and electric- or steam-heated coil, mounted on top of a dishwasher for quick drying of ware at the end of the final rinse cycle.

Blower (Evaporator) Coil. *See* Unit Cooler.

Board. A rectangular or round board, small for easy handling, set on a hard surface or counter top, to prevent dulling of the knife blade when cutting food. It can be made of laminated or solid hard rock maple or of rubber or thermal plastic material. Usually furnished with a handle or grip. Sandwich and steam table boards are rectangular and narrow; they are mounted on a sandwich unit or the corresponding section of a counter top. Also called workboard in preparation areas of a kitchen.

Boil-In-Bag. A clear plastic waterproof pouch containing foods that are heated by immersing the package in boiling water.

Bone Saw. *See* Meat and Bone Saw.

Booster. *See* Hot-Water Booster.

Bottle Breaker. Motor-driven device with revolving, horizontal, open-top pan in which empty glass bottles are safely flogged with steel bars.

Bottle Chute. Flexible cylindrical tubing to convey empty bottles from bar to bottle storage bin or breaking or crushing device. Load end is usually located at the cocktail mix station.

Bottle Crusher. Motor-driven device with rollers or reciprocating plate(s) to crush bottles, plastic containers, and cans. The unit is mounted on a stand with a waste receptacle beneath to receive crushed and broken articles. The loading chute is provided with a spring-loaded or gravity-hinged door.

Bottle Disposer. System consisting of bottle chute and storage bin, bottle breaker, or bottle crusher.

Bottle Trough. Trough suspended along the front of a bar workboard, usually at the cocktail mix station, to hold various bottles of liquor or mixer used often. Also called speed rail.

Bowl. A round-bottomed container open at top for mixing food. The salad bowl is a shallow type for mixing and displaying leafy vegetables. A coffee bowl is the lower of a two-piece, siphon-type coffee maker, used as a decanter.

Braising Pan, Tilting. *See* Fry Pan, Tilting.

Breading Machine. Horizontal rotating cylinder set on a base with a drive motor and filled with breading mix. Food is placed in one end, carried through the cylinder by an internally mounted auger, and discharged at the other end. Food is tumbled in breading mix.

Bread Molder. Machine with a series of rollers and conveyor belts to shape a ball of dough to pan bread, hearth bread, or long rolls of varied length.

Bread Slicer. (1) Motor-driven machine with a multiple set of reciprocating knives in a single frame through which bread is pushed, or vice versa. (2) Motor-driven or hand-operated machine with a single revolving knife to slice single slices while a bread loaf is moved along in a chute by a gear driven plate. Slice thickness may vary.

Breath Guard. *See* Display Case.

Briquette. One of the coal-size pieces of permanent refrac-

tory material used in open-hearth gas-fired grills to provide radiant broiling heat.

Broiler, Backshelf. Broiler with gas-heated ceramic radiants or electric heating elements, having an adjustable sliding grill. The unit is normally mounted on a panel and brackets above the rear of the range. Also called salamander broiler.

Broiler, Charcoal. Horizontal-type unit with removable bottom pan containing glowing charcoals to radiate high heat into the bottom of foods set on a grill above. Mounted on stand or enclosed cabinet or masonry base.

Broiler, Char or Open-Hearth. (1) Horizontal-type unit with gas-heated briquettes under a grill at the top. (2) Horizontal-type unit with nonglowing electric strip heaters at the top. May also be equipped with an adjustable electric grill above the top grill to broil both sides at once.

Broiler, Conveyor. (1) Horizontal-type unit with openings at both ends, using a motor-driven grill-type conveyor to transport food between or under gas-fired ceramics or electric heaters. (2) Horizontal-type unit, open at both ends, using a motor-driven, revolving, heated griddle to transport food under gas-fired ceramics or electric heaters.

Broiler-Griddle, Combination. (1) Unit with front opening with griddle plate set into top, equipped with gas-heated radiants under the griddle. Radiants heat food and griddle simultaneously. (2) Unit with front-opening door(s) having gas-heated radiants at the top of the cavity and food placed on a sliding or swinging type griddle plate set below.

Broiler, Pop-Up. Enclosed horizontal-type unit with a slotted opening in the top and gas-heated radiants on both sides of the cavity. Food is placed in an elevating mechanism and broiled on both sides at the same time. Similar to a pop-up toaster.

Broiler, Pork and Spare Rib, Chinese. Counter- or stand-mounted narrow-depth broiler with two or three decks, each having gas burners and radiants, for cooking pork slices and spare ribs in metal platters.

Broiler, Upright. Vertical-type unit with an opening at the front and gas-heated radiant ceramics or electric heating elements at the top of the cavity. Food is placed on a sliding adjustable grill set under the radiants. May be mounted on counter top, oven or cabinet base, or stand. Often aligns with ranges. May be equipped with removable charcoal pan.

Buffet Unit. One or more mobile or stationary counters having flat surfaces, with cold pans or heated wells at the top, on which chafing dishes, canapé trays, or other food displays can be placed for self service.

Bun Divider. *See* Roll Divider.

Butcher Block. Rectangular or round shape—6, 10, 14, or 16 inches thick—consisting of hard rock maple strips, kiln dried, hydraulically pressed together, glued, and steel-doweled through. Work surface of block is smoothed surface of ends of strips. Block mounted on open-type wood or steel legs.

Butter Chip Dispenser. Enclosed insulated unit with mechanical refrigeration or ice to hold tiers of butter pats placed on chips and dispensed one at a time. Normally set on a counter top. Also called butter chip cooler.

Cafeteria Counter, Serving Counter. In a cafeteria, top which is usually provided with recessed cold pans, recessed pans for hot foods section, display and protector cases, and drain troughs for beverages; set on legs or masonry base with enclosure panels, semi- or fully enclosed cabinets with refrigeration or warming units beneath; all as required to accommodate foods to be served. Unit may be equipped with tray slide.

Can Crusher. Motor-driven machine with rollers or reciprocating plates or arms to crush cans and break bottles. Unit mounts on stand with space under for refuse receptable to receive crushed articles. Also called can and bottle crusher.

Can Opener. (1) Hand-operated or motor-driven device fastened to the top of a table, wall, cabinet, etc., to open individual cans. (2) Portable motor-driven device capable of opening cans while still in case.

Can Washer. (1) Enclosed cabinet with spray heads for washing the interior and exterior of a can, mounted on open legs. (2) Round platform with a rotating spray head at its center for washing the interior of a can, mounted on a stand with foot-operated water valves. (3) Rinse nozzle built into a floor drain and connected to a hand-operated quick-opening mixing valve.

Can Washer and Sterilizer. Enclosed cabinet with spray heads for washing the interiors and exteriors of cans, mounted on open legs, provided with detergent dispenser and 180°F hot-water rinse or steam-mixing valve for final rinse. *See* Pot and Pan Washer.

Carbonated Beverage System. *See* Soda System.

Carbonator. Motor-driven water pump, with tank and control valves, to combine cold water and CO_2 gas in a storage tank, producing soda water. Used for soda fountains, carbonated beverage dispensers, and dispensing systems.

Carrier. A unit for carrying food, beverages, and ware by hand for short distances, furnished with grip(s) or handle(s). Could be an enclosed cabinet, insulated, heated or refrigerated; or a wire basket or rack.

Cart. Mobile unit of varying structure: as an open shelf or shelves; a semi- or fully enclosed cabinet with single or multiple compartments that may be insulated. Used for transporting food or ware and for cleaning and storage.

Cash Drawer. Shallow drawer located under a counter top at the cashier end. Often provided with removable compartmented insert for currency and coins.

Cashier Counter. *See* Checkout Counter.

Cashier Stand. Mobile or stationary stand with solid top set on four legs, or semienclosed body open at bottom. May be provided with foot rest, cash drawer, and tray rest on one or both sides.

Cereal Cooker. Rectangular-shaped unit with heated water bath, having one or more openings in top with lug holders, into which pots with lugs are fitted to prevent the pot from floating. Cooker may be gas-, electric-, or steam-heated. Unit may be floor- or wall-mounted and equipped with water filler and gauge.

Checkout Counter. Counter located between a cafeteria serving area or kitchen and a dining room, for use by checker and/or cashier. Also called cashier counter.

Chinese Range. Range with one or more large-diameter gas burners on an inclined top and a raised edge around each burner opening. Food is cooked in shallow bowls called woks. Range top is cooled by water flowing from a front manifold to a rear trough, with strainer basket at one end. A swing-spout faucet mounted on high splashguard at rear fills the bowl when the spout is turned ninety degrees.

Chopping or **Cutting Block.** *See* Butcher Block.

Clam Opener. Device with hand-operated, hinged knife and fixed, V-shaped block attached to a table top.

Cleaning Cart. Mobile unit with one or more compartments for soiled linen, waste, and water for mops and wringer.

Cocktail Mix Station. Section of bar workboard where drinks are poured or mixed. Usually includes open-top ice storage bin and wells for mixer bottles and condiments.

Coffee Filter. Perforated metal container or disposable paper or muslin bag in coffee maker or urn to hold bed of coffee grounds.

Coffee Grinder. (1) Bench-mounted hand- or motor-driven machine with bean hopper at the top, grinding mechanism, and discharge chute with holder for container or filter beneath. (2) Coffee-grinding attachment for a food machine.

Coffee Maker. (1) Hand- or automatically operated electric-heated unit in which a measure of hot water at the proper temperature is poured over a measured bed of coffee grounds contained in a filtering unit. The extracted beverage is discharged into a container and/or serving unit. (2) Hand- or automatically operated electric-heated unit in which a measure of hot water at the proper temperature is combined with a measure of instant coffee mix and discharged into a container. (3) Unit consisting of one or more sets of upper and lower bowls set on gas- or electric-heated range. The measure of water boiled in the lower bowl is forced by pressure into the upper bowl containing measured coffee grounds. When the set is removed from the heat source, the cooling lower bowl creates a vacuum, causing the liquid to flow back down through a filter in the bottom of the upper bowl. The upper bowl is then removed to permit use of the lower bowl as a server or decanter.

Coffee Mill. *See* Coffee Grinder.

Coffee Percolator. Covered cylindrical container with up to 120-cup capacity, electric or gas heated. Percolating device in center causes heated water to flow over measured bed of coffee grounds contained in a filtering basket at top. Unit is normally hand filled. Heating unit keeps coffee warm for serving. Bottom has draw-off faucet.

Coffee Range. Counter unit consisting of one to four low-rated gas or electric burners for making coffee with siphon-type coffee makers.

Coffee Urn. Enclosed container of water with jar (liner) set into top. Urn water is heated by gas, electric or steam. A measure of hot water at proper temperature is poured over measured bed of coffee grounds contained in a filtering unit. Beverage collects in jar and is discharged through bottom connection to draw-off faucet. Urn water is not used for coffee making. Equipped with water inlet valve to fill urn body.

Coffee Urn Battery. Assembly of units consisting of one or more water boilers and one or more coffee urns heated by gas, electricity, or steam. Battery is complete with piping, fittings, and controls between boiler(s) and urn(s).

Coffee Urn, Combination. (1) Coffee urn with water inlet valve and additional draw-off faucet for hot water, to make tea and instant beverages. (2) Pressure siphon type has sealed water and hot-air chambers with piping control between water jacket and jar. (3) Twin type has two coffee jars set into top of single container. Urn body is usually rectangular in shape. (4) Automatic type has electrically operated device to pump and measure hot water at thermostatically controlled temperature.

Coffee Warmer. Counter-top range with one or more gas, electric, or canned heaters to maintain coffee at serving temperature; each with coffee bowl or decanter. Also called coffee server.

Cold Beverage Dispenser or **Urn.** See Iced Coffee/Tea Urn.

Cold Pan. Insulated depressed pan set into a table or counter top; provided with waste outlet; may be refrigerated with crushed ice, refrigeration coil fastened to the underside of the lining, or a cold plate. A perforated false bottom is provided when ice is used.

Combination Steam Cooker and Kettle. See Cooker and Kettle, Combination.

Compressor, Refrigeration. See Condensing Unit, Refrigeration.

Condensate Evaporator. Finned coil through which compressed refrigerant flows, absorbing the heat inside refrigerator or freezer.

Condensing Unit, Refrigeration. Assembly consisting of mechanical compressor driven by electric-powered motor with either air or water-cooling device. (1) Open-type unit has major components separate but mounted on same base. (2) Hermetic-type unit has major components enclosed in same sealer housing, with no external shaft, and motor operating in refrigerant atmosphere. (3) Semihermetic-type unit has hermetically sealed compressor whose housing is

sealed and has means of access for servicing internal parts in field.

Condiment Cabinet. Semi- or fully enclosed cabinet, mobile or stationary, having several removable or intermediate shelves to store cook's or baker's condiments and spices in the cooking and preparation areas.

Condiment Shelf or **Rack.** Shelf or rack mounted above or under a table top to hold several condiment items for use by the cook or baker.

Condiment Stand. Standard-height mobile or stationary stand having a solid top with receptacle for holding condiment containers, and tray rest on one or both sides. May be open type with legs, enclosed type with cabinet base and shelves, or may have insulated cold pan and refrigerated base.

Confectioner's Stove. See Pot Stove.

Container, Food and Beverage. See Bin; Carrier.

Convection Oven. Gas- or electric-heated. Heat is circulated through the oven interior with fan or blower system. Interior may be equipped with racks and/or shelves. Ovens may be stacked or set on stand. Oven bottom may be constructed as part of the platform of a mobile basket rack cart.

Convenience Food. Any food item that has been processed by any method from the raw state and packaged for resale and/or further processing or use at later date.

Cooker and Kettle, Combination. One or more steam-jacketed kettles with one or more steam cookers mounted in top of single cabinet base or tops of adjoining cabinet bases. May be for direct steam operation or provided with steam coil, gas- or electric-heated steam generator in the base under the steam cooker(s).

Cooker/Mixer. Direct steam-, gas-, or electric-steam-jacketed kettle, with hinged or removable agitator mounted to supporting frame or brackets.

Cookie Dropper. Motor- or hand-driven machine used to portion and shape drops of cookie dough using dies. Unbaked cookies are dropped onto baking sheet pans or conveyor belt. Also called cookie machine.

Cook's Table. Table located in the cooking area of kitchen for cook's use.

Corn Popper. Enclosed unit with transparent front and ends, transparent doors on the working side, electrically heated popcorn popper suspended from the top, and warming heaters for storage of finished popcorn. May be mounted on counter or enclosed base.

Cotton Candy Machine. Machine with round tub and spinning unit and electric heating unit for converting sugar into cotton candy. May be set on counter top or stand.

Creamer. (1) Insulated container for cream, having ice or mechanical refrigeration, and provided with adjustable draw-off faucet for each cream measure. Often anchored to counter or wall. Also called cream dispenser. (2) Soda fountain unit with self-contained ice cream cabinet.

Creamer Rack. Rectangular basket of wire or plastic with compartments to fit glass creamers. Used to wash, fill, and store creamers.

Crusher. *See* Bottle Crusher; Can Crusher; and Ice Crusher.

Cryogenic Freezer. *See* Freezer (3).

Cubing Machine. *See* Dicing Machine.

Cutlery Box. Unit consisting of one or more compartments for storage and dispensing of flatware (knives, forks, spoons). Often set on a counter or table top, and sometimes built into the front of a cabinet under the top, or as a drawer.

Cutting Board. *See* Board.

Deep Fat Fryer. *See* Fryer.

Defrost System. Refrigeration system for a freezer consisting of a blower evaporator coil, heating unit, and controls. Electric type employs heating elements; hot gas type uses heat exchanger to remove frost from the coil and allow condensate to flow to the drain pan under the coil.

Dessert Cart. Cart with several shelves for display and serving of desserts. May be equipped with mechanical or ice-refrigerated cold pan or plate and with transparent domed cover.

Detergent Dispenser. Device mounted on a dishwasher or sink for storage and dispensing of liquid detergent or mixture of powdered detergent and water into the wash tank of the unit through the pump manifold or incoming water line. Some units are equipped with control device, electrically operated, to detect detergent strength in tank.

Dicing Machine. Bench-mounted hand- or motor-driven two-operation machine that first forces food through a grid network of knives in a square pattern and then slices the food the same length as the side of the square. May be attached to food mixing or cutting machine. Also called dicing attachment or cubing machine.

Dish Box. *See* Carrier.

Dish Cart. Cart for storage and dispensing of clean or soiled dishes. Usually of height to roll under counter or table top.

Dish Table. Work surface with raised sides and end(s) having its surface pitched to a built-in waste outlet, adjoining a sink or warewashing machine. There may be a soiled table used for receiving, sorting, and racking ware, located at load end of the sink or washing machine, and a clean table at unload end for draining of rinse water, drying, and stacking ware.

Dispenser. Unit for storage and dispensing of beverages, condiments, food, and ware. May be insulated and refrigerated or heated. May be provided with self-leveling device. May be counter- or floor-mounted, stationary or mobile.

Display Case. A semi- or fully enclosed case of one or more shelves, mounted on counter top or wall, for display of desserts. Semienclosed types have transparent end panels and sneeze guards along customers' side to protect uncovered foods. Refrigerated types have insulated transparent panels and doors. Heated types are usually provided with sliding doors and electric heating units, with or without humidifier.

Dolly. Solid platform or open framework mounted on a set of casters, for storage and transportation of heavy items. May be equipped with handle or push bar.

Dough Divider. Motor-driven floor-type machine to divide dough (usually for bread) into equally scaled pieces. Pieces are removed from work surface by conveyor to next operation. Normally used for bread dough. Also called bread divider.

Dough Mixer. (1) Motor-driven machine with vertical spindle to which various whips and beaters are attached. Bowl is raised to the agitator. Mixers of 5- to 20-quart capacity are bench mounted. Mixers of 20- to 140-quart capacity are floor type. (2) Motor-driven, floor-type horizontal machine with tilting-type bowl and horizontal agitator(s) for a large dough batch. Also called kneading machine or mixer.

Dough Molder. *See* Bread Molder.

Doughnut Fryer. *See* Fryer.

Doughnut Machine. Unit consisting of hand- or motor-driven batter dropper and shallow fryer. Doughnuts are conveyed through heated cooking fat or oil bath, turned over, and discharged out of bath into drain pan.

Dough Proofer. *See* Proof Box or Cabinet.

Dough Retarder. May be upright reach-in, low-counter bench-type, or walk-in refrigerator with series of racks or tray slides and/or shelves, in which dough is kept cool, to retard rising.

Dough Rounder. Motor-driven floor-mounted machine into which a piece of dough is dropped and rounded to ball shape by means of a rotating cone and fixed spiral raceway running from top to bottom. *See* Roll Divider.

Dough Sheeter. Motor- or hand-driven machine with a series of adjustable rollers to roll dough to sheets of even thickness. Also called pie crust roller.

Dough Trough. Large tub with tapered sides, usually mounted on casters, for storing and transporting large batches of dough. Some troughs have gates at the ends for pouring dough when the trough is lifted above a divider and tilted.

Drainer. *See* Kettle Drainer.

Drink Mixer. Vertical counter-type unit with one or more spindles with motor at top. Switch is activated by drink cup when placed in correct position. Also called malted mixer.

Drop-in Unit. Any warming, cooling, cooking, or storage unit that is dropped into an opening in a counter or table top and is fitted with accompanying mounting brackets and sized flange.

Dunnage Rack. Mobile or stationary solid or louvered platform used to stack cased or bagged goods in a storeroom or walk-in refrigerator or freezer.

Egg Boiler. Electric-, steam-, or gas-heated unit with removable timed elevating device(s) to raise basket(s) or bucket(s) out of boiling water bath. Containers are lowered by hand.

Ferris-wheel-type unit will automatically lower and raise baskets through water bath. Also called egg timer.

Egg Timer. *See* Egg Boiler.

Electronic Oven. *See* Microwave Oven.

Evaporator. *See* Condensate Evaporator; Unit Cooler.

Extractor. (1) *See* Juice Extractor. (2) *See* Grease Filter. (3) *See* Water Extractor.

Extruder. *See* French Fry Cutter.

Fat Filter. (1) Gravity type has disposable paper or muslin strainer set in holder on top of fat container. Unit is placed under drain valve of fat fryer. (2) Siphon type uses disposable paper or muslin strainer over fat container, attached to rigid siphon tube mounted on fat fryer, with other end of tube in fat tank. (3) Motor-driven pump type, portable or mobile, uses disposable paper strainer. Has flexible hose from fat tank to strainer. Strainer set on fat container.

Filter. (1) *See* Coffee Filter. (2) *See* Fat Filter. (3) *See* Grease Filter.

Finishing Oven. *See* Au Gratin Oven.

Fire Extinguisher. Hand operated, sealed with chemical inside, most commonly wall mounted and provided with control and directional hose, or horn.

Fish and Chip Fryer. *See* Fryer.

Fish Box. (1) Ice-refrigerated insulated cabinet with counterbalanced hinged or sliding door(s) at the top, and drawer(s) at the bottom front. (2) Ice or mechanically refrigerated cabinet with tier(s) of self-closing drawers with insulated fronts. Also called fish file.

Fish File. *See* Fish Box.

Flatware. Knife, spoon, and fork used by the diner.

Floor Scale. (1) Unit fixed in a pit, its platform flush with finished floor. May have dial or beam mounted on top of the housing at the rear of platform framing, plus tare beam. Used for weighing heavy objects on mobile carriers. (2) Mobile type. *See* Platform Scale.

Food Carrier. *See* Carrier.

Food Cutter. (1) Motor-driven bench- or floor-mounted machine with a rotating shallow bowl to carry food through a set of rotating horizontal knives whose axis is perpendicular to the radii of the bowl. Knives are set under hinged-up cover. (2) Motor-driven floor-mounted high-speed machine with vertical tilting bowl having a vertical shaft with rotating knife. Also called vertical cutter/mixer or sold under various brand names.

Food Freshener. Electrically operated unit that introduces live steam to the exterior or interior of food, heating it to serving temperature without loss of moisture. Cabinet type has a hinged cover or drawer for warming the exterior of foods. Hollow-pin type heats food interior through injection.

Food Merchandiser. Refrigerated, heated, or noninsulated case or cabinet with transparent doors and possibly transparent ends. Used for display and sometimes self-service of foods.

Food Shaper. (1) Motor-driven unit with loading hopper, bench or floor mounted. Shapes food into rectangular or round patties of varying thickness. May be equipped with paper interleaving, removing, and conveying devices. (2) Attachment to meat chopper to shape ground food into rectangles of varied thickness. Also called food former.

Food Warmer. (1) Insulated mobile or stationary cabinet with shelves, racks, or tray slides, having insulated doors or drawers. May be electric, steam or gas heated and provided with humidity control. (2) Infrared lamp or electric radiant heating element with or without a glass enclosure, mounted above the serving unit in a hot-food section.

French Fry Bagger. Motor-driven machine to convey, measure, and insert french-fried potatoes into paper bag blown open to receive product.

French Fry Cutter. Hand-operated or motor-driven machine or attachment to food machine, that pushes potato through grid of knives set in square pattern in frame.

French Fryer. *See* Fryer.

Fryer. Floor- or bench-mounted unit heated by gas or electricity with tank of oil or fat into which foods are immersed. Common type has deep tank. Special types have shallow tanks for fish, chicken, doughnuts, etc., and basket-conveyor type has a shallow tank for draining with baskets, arms, mesh-type belt, or rotating auger to move foods through the bath. Pressure type has a lift or hinged cover to seal the top of the fryer tank.

Fry Pan, Tilting. Rectangular pan with gas- or electric-heated flat bottom, pouring lip, and hinged cover. Floor mounted on a tubular stand or wall mounted on brackets with in-wall steel carriers. A small electric pan may be table mounted on legs. Also called braising pan, tilting griddle, or tilting skillet.

Fudge Warmer. Counter-mounted electrically heated insulated pot with hinged or lift-off cover and ladle.

Glass Washer. (1) Multitank horizontal machine with hand-activated rinse nozzle in one tank, revolving brushes in a second tank, and final rinse nozzles in a third. (2) Single- or double-tank door-type or rack-conveyor-type dishwasher.

Grater. (1) Bench-mounted hand- or motor-driven machine in which food is forced against the face of a revolving grater plate by a pusher or hopper plate. (2) Part of vegetable-slicing attachment to food machine.

Grease Filter or **Extractor.** (1) Removable rectangular or round frame having several layers of wire mesh or baffles and mounted in the exhaust equipment above or behind cooking units. (2) A series of baffles mounted in exhaust equipment, from whose surfaces grease deposits are flushed with wash water into a waste outlet. (3) Manifold-mounted water nozzles in exhaust equipment producing a fine spray mist that collects grease from laden air and drains through a waste outlet.

Griddle. Extra-thick steel plate with a ground and polished top surface, heated by gas or electricity. Surface edges are raised or provided with gutters and drain hole leading to catch trough or pan. May be set on counter top with legs, stand, or oven base.

Grill. Bench-mounted unit with fixed lower and hinged upper electrically heated plates. Plates have a waffle pattern for waffles, grooves for steaks, and are smooth for sandwiches.

Grill, Charcoal. *See* Broiler, Charcoal.

Grinder. (1) *See* Meat Chopper. (2) *See* Coffee Grinder.

Hamper. *See* Linen Hamper.

Heat Exchanger, Steam. Boiler with coils to generate clean steam with possibly contaminated house steam. Used for steam cooking units.

High-Speed Cooker. *See* Steam Cooker.

Hors d'Oeuvre Cart. Cart with platforms on ferris wheel having several food containers on each platform. Used for display and service.

Hot Chocolate Dispenser or **Maker.** (1) Counter-mounted electrically heated glass bowl with agitator or insulated tank with agitator for dispensing premixed hot chocolate. (2) Counter-mounted electrically heated unit that combines measure of heated water with measure of chocolate mix and dispenses mixture at touch of button.

Hot Dog and Hamburger Broiler. Semi- or fully enclosed cabinet with glass doors and panels for display. An electric heater under the top radiates onto hot dogs in baskets or on pins on wheel, or onto hamburgers laid on platforms mounted on motor-driven ferris wheel. Food rotates while cooking.

Hot Dog Steamer. Counter-mounted cabinet with transparent display panels and hinged covers or doors. The unit is electrically heated with a water bath and immersion device to generate steam for heating hot dogs and dry heat for warming rolls.

Hot Food Cabinet. *See* Food Warmer; Carrier.

Hot Plate. Counter-top and floor-mounted unit with one or more open gas or tubular electric burners arranged left to right and/or front to rear. French hot plates are round or square solid steel plates, gas or electrically heated.

Hot-Water Booster. Electric-, steam-, or gas-heated insulated tank or coil used to raise the incoming hot water from house temperature to sanitizing temperature, as required by code. Booster may be mounted inside housing or at end of warewashing machine, under warewashing table, or may be remotely located.

Housekeeping Cart. Cart with one or more semi- or fully enclosed compartments for clean linen, a compartmented tray at the top for supplies, a cloth hamper for soiled linen, and a waste receptacle.

Humidifier. Electric-, steam-, or gas-heated unit used to evaporate and distribute water inside proofing equipment and hot food warmers. May be fixed or removable attachment.

Ice Breaker. *See* Ice Crusher.

Ice Chest. *See* Ice Storage Bin.

Ice Cream Cabinet. (1) Mechanically refrigerated low-type chest with removable, hinged, flip-flop covers, used for storage and dispensing of ice cream. (2) Mechanically refrigerated upright cabinet with hinged door(s), for storage of ice cream.

Ice Cream Display Cabinet. Ice cream cabinet with sliding or hinged transparent doors or covers. Mostly used in self-service stores.

Ice Cream Freezer. Floor- or counter-mounted machine with mechanically refrigerated cylinder, having a dasher to mix and refrigerate an air and ice cream mix to flowing ice cream. The product is then placed inside a hardening cabinet.

Ice Cream Hardening Cabinet. Low cabinet with a lid(s) or upright cabinet with hinged door(s), insulated and refrigerated at a very low temperature to set ice cream hard.

Ice Crusher. (1) Motor-driven or hand-operated floor- or counter-mounted machine with spiked rollers, to crush large pieces of ice or ice cubes. (2) Attachment mounted between an ice-cube-making machine and an ice storage bin, having a damper for directing cubed ice to motor driven rollers with spikes to crush ice as required.

Ice Cuber. *See* Ice Maker.

Iced Coffee/Tea Urn. Urn with stainless steel or transparent glass jar and draw-off faucet. Stainless steel type may be insulated. Glass jar may be equipped with ice compartment suspended from cover. Also called iced tea/coffee dispenser.

Ice Dispenser. A floor-, counter-, or wall-mounted stationary ice storage bin with motor-driven agitator and conveyor mechanism or gravity feed, that dispenses a measure of ice (cubed or crushed) through a discharge chute into a container at working level.

Ice Maker. Floor-, counter-, or wall-mounted unit containing refrigeration machinery for making cubed, flaked, and crushed ice. Maker may have integral ice storage bin. Larger-capacity machines generally have a separate bin in which ice is received via a connecting chute. Capacity is rated in pounds of ice per twenty-four-hour day.

Ice Maker and Dispenser. Floor-, counter-, or wall-mounted ice maker with storage bin and dispensing mechanism. *See* Ice Maker; Ice Dispenser.

Ice Pan, Display. *See* Cold Pan.

Ice Plant. (1) An assembly consisting of a large-capacity ice maker that empties into a walk-in freezer or ice storage bin(s) on the floor below via directional chute(s). (2) A large-capacity, floor-mounted ice maker, having a small-capacity bin connected to vertical and horizontal conveyors with insulated sleeves for transporting ice to large capacity bin(s).

Ice Shaver. Hand-operated or motor-driven floor- or bench-mounted machine whose rotating plate or wheel has a sharp knife that produces icelike snow when forced against the face of a cake of ice. Also called snowcone machine.

Ice Storage Bin. Insulated mobile or stationary cabinet of one or more compartments with hinged or sliding door(s) or cover(s). It is commonly mounted under an ice-making machine, with opening(s) in the top to receive product(s), and is fitted with a waste outlet in the bottom. Ice is normally scooped out of bin. Unit may be built into counter.

Ice Vendor. Floor-mounted, mechanically refrigerated freezer with a coin-operated mechanism to release a measure of loose or bagged ice cubes at working level.

Infrared Heater or **Warmer.** Unit consisting of one or more lamps or electric strip heaters, with or without protective covering or reflector, mounted in a bracket or housing. Usually set over hot-food serving and display areas or inside enclosed displays. Unit produces infrared heat to keep food warm.

Infrared Oven. Oven having heat generated and radiated from electric infrared heating elements encased in a glass tube or from an exposed quartz infrared plate.

Injector, Rinse. *See* Rinse Injector.

Insert. Rectangular pan or round pot set into the top of a steam or hot food table.

Juice Extractor. (1) Counter-mounted motor-driven ribbed cone having base with drain hole for juice. Half of fruit is pressed by hand, down onto cone. (2) Bench- or floor-mounted motor-driven machine that slices fruit in half, and squeezes halves between nesting cones. (3) Hand-operated bench-type machine that squeezes fruit halves between inverted cones. Also called juicer.

Kettle Drainer. Mobile sink with screen or strainer basket, waste outlet with adjustable tailpiece, and push handle.

Kettle, Electric Heated. (1) Stationary or tilting two-thirds steam-jacketed, or stationary full-steam-jacketed kettle with electric immersion heater in water between shells. Kettle is floor mounted inside housing or attached to housing with tilting mechanism. Tilting device may be hand or power operated. Stationary unit is provided with water filler, hinged cover, and drawoff valve. Tilting type has pouring lip and may have drawoff valve, hinged cover and water filler. (2) Stationary or tilting two-thirds steam-jacketed kettle set into top of cabinet base with remote electric-heated steam generator adjoining kettle. Kettle provided with hinged cover, water filler, and drawoff valve.

Kettle, Flat Bottom. Rectangular pan with flat bottom having inner and outer shells. Live steam is introduced between shells, heating inner shell for cooking. Kettle is tilting type, floor mounted on tubular stand or wall mounted with brackets and in-wall steel chair carriers. Kettle front has pouring lip. Top has hinged cover.

Kettle, Gas Heated. (1) Stationary full or two-thirds steam-jacketed kettle with a gas burner under the bottom of its outer shell to heat water between shells. The kettle is floor mounted inside housing and provided with a water filler and hinged cover. (2) Stationary or tilting two-thirds steam-jacketed kettle set into the top of a cabinet base with remote gas-heated steam generator adjoining the kettle. The kettle is provided with hinged cover, water filler, and drawoff valve.

(3) Stationary floor-type direct-fired kettle with a single shell, mounted inside insulated housing, with a gas burner under bottom of shell, drawoff valve, and hinged cover.

Kettle, Steam-jacketed. Kettle having live steam introduced between the inner and outer shell to heat the inner shell for cooking. Deep-type kettle generally is two-thirds jacketed. Shallow-type kettle generally is fully jacketed. May be mounted to the floor with tubular legs or pedestal base, or mounted to the wall with brackets and in-wall steel chair carriers. Tilting- or trunion-type may be floor or wall mounted, having a worm gear device for hand operation. The stationary kettle has a drawoff valve. The tilting kettle has a pouring lip and may have a drawoff valve. The kettle may be equipped with lift-off or hinged cover, filling faucet, water-cooling system, thermostat, etc.

Kettle, Table Top. Two-thirds steam-jacketed kettle, tilting type, with operating lever up to 20-quart capacity, or tilting worm gear device for 40-quart capacity; all direct steam, electric heated. All kettles have a pouring lip. Tilting types have 20- and 40-quart capacity with a lever handle. Oyster stewing kettle is shallow tilting-type kettle.

Kettle, Tilting or Trunion. *See* Kettle, Steam Jacketed; Kettle, Flat Bottom.

Kneading Machine or **Mixer.** *See* Dough Mixer.

Knife Rack. Slotted wood or stainless steel bar set away and attached to edge of table top or butcher block. This forms a slot into which cutlery blades are inserted and held up by handles of same while the handles protrude at the top.

Knife Sharpener. (1) Bench-mounted motor-driven machine with rotating stones forming a V to grind edges on both sides of a blade. (2) Attachment to slicing machine. (3) Grinding-wheel attachment to food machine, having an attachment hub.

Linen Cart. Cart with several compartments for storage of clean linen. May be semi- or fully enclosed.

Linen Hamper. (1) Stationary or mobile metal cabinet with hinged metal cover. (2) Stationary or mobile framework with round cloth bag or cloth sides, ends, and bottom.

Lobster Tank. Transparent tank open at the top and with a water wheel at one end. Tank bottom is lined with special salt. Mounted on a stationary or mobile enclosed base with a filtering and mechanical refrigeration system for tank water. Also called trout tank, with salt omitted.

Machine Stand. Mobile or stationary stand with solid or open-frame top, mounted on open legs or cabinet base, with adjustable dimensions to suit a specific machine or device.

Malted Mix Dispenser. Counter- or wall-mounted unit with a transparent covered hopper, having a lever for dispensing a measure of malted mix powder.

Meat and Bone Saw. Floor-mounted motor-driven band saw with upper and lower pulleys, stationary cutting table with gauge plate, and movable carriage.

Meat Chopper. Table- or floor-mounted hand- or motor-driven horizontal machine. Food placed in top-mounted hopper is fed by a stomper into cylinder with tight-fitting auger to drive food against rotating knife and perforated plate. Also called meat grinder.

Meat Grinder. *See* Meat Chopper.

Meat Hook Rack. One or more wood or metal bars mounted on a wall or floor stand, with fixed or removable sharp pointed metal hooks. Also called meat rail.

Meat Roaster, Steam-jacketed. Shallow steam-jacketed kettle with cover and drawoff valve.

Meat Tenderizer. Counter-mounted machine having two sets of round knives with spaced cutting edges, set apart on slow-speed rollers. Meats are inserted into a slot in the top, pass through the rollers, and are discharged at the bottom front through which the meats to be tenderized pass.

Menu Board. Sign with fixed or changeable letters, or removable lines listing the food items and prices.

Mexican Food Machine. Device used to hold a V-shaped tortilla when filling it to make a taco.

Microwave Oven. Stand- or counter-mounted oven in which foods are heated and/or cooked when they absorb microwave energy (short electromagnetic waves) generated by magnetron(s).

Milk Cooler. (1) Low insulated chest with mechanical or ice refrigeration, for storing and dispensing ½-pint to 2-quart containers of milk. (2) Counter- or stand-mounted refrigerator with one or more 2- to 10-gallon containers equipped with sanitary tube connections that extend through flow-control handles for dispensing loose or bulk milk.

Milkshake Machine. *See* Drink Mixer; Shake Mixer.

Mix Cabinet. Low counter-type or upright reach-in refrigerator in which the mix for frozen shakes or ice cream is stored.

Mixer, Dough. *See* Dough Mixer.

Mixer, Drink. *See* Drink Mixer.

Mixer, Food. Motor-driven machine with vertical spindle having several speeds on which various whips and beaters are mounted. Bowl is raised up to agitator. Mixers of 5- to 20-quart capacity are bench type. Mixers of 20- to 140-quart capacity are floor type.

Mixer Stand. Low-height stationary or mobile stand with four legs and a solid top to support a mixer up to 20-quart size. May be provided with undershelf and vertical rack for mixer parts.

Mixer, Vertical Cutter. *See* Vertical Cutter/Mixer.

Mixing Tank. Vertical type has center-, bottom-, or side-mounted agitator assembly. Horizontal type has end-agitator assembly. All are floor mounted and provided with removable or hinged cover and drawoff valve. Tank may be provided with recirculating pump and filtering system.

Modular Stand. Low-height open stationary stand with four or more legs, having an open framework top, to support heavy-duty modular cooking equipment.

Molder, Food. *See* Food Shaper.

Napkin Dispenser. Counter-top unit for storage and dispensing of folded paper napkins. Napkins forced to headplate by spring.

Order Wheel. Metal- or wood-spoked wheel with clips or hooks on its perimeter, located between cooks' and servers' areas, on which order slips are placed to maintain rotation and visibility.

Oven. Fully enclosed insulated chamber with gas-, electric-, or oil-fired heat, provided with thermostatic control. Deck-type units have chambers or sections stacked one above the other. Bake-type decks are approximately 7 inches high inside. Roast-type decks are 12 to 14 inches high inside.

Oyster Opener. *See* Clam Opener.

Pan and Utensil Rack. (1) One or more bars and braces suspended from a ceiling or mounted on posts or a wall, housing fixed or removable hooks for hanging pots, pans, and utensils. (2) Upright mobile or stationary unit, open or semienclosed, with tiers of angle- or channel-shaped slides to support pans. (3) Heavy-duty rectangular wire basket to hold pans and utensils upright in a pot washer.

Pan Washer. *See* Pot and Utensil Washer.

Pass-through Window or **Opening.** Trimmed opening between kitchen and serving areas having a shelf for a sill. May be equipped with hinged or sliding door or shutter.

Peanut Roaster. Electrically heated enclosed display case with hinged cover at the top.

Peeler. Floor- or bench-mounted machine having a vertical, stationary, abrasive-lined cylinder open at the top, a motor-driven agitator bottom plate, and an over-the-rim water supply. Product discharged through door in cylinder side. Waste water is discharged at bottom and may be equipped with a peel trap basket that can be hung on a pipe over sink or set inside a cabinet base under the peeler. May also be equipped with garbage disposal unit.

Peeler Stand. (1) Special-height mobile stand, open type, with four legs. (2) Special-height enclosed cabinet with adjustable legs, a door designed to house a trap basket, and a waste outlet.

Pellet Heater. Counter-mounted electric-heated, insulated cabinet having one or more vertical cylinders in which metallic discs, inserted at the top, are heated. Discs are dispensed at the bottom through drawer-type device.

Pie and Pastry Case. *See* Display Case.

Pizza Oven. Baking-type oven of one or more decks, gas, electric, or oil fired, having temperature range from 350° to 700°F. Deck(s) are of heat-retaining masonry material.

Pizza Sheeter. *See* Dough Sheeter.

Platform Scale. Mobile unit with a dial or beam, for weights up to 1,500 pounds. May be floor or stand mounted.

Platform Skid. *See* Dunnage Rack.

Popcorn Machine. *See* Corn Popper.

Pot and Utensil Washer or **Pot-washing Machine.** Machine of one or more tanks with hood or wash chamber above, inside which large ware is washed, using very big, high-pressure pumps. Water is pumped from tanks and sprayed over ware placed in racks or set on a conveyor or platform. One or more final fresh-water rinses sanitize ware. Machine has a 34- to 36-inch working height. (1) Door-type single-tank machine has power wash and final rinse only. (2) Door-type two-tank machine has power wash and power rinse tanks and final rinse. (3) Belt-conveyor machine is straight-through-type machine having one to three tanks plus final rinse. Ware is set directly on a belt. (4) Revolving tray-table type has two to three tanks plus final rinse. Ware is set directly on turntable platform.

Pot Filler. Faucet or valve with a hose mounted at a range, pot stove, or kettle to fill a vessel direct.

Pot Stove. Low, floor-mounted single-burner stove with high Btu or kW rating for use with large stock pots.

Prefabricated Cooler. Walk-in refrigerator or freezer having insulated walls, ceiling, and floor fabricated in a shop and assembled on the job site. The insulated floor and base of the walls may be constructed as part of the building.

Preparation Table or **Counter.** Unit located in the preparation area of a kitchen, for cutting, slicing, peeling, and other preparation of foods.

Prerinse or **Prewash Sink.** Sink constructed as an integral part of a soiled dish table, located near a dishwashing machine, and furnished with removable perforated scrap basket(s) and spray hose.

Pressure Cooker. *See* Steam Cooker.

Pressure Fryer. *See* Fryer.

Prewash. Separate machine or built-in section of a warewashing machine with tank and pump or fresh-water supply. Pump recirculates water over ware; fresh-water type sprays over ware; before pumped wash section of machine.

Proof Box or **Cabinet.** Fully enclosed cabinet with gas, steam, or electric heater and humidifier. Sometimes unit may be insulated type with thermostatic and humidity controls. Box may be mobile. Traveling-type proofer has a conveying mechanism inside the overhead cabinet, as in large commercial bread bakery.

Protector Case. A single shelf mounted on posts with transparent shield at the front or at front and ends. Mounted over a counter top at hot-food or sandwich sections to protect uncovered food.

Pulper. Floor-mounted garbage and waste disposal machine with a vertical cylinder, grinder plate, knives, and sump compartment for nongrindable matter. Waste material is ground in a deep-water bath to form a slurry that is piped to a water extractor. Water from the extractor is recirculated to the pulper.

Quartz Oven. Oven that employs an electrically heated quartz plate or infrared quartz element inside a glass tube to generate heat. Also called infrared oven.

Rack: Cup, Dish, Glass, Plate, or Tray. (1) Rectangular or round basket of wire or plastic construction, with or without compartments or intermediate lateral supports, used for washing and/or storage of small ware. Racks are self-stacking for cups and glassware. (2) *See* Tray Rack for upright unit.

Rack Pan. *See* Pan and Utensil Rack.

Rack Washer. Machine of one or two tanks with hood or wash chamber over, with one or two doors, using large-size high-pressure pumps and final sanitizing rinse. Steam- or electric-heated water is pumped from tanks and sprayed over racks wheeled onto tracks inside washer. Machine is made to recess into floor to have tracks set flush with finished floor.

Range. Unit with heated top surface or burners that heat utensils in which foods are cooked, or cook foods directly. Some ranges are equipped with an insulated oven base. Hot or even-heat tops and fry or griddle tops are gas or oil fired or electrically heated. Open or hot-plate tops have electric or gas burners.

Reel Oven. *See* Revolving Tray Oven.

Refrigerated Table. Table top mounted on counter-type refrigerated base.

Refrigerator Shelves. Shelves of wire, solid, embossed, or slotted material with reinforced hemmed edges, mounted on tubular posts with adjustable sanitary brackets. May be in stationary or mobile sections.

Revolving Tray Oven. Gas-, electric-, or oil-heated oven with a motor-driven ferris wheel device inside having four or more balanced trays. Bake or roast pans are loaded and unloaded from a single opening with a hinged-down door. Steam may be added for humidity requirements of products.

Rinse Injector. Device mounted to top or side of washing machine for storage and automatic dispensing of liquid water softener into the final rinse manifold.

Roaster, Meat, Steam-jacketed. *See* Meat Roaster, Steam-jacketed.

Roast Oven. *See* Convection Oven; Oven; Revolving Tray Oven.

Roll Divider. Hand- or motor-operated machine that divides a ball of dough into equal pieces. Hand-operated unit is stand or table mounted. Motor-driven unit is floor mounted with a cabinet base and may be combined with a rounding device. Also called bun divider.

Roll Warmer. (1) Enclosed cabinet with a telescoping cover, heated by pellet or glowing charcoal under a false bottom. (2) Enclosed insulated cabinet with electric heating elements and humidity controls. The unit is provided with one or more drawers in a tier at the front; it sets on a counter top, legs or a stand, or is built into a counter. Also called bun warmer.

Rotisserie. (1) Upright enclosed cabinet with a vertical grill having gas-fired ceramics or electric heating elements. A side-mounted motor drives revolving spits set in a tier in front of the heaters. The unit has hinged or sliding glass doors. (2) Upright enclosed cabinet containing a motor-driven ferris wheel provided with food cradles or baskets passing under gas-fired ceramics or electric heating elements. (3) Enclosed, square, upright cabinet with meat suspended from top in center revolving motor-driven cradle, heated by four infrared lamps radiating from the corners. (4) *See* Hot Dog and Hamburger Broiler.

Salad Case. Unit consisting of a refrigerated counter with refrigerated food pans set into the top, and a refrigerated or nonrefrigerated display case mounted on the counter top.

Salamander. A backshelf or cabinet mounted over the rear of a range or steam table, absorbing the heat to keep foods on it warm.

Salamander Broiler. *See* Broiler, Backshelf.

Saw, Meat and Bone. *See* Meat and Bone Saw.

Scale. *See* Floor Scale; Platform Scale.

Self-Leveling Dispenser. *See* Dispenser.

Service Stand. A stationary cabinet with a solid top at a working height used in a restaurant; may have shelves, bins, drawers, and refrigerated section for storage of linen, flatware, glassware, china, condiments, water, and ice.

Settee Bench. Bench with upholstered seat and upholstered back.

Shake Maker. Floor- or counter-mounted machine with one or two mechanically refrigerated cylinders, having dashers to mix and refrigerate an air and milk mixture to a flowing frozen dessert beverage. Unit may be equipped with syrup tanks and pumps, and mixing spindle to blend various flavors in shakes.

Shrimp Peeler and Deveiner. Bench-mounted, motor-driven machine that removes vein and shell from shrimp and prawn.

Silver Burnisher, Holloware and Flatware. Machine with a tumbling barrel or vibrating open-top tub filled with steel balls and compound, in which silver-plated utensils are placed. Tumbling or vibrating action causes steel balls to roll down plating onto base metal. Units may be bench or floor mounted or made mobile to roll under a table top.

Silver Washer and Drier. Floor-mounted machine with a fixed or removable tumbling drum set inside a wash chamber with a hinged cover for washing, sterilizing, and electrically drying flatware. The removable drum has a perforated bottom and top cover. The fixed drum has a hinged cover and perforated ends. Machine has wash, rinse, and final sterilization rinse cycles. Electrically heated air is blown through wash chamber and drum to dry flatware.

Sink. (1) Preparation, cook's or utility: one- or two-compartment type with drainboard on one or both sides, each compartment averaging 24 inches square. (2) Pot and pan or scullery: two-, three-, or four-compartment type with drainboard on one or both sides, and possibly between, compartments. Each compartment should be minimum 27 inches left to right, and average 24 inches front to rear.

Slaw Cutter. Floor- or bench-mounted machine with revolving slicer plate and hopper. Cored and quartered cabbage heads inserted in hopper are forced against slicer plate and discharge through chute below.

Slicer. Bench- or stand-mounted machine with a stationary motor-driven round knife and slice-thickness gauge plate, and reciprocating feed trough or carriage. Flat trough may have hand and/or spring-pressure feed plate. Gravity trough may have hand or automatic feed plate. Trough may be hand operated or motor driven. Slicer can be equipped with automatic stacking and conveying device.

Slicer, Bread. *See* Bread Slicer.

Slicer, Vegetable. *See* Vegetable Slicer.

Slush Maker. Floor- or counter-mounted machine with one or two mechanically refrigerated cylinders having dashers to mix and refrigerate a water mixture to a flowing frozen dessert beverage.

Smokehouse, Chinese. Floor-mounted, enclosed, insulated roasting cabinet with gas burners and baffle plates, hinged door(s), duct connection, and flue at top, and removable grease pan inside the bottom. Meat, fish, and poultry are mounted on skewers inside. Interior walls and door have deflector plates to direct drippings into the grease pan.

Sneeze Guard. *See* Display Case.

Snowcone Machine. *See* Ice Shaver.

Soda Dispenser. (1) Part of soda-making and refrigeration system: dispensing head attachment for mounting on a soda fountain, bar, counter, or at a waiter station, complete with drainer. (2) Enclosed cabinet, ice or mechanically refrigerated, to dispense premixed soda or combine soda water and syrup stored in a cabinet or remote tanks. (3) Floor- or counter-mounted cabinet with a self-contained soda and refrigeration system having remote or self-contained syrup tanks.

Soda Maker. Unit consisting of mechanical refrigeration system, carbonator, and soda storage tank.

Soda System. Assembly consisting of soda maker, syrup tanks, syrup, soda and refrigeration tubing, and soda-dispensing head(s) and/or cabinet(s). Also known as carbonated beverage system.

Soft-Ice Cream Maker. Floor- or counter-mounted machine with one or two mechanically refrigerated cylinders having dashers to mix and refrigerate air and ice cream mix to a flowing frozen dessert. Unit is equipped with hand or foot-operated dispensing head or control.

Soiled Dish Pass Window. Trimmed opening in a partition between dishwashing and serving areas, having the soiled dish table as a sill. The opening may be equipped with hinged or sliding door or shutter.

Soup Station. Section of cook's table or cafeteria counter with a hot-food receptacle, rectangular or round, set into the top.

Speed Rail. *See* Bottle Trough.

Spice Bench. Table with stationary cabinet above rear or below top, or mobile cabinet(s) under the top. Cabinet(s) have two or more spice drawers or bins.

Squeezer, Juice. *See* Juice Extractor.

Steam Cooker. Enclosed cabinet with one or more sealed compartments having individual controls into which (chemically clean) steam is introduced for cooking or heating. Cooker may be direct-connected or equipped with gas-fired, electric, or steam coil generator in the base. (1) A cooker with compartments in tiers cooks with low-pressure steam. Each compartment has a hinged door with a floating inner panel and a sealing gasket made tight with a wheel screw. Unit is floor mounted, or if direct connected, may be wall mounted. (2) Cooker with high pressure has self-sealing door(s) with a gasket made tight by interior steam pressure. May be floor, counter, or wall mounted. Also called high-speed cooker.

Steamer, Dry. *See* Food Freshener.

Steamer, Hot Dog. *See* Hot Dog Steamer; Steam Cooker.

Steam-Jacketed Kettle. *See* Kettle, Steam-jacketed.

Stock Pot Stove. *See* Pot Stove.

Storage Rack. Unit consisting of one or more shelves mounted on angle, channel, or tubular posts, for storage of goods or ware.

Stove. Floor- or counter-mounted unit with one or more open gas or electric burners. Also called hot plate.

Swill Trough. (1) Depression in dish table approximately 6 to 9 inches wide, and 2 to 6 inches deep, equipped with waste outlet, strainer basket, and perforated cover. (2) Extra sink compartment of shallow depth located between compartments of pot-washing sink, equipped with strainer basket.

Table. Top with solid flat surface, mounted on floor with legs, on wall with brackets and legs, or on semi- or fully enclosed cabinet. May be stationary or mobile. May have shelves under, shelves over, and tool drawer(s).

Tea Maker or Dispenser. (1) *See* Coffee Urn. Same as coffee urn with tea laid in strainer. (2) Counter-mounted unit used to combine instant tea mix with heated water for hot tea or cold water for ice tea.

Tenderizer. *See* Meat Tenderizer.

Timer, Egg. *See* Egg Timer.

Toaster. (1) Counter-mounted pop-up type has two- or four-slice capacity. Electric only. (2) Counter-mounted conveyor type with a motor driven conveyor carries the product between electric or gas-fired radiants. (3) Sandwich type: *see* Grill.

Tray Make-up or **Assembly Conveyor.** Motor-driven or gravity-type horizontal conveyor used to transport trays between various food loading stations.

Tray Rack. Upright mobile or stationary unit, open or semienclosed, having angle, channel, or tubular posts and one or more tiers of angle- or channel-shaped slides to support trays or pans. Rack may be built into cabinets or suspended from under table tops.

Tray Slide or **Rail.** Horizontal surface that accommodates the width of a tray, extended out from, and running the length of, cafeteria counter top. May be constructed of solid material with or without raised edges and V beads; or of several tubular or solid rails or bars. Mounted on and fastened to brackets secured to counter top and/or counter body. Also called tray rest.

Tray Stand. Low-height, mobile or stationary four-legged stand with solid top. Top may have raised back and sides to prevent tray stacks from falling over.

Trough, Swill. *See* Swill Trough.

Trout Tank. *See* Lobster Tank.

Truck. *See* Cart.

Under-counter Sink Workboard. *See* Bar Workboard.

Unit Cooler. Semienclosed cabinet open at front and rear or top and bottom, depending on air flow, with a motor-driven fan blowing air through a mechanically refrigerated finned coil. Device is normally suspended inside a refrigerator or freezer. Also called blower (evaporator) coil.

Urn, Coffee/Tea. *See* Coffee Urn.

Urn Stand. Stationary stand with a solid top having raised edges all around, recessed drain trough(s) with waste outlet, and a drainer plate flush with the top. Raised, die-stamped openings are used to connect lines to an urn. Top set on open base with shelf, semienclosed cabinet with bottom (and intermediate) shelf, or enclosed cabinet with bottom (and intermediate) shelf and door(s). May also be equipped with fold-down step.

Vegetable Peeler. *See* Peeler.

Vegetable Slicer or Cutter. (1) Hand- or motor-driven counter-mounted machine having rotating removable plates with varied knives. Product is forced against plates and knives for slicing, dicing, grating, shredding, etc. (2) Similar attachment to a food machine with rotating removable plates and knife arrangements.

Vegetable Steamer. *See* Steam Cooker.

Vertical Cutter/Mixer. Floor-type machine with a vertical tilting mixing bowl having a 25- to 80-quart capacity. The bowl is equipped with a two-speed motor and a high-speed agitator shaft at bowl bottom with cutting/mixing knife. A hand- or motor-driven stirring and mixing shaft is fixed to the bowl's cover. A strainer basket may be included.

Waffle Baker. *See* Grill.

Water Boiler. (1) One or more urns of coffee urn battery, heated by gas, steam, or electricity, to bring water to boil for making beverages. Usually connected to other urns with water piping and controls. Can be used separately. (2) Gas-, electric-, steam-, or oil-fired unit to heat water for use in kitchen.

Water Extractor. Floor-mounted machine located at the terminal of a waste pulping system. The device augers pulp in a slurry out of the tank to a pressure head at the top, extracting water that is then recirculated into the system. The pulp is discharged into a chute to a waste receptacle.

Water Heater. Counter-mounted instant electric heating device with faucet for making tea and hot chocolate drinks.

Water Station. Section of a counter or stand with a glass- and/or pitcher-filling faucet and drain trough.

Window, Soiled Dish Pass. *See* Soiled Dish Pass Window.

Wine Rack. Fixed or portable folding unit with alternating stacked compartments open at front and rear to support wine bottles in a horizontal position for storage and display.

Wok. *See* Chinese Range.

Wood Top. Table top constructed of kiln-dried laminated hard rock maple strips, hydraulically pressed together, glued, and steel doweled through.

Workboard. *See* Bar Workboard.

Work Table. *See* Preparation Table.

BIBLIOGRAPHY

Aceti, Diana M. "Passage to India: In a Connecticut Retail Center, Theatrical Flair Enhances an Authentic Atmosphere." *Restaurant and Hotel Design* 7:70 (January/February 1985).

———. "Puttin' on the Ritz." *Restaurant and Hotel Design* 6 (1): 52-53 (January/February 1984).

"Acki's Emporium: New Wave in Seafood: Ethnic Styles Range from Chinese to Iberian—Kitchen Ranges Are Exclusively Gas." *Restaurants and Institutions* 97 (9): 150-53 (April 15, 1987).

"Adapting a Historic Site to Contemporary Cuisine." *Independent Restaurants,* 34-36 (March 1985).

Ashton, Robin. "Unusual Design Projects Require Special Solutions." *Foodservice Equipment and Supplies Specialist* 40 (5): 121-28 (September 25, 1987).

Askin, Patricia. "1984 Designers Circle Awards." *Lodging Hospitality* 40 (10): 47-75 (November 1984).

Bain, Laurie. "Manufacturing Program Builds Revenues for Church's: Selling Prefabricated Mini-Stores Is Proving Profitable for the Chain." *Restaurant Business* 85:126 (November 20, 1986).

Baraban, Regina. "Abstracting a Waterfront Theme." *Restaurant and Hotel Design,* 31 (March/April 1983).

———. "East Meets West: Euro-Japanese Influences Inspire a Dynamic Design." *Restaurant and Hotel Design,* 60-62 (March/April 1983).

———. "Hollywood Romance: The Show Biz Sensibility of an Entertainment Mecca." *Restaurant Design,* 52-55 (Spring 1982).

———. "McDonald's at Vineland, N.J.: Meeting Fast Food Changes and Challenges." *Restaurant Hospitality* 70:138 (July 1986).

———. "Mixed Metaphors: Fresh Concepts and Promising Trends in California Restaurants." *Restaurant Design,* 39-49 (Summer 1982).

———. "Palazzo Della Pizza." *Restaurant Design,* 46-47 (Summer 1982).

———. "A Psychological Primer on Restaurant Design." *Lodging* 9 (7): 96-100 (April 1984).

———. "The Psychology of Design." *Restaurant Hospitality* 69 (9): 95-102 (September 1985).

———. "Saddle Shoes and Swing: A Sassy Diner Enlivens a Northern California Fashion Mall." *Restaurant Design,* 48-49 (Summer 1982).

———. "Second Avenue Cafe: A Warm, European Atmosphere Distinguishes This Informal Spot." *Restaurant and Hotel Design,* 56-57 (March/April 1983).

———. "Successful Transformation of a Fast Food Image." *Restaurant and Hotel Design,* 21 (July/August 1983).

———. "The View's the Thing: Manhattan's Skyline Inspires Restrained Interiors." *Restaurant and Hotel Design,* 72-75 (September/October 1983).

Bayles, Soni. "Jolly Roger Charts Course for Image Change." *Restaurant Business* 83 (2): 56-70 (January 20, 1984).

Beaudin, Richard. "Maximize Space, Service and Profits in a City-Center Fast-Food Kitchen." *Hotels and Restaurants International* 21 (7): 131-32 (July 1987).

Bertagnoli, Lisa. "Basic Business Sense Dominates 1985 Design Award Winners." *Foodservice Equipment Specialist* 38:73 (July 25, 1985).

———. "FES Layout and Design: U-Shape Distinguishes Marie Callender's Kitchen." *Foodservice Equipment Specialist* 38:71 (October 24, 1985).

Birney, Dion. "Back in the Pink: [Guthrie] Medical Center Provides a Step-Down Care Facility and an Inn for Its Community [Sayre, Pennsylvania]." *Restaurant and Hotel Design* 9 (8): 36-39 (August 1987).

———. "Deja View: A Seasonal Cape Cod Hot Dog Stand Grows Up and Out to Become a Year-Round Dining Attraction." *Restaurant and Hotel Design* 9 (5): 70-73 (May 1987).

Blair, Marilaine. "Countryside: Stone Mountain Inn's Rebirth in Indiana." *Restaurant Management* 1 (5): 40-41 (May 1987).

Boyle, Kathy. "Kitchens Out in the Open: Restaurants Are Opening Their Kitchens to Diners as Never Before—And Customers and Staff Are Loving It." *NRA News* 6:26 (May 1986).

———. "Your Restaurant's Image: More Than a Sum of Its Parts." *NRA News* 4 (2): 6-9 (February 1984).

Branca, Margaret. "Renovations: An Innovative Trend: Historic Dining in

Minneapolis/St. Paul." *Cooking for Profit*, no. 410:7 (March 1985).

"Brand New Look, Same Good Name Spell Success for Cascone's." *Independent Restaurants* 46 (11): 44-48 (November 1984).

"Breaking with Tradition." *Nation's Restaurant News: Restaurant Interiors*, 30-33 (June 6, 1983).

Brotman, Ellen. "Debunking Five Restaurant Design Myths." *NRA News* 6:18 (January 1986).

Bruin, Florence. "Paris Match: Two Famed Designers Team to Create the Grand Interiors of a Luxury Liner." *Restaurant and Hotel Design* 8:82 (November 1986).

"Burger King: New Image/New Locations Spell Expansion." *Cooking for Profit*, no. 427:7 (October-December 1986).

"Burger King's Floor Plan for Increased Productivity." *Restaurants and Institutions*, 149-151 (March 1, 1983).

Byrne-Dodge, T. "Urban Oasis: In High-Rise Houston, a Onetime Country Home Is a Popular Restaurant." *Restaurant and Hotel Design* 7:74 (March 1985).

Caprione, Carol. "Renovations: Big Return on Investment." *NRA News* 4 (3): 22-24 (March 1984).

Cohen, Edie Lee. "50s Revisited: Edwin Bronstein, AIA, Interprets the Decade for the Heartthrob Cafe and Philadelphia Bandstand." *Interior Design* 57:266 (October 1986).

———. "Le Papillon: A Club by Adam Tihany in Boston's Back Bay Hilton." *Interior Design* 57:276 (October 1986).

Colgan, Susan. "Dining Out: A Swiss Restaurant Puts a Cover on a Piece of a Park." *Restaurant and Hotel Design* 8:70 (June 1986).

———. "French Original: This Pared-Down Restaurant Breaks Successfully with Tradition." *Restaurant and Hotel Design* 8:76 (November 1986).

———. "Light Fantastic." *Restaurant and Hotel Design* 9 (4): 36-39 (April 1987).

———. "Logging It: Catering to Skiers, a Colorado Mountaintop Restaurant Recreates the Look of an Historic Early Homestead." *Restaurant and Hotel Design* 9 (9): 66-69 (September 1987).

———. "Making a Splash: A New-Concept Benihana Prototype Appeals to the Trendy." *Restaurant and Hotel Design* 8:58 (July/August 1986).

———. "Redesigning a Landmark: On Boston's North End, a Famous Italian Restaurant Gets a Bright New Look." *Restaurant and Hotel Design* 8:54 (January/February 1986).

———. "Simply Successful: Bright Mexican Artifacts Rev Up a Cost-Saving Architectural Plan." *Restaurant and Hotel Design* 8:66 (July/August 1986).

———. "Something Sleek: In This Atlantic Bistro, a Long Narrow Space Becomes an Architectural Asset." *Restaurant and Hotel Design* 8:58 (March 1986).

———. "Theming It Up: Imagination Takes the Driver's Seat in a Maryland Restaurant for Auto Buffs." *Restaurant and Hotel Design* 8:70 (March 1986).

———. "Third Annual Design Competition: Best of Competition: Best Full Service Restaurant: Indian Oven Restaurant." *Restaurant and Hotel Design* 8:54 (October 1986).

———. "Third Annual Design Competition: Best Restoration: Hop Brook." *Restaurant and Hotel Design* 8:68 (October 1986).

———. "Windows on the Water: A Renovated Restaurant Makes the Most of Its Intracoastal View." *Restaurant and Hotel Design* 8:62 (April 1986).

"Collins Turns Landlord." *Restaurants and Institutions*, 149-54 (May 1, 1983).

"Colony Inn: Face-Lift Puts Foodservice Up Front." *Restaurant Business* 84:223 (March 20, 1985).

Cooper, Jerry. "Artful Blend: A Hybrid Aesthetic Formula Suits a Suburban Brasserie." *Restaurant and Hotel Design* 7:76 (September 1985).

———. "Hi-Tech Rock and Roll." *Restaurant and Hotel Design* 6 (1): 48-50 (January/February 1984).

———. "La Differance: Capturing the Ambience of Its Paris Predecessor." *Restaurant Design*, 13-20 (Summer 1982).

———. "Modernism Meets Post Modernism: Blending Architectural Styles in a New Haven Restaurant." *Restaurant and Hotel Design*, 66-69 (September/October 1983).

———. "Raising the Curtain: Portland's Sleek Heathman Hotel Restaurant Makes a Timely Debut." *Restaurant and Hotel Design* 7:60 (March 1985).

———. "Restaurants by Great Architects." *Restaurant and Hotel Design* 7:55 (June 1985).

———. "Village Vernacular: Small Town Charm Infuses This Exurban Restaurant." *Restaurant and Hotel Design* 68-71 (May/June 1983).

———. "West Side Kosher Bakery: Dramatic Architecture Amplifies an Urban Theme." *Restaurant and Hotel Design*, 48-49 (March/April 1983).

Coutts, Cheryl. "All Aboard at the Greenwood Grille." *Restaurant Business* 86 (6): 272-76 (April 10, 1987).

———. "Hamburger Harry's: Quick Service and Casual." *Restaurant Business* 86 (1): 120-22 (January 1, 1987).

Curran, George. "Cafeteria Service: Design Firm Vaults Over Space Problems: Public Corridor Separating Kitchen and Service Areas Poses Trafficking Challenge at SOHIO Headquarters." *Restaurants and Institutions* 97 (18): 190-92 (August 19, 1987).

Cuttler, Elyse. "Design: A Language You Need to Speak." *NRA News*, 13-16 (February 1983).

"Decor Makes the Difference for McDonald's Franchise." *Restaurant Business* 84:130 (June 10, 1985).

"Denny's New Image Is a Reflection of the Past." *Restaurants and Institutions*, 183-85 (May 1, 1983).

"Designer Q & A: Brad Elias: The Bistro: The New American Watering Hole." *Restaurants and Institutions* 97 (2): 126 (January 21, 1987).

"Designer Q & A: Juerg Schmid: Designing for the Future: The Designers of the New Carl's Jr. Modeled the Interior for the 1990s." *Restaurants and Institutions* 97 (13): 212 (June 10, 1987).

"Designers Circle Awards 1985." *Lodging Hospitality* 41:51 (November 1985).

"Design Forecast: Restaurant Designers Point to 'No Nonsense' Concepts for the Year Ahead." *Independent Restaurants* 48:52 (January 1, 1986).

"Design Lines." *Restaurant Hospitality* 69:111 (May 1985).

"Design That Works from the Kitchen Out." *Independent Restaurants* 46

(11): 40-42 (November 1984).

Devins, Kim J. "Carolina Eclectic: Sleek Deco Style Replaces Stereotypical Southern Charm in Formal Hotel Dining." *Restaurant and Hotel Design,* 75-157 (May/June 1983).

———. "Classic Revival: A California Entrepreneur Renews the Spirit of a Legendary Design." *Restaurant and Hotel Design* 7:70 (June 1985).

———. "Pure Theater: An Old Movie House Brings Back the '50s for McDonald's in Raleigh." *Restaurant and Hotel Design* 8:64 (May 1986).

———. "Seeing Red: Vibrant Color Paces a High-tech Concept in an Atypical Chinese Eatery." *Restaurant and Hotel Design* 7:66 (June 1985).

Dilling, Mary E. "Redesign Perks Up Coffee House." *Lodging Hospitality* 41:56 (September 1985).

Draheim, Charlene. "Variation on a Theme: La Fonda Restaurants." *Restaurant and Hotel Design,* 24 (July/August 1983).

Eaton, William. "Behind the Scenes: Designing for Labor Efficiency." *Restaurant Management* 1 (2): 84-88 (February 1987).

———. "Facilities: Excellence by Design." *Restaurant Management* 1 (7): 92-93 (July 1987).

———. "How to Retrofit Your Restaurant for Takeout Service." *Independent Restaurants* 48:38 (October 1986).

———. "Making the Most of Your Facility: Building Within Physical Constraints" *Independent Restaurants* 47:49 (December 1985).

———. "Rules of Thumb for Estimating Facility Space Requirements." *Independent Restaurants* 46 (10): 84-87 (October 1984).

"An Elegant Swamp in the Sky." *Nation's Restaurant News: Restaurant Interiors,* 14-15 (June 6, 1983).

"Excellence in Kitchen Design." *Restaurant Hospitality* 79 (2): 37-64 (February 1985).

Faulkner and Weinstein. "1986 Growth Chains: Diners: Nothing Could Be Finer than a Taste of Simpler Times." *Restaurants and Institutions* 96:120 (November 12, 1986).

———. "1986 Growth Chains: Drive-Thru Limited Menu with a Little Service on the Side." *Restaurants and Institutions* 96:102 (November 12, 1986).

"Feast for the Eyes: Six Restaurant Designs with Interior Motives." *Restaurants and Institutions* 96:157 (March 19, 1986).

Festa, Gail. "Design Directions." *Restaurant Hospitality,* 86-90 (April 1983).

———. "Design/Interiors: Seafood Shanty." *Restaurant Hospitality* 68 (7): 56-57 (July 1984).

———. "Diner on Sycamore: Distinctive Diner Design." *Restaurant Hospitality* 70:123 (September 1986).

———. "Interior Design Awards 1987." *Restaurant Hospitality* 71 (5): 137-52 (May 1987).

———. "King Charles: Renovated and Regal." *Restaurant Hospitality,* 68-69 (August 1983).

———. "The Magnolia Room Blossoms with a Redesign." *Restaurant Hospitality* 68 (8): 104-6 (August 1984).

———. "New Wave: Nostalgia." *Restaurant Hospitality* 70:99 (May 1986).

———. "1985 Interior Design Awards." *Restaurant Hospitality* 69 (5): 69-102 (May 1985).

———. "1986 Interior Design Awards." *Restaurant Hospitality* 70:107 (May 1986).

———. "North Star: Bringing a Bit of Britain to Manhattan's South Street Seaport Area." *Restaurant Hospitality* 69:113 (August 1985).

———. "Penrod's: Where Customers Can Drink to the Success of Its Dining Operations." *Restaurant Hospitality,* 122-24 (March 1983).

———. "Sidewalk Cafe: Where the Past Mingles with the Present." *Restaurant Hospitality* 69:111 (June 1985).

———. "Steven, Lake Tahoe: A Blend of Ambience and Efficiency." *Restaurant Hospitality* 69:49 (February 1985).

———. "First Stop 54th and Madison: Manhattan's Hottest New Restaurants Sizzle with Vitality." *Restaurant and Hotel Design,* 40-65 (March/April 1983).

"Foodservice for the Airport of the 21st Century." *Restaurants and Institutions* 96:193 (May 28, 1986).

Forgac, Janie. "Casa Diego: Fine Mexican Food Need Not Come Only to Those Who Wait." *Restaurant Hospitality* 69:121 (August 1985).

———. "Hotel du Pont's Green Room." *Restaurant Hospitality* 69:89 (April 1985).

———. "Palma's: A How-To Example of Space Saving in a Long, Narrow Kitchen Area." *Restaurant Hospitality* 69:55 (February 1985).

———. "Panache: Doing It All: Intermingling Dining and Display Merchandising." *Restaurant Hospitality* 71 (3): 137-40 (March 1987).

———. "Viking Lodge and Restaurant." *Restaurant Hospitality* 70:95 (February 1986).

Forman, Gail. "Hausner's Restaurant: New Kitchen Brings New Efficiency." *Cooking for Profit* 421:7 (February 15, 1986).

Fournier, Larry. "Tacking and Coursing." *Restaurant Hospitality* 70:32 (December 1986).

Fox, Jill. "American Graffiti: Focus of This California Pizza Place Is the Handwriting on the Walls." *Restaurant and Hotel Design* 8:68 (May 1986).

———. "Magic, Etc.: Mondrian-Style Decor and a New Geometric Plan Revitalize an Amusement Park's Flagship Concession." *Restaurant and Hotel Design* 9 (5): 78-80 (May 1987).

———. "On Site: Los Angeles: In L.A., Opposites Attract." *Restaurant and Hotel Design* 9 (3): 124 (March 1987).

———. "Third Annual Design Competition: Best Low-Budget Project: City Spirit Cafe." *Restaurant and Hotel Design* 8:70 (October 1986).

"Functional Space Opens Opportunities for 75-Seat Operation." *Independent Restaurants,* 59-61 (October 1985).

Gamrecki, John. "Philadelphia Restaurant: The Dining Car." *Food Management,* 96-103 (April 1983).

———. "St. John Hospital's Restaurant: The Courtyard." *Food Management,* 101-3 (January 1983).

Garvey, Audrey. "Equipment Tied to Service and Menu: Pickup Stations Are Designed to Deliver with Clean-Cut Efficiency." *Restaurants and Institutions* 96:124 (December 1986).

Gary, Stephen. "City Bites." *Restaurant*

Hospitality 68 (6): 140-42 (June 1984).

Gavron, Darlene. "Bar Design: Viva La Difference." *Restaurants and Institutions* 97 (10): 138-40 (April 29, 1987).

Gay, Bruce. "Designing for Profit: Banana Max Plays Soft Theatre." *Restaurant Management* 1 (7): 54-57 (July 1987).

Geran, Monica. "Art Institute of Chicago: The Center's Public Restaurant and Member's Rooms Designed by Norman DeHaan Associates." *Interior Design* 57:272 (October 1986).

———. "South China: A Western-style Dining Facility in [formerly] Canton by Alfred Mok Designs Ltd." *Interior Design* 57:270 (October 1986).

Gindin, Rona. "Chance to Snap Up Profits: Central Park." *Restaurant Business* 85:184 (August 10, 1986).

Gottlieb, Leon. "Working Smarter, Not Harder: Want an Efficient Kitchen? Get Your Staff Involved in the Planning." *Restaurant Business* 84:92 (December 10, 1985).

Henderson, Justin. "Center City Jazz: City Lights, a Philadelphia Hot Spot." *Restaurant Design*, 58-60 (Spring 1982).

———. "Discovering a Pearl: Designers Find an Architectural Gem Perfect for a Classic Oyster House." *Restaurant and Hotel Design* 7:74 (July/August 1985).

———. "Downtown Uptown: Mixing Neighborhood Vernaculars in New York City." *Restaurant and Hotel Design* 7:74 (January/February 1985).

———. "Pacific Coast Minimalism: High Style and a Relaxed California Attitude Enhance Beachside Location." *Restaurant and Hotel Design*, 78-156 (May/June 1983).

———. "Style and Synthesis: A 'Low-Tech Generic Deli' Suits Southern California's Eclectic Style." *Restaurant and Hotel Design* 7:64 (March 1985).

———. "Three That Break the Mold." *Restaurant and Hotel Design* 6 (1): 69-74 (January/February 1984).

———. "Village Savoir-Faire: Raoul's, Continental Polish in Nyack, New York." *Restaurant Design*, 64-66 (Spring 1982).

"Historic Winery Converted: The Sherry Oven Restaurant and Seafood Bar." *Cooking for Profit*, no. 428: 7-9 (January 1987).

"Intimacy and Comfort: Tomorrow's Watchwords: A Restaurant's Design Should Provide Customers with a Feeling of Well-being." *Restaurants and Institutions* 96:204 (October 29, 1986).

"Japanese Fast Food: Making an American Invention Even Better." *Restaurants and Institutions*, 139-40 (October 1, 1983).

Kass, Monica. "Restaurant Bar Design: Murals, Mirrors, Glass and Chrome." *Restaurants and Institutions* 97 (12): 203:32 (May 27, 1987).

Kazarian, Edward. "Controlling Noise Helps Create a Pleasant Dining Atmosphere." *Independent Restaurants* 46 (4): 28 (April 1984).

Keane, Robert. "Design Portfolio: Looking Down on Columbus Avenue: Now a Restaurant, Cameos Was Once a Storeroom." *Restaurants and Institutions* 97 (13): 210 (June 10, 1987).

———. "Up-and-Coming: Union Square Cafe Eschews the Trendy." *Restaurants and Institutions* 97 (12): 176-77 (May 27, 1987).

Kerth, Al. "How to Improve the Image of Your Pizza Restaurant." *Pizza Today* 4:25 (January 1986).

Kissler, Stephen J. "Change Atmosphere —Change Profit." *Hospitality Education and Research Journal* 10 (2), 11 (1): 154-55 (1987).

"Kitchen Design: American Grill: Stylish Display; Marco Polo: Double Challenge; Wendy's: Prototype for Profit." *Restaurant Business* 84:135 (March 1, 1985).

Knox, Barbara. "Architectural Moxie: Vim, Vigor, and Verve in Oakland." *Restaurant and Hotel Design*, 38-41 (July/August 1983).

———. "Design's Quantum Leap: Will Computers Transform the Design Process?" *Restaurant Design*, 41-46 (Spring 1982).

———. "Nautical Interpretation." *Restaurant Design*, 80-81 (Fall 1982).

———. "New England Vernacular: Legal Sea Foods Opens a Fourth Store in Cambridge." *Restaurant and Hotel Design*, 60-63 (September/October 1983).

———. "New Midtown Classic: Bold Interior Architecture Enhances Haute Cuisines." *Restaurant and Hotel Design*, 42-65 (March/April 1983).

———. "Sophisticated Bar and Grill: Richly Detailed Architecture Distinguishes This Minneapolis Cafe." *Restaurant and Hotel Design*, 66-67 (May/June 1983).

———. "Top of the Line: Campton Place's Restaurant Establishes a Luxurious Ambience." *Restaurant and Hotel Design* 7:72 (June 1985).

———. "Tribeca Oasis: Lower Manhattan Hotspot Adds Vigor to an Up-and-Coming Neighborhood." *Restaurant and Hotel Design*, 54-55 (March/April 1983).

———. "Urban Dimensions: Les Quartres Amis, Contemporary Style in Minneapolis." *Restaurant Design*, 61-63 (Spring 1982).

———. "Variation on a Theme: Contemporary Interiors Complement Traditional French Fare." *Restaurant Design*, 82 (Fall 1982).

Kolb, Patricia. "What's New in Drive-Throughs." *Restaurant and Hotel Design* 8:67 (January/February 1986).

Kooser, Ron. "Restaurant Redesign: Realizing Off-Premise Potential." *Restaurant Hospitality* 70:155 (May 1986).

Kristal, Marc. "All Things Considered: High Style Design Distinguishes a Fast Food Cluster." *Restaurant and Hotel Design*, 46-49 (July/August 1983).

———. "American Idyll: Art Provides the View in This Manhattan Cafe." *Restaurant and Hotel Design* 7:74 (November 1985).

———. "Anatomy of a Restaurant: Huckleberry's, Stuart, Florida." *Restaurant and Hotel Design*, 88-93 (September/October 1983).

———. "The Ballad of the Glass Cafe: Greenhouse Cafes in New York City." *Restaurant and Hotel Design*, 81-83 (September/October 1983).

———. "Continental Flair." *Restaurant and Hotel Design* 7:68 (July/August 1985).

———. "Redesigning an Acclaimed Space: Award-Winning Johnny's Restaurant Gives Way to Successor." *Restaurant and Hotel Design*, 90-91 (May/June 1983).

———. "A Second Look: How Design Plays a Part in the Success or Failure of Restaurants." *Restaurant and Hotel Design*, 89-94 (May/June 1983).

———. "Working Out the Kinks: Alterations Spur New Success for Reflections." *Restaurant and Hotel Design*, 94 (May/June 1983).

Lamalle, C. "Riveranda: Shaping Up a Shipboard Kitchen." *Restaurant Hospitality* 69:38 (February 1985).

Lambert, Carolyn U., and Karen Watson. "Restaurant Design: Researching the Effects on Customers." *The Cornell Quarterly* 24 (4): 68-76 (February 1984).

Lang, Joan. "Face-Lifts Favor Venerable Chains: Some of the Industry's Oldest Concepts Are Also Its Newest." *Restaurant Business* 84:194 (March 20, 1985).

———. "Fast-Finish Approach: Construction Is Begun During the Design Stage, Rather Than After, Saving Time and Money." *Restaurant Business* 85:226 (May 20, 1986).

———. "Newport Turtle." *Restaurant Business* 83 (4): 118-20 (March 1, 1984).

"Let the Sunshine in with a Solarium." *Restaurants and Institutions* 96:203 (May 28, 1986).

Lewis, Pamela. "Country Charm in the City." *Restaurant and Hotel Design* 7:56 (April 1985).

Liebs, Chester H. "Don't Throw Away Your Architectural Treasures." *Restaurants USA* 6:26 (November 1986).

Long, Rachel. "Atrium Trio: Bar, Cafe, and Restaurant Mix Under a Skylight Grid." *Restaurant and Hotel Design* 9 (5): 66-69 (May 1987).

———. "Fast Food Design Trends: Beefing Up an Image: In the Competitive Fast Food Business Creative Designers Are on a Roll." *Restaurant and Hotel Design* 9 (9): 76-81 (September 1987).

———. "Healthy Changes: A Complete Renovation and a New Name Put a Chicago Institution [John F. Kennedy Medical Center] Back into a Competitive Healthcare Market." *Restaurant and Hotel Design* 9 (8): 44-47 (August 1987).

———. "Home on the Range: Greystone Restaurant: Oklahoma City." *Restau-*

rant and Hotel Design 9 (2): 68-69 (February 1987).

———. "New Ambience: Natural Materials and Light Transform a Landmark Restaurant in Downtown Houston." *Restaurant and Hotel Design* 9 (5): 62-65 (May 1987).

———. "New Breed: This Softly Colored, Sunlit Restaurant Breaks with Wall Street's Clubby Tradition." *Restaurant and Hotel Design* 8:62 (July/August 1986).

———. "Seven-Day Wonder: Closed for Just a Week During Renovation, Breakaway Establishes New Sophistication." *Restaurant and Hotel Design* 8:66 (March 1986).

———. "Take-Away Chic: The Storefronts of the Italian Riveria Inspire the Design Theme of a Narrow Groceria." *Restaurant and Hotel Design* 8:56 (May 1986).

———. "Third Annual Design Competition: Honorable Mention: Full Service Restaurant: Willow Tea Room." *Restaurant and Hotel Design* 8:76 (October 1986).

———. "Winning Combination: Three World-Famous Chefs Cook Up a French Country Setting in Central Florida." *Restaurant and Hotel Design* 9 (1): 72-75 (January 1987).

Lovell, J., and C. Senkler. "Bar Design Part I: The Elements of Success: Many Diverse Ingredients Make Up the Operation of the Bar/Lounge." *Restaurant Business* 84:112 (March 20, 1985).

———. "Bar Design Part II: The Elements of Space Planning: Three Concerns Must Be Considered in Space Planning." *Restaurant Business* 84:165 (April 10, 1985).

———. "Bar Design Part III: Programming Entertainment: People Interacting with Other People Is an Important Aspect of Entertainment." *Restaurant Business* 84:268 (May 1, 1985).

———. "Bar Design Part IV: The 'People' Element: The Staff, from Management on Down, Needs to Be a Finely-Tuned Instrument." *Restaurant Business* 84:182 (June 10, 1985).

McCall, Celeste. "Lighting Up a Restaurant's Profits." *NRA News* 5 (6): 27-30 (June/July 1985).

McCall, Peter. "Making Restaurants

Accessible." *NRA News* 5:32 (October 1985).

———. "Noise Control Striking the Right Acoustical Balance." *NRA News* 5:22 (September 1985).

McCarthy, R. "FM Design: Westminster Village: Dining Facilities." *Food Management* 20:117 (February 1985).

Madigan, Mary Jean. "Images of Freedom: Seagulls—and Spirits—Soar in a Sun-Drenched Waterside Cafe." *Restaurant and Hotel Design* 8:54 (March 1986).

———. "Prototypes: The Designer's Viewpoint." *Restaurant and Hotel Design* 7:82 (July/August 1985).

———. "Stop the Presses: Extra! Extra!: New York City." *Restaurant and Hotel Design* 9 (2): 58-61 (February 1987).

———. "Sushi Space: Old Japan Inspires a Modern Seattle Grill." *Restaurant and Hotel Design* 9 (1): 76-77 (January 1987).

———. "Take-Out Foods Have Become Big Business." *Restaurant and Hotel Design* 8:80 (May 1986).

———. "Tuscan Trilogy: Italian Design, Materials, and Craftsmanship Elevate a New York Restaurant to 'Classic' Stature." *Restaurant and Hotel Design* 9 (9): 48-51 (September 1987).

———. "World Class Flash." *Restaurant and Hotel Design* 9 (4): 46-49 (April 1987).

Major, M. "No End to Trends at Westin." *Restaurant Hospitality* 69:99 (October 1985).

"Mama Mia! It's Fast: This Snazzy Quick-Service Eatery Takes Its Design Cue from the River It Overlooks." *Restaurant and Hotel Design* 7:56 (May 1985).

"The Mansion on Turtle Creek." *Restaurants and Institutions*, 115-17 (April 1, 1983).

Marshall, Kathleen. "Chicken Kitchen Plucks Up a Design Award." *Restaurants and Institutions* 95:235 (July 24, 1985).

———. "Consistency in Mallard's Design Merits R&I Interior Design Award." *Restaurants and Institutions* 95:247 (May 1, 1985).

———. "Deli Captures New York Style, Energy." *Restaurants and Institutions* 96:222 (September 17, 1986.)

———. "Design Combats Fast-food Sameness." *Restaurants and Institu-*

tions 96:220 (September 17, 1986).

———. "Design Exudes Youthful Yet Cosmopolitan Sophistication." *Restaurants and Institutions* 96:191 (August 20, 1986).

———. "Design: Rose Room Tops at Sheraton: Restaurant Design Projects a Colorful Image." *Restaurants and Institutions* 96:176 (November 26, 1986).

———. "Diner Takes a Step Back in Time." *Restaurants and Institutions* 96:193 (August 20, 1986).

———. "Fine-Tuned Decor, Right Down to the Menu." *Restaurants and Institutions* 95:211 (September 18, 1985).

———. "Food and Design Are No. 1 at Pizzeria Uno." *Restaurants and Institutions* 95:237 (July 24, 1985).

———. "Interior Design Awards: Basement Location Doesn't Mean a Drab Design: Light, Open Cafeteria Keeps Employees In-House for Lunch and Breaks." *Restaurants and Institutions* 97 (18): 184 (August 19, 1987).

———. "Interior Design: The '50s and '60s Revisited." *Restaurants and Institutions* 97 (12): 236 (May 27, 1987).

———. "Interior Design Showcase: Michelle's Sets Elegant Tone for Downtown Atlanta Office Center." *Restaurants and Institutions* 94 (9): 277 (May 9, 1984).

———. "Interior Design Showcase: Serving Food Fast from a '30s Gas Station." *Restaurants and Institutions* 94 (23): 207 (November 21, 1984).

———. "Kentucky Fried Chicken Does Design Right, Too." *Restaurants and Institutions* 95:239 (August 21, 1985).

———. "Larchmont's McDonald's Design Is a Winner: Exacting Design Is Possible Prototype for Stores." *Restaurants and Institutions* 97 (1):206 (January 7, 1987).

———. "Look into the Past Creates a Modern Design: Simplicity and Nostalgia Are the Key to Brigham's Design Success." *Restaurants and Institutions* 96:166 (December 10, 1986).

———. "Marie Callender's: A Design with Special Distinction." *Restaurants and Institutions* 96:243 (July 23, 1986).

———. "Marketplace: Reflections on Design: Designer Glass Can Help to Polish a Restaurant's Image." *Restaurants and Institutions* 96:208 (November 26, 1986).

———. "A Modern Interpretation of Classic Art Deco." *Restaurants and Institutions* 94 (19): 216 (September 26, 1984).

———. "Oriental Design Receives 'Honorable' Mention." *Restaurants and Institutions* 95:209 (September 18, 1985).

———. "Puttin' on the Ritz." *Restaurants and Institutions* 94 (5): 205 (March 14, 1984).

———. "Schlotzsky's: Before and After: Design Transformation Creates a Lively, Playful Dining Ambience." *Restaurants and Institutions* 96:164 (December 10, 1986).

———. "Trucks Stop Here: Return on Investment Is a Major Design Plus." *Restaurants and Institutions* 96:126 (December 24, 1986).

Martin, Richard. "Los Angeles Skyscraper Showcases McDonald's for Yuppies." *Nation's Restaurant News* 21 (34): F13 (August 17, 1987).

Mautner, Julie. "Dakota's: Dining Has Gone Down Under in a Unique Beneath-the-Street Dallas Restaurant." *Restaurants and Institutions* 96:167 (October 15, 1986).

———. "Design: Duck & Decanter: A Deli and Gourmet Shop in Scottsdale's Camelview Plaza." *Restaurants and Institutions* 96:171 (November 26, 1986).

———. "Design: Frog: Soft Color, Oriental Touches and a Neon Surprise." *Restaurants and Institutions* 96:172 (November 26, 1986).

———. "Design: Mick's: The Peasant Group's Award-Winning Atlanta Diner." *Restaurants and Institutions* 96:170 (November 26, 1986).

———. "Designer Lee Gamble Creates an Elegant Spot for Dining and Entertainment." *Restaurants and Institutions* 96:200 (October 29, 1986).

———. "Design Gallery: When Two Restaurants Become One: The Venerable Quilted Giraffe Moves in with Its Younger, Flashier Sister." *Restaurants and Institutions* 97 (18): 176-78 (August 19, 1987).

———. "Design Techniques: Jesse's St. Louis Saloon." *Restaurants and Institutions* 97 (14): 140-41 (June 24, 1987).

———. "Design Techniques: Wall Things Considered." *Restaurants and Institutions* 97 (5): 160-63 (March 4, 1987).

———. "Doyenne of Dramatic Restaurant Design [Lazaroff]." *Restaurants and Institutions* 96:218 (December 10, 1986).

———. "High-Styled Ceremony: Sushi-Zen." *Restaurants and Institutions* 96: 198 (October 29, 1986).

———. "Hotline: The Grill Who Has Everything." *Restaurants and Institutions* 97 (19): 138 (September 2, 1987).

———. "Jack's and No. 1022: An Intimate Restaurant and an Elegant Inn Are Edward J. Safdie's Latest Creations." *Restaurants and Institutions* 96:165 (September 17, 1986).

———. "Knowlwood's: A Culinary Homage to a Bygone Era." *Restaurants and Institutions* 96:245 (May 28, 1986).

———. "Open Kitchens: The Joy of Looking." *Restaurants and Institutions* 97 (6): 138-39 (March 18, 1987).

———. "Responsive Restaurants: An Architect by Training, Ed Bronstein Brings an Unusual Perspective to Restaurant Design." *Restaurants and Institutions* 97 (4): 160 (February 18, 1987).

———. "Three Distinct Goals, Three Distinct Designs." *Restaurants and Institutions* 96:208 (November 12, 1986).

———. "Trio of Bistros: New York Designer Adam Tihany Creates Three Show-stopping European Cafes for Omni Hotels." *Restaurants and Institutions* 97 (4): 156-58 (February 18, 1987).

Mazzurco, M. "Lighting Keys a Dramatic Scheme." *Restaurant and Hotel Design* 7:60 (January/February 1985).

Mazzurco, Philip. "Breaking the Rules: Interiors for the Winnetka Grill Draw on the Whole of Design History." *Restaurant and Hotel Design* 7:67 (January/February 1985).

———. "Out on the Edge: Glamour Gains a Foothold in a Reviving Manhattan Neighborhood." *Restaurant and Hotel Design* 7:82 (June 1985).

———. "Replicating Southern Traditions in the Low Country." *Restaurant and Hotel Design* 7:58 (January/February 1985).

"Metropolis' Gas Rotisserie Turns a Meaty

Profit." *Foodservice Equipment and Supplies Specialist* 39 (9): 82-85 (January 25, 1987).

Michaelides, Stephen. "How Now Redesign?" *Restaurant Hospitality,* 16-21 (July 1983).

Minno, Maurice, and others. "The Project Planning Team: Planning a New Restaurant." *NRA News* 5 (6): 24-26 (June/July 1985).

"Move Over Columbus Avenue—Here Comes Midtown South." *Restaurants and Institutions* 96:164 (October 29, 1986).

Nelson, Ibsen. "A Dynamic Collaboration of Owner/Architect." *Restaurant Design,* 31 (Summer 1982).

"New Directions." *Restaurants and Institutions* 94 (20): 161-67 (October 10, 1984).

Nickel, C. Russell. "An Alternative for Self-Service Restaurants." *Restaurant and Hotel Design,* 105-6 (September/October 1983).

Niepold, Cecelia. "America's Star-Spangled Diners." *Restaurants USA* 6:20 (November 1986).

———. "Bye Bye Plastics, Hello Natural: Fast Food Design." *NRA News* 6:26 (March 1986).

———. "Murals: A Restaurant's Exclamation Point." *Restaurants USA* 7 (3): 24-29 (March 1987).

———. "Redesigning Your Restaurant: Black and White and New All Over." *NRA News,* 21-26 (November 1983).

"1985 Interior Design Awards." *Restaurant Hospitality* 69:69 (May 1985).

"Old West Goes Postmodern: Cowboy Character Is Evoked by Use of Redwood and Stone at Cadillac Grille." *Restaurant and Hotel Design* 8:38 (January/February 1986).

"Oriental Fantasy California Style: Barbara Lazaroff and Wolfgang Puck Stage (and Star in) an Extravaganza Called Chinois on Main." *Restaurants and Institutions* 96:158 (December 10, 1986).

Overbagh and Woodburn. "How New Concepts Can Change the Operation Design." *Restaurants USA* 6:16 (November 1986).

Papa, Anne. "Restaurant Design: Finding the Right Look." *NRA News* 6:12 (January 1986).

Person, Sarah. "Aurora: Postmodern

Elegance." *Restaurant Business* 85:272 (October 10, 1986).

———. "Bar Lui's Blues Put It in the Black: With Its Unusual Design and Distinctive Menu, Bar Lui Has Become a Hot Spot in New York." *Restaurant Business* 84:172 (December 10, 1985).

———. "Cutting Edge of Kitchen Design." *Restaurant Business* 85:102 (March 20, 1986).

———. "East Meets West at Chaya Brasserie." *Restaurant Business* 85:322 (October 10, 1986).

———. "Fast Food Design: A New Approach." *Restaurant Business* 86 (6): 150-54 (April 10, 1987).

———. "Focus on Design: Supporting Hotel Foodservice." *Restaurant Business* 86 (3): 248-50 (February 10, 1987).

———. "French Designer Patterns Maxim's After Paris Eatery." *Restaurant Business* 84:138 (November 20, 1985).

———. "Good Design: Doesn't Have to Cost Millions." *Restaurant Business* 85:254 (August 10, 1986).

———. "Great Rooms: The Pump Room." *Restaurant Business* 85:104 (July 20, 1986).

———. "Lively Atmosphere Promotes Tutti's Sales: (The Concept of a 'Neighborhood Place' Dictated a Convivial Design)." *Restaurant Business* 86 (6): 142-43 (April 10, 1987).

———. "Perino's Restaurant." *Restaurant Business* 85:86 (September 1, 1986).

———. "Redwood Room Sparkles as Clift Hotel's Jewel." *Restaurant Business* 85:110 (January 1, 1986).

———. "Russian Tea Room: A Cultural Legacy: For Five Decades, This Manhattan Institution Has Hosted the Rich and Famous." *Restaurant Business* 85:184 (February 10, 1986).

———. "A Star Is Born in America." *Restaurant Business* 84:200 (May 1, 1985).

Picard, Maureen, "American Bar: Just Off Manhattan's Madison Avenue, Charley O's Restaurant Gets a Punchy New Identity." *Restaurant and Hotel Design* 8:66 (June 1986).

———. "City Roadhouse: New York City's Upper East Side Gets Some Down-Home Southwestern Funk."

Restaurant and Hotel Design 9 (6): 76-78 (June 1987).

———. "Dining at Water's Edge." *Restaurant and Hotel Design* 9 (6): 33-38 (June 1987).

———. "Hey, Ba-Ba-Reeba: A Patchwork of Motifs from Spain and the '50s Enlivens Chicago's First Tapas Restaurant." *Restaurant and Hotel Design* 8:72 (May 1986).

———. "Industrial Style: Inspired Fakery Yields a 'Warehouse' Pizza Restaurant in Chicago." *Restaurant and Hotel Design* 9 (5): 74-77 (May 1987).

———. "Neat Seats: Booths and Banquettes." *Restaurant and Hotel Design* 9 (2): 15-18 (February 1987).

———. "A Plan for the Aging: A Congregate Care Facility Offers Full and Pleasant Living." *Restaurant and Hotel Design* 9 (8): 40-43 (August 1987).

———. "Reflecting on Design." *Restaurant and Hotel Design* 8:39 (September 1986).

———. "Small Change: The Beverly Hills Piret's Pivots between Retail and Restaurant." *Restaurant and Hotel Design* 9 (7): 48-51 (July 1987).

———. "Solutions: Designing for the Elderly: Tips for Congregate Living Facilities." *Restaurant and Hotel Design* 9 (8): 25-26 (August 1987).

———. "Solutions: Designing with Signage: Creating a Theme with Theatrical Signs." *Restaurant and Hotel Design* 8:47 (March 1986).

———. "Solutions: The Kitchen as a Focal Point." *Restaurant and Hotel Design* 8:43 (May 1986).

———. "Solutions: Lighting Sets the Mood." *Restaurant and Hotel Design* 9 (4): 29-32 (April 1987).

———. "Table Talk: A Comfortable, Intimate Atmosphere Encourages Lots of Dinner Conversation." *Restaurant and Hotel Design* 8:68 (July/August 1986).

———. "Timeworn Appeal: . . . Packs Them in at Lettuce Entertain You's Nostalgic Italian Eatery." *Restaurant and Hotel Design* 9 (5): 58-61 (May 1987).

———. "Variations on a Mexican Theme: Crafts Shape an Ethnic Experience." *Restaurant and Hotel Design* 7:27 (September 1985).

———. "Wine Country Winner: The

Grape Is the Theme of This Napa Valley Inn." *Restaurant and Hotel Design* 8:54 (September 1986).

———. "Wit and Wisdom: Clever Sculpture and Lighting Animate a New York City Pizzeria Prototype." *Restaurant and Hotel Design* 7:72 (July/August 1985).

Piera, Nancy. "Dealing with Too Much Success: Sawgrass Resort Beach Club, Florida." *Restaurant and Hotel Design*, 41 (May/June 1983).

"Po Folks Profits from Big Family Meals: Testing and Procedures Provide Consistent Quality." *Cooking for Profit*, no. 414: 7 (July 1985).

Price, Laurence. "A Case Study: The Big Turnaround in Hotel Food Rooms." *Lodging* 13 (1): 77-82 (September 1987).

"Problem Solving Design: Functional Space Opens Opportunities for 75-Seat Operation." *Independent Restaurants* 47:59 (October 1985).

Raffio, Ralph. "Marketing to a New Urban Niche." *Restaurant Business* 84:159 (February 10, 1985).

———. "Old Ebbitt Grill." *Restaurant Business* 83 (4): 132-34 (March 1, 1984).

"Relocated Nankin Cafe Retains Past Ambience." *Restaurants and Institutions*, 129 (August 1, 1983).

"Remodeling Profile: An Industry Profile." *Nation's Restaurant News: Restaurant Interiors*, 4-13 (October 24, 1983).

"Resource Listing: Arranged by Product Category." *Restaurant and Hotel Design* 8:60 (December 1986).

"R&H's 2nd Annual Design Recognition Awards." *Restaurant and Hotel Design* 7:38 (October 1985).

"Restaurant Design Pros: Twenty-six of the Best." *Restaurant and Hotel Design* 7:34 (September 1985).

"Restaurant Design: Staying Ahead of the Game." *Nation's Restaurant News: Restaurant Interiors*, 4-12 (June 6, 1983).

"Restaurant Enterprises Group Tests Cogeneration." *Restaurants and Institutions* 97 (4): 186-87 (February 18, 1987).

Richards, Greg. "Diner Dishes Up Nostalgia in Compact Layout: Designers Hid High Production Kitchens and a

Bakery." *Foodservice Equipment Specialist* 38:91 (April 1986).

———. "LeBow Thrives in Fertile D.C. Market: A Zeal for Planning and Youthful Management Make for Success." *Foodservice Equipment Specialist* 38:47 (February 25, 1986).

———. "Pulling All the Stops: Schweppe & Sons Tackles a Million-Dollar Job at Chicago-Area Drury Lane." *Foodservice Equipment Specialist* 37:50 (March 25, 1985).

"Ron Kooser: Excellence in Kitchen Design. Part 3." *Restaurant Hospitality* 71 (5): 165-67 (May 1987).

Salmen, John. "How to Make Restaurants More Accessible to the Physically Disabled." *NRA News*, 28-29 (August 1983).

"A Sanitary Kitchen Is Born, Not Made." *Restaurants and Institutions*. 251 (May 15, 1983).

Sanson, Michael. "Kitchen Design: The Golden Touch." *Restaurant Management* 1 (5): 82-83 (May 1987).

———. "World According to Joe Baum." *Restaurant Management* 1 (5): 43-49 (May 1987).

Sasanow, Richard. "Now on Exhibit at the Met . . . The Fountain Restaurant at the Metropolitan Museum of Art." *Restaurant and Hotel Design*, 50 (May/June 1983).

———. "Windy City Interpretation: New York's Jazz Age Elan Inspires a Glamorous Chicago Nightspot." *Restaurant and Hotel Design*, 82-84 (May/June 1983).

Schirmbeck, Egon. *Restaurants, Architecture, and Ambience.* New York: Architectural Book Publishers, 1983.

Schlossberg, Howard. "Converting for Profit: Sales Get a Shot in the Arm from Quick and Efficient Remodeling of Former Concepts." *Restaurants and Institutions* 96:161 (October 15, 1986).

———. "Life in the Fast Lane: A New Group of Chains Creates a Segment Catering to Those Who Dine on Wheels." *Restaurants and Institutions* 96:149 (September 3, 1986).

"Seattle Salty's More Than a Pretty View: Features Gas Equipment Up Front; Energy-saving Heat-recovery System Behind the Scenes." *Foodservice Equipment and Supplies Specialist*

39 (10): 66-69 (February 25, 1987).

Sellers, John. "Winning Design Raises Stock of Wall Street Firm." *Foodservice Equipment and Supplies Specialist* 40 (5): 113-16 (September 25, 1987).

"Sense of Place Marks the Hartford Landmarks of the Restaurant Group." *Restaurants and Institutions* 96:170 (March 19, 1986).

"Setting the Stage for 1985." *Independent Restaurants* 47:62 (January 1985).

Shade, C. Edwin. "Design Factor in Food and Beverage Areas." *Hotel and Resort Industry* 10 (5): 84-86 (May 1987).

Shankman, Sarah. "Joe Baum's Aurora Glows in Manhattan." *Restaurants and Institutions* 97 (8): 142-44 (April 1, 1987).

Slater, David. "Nine Top Designers Speak Out: New Directions in Restaurant Design." *Restaurants USA* 7 (6): 22-26 (June/July 1987).

Slinker, Barry H. "Solving the Puzzle: New Look for Columbus Avenue." *Restaurant and Hotel Design* 6 (1): 60-63 (January/February 1984).

———. "Turning Problems to Advantage in Boston's Back Bay Area." *Restaurant and Hotel Design*, 37 (September/October 1983).

Spazzoli, Adriana. "Church Work: In Pavia, Italy, a Trendy Club Takes Shape Within the Walls of a Deconsecrated 13th-Century Church." *Restaurant and Hotel Design* 9 (9): 56-59 (September 1987).

———. "Going Underground: One Level Below the Street, Sunny Colors and Good Lighting Brighten Up a Milanese Cafeteria." *Restaurant and Hotel Design* 9 (9): 52-55 (September 1987).

———. "Milanese Flair: Elegant Fast Food? Yes, in Urban Italy." *Restaurant and Hotel Design* 8:62 (September 1986).

Storey, Alice. "Goldberg Produces Showtime at Woods." *Restaurant Business* 84 (8): 184-92 (May 20, 1985).

"Third Annual Design Competition." *Restaurant and Hotel Design* 8:52 (October 1986).

"Update: Top Restaurant Designers." *Restaurant and Hotel Design* 8:87 (June 1986).

Waskey, F. H. "The Loan Package: Situation No. 2: Assessing Restaurant

Square Footage." *Club Management* 66 (9): 38-39 (September 1987).

Wasserman, Natta L. "Interior Design Opens New Horizons." *Foodservice Equipment Specialist*, 46-48 (July 1983).

Wayman, Doyle. "When Design Success Is the Name of the Game." *Restaurant Hospitality* 709:56 (February 1986).

Wayman and McKerrow. "Building a Restaurant Bar That Builds Business." *Restaurant Hospitality* 70:64 (October 1986).

Webb, Michael. "Chinese Fantasia: A New Look for Sacramento's Favorite Hangout." *Restaurant and Hotel Design* 7:68 (September 1985).

———. "Grandallusion: References to Classic Architecture Inform and Animate a Witty Oakland Renovation." *Restaurant and Hotel Design* 8:60 (May 1986).

———. "Impressionist Chic: This Casual L.A. Restaurant Recreates the Mood of Monet's Dreamy Canvases of Water Lilies." *Restaurant and Hotel Design* 8:46 (September 1986).

———. "New Wave Sushi: Terse Geometrics and Vivid Colors Carry This Restaurant a Step Beyond the Ordinary." *Restaurant and Hotel Design* 8:58 (April 1986).

———. "Now for Something Different: Two New Restaurants by Morphosis Reject the California Vernacular." *Restaurant and Hotel Design* 7:78 (March 1985).

———. "Orderly Retreat: A Refined Restaurant Beckons from Beneath a Corporate Tower." *Restaurant and Hotel Design* 8:74 (March 1986).

———. "Oriental Light: Chinatown [Restaurant]: Irvine, California." *Restaurant and Hotel Design* 9 (3): 62-65 (March 1987).

———. "Sassy and Streamlined: Bubbles [Restaurant]: Balboa, California." *Restaurant and Hotel Design* 9 (3): 72-75 (March 1987).

———. "Sleek Classic: Brass Fittings and Polished Woods Evoke the Image of a '30s Dining Car." *Restaurant and Hotel Design* 8:62 (June 1986).

———. "Soft Touch: Hilton Renovates Its Beverly Hills Property to Luxury Standards." *Restaurant and Hotel Design* 9 (9): 60-65 (September 1987).

———. "Third Annual Design Competition: Best Quick Service Restaurant: Mrs. Garcia's." *Restaurant and Hotel Design* 8:62 (October 1986).

"What's a Nice Restaurant Like You Doing in a Place Like This?" *Restaurants and Institutions*, 83-97 (August 1, 1983).

"When Kitchens Come Out of Hiding: Open Kitchen Design a la Fuddruckers." *Foodservice Equipment Specialist* 38:110 (October 25, 1985).

Wines, Leslie. "Firehouse Turned Restaurant in New Haven." *Restaurant and Hotel Design*, 38 (September/October 1983).

Wolson, Shelley. "1985 Interior Design Awards." *Restaurants and Institutions* 95 (17): 105-40 (August 21, 1985).

———. "1986 Food Facilities Awards." *Restaurants and Institutions* 96:171 (September 3, 1986).

———. "Show Must Go On: All the Restaurant's a Stage When Operators Use Display Kitchens." *Restaurants and Institutions* 96:151 (February 5, 1986).

Wynn, Joyce. "How to Find a Designer." *Restaurant Management* 1 (7): 57 (July 1987).

"York's Choices: Changing a Chain Restaurant's Image." *Restaurant Hospitality* 69:110 (July 1985).

Ziolkowski, Dennis J. "Systems: Decisions Depend on Menu: Operators and Designers Must Work Together to Create the Decor for a Successful Restaurant." *Restaurants and Institutions* 96:148 (November 26, 1986).

INDEX